Praise for

TAKING OUR PLACE IN HISTORY: THE GIRLS WRITE NOW 2020 ANTHOLOGY

"Girls Write Now is an urgent need—the world needs women's voices, and when they are mentored young, they start strong. Girls Write Now gives girls the strength to speak their voices—and we need their voices to strengthen our world."

> **—GINA APOSTOL**, author of *Insurrecto*

"What a gift to read such luminous and fearless prose from a new generation of fierce women writers."

> **—MAISY CARD**, author of *These Ghosts Are Family*

"What an honor and joy it is to be a part of this wonderful organization! I was raised by a remarkable single mom who loved books and writing and who went back to school to earn her master's degree in counseling while raising three children. I am as proud of her as I am of my own daughter, Gillian, who at the age of ten already has found her voice through poetry. It's a joy to share my story with you, and I'm grateful to Girls Write Now for encouraging so many young women to express themselves as my mother did for me."

> **—ROBYN CRAWFORD**, author of *A Song for You: My Life with Whitney Houston*

"We are proud to align with Girls Write Now because their mission is our mission: to ensure the voices of girls and women are centered and elevated to tell their own stories, especially those girls and women who have been silenced because of their immigration and socioeconomic statuses."

> **—ROSAYRA PABLO CRUZ AND JULIE SCHWIETERT COLLAZO**, authors of *The Book of Rosy: A Mother's Story of Separation at the Border*

"I shout out and whisper and sing and pray in gratitude for the gift and hard work of Girls Write Now. I've been in the group's physical space and felt the love and the power. I know some of the mentors. All over the world the voices of girls are creating waves of possibility. These utterances and transcriptions and living archives are essential. Every time the voice, the pen or pencil, the dare, dream, the imagined, and conjured reaches the air, paper, stone, dirt . . . another . . . the world becomes a little safer, more beautiful, more sustainable."

—KATHY ENGEL, author of *The Lost Brother Alphabet*

"Reading these honest, passionate stories of girls grappling with who they are and who they will become is a true pleasure. These young writers are triumphantly taking their place in history, and we will all be the better for it."

—LAURA HANKIN, author of *Happy & You Know It*

"Girls Write Now gives young women guidance and tools to amplify their voices. I am thankful to have their stories in the world."

—VICTORIA JAMIESON, author of *Roller Girl*

"In a world that is designed to crush the spirits and ambition of young women, Girls Write Now prevails as a necessary organization where members can claim the narratives over their own stories and receive the shepherding to get their voices out in the world. This anthology is a continuation of that important chronicling."

—MORGAN JERKINS, author of *Wandering in Strange Lands: A Daughter of the Great Migration Reclaims Her Roots* and *This Will Be My Undoing*

"For too long women have been written out of history. Girls Write Now is an exciting collection of voices tearing up the old ways and taking their rightful place."

—CHRISTINA LAMB, author of *Our Bodies, Their Battlefield*

"The voices of girls and gender-nonconforming youth have historically been downplayed, belittled, or lost to us—but they refuse to disappear any longer. Girls Write Now is giving a loudspeaker to these crucial voices, their wants and desires, and preserving them, putting them right in the stream of history, where they have always belonged."

—ILANA MASAD, author of *All My Mother's Lovers*

"Every story in this collection is affecting, revelatory, and edifying. Within these pages are the premier words of the next generation of women writers."

—BERNICE L. McFADDEN, author of *Praise Song for the Butterflies*

"The urgent voices of the young writers in the latest Girls Write Now anthology forces open once-silenced mouths into the forefront of necessary conversations. These stories—a balm to heal wounds, a life-giving tonic for humanity we so desperately need today. When we give girls the freedom to write, the power to *know* they are writers, and to tell us, with their own fearless language, they exist—this is how we change the world together for the better."
    —JESSICA CARE MOORE, author of *We Want Our Bodies Back*

"Girls Write Now is an organization that is changing the course of history by lifting up the voices of girls that have been left out, so it is apt that this year they'd focus on their place in it. If this generation is remembered for anything, it's going to be the bravery of girls and young women that spoke truth to power. There is no better example of this than in the essays in this collection."
    —SAMHITA MUKHOPADHYAY, executive editor of *Teen Vogue* and
    author of *Outdated: Why Dating Is Ruining Your Love Life*

"The girls whose words fill this remarkable anthology are not only taking their places in history: They are making their own historic paths, carving out their own directions, as they select, place, and contextualize the powerful words that share with the readers their mighty aspirations, victories, visions, stories. There can only be one direction for these future writers, teachers, leaders, poets, inspirers: formidably forward, on their own paths."
    —VICTORIA ORTIZ, author of *Dissenter on the Bench: Ruth Bader Ginsburg's Life & Work*

"The young women and gender-nonconforming youth whose work fills these pages are not only tomorrow's greatest writers, speakers, activists, and thinkers—they are also today's. Here are the voices shaping the world."
    —JULIA PHILLIPS, author of *Disappearing Earth*

"The Girls Write Now anthology is a testament to what we know to be true: that stories have the power to change lives, both readers' and writers'. There's nothing more affirming than finding your voice, and expressing it, or seeing yourself and your experiences reflected back to you in the pages of a book. That is the beauty of this anthology: a kaleidoscope of creativity, a celebration of girl power, a beacon of our future."
    —CHRISTINE PRIDE, author of *We Are Not Like Them*

"Girls Write Now is rich with a captivating raw honesty that the writers earned by choosing to find and amplify their voices. These young people will not only take their place in history, they will make history."
 —SARAH RUDEWALKER, author of *Revolutionary Poetics: The Rhetoric of The Black Arts Movement*

"Girls Write Now is a powerful and important platform that amplifies the young voices that need, deserve, and, most important, demand to be heard. Reading their words and hearing their stories gives me goose bumps, a reality check, and a glimmer of hope for our future—all at once."
 —JENNIFER ANN SHORE, author of *New Wave*

"The written word has often been the only outlet for women and girls to express their authentic stories and unique voices in so many societies across the globe. Girls Write Now harnesses that power, nurtures it, and amplifies it so that these singular voices can become generations."
 —ROBIN THEDE, creator, writer, executive producer, and star of *A Black Lady Sketch Show*

"It is a pleasure to be here with Girls Write Now. I am a girl writing now, and I dare say it is better late than never . . . In my community, the word 'girl' is powerful and used as a term of endearment. If you are 'my girl,' you are humble, beautiful inside and out, bright, warm, kind, respectful—of yourself, others, and this dear earth."
 —CICELY TYSON, author of *Just As I Am*

"Whenever I think of the wonderful mission of Girls Write Now, it fills my heart with so much hope. By encouraging girls and gender-nonconforming youth to tell their stories, you are showing them their power. In teaching them that their voices matter, you are doing revolutionary work that will change our world for the better."
 —LAUREN WILKINSON, author of *American Spy*

TAKING OUR PLACE IN HISTORY

THE GIRLS WRITE NOW
2020 ANTHOLOGY

TAKING OUR PLACE IN HISTORY

THE GIRLS WRITE NOW 2020 ANTHOLOGY

Introduction by
CHRISTINE BALL

Poem by
RUPI KAUR

Rupi Kaur's poem is made possible by arrangement with Rupi Kaur and Andrews McMeel
Publishing

Published 2020

Printed in the United States

Print ISBN: 978-0-9962772-4-2

E-ISBN: 9781936932917

Library of Congress Control Number: 2020900258

Cover design by Kaitlin Kall

For information, write to:

Girls Write Now, Inc.
247 West 37th Street, Suite 1000
New York, NY 10018

info@girlswritenow.org
girlswritenow.org

TAKING OUR PLACE IN HISTORY

The Girls Write Now 2020 Anthology

If I had to pinpoint the moment my mentee Kaya and I really, deeply clicked, it was probably during a conversation about history. We met at our usual spot in Brooklyn, unpacking the contents of our respective days, and somehow the conversation got around to the things we wished we'd learned in school. As a Black girl growing up in a small Michigan town in the 1990s, stories by authors who looked like me were never on the curriculum. When I went to college, my entire universe exploded. I was exposed to so many histories, stories, and experiences through the books I read that completely altered my view of the world, and the place I saw for myself within it. I learned that for Kaya, a Black girl growing up in New York City in the 2010s, our experiences may not have been so different. She told me that she also felt like there were crucial things left out of the lessons she was taught during Black History Month, or in her American history or government or English classes.

We started talking about Audre Lorde, Octavia Butler, Angela Davis, Ida B. Wells, and others—women who wrote or spoke themselves into history as a radical act of visibility, as a demand to be seen. And this, I think, is what taking your place in history means:

using your own unique voice to unapologetically proclaim, *Here I am*. The anthology you hold in your hands wonderfully demonstrates just that.

Each of the stories in this collection are powerful declarations by the current class of Girls Write Now mentees. They use poetry and prose, personal essay and fiction, to write their truths into existence. Make no mistake, this is no easy thing. Writing in this way, laying out so many vulnerabilities, hopes, and fears for others to read—it takes courage. But by doing so, these young writers are stepping into a powerful legacy of truth-tellers—the Audre Lordes and Octavia Butlers and [insert your favorite badass!]—who dared to do the same. Let us all find inspiration in these pages, then go out into the world and boldly, loudly, fearlessly take our place. These Girls Write Now mentees are leading the way.

MAYA MILLETT *is an independent nonfiction writer, editor, and audio producer, and the founder of Race Women, an archive research project honoring nineteenth-century Black feminist trailblazers. Maya is also a Girls Write Now mentor alum and co-chair of the Girls Write Now anthology committee.*

ANTHOLOGY EDITORIAL COMMITTEE

Molly MacDermot

Rosalind Black
Spencer George
Jisu Kim
Maya Millett

Grace Aneiza Ali
Annie Bryan
Shannon Carlin
Mary Darby
Nadia DeLane
Erica Drennan
Morayo Faleyimu
Amy Flyntz
Kristen Gaerlan
Catherine Greenman
Donna Hill

Kate Mulley
Livia Nelson
Carol Paik
Nikki Palumbo
Jennifer Rowe
Hannah Sheldon-Dean
Marissa Silverman
Carina Storrs
Jen Straus
Maryellen Tighe
Lauren Vespoli

Spencer George
Katherine Goldblum
Alexandra Harris
Muneesh Jain

Teresa Mettela
Jennyfer Parra
Lisbett Rodriguez
Richelle Szypulski

CONTENTS

The Girls Write Now 2020 Anthology

INTRODUCTION

CHRISTINE BALL

As I think about this amazing organization, I find myself reflecting on the mentors I have had in my own life. And one woman, who was all of four-foot-ten, stands tall among them. That is Miss Five, my fifth-grade teacher, who changed the trajectory of my life.

Growing up, I was painfully shy. I hid in the back of the classroom and tried not to get called on. Math and science were my preferred subjects because there was little chance of interpretation or having to speak up or express myself. There was just one right answer and I could go about it quietly. So when Miss Five had us write poems for one of her lessons, I literally froze.

I distinctly remember the panicked feeling I had looking down at my sheet of lined paper while all of my classmates were furiously writing away. My mind was blank—I couldn't even come up with a subject to write about. I think about it now and it was probably akin to that feeling you get when you accidentally send an email to the wrong person—you know, when everything goes black and your stomach drops out . . . Well, that is what I felt like back then.

My struggle must have been apparent to Miss Five, because next thing I knew she was crouching by my desk and started by calming me down. She then asked me to come up with an image, just one image, and I managed to spit out the word "lightning."

She asked me questions: *What does it look like? Feel like? Sound like? Smell like?* and had me write a paragraph. Then, together, we crossed out the extra words—the ors, ands, the ifs, the buts—and we physically rearranged it into a short poem.

I get goose bumps just thinking about the pride I felt looking at my first poem! In that moment, I felt like my whole world opened up, but I could never have imagined to what extent. Miss Five's mentorship did not stop there; afterward she encouraged me to be bold enough to submit the poem to be judged for a very small award.

Then, a couple years later, when she wrote a book on teaching creative writing, there was my poem, in print, actually published as the opening to one of her chapters.

While this was only elementary school, Miss Five had opened a door to me that I may never have discovered without her encouragement. And it turns out the joy I discovered writing my first poem and expressing myself is something I would come back to again and again in my life.

Skipping ahead to college, I found myself at this same crossroads. While I was strongly encouraged to pursue math and science by my engineering professor, at the last second, I veered and became an English major. This was no easy road for me, but it was what made me happy. I traded formulas for trying to decipher William Blake's mythology, and there were many late nights alone in my room when I wanted to pull my hair out and scream, "I don't get it!"

Truly wanting to follow in Miss Five's footsteps, I became certified to teach secondary English—which required me to stand up and teach in front of my peers. And even though I didn't ultimately pursue teaching, I think this is where I finally came out of my shell and got comfortable talking in front of a group.

When I was about to graduate college and had a teaching gig lined up, I got a call from Penguin, where I had interned a while back. They wanted to know if I could come work in their publicity department. This shy girl would have to get on the phone to cold-call media and pitch books, not to mention move to New York. At this point, teaching and lesson plans felt safer than doing something more creative and less structured. But I remembered Miss Five's lesson with the poem—to take it one step at a time and go from there. I followed my gut, brashly and boldly, and five days later I was at my first job in the big city. I told myself I would try it for a year and see what happened.

That was twenty years ago and I am happy to say it was the best choice I ever made. I am surrounded by people smarter than I am;

I get to publish writers, thinkers, communicators, and creators like all of you, and though it can be a challenge, I still love what I do every single day.

As Girls Write Now embarks on its third decade, I can't help but think back to more than thirty years ago and the ten minutes Miss Five took with me to go the extra mile.

I am not a writer, but Miss Five gave me a voice that I didn't know I had. She gave me the courage to follow what was for me a harder path but one that has brought me pure joy. She gave me the gift of creativity and communication, and taught me how to challenge myself.

Girls Write Now helps thousands of girls every year. Not to mention, they're doing this in a moment when helping young women speak their truth is more important than ever. If ten minutes with Miss Five could change the path of my life, I can only imagine the resounding impact of the lifelong mentorships Girls Write Now facilitates.

Thank you to this organization, for fostering such long-lasting mentor/mentee relationships that go well beyond just writing. Thank you to the mentors, for helping these young women blaze their trails into the world. And thank you to the mentees, for being brave enough to think big.

CHRISTINE BALL *is the senior vice president and publisher at Dutton and Berkley, two imprints within the Penguin division of Penguin Random House, where she has been since 2005. Christine is a champion of women's voices and has shepherded through the production of Girls Write Now's award-winning annual anthology for the past three years. Christine and her team have showcased hundreds of stories from our mentees, and we thank her!*

© BALJIT SINGH

A POEM

RUPI KAUR

Dedicated to the young writers of Girls Write Now

you tell me to quiet down cause
my opinions make me less beautiful
but i was not made with a fire in my belly
so i could be put out
i was not made with a lightness on my tongue
so i could be easy to swallow
i was made heavy
half blade and half silk
difficult to forget
and not easy for the mind to follow

RUPI KAUR *is an internationally bestselling poet, author, illustrator, and performer. Her second book,* the sun and her flowers—*an instant global bestseller—is an artistic sibling to her debut,* milk and honey—*one of America's bestselling books of 2017.* milk and honey *has sold more than five million copies, has been translated into more than forty-two languages, and was on the* New York *Times Best Sellers list for more than three years.*

GIANA ADOTE

YEARS AS MENTEE: 1
GRADE: Freshman
BORN: Queens, NY
LIVES: Queens, NY

MENTEE'S ANECDOTE: *When my mentor Dayna and I meet, the objective isn't just to get the work done and go. Every time we meet we learn something new about each other. For example, she has a sweet tooth, like me, and she loves dogs, like me (she actually got one and I'm so jealous). But she's actually taught me so much and her writing really inspired me to use more descriptive words and edit my short stories, so I included the really important parts that made up the story. She's always so understanding and helpful and I'm really thankful for her.*

DAYNA SASON

YEARS AS MENTOR: 1
OCCUPATION: Human Resources Business Partner, Johnson & Johnson
BORN: Ridgewood, NJ
LIVES: Jersey City, NJ

MENTOR'S ANECDOTE: *The first time I met Giana, I knew she had a story to tell. We met every week in a coffee shop to catch up on the highs and lows of our weeks, bond over our love of sweets and dogs, and give each other prompts to get us writing. We talked about how writing gets easier the more you do it, learned how to get going with prompts and questions, and explored different tones and techniques to help her find her voice as a writer. Giana is incredibly smart and passionate, and I can't wait to see what she gets up to in the world.*

EVENING DISTRACTIONS

GIANA ADOTE

For this flash-fiction exercise, we started with a prompt and edited down to 100 words. I cut out words that didn't hold as much significance to the story, and what's left was intentionally included to help show the reader instead of telling them.

Sitting at my favorite coffee shop, my fingertips brush the delicate pages of my book as I sip on the velvety hot chocolate. In the middle of a plot twist, a woman wearing a winter jacket with black knee-high leather boots and a gray knit beanie walks in looking straight out of a magazine. Her perfectly filled-in red lips order. She stands there fiercely texting, lips pursed and eyebrows scrunched. Drink in hand, she struts out of the shop. Minutes later, my mind is still on her; where'd she come from? Why did she look so upset?

OBENEWA ADU

YEARS AS MENTEE: 1

GRADE: Junior

BORN: New Haven, CT

LIVES: Queens, NY

PUBLICATIONS AND RECOGNITIONS: Designed The Help App

MENTEE'S ANECDOTE: *My mentor Tracy is a role model to me. In many ways we share similar views and have similar interests, such as medicine and writing. Our weekly meetings at Starbucks are often the highlight of my week because Tracy opens my eyes to new styles of writing and new perspectives on life. In the past year with Girls Write Now, I have accomplished so much and I thank Tracy for helping me throughout the process. Tracy has definitely helped me take my place in history.*

TRACY MILLER

YEARS AS MENTOR: 3

OCCUPATION: Director of Digital Communications, NYU Langone Health

BORN: Columbus, OH

LIVES: Queens, NY

MENTOR'S ANECDOTE: *Obenewa and I have had the most fun in our weekly meetings this year just talking—about books we're reading, TV shows we're watching, our families, and where we grew up. This year she has explored identity, family, and culture through her writing, and that's helped me to get to know her better as a person. I'm glad I can be there for her as a mentor, and she's there for me, too, whether it's giving me a tour of TikTok or loaning me Michelle Obama's memoir.*

TALES OF A MIXED GIRL

An Open Letter to All the Mixed Girls
Struggling to Find Their Identity

OBENEWA ADU

A person's identity is shaped by many factors, such as nationality, race, ethnic group, physical appearance, talents, interests, language, religion, and especially culture. Here is a deeper insight to my growth as a mixed girl: My History.

I am the proud offspring of a Ghanaian man and an Irish–Puerto Rican woman. Being mixed does not come as easy as people are led to believe. Many people believe that mixed people are given special treatment or receive more privileges, but in all reality, just because I am mixed with white doesn't mean I actually get the same treatment white people receive. When people look at me they still see a black person.

For most of my life I found myself in an identity crisis, split between two totally different ethnic groups. Too light to fit in with my dad's family, yet too dark to feel close to my mom's family.

I am among the many mixed girls who started to straighten their hair at a young age to fit in with the other girls in class. Every week, I begged my mother to straighten my dark brown curls until they wouldn't coil anymore. I was surrounded by kids who looked nothing like me, and it led to me feeling uncomfortable and ashamed in my own skin.

I wanted nothing more than to fit in with my peers. I was caught between identities, remolding myself with every different crowd. Constantly checking my tone to make sure it wasn't too "ghetto" and always remaining calm or tame so no one could call me the angry black girl. Many times I have struggled with not being the typical beautiful and exotic Ghanaian woman, not fully understanding the morals or language because I was raised here. And after several Spanish classes, I still wasn't fluent in one of my family's many languages.

I was constantly asked to shorten my "ethnic" name because it was "too much work to say." I was no longer Obenewa Afia Adu, I was O.A., Obe, or sometimes even just O. At first, it was fine. I didn't mind until I realized people around me could learn names like Madison or Natalie. Seven letters just like mine, but for some reason, no one was eager to learn my name or pronounce it correctly.

I had no one to turn to with the thoughts racing through my mind. My white mother with silky straight hair and pale freckled skin would never understand my struggles. My Ghanaian father considered me privileged, and I don't blame him in this society. I hated everything—from my dark brown curly hair, to the gap in between my front teeth, to my caramel skin that changes with the seasons.

It took me a long time to realize the beauty of being multiracial and the three different amazing cultures that I belong to. I started to notice where my features came from and it helped me connect. My curly hair and hooded eyes either from my Puerto Rican or Irish ancestors, my flat nose and the gap in between my teeth from my Ghanaian ancestors. I started to eat more of my countries' different foods, and whenever I got the chance I would write essays about where I was from, owning the fact that I was multiracial and highlighting all the amazing things my countries had to offer. I spent hours upon hours Google-searching all the places I am from, trying to get a deeper understanding of who I really am.

I have grown to embrace both cultures and be proud of who I am, which was not easy.

Growing up, I watched *Hannah Montana* on TV every day, the story of a girl with two identities. Hannah is a normal kid by day and a superstar at night. Now I see that in my own way, I am like Hannah, getting the best of both worlds.

I know that being of multiple races does not mean I am any less "full-blood," and it does not mean I am "washed out."

I can't imagine life without my iconic Irish step-dance classes, jollof rice for dinner, and arroz con leche for dessert.

I have learned to stick up for myself and love who I am.

I am proud of my growth and now I know that only I can define myself.

My name is Obenewa Afia Adu.

AFIWA AFANDALO

YEARS AS MENTEE: 1

GRADE: Senior

BORN: Aklakou, Togo

LIVES: Bronx, NY

MENTEE'S ANECDOTE: *Are you familiar with The Sun Is Also a Star by Nicola Yoon? If yes, then you know Natasha's love story began when she was standing in the middle of Grand Central Terminal while gazing up at the ceiling. I was also standing in Grand Central not long ago, with my mentor Caroline. We were looking for a dark spot my teacher had said was in the corner of the ceiling. Lesson to take away: No matter what you are looking for, the person supporting you is what matters the most.*

CAROLINE PRESTON

YEARS AS MENTOR: 1

OCCUPATION: Senior Editor, *The Hechinger Report*

BORN: Charlottesville, VA

LIVES: Brooklyn, NY

MENTOR'S ANECDOTE: *I met Afiwa for our first pair session at a café in the Bronx. I thought it would take a few weeks, maybe months, before we found a rhythm to our conversations. But Afiwa has a way of making me—and everyone—feel comfortable from the start. She gave me a big hug, as if we'd grown up together. Afiwa has a way of assuring others that there's little to worry about, even when I've just come close to choking on a grilled cheese sandwich or neither of us can figure out Glitch. I find this same quality in her writing. She creates worlds that are warm, hopeful, that you want to inhabit.*

PNEUMA

AFIWA AFANDALO

This poem is dedicated to all the girls who are forced, by circumstances, to hide their identity so they can be present for those around them. One reminder: You need to be your authentic self. Go out, find your flame, and take your place in history.

Phoenix!!!!
Can you hear me?
I am looking for my flame.
It disappeared when my small, oval eyes met the desperate
  crocodile tears of the blue, dark, and infinite ocean.
My flame, I painted it with a red and yellow tint
A red so dashing, it is trending on all of social media,
A yellow so luminous, even the brightness of the sun at noon
  can't compete
You might have seen other flames around here.
However, my flame is uncommon.
It has a strike of black—
A black, dark as midnight,
It holds the secrets of unspoken things.
A darkness, clear as clean water
It shines and moves in glory at all times
Phoenix!!!
My flame has been lost for a while now.
Without it,
I feel like a desert without sand,
I feel like a home without a family
I feel empty.
Phoenix!!
I came in hope that you will help me find it.

When you find it,
Please
Tell it that I promise to no longer look into the blue, dark, and
    infinite ocean,
Tell it that I promise to protect it
Phoenix!
Can you hear me?
I am looking for my soul.

ONYEKA AGWU

YEARS AS MENTEE: 1

GRADE: Senior

BORN: Bronx, NY

LIVES: Bronx, NY

MENTEE'S ANECDOTE: *As I struggled to find the right words, there she was right next to me reminding me of how great my piece was already. When I began to doubt my work, Kelsey encouraged me by reminding me of how important my story was and how a little can do a lot.*

KELSEY WEEKMAN

YEARS AS MENTOR: 2

OCCUPATION: Writer, Verizon Media

BORN: Raleigh, NC

LIVES: Brooklyn, NY

MENTOR'S ANECDOTE: *Onyeka and I are both chronically early to everything. At our first meeting, we sat together for an extra half-hour talking about things, and I didn't feel the time pass by. I said, "You know, you're really easy to talk to." She said the same back to me. I've felt that way in each of our meetings—she's so bright and is so good at opening up to the world. She finds inspiration all around her, easily identifies those she can learn from and portrays them beautifully. As she writes about those people, she's writing herself into history as well.*

BLACKBIRD

ONYEKA AGWU

Like blackbirds we lived in a constant state of struggle trying to survive. Every time we tried to fly there were others pecking away at our wings. Like that bird, fueled by our need to survive, we learned to soar.

Their eyes bore into her, while the question "Why you wanna fly, Blackbird?" begged to be answered. As the silence grew, the words "You ain't never gonna fly" rang in her head, revealing the unspoken truth.

Sitting in the front of the room surrounded by books, she began. At the drop of each note, a melody ensued and the voice of twelve-year-old Eunice followed. Turning, her eyes glossed over the crowd in search of her parents, but they were nowhere to be seen. As she was about to return to her piano, there they were, relegated to the back and constrained by their complexion.

Blackbird. A species of birds with strong beaks and one not to be confused with another species. Their blackness is a symbol of pure potential. However, common blackbirds spend their time looking for food on the ground, where they are infected with ticks. This leaves them exhausted and worn out. Despite their troubles, these birds maintain a high level of alertness even in areas of high predation.

As a black woman, Eunice faced the complex struggles of class, race, and gender. Like a blackbird, she was filled with pure potential but found it hard to experience it because of the pressures of society keeping her down. Although Eunice's experiences left her brimming with rage, it was this anger that fueled her. Her rage kept her afloat and alert to inequality and racism around her. Using her musical talent, Eunice discovered her identity and full potential as she fought for racial justice.

In 1963, after the assassination of Medgar Evers and the Birmingham church bombing that left four young black girls dead, Eunice, who was now known as Nina Simone, wrote the song "Mississippi Goddam." Although her song was denied on many radio stations, she used the anthem to raise awareness of racism and inequality. Nina understood that living life in fear was a waste of life. In the song "Turn! Turn! Turn!," Nina chants about the passage of life and that there is a time to break down and a time to build up. These verses were ones Nina lived by. Despite the risk of losing her life and being blackballed in the music industry, Nina continued to protest. As an image of "black rage," she openly expressed her contempt for America and her lack of hope for the future.

Though Simone lived a life of struggle, her fearlessness and passion to uncover the truth taught her that she didn't need society's permission before learning how to fly. By living true to herself, she found her passion and reached the potential the world had tried to suppress. Even in a time of severe oppression, Simone lived with a conviction that allowed her to fly, silencing the doubts of the Blackbird's capabilities.

|

UGONNA AGWU

YEARS AS MENTEE: 1

GRADE: Sophomore

BORN: Bronx, NY

LIVES: Bronx, NY

MENTEE'S ANECDOTE: *This is my first year at Girls Write Now and so far, so good. My mentor Kate has helped me broaden my experience with writing. I really enjoyed writing my short story "If Walls Could Talk," which is the beginning of a book I am definitely planning to continue. Kate helped me find a passion in poetry, which I really enjoy writing, and for this I owe a huge thanks to her.*

KATE NEWMAN

YEARS AS MENTOR: 3

OCCUPATION: Content Strategy Manager at *The Washington Post*

BORN: Washington, D.C.

LIVES: Brooklyn, NY

MENTOR'S ANECDOTE: *I am astonished by Ugonna's creativity and willingness to try different kinds of writing. My favorite pair session was our first experiment with found poetry, when we cut words out of used books to shape into our own stories. The depth of feeling in Ugonna's first poem blew me away—and she's only continued to impress me with her thoughtful choice of words for every piece of writing! I'm very excited to see her explore more forms and genres in our future years together.*

IF WALLS COULD TALK

UGONNA AGWU

This is a fantasy story that I wrote in one of our pair sessions. This piece is only the first chapter of a novel I am working on.

After escaping her home, which she hated, Hazel moved into a home with her grandmother.

Although most people wouldn't see it as a home, to Hazel the house was everything she had ever wished for. It was run-down and the exterior looked like it hadn't been occupied for ages. The loud creaks on the steps always made it seem as if the house was a hide-out for a witch, but Hazel felt at peace when she was there. Ever since she moved in with her grandmother, she had never felt alone. Even after her grandmother died—three months after she moved in—she always felt like there was someone near watching her.

That was, until she realized she wasn't alone.

After coming home from the bakery owned by her grand-mother's close friend, Hazel whisked up her favorite meal—tomato soup—with the bread she brought.

As she was cooking, she heard someone say, "Mmm, that smells wonderful." Hazel jumped back in astonishment, grabbed a pan, and shrieked, "Who said that!" She took a look around her in search of the intruder, but an empty kitchen stared back at her.

"How can she hear us?"

"I will swing it, I swear," she threatened.

"Put down the pan, Hazel. No need to get so worked up, you're gonna hurt yourself."

"I know how to use a pan, what are you implying? And how do you know my name, who are you, who do you work for!!!"

The voice stayed silent. She screamed in frustration.

"Okay, okay, we'll tell you."

But then Hazel passed out.

When she woke up, she was in an unfamiliar blank room. She sat there trying to place where she was. But she could only hear voices—a lot of voices.

She scrambled up from the floor. The voices sounded panicked: "Take her to the king!" "She must be executed!" "Who is this?" Hazel didn't know what to do, but she didn't scream. She couldn't.

How do I get out of here? she thought.

Then she saw a pair of glasses on the floor, and as soon as she put them on, she saw every person in the room. Except they were not quite people: They had skin rough like sandpaper, the color of bluegrass. They were nothing like the creatures you have seen in movies or heard about in books. Their eyes were completely white and teeth brown like wood.

"What are you things? And where am I? What's going on?"

One replied, crossing its arms, "Umm, rude. We are not things."

Then another replied, "We are wall people, and we live in your walls."

Hazel burst into laughter. "Wall people? That's the most ridiculous thing I have ever heard!" The room was completely silent.

"Oh, you're serious."

One said, "Um, boss, when can we kill her off?" and the rest of the crowd muttered in agreement. Then a bigger wall person walked out from among the crowd, and raised his hand, which seemed to shut them up. He lifted Hazel up and took a good look at her: "Send her back, she's no harm."

Hazel was very frightened. "Please, just take me back home."

"All right, then." He proceeded to close his eyes and snap his fingers. She waited, but she was still in the same room. "Can you get me out of here?"

"I'm trying." He waved his hand but nothing worked. He tried snapping his fingers and used ridiculous words like "alakazam" or "wazoo," but still nothing happened.

Suddenly everyone panicked and ran. "What's going on?" she wondered. Someone shouted, "Big boss is coming!" It was complete chaos—with everyone moving in different directions, it could have been easily mistaken for a circus or a mass murder.

Hazel didn't know what "big boss" meant, but she was pretty sure it wasn't a good thing, so she started running with the crowd. However, she didn't make it very far. Something dragged her in the opposite direction.

Before she could react, she was in a beautiful place with stained-glass windows and walls drenched with murals.

She noticed a lavender pearl perched in an open oyster right in front of her. It sparkled like it had been washed several times before she got there. The light that reflected off of the pearl was almost blinding. There was a piece of papyrus under the pearl with words written on it in a fancy font. Hazel took the paper and the oyster immediately shut—so quickly that if she had waited any longer, her hand would have been flatter than the paper in front of her. The paper itself was covered in dust, as if it had waited upon Hazel's arrival for quite some time.

Written inside of it were the words: "Keep your enemies close, and your friends closer." Hazel knew this was not the original phrase and this confused her a lot. She demanded more information from the pearl, and when the oyster opened again, another piece of paper appeared with four written words: "The oracle has spoken."

EMMANUELLA AGYEMANG

YEARS AS MENTEE: 1

GRADE: Sophomore

BORN: Bronx, NY

LIVES: Bronx, NY

MENTEE'S ANECDOTE: *I remember applying to Girls Write Now, and in my essay I mentioned that having a mentor meant having a guardian angel. My mentor, Grace, is all that I have hoped for in a mentor. She has a warm and welcoming energy that constantly surrounds her. Our pair sharings are something that I will forever carry with me because I was able to grow as a writer and as a person through her words to me. When I get all old and wrinkled, I will remember our pair sharings as my humble beginnings and a part of me growing.*

GRACE ANEIZA ALI

YEARS AS MENTOR: 2

OCCUPATION: Professor, New York University

BORN: Georgetown, Guyana

LIVES: New York, NY

MENTOR'S ANECDOTE: *Emmanuella and I share many firsts. We are first-generation immigrants. We are the first in our family to go to college. We are the first in our families to be published writers. As I watch her soar, I also witness her come to know that to take her place in history is not an individual journey, but a journey of community, friendship, and service to others. As she writes in her poem, "I am taking my place in history / Like women who have done it before me."*

TO THE ONES WITH SKIN AS DARK AND BEAUTIFUL AS NIGHT

EMMANUELLA AGYEMANG

"To the Ones with Skin as Dark and Beautiful as Night" comes from a time when I didn't feel so confident. Lupita Nyong'o is a huge part of me realizing that I am beautiful, as she took her place in history, and I soon took my own place in history.

Look into our dark brown eyes,
Do you see the tears we cried?
Or the way we looked at ourselves in the mirror
Agonized by our sorrowful reflection.
Do you see the tear-stained pillows?
The long nights where we scrubbed our skin,
Wishing we were lighter.
Do you see the faces of our so-called friends?
When we tell them we are African.
When we tell them we are Ghanaian.
When we tell them we are Kenyan.
When we tell them we are Nigerian.
Do you hear the shatter of our hearts, followed by silence?
Never again daring to mention that we belong to Africa.

I see a girl who looks like me.
I am mesmerized by her beauty.
Lupita.
Her name means valley of the wolf
She embodies the strength of little black girls.
The colors of an African sunset adorn her flowy dress,
As she walks effortlessly, gracefully,

To collect the Academy Award for Best Supporting Actress
The first African.
The first Kenyan.
She will not be the last.

I see myself
I am mesmerized by my power.
Emmanuella
My name means God is with us.
I will not fail.
I see my cocoa-colored skin
My delicate dark brown eyes
The first to go to college in my family.
The first published writer.
I am taking my place in history
Like women who have done it before me
Like all the girls like me
Whose skin is as dark and beautiful as night.

ANNEMARIE ALMS

YEARS AS MENTEE: 2

GRADE: Sophomore

BORN: New York, NY

LIVES: New York, NY

PUBLICATIONS AND RECOGNITIONS: Scholastic Art & Writing Awards: Honorable Mention

MENTEE'S ANECDOTE: *Who would I be had I not met Kate? I wouldn't know who Kathleen Hanna is or what postmodernism really entails or how much caffeine a person can physically consume over the course of twenty-four hours. I probably still would've been as shy and indecisive as I was two years ago. But meeting with Kate every week (the highlight of every week, I should note!) has molded my confidence into a visible thing. Because that's exactly what Kate exudes: confidence. Like, learning-how-to-skateboard-in-her-late-twenties confident. Wearing-unbelievably-awesome-furry-coats confident. Rebel-girl confident. She continues to amaze and empower me at every turn!*

KATE NAPOLITANO

YEARS AS MENTOR: 2

OCCUPATION: Senior Editor, Houghton Mifflin Harcourt

BORN: Seaside Park, NJ

LIVES: Queens, NY

MENTOR'S ANECDOTE: *When I first met Annemarie in 2018, I knew I had encountered a special person: She was smart and observant and kind and had a subtly subversive sense of humor that always managed to surprise me. I've watched her writing flourish over the past two years, both in prose and poetry, and her enduring curiosity has served only to strengthen these skills. Annemarie's anthology piece is indicative of the way in which she has continually pushed her creative limits.*

BERLIN, ETERNALLY

ANNEMARIE ALMS

Despite dating back to the thirteenth century, Berlin is such a mysteriously modern place. It was destroyed by bombs. And so, in the city, you feel the weight of these ghosts. Their blood suspended in the air: an antiwar cry. An anthem. A glimmer of hope.

3 a.m.
Cobblestone soaking moonlight
beneath a closed window. Little
nuns rush to bolt her door.

So—she'd rinse with
Vinegar. Between mouthfuls: "Calm yourself.
All's well in limelight, in the corner of this room."
    With her

thighs ballooning out on
the wooden floor. Legs, her legs, like perfect
halves of a coffee bean.

Blue eyes and
Lips like stapled sheets.
—She imagines—
Melting sunlight on cold
grass. Mourning doves Gazing
down, Away, a
world Away. Separating
her
from their feathers.

Empty, now, she
breathes. Spreads her hand across an Ugly
blanket. an Uneven, Corkscrewed
thing. layered among the Ash,
Dust, and Rubble.

"Make your bed," she
whispers. But
Imagines—She imagines—can only
imagine:
Cloudless sky. and
Cursive wind spiraling through her feathers.

MIKAYLA AUGUSTIN

YEARS AS MENTEE: 1

GRADE: Senior

BORN: Travis, TX

LIVES: Queens, NY

PUBLICATIONS AND RECOGNITIONS: LEAP, First Place, Spoken Word; Amari, *Much Ado About Nothing*, Off-Broadway; NYC Mock Trial Lawyer, Semifinalist

MENTEE'S ANECDOTE: *Writing with my mentor is absolutely amazing. It's almost like exploring your very first fair or amusement park and being ready to ride anything. At first, I honestly didn't know what to expect, but as I opened myself up, I was taught to be brave, funny, and creative; and I was encouraged through it all. It's because of my mentor Kate and all we did for the sake of our pair writing, our other projects, and just for the sake of trying new things.*

KATE RILEY

YEARS AS MENTOR: 1

OCCUPATION: Fundraiser

BORN: Hartford, CT

LIVES: Huntington, NY

MENTOR'S ANECDOTE: *The Girls Write Now algorithm kicked out a winning combination when I was matched with Mikayla. While she was somewhat soft-spoken at first, we got over that real quick. She attacked our first workshop assignment by interviewing me, drafting a profile, and bravely sharing it with the room. And she continues to impress by voicing her ambitions, frustrations, and visions of a better world over ramen and tacos. Her powerful poetry is where she has chosen to tackle knotty social issues, and I'm grateful to have been part of that journey.*

NOTE TO SELF

MIKAYLA AUGUSTIN

"Note to Self" is a poem that was written in the midst of a wave of high self-esteem that shows itself rarely. This is when the power of Melanin Beauty reveals itself unapologetically.

One
Beauty given straight to her
She's a gift from God
Wait i messed up the first line
Beauty is her first name
She gave it meaning
There's nothing to compare

Two
Language owned
Projected in different ways
Neck Rolls aren't to be taken lightly
Hand Gestures makes our point wildly
We have our own grammar
Dictionary thicker than anything made about us to make us
    frown

Three
Essential Hair
A needed topic of its own
May i say
I'll let you touch it before you speak
But don't look at me like i'm a petting-zoo animal

Four
Sun-Kissed by the sun so much
Yea i'm dark as hell
The sun couldn't help itself
It's addicted to melanin
Wanted to share that type of love with the world
It gave us different shades

You see a room full of black women
You gotta take a breath
A step
A sip of water
Take a seat
It's okay, we get it
The beauty is so mesmerizing, it knocks the breath out of you
Just like an eighteen-mile run
Run down
Get a camera
A picture lasts longer

Black Women
Of all shades
all sizes
With nothing but positivity is a sight to be seen by everyone

Five
Sacrifice
Something embedded into our lives
From black baby to black woman
It's like a weird middle name
It'll bring you pain
But makes the victory from your history so much better

Live, Do your thing
You're so blessed to be who you are
You're a dark young lady shipped from heaven

Your pain ain't nothing but a chapter
A chapter to make the history books made about you much better

Merge the fork in the road
Make it your own
You're a goddess
Don't let anybody sit in your throne

Take your joy back
And note to self
Beauty is within the eyes of the beholder
And baby girl
You're isis
Fuck if the world falls for you

LUNA AZCURRAIN

YEARS AS MENTEE: 2

GRADE: Junior

BORN: New York, NY

LIVES: New York, NY

PUBLICATIONS AND RECOGNITIONS: The Moth All-City Slam; Columbia University High School Law Institute

MENTEE'S ANECDOTE: *I have had the pleasure of working with Carina for two years now and I couldn't have been paired with a better mentor! She makes the time no matter what to consult with me and talk about my work. Her feedback is always well thought out and teaches me so much about the writing world. The positive energy she brings makes it so easy to work with her. I look forward to many more Wednesdays at Pret a Manger!*

CARINA STORRS

YEARS AS MENTOR: 2

OCCUPATION: Freelance Science Journalist and Writer

BORN: Tallahassee, FL

LIVES: New York, NY

PUBLICATIONS AND RECOGNITIONS: *Health Affairs, Nature News*

MENTOR'S ANECDOTE: *Luna and I clicked right from the start over our love of travel and food. But we really connected toward the end of our first year over our similar experiences having divorced parents. I was thrilled when Luna started putting these down on paper during one of our meetings at whichever Union Square coffee shop had an open table that day. She has a gift for portraying the bittersweetness of family relationships. I hope many more people will read her words! Our second year working together has just made me more in awe of Luna's understated talent. I will not be remotely surprised when she heads out and changes the world.*

ABUELO, APPLES & ME

LUNA AZCURRAIN

This piece looks at the way an unexpected Thanksgiving tradition was able to bring me and my grandfather closer.

I was on my way to work when I remembered that it was going to be Thanksgiving tomorrow. Thanksgiving in my family is not your traditional Thanksgiving. Half of my family is from Spain, so we like to add our own spin to it. We have tortilla de patata, croquetas, and Manchego, but the one thing that stood out to me every year was the apple cake. Thanksgiving was typically held at my aunt's house, so I always assumed she was the mastermind behind it, but I soon learned it was actually my grandfather, which completely surprised me because I had only ever seen him reading the French newspaper or watching the Spanish news channel. When I found out it was him my first reaction was that: for one, I would finally be able to get closer with my grandfather; and two, I would finally get my hands on this recipe. As I approached work I got excited about the cake me and my grandfather would be making the next day; it has become a tradition over the last few years.

As I begin to close up at work, my mom calls me and says my grandfather has been admitted to the hospital. He needs to get a pacemaker put in, it's going to be a minimal surgery, and he is going to be okay, but we will be having Thanksgiving in the hospital this year. I have to admit part of me was worried about him, but I was also worried about who was going to make the cake. I know that if we don't have the apple cake, it won't be Thanksgiving, so I decide I will make it alone for the first time this year.

I get home and I'm staring at these apples my mom had just picked out from the farmer's market as my mind slips away, and I completely forget how to do everything. I can't remember if he cuts the apples into slivers or chunks. If they are big or small. I just remember being mesmerized by the fact that he could peel an apple in one entire strip. We would have this old recipe book in between us as I would mix the wet and the dry ingredients together. He would always double-check my measurements and as I look down at the bowl in front of me I realize no one has checked if there really is a cup and a half of flour in mine. Nothing seems to come out right. I keep making this cake with a huge cloud of doubt hanging over my head, *I'm making it wrong, it's not going to taste the same.* All I want is for it to feel like I was baking with my grandfather again. The house would instantly smell like apples and cinnamon. As soon as it came out at the end of the night, everyone got that thick slice. My family would applaud and give us never-ending praise for it being the perfect palate cleanser and having just the right amount of sweetness. My grandfather and I would look at each other as everyone was enjoying their slice. We would smile and nod like, *Yeah, we did that.* It was a moment I looked forward to every year. My opportunity to bond with my grandfather. This year we couldn't do that.

I finish off the rest of the cake, put it in the oven, and just wait. I reminisce about all the times I was little and had the chance to share this moment with him. Having abuelo by my side and connecting with me was what made making the apple cake so special. *Beep beep beep,* the oven rings, reminding me that this no-longer-perfect cake was done. I am hesitant to bring the cake over to the hospital. I know it is not the same. It doesn't have his touch, but of course my mother insists. As we enter the hospital this waft of medicine fills our noses and the cool air leaves goose bumps on our skin, but as we approach my grandfather's room I see my whole family surrounding him, creating some warmth. I pull out the bag of apple cake from behind me and hand it to my grandmother. She takes the cake and exclaims, "Look, Luna made apple cake!" as she places it on my grandfather's lap. He looks down at the apple cake and back up at me and I swear I feel this rush of memories flow, of us making the cake together year after year and our bond getting tighter. At that moment, even though he was in the hospital, it still felt like he made it with me. We had done it once again.

MAXINE BABB

YEARS AS MENTEE: 2

GRADE: Sophomore

BORN: New York, NY

LIVES: Bronx, NY

MENTEE'S ANECDOTE: *Agnes shows me that women can do anything they put their minds to by being adventurous and trying new things all the time. She definitely takes her place in history by being a dedicated athlete and an even better writer. She also shows that women can do anything men can do. Agnes, many other women, and I have experienced toxic masculinity and it needed to be brought to light. Toxic masculinity is a real thing and can be dangerous in some instances. Let's all come together and take our places in history by showing men who the bosses are!*

AGNES BANNIGAN

YEARS AS MENTOR: 2

OCCUPATION: Writing Editor, Great Minds

BORN: Cheverly, MD

LIVES: New York, NY

PUBLICATIONS AND RECOGNITIONS: 2018–2019 Alderworks Alaska Writers and Artists Retreat Residency Recipient

MENTOR'S ANECDOTE: *If any girl is primed to take her place in history and make a mark on the future, it's my mentee Maxine. In her second year at Girls Write Now, she continues to be courageous and sharp in her writing and her commitment to amplifying girls' and women's voices. Her writing is always pushing limits. Her anthology piece in particular uses suspense fiction to explore how toxic masculinity is a dangerous epidemic, a powerful and creative commentary on the past and a call to action for our future. As we like to say, "The future BEEN female!"*

A PAINTER'S JOB

MAXINE BABB

John, an excessive, narcissistic, psycho painter, finds himself liking Al-
lisa, who just happens to be the girl whose house he's painting, but just
how far will he take this liking?

For three days we've been painting this wall white. Oh, I'm sorry, Marshmallow White, because it's so important to Duke that I include the "marshmallow" in that sentence. We are literally painting white on top of white.

Honestly, I would do anything to see pretty Lisa, though. Her real name is Allisa, but I like calling her Lisa. Everything is perfect about her—perfect eyes, perfect smile, perfect lips, perfect age. She is twenty-six and living by herself. Lisa needs a man to stay here with her and protect her. I'm going to be that man and I won't let anybody else take my job. For now, though, my one and only job is to take as long as I can with painting this room and find out as much as I can so that I can be that man she clearly wants. If only you could see what she wears in the house knowing there are men in her new house; she wants a man's attention.

"C'mon, Johnny. You've been working on that one wall for almost three days. If I can finish a whole house in two days, then you can at least finish this room by the end of this week," Duke says, interrupting my daydreaming.

I hated Duke. You haven't really worked at Junior's painting business until you've heard Duke's record-breaking painting story. I honestly should be Duke's boss. I've been working at Junior's Painting Company way longer than he has, but instead I'm known as that weird guy who barely anybody associates with. They don't think I know, but I know. I guess I'm okay with it. I was always an outcast back in grade school. Sometimes I wonder if this was the right business to work in. Don't get me wrong, I love painting and it will always be my passion, but jerks like Duke make me want to become an accountant or something. Whenever I see Lovely Lisa, though, I feel completely different, like God sent me here to come sweep her off her feet. Angels like her make me love my job. Today she's wearing pink and gray leggings with a gray spaghetti-strap tank top that says "Sunshine Away." Lisa has her earbuds in with music already blasting. She's going on her daily run. She's perfect.

"I'm going out for a run. Everything good here, Duke?" she asks, screaming over her music with her thumbs up.

Duke replies, "Of course, pretty lady. We've got you covered."

Lisa giggles and then runs out while waving to him with her music still on one hundred. If I was her boyfriend I'd tell her to not run with her music so loud. Sometimes I feel like I'm invisible to her. I don't think we've ever had a full-blown conversation (unless the conversations in my head count). I don't know if she's ever even looked my way. I'm pretty sure Duke is trying to flirt with Lisa. I mean, even if I would let their relationship happen it wouldn't last a week. Being a witness of Duke's last relationship, I can tell that out of all the things Duke is toxic at, he is the most toxic in relationships. His girlfriend of three weeks just dumped him, and he's trying to use my Lisa as a rebound.

I look at my watch, and it's finally five o'clock. I could go home to my cozy, lonely apartment, just the way I like it. I have a bunch of unread books waiting for me. Ever since I was a kid, my whackjob mom could not stress enough to me the importance of books. Since I was ten, she made me read half of a novel by myself every night before I went to sleep. I actually ended up developing a love for reading. Every night as soon as I get home I make dinner and then read a book. Right now I'm reading *The Hedevil.* Currently I'm at the part where Stanley is at Heilda's house watching her, and any second now he's going to pop out and declare his love for her as she sits at the fire and longs for a lover of her own. When he pops out, at first she'll be startled and reject him, but he won't take no for an answer. As she resists him and tells him to leave her house, she suddenly realizes that she needs him and starts to embrace him. As you can tell, I've read this book about a thousand times. I love the romance of it all.

As I'm preparing for my dinner, I realize that I don't have milk and I need milk. It's a simple necessity.

As I'm driving around, all I can think about is Lisa, wondering if she has milk in her house, considering she just moved in. Stupid of me, I know, but when you're in love like this you want to make sure your partner is secure. When I finally stop my car, I find myself in front of Lisa's house AGAIN!

NYASIA BAILEY

YEARS AS MENTEE: 1

GRADE: Junior

BORN: New York, NY

LIVES: New York, NY

MENTEE'S ANECDOTE: *When Girls Write Now told us we would each get our own mentor, I was excited about the idea of having a personal guide to help me navigate through my first year. It was a bit nerve-racking meeting Jazmyn the first time and I was worried that I didn't measure up to what she was expecting. After the first couple of our meetings, I realized that her expectations for me were to see me reach my personal milestones. Jazmyn always wants me to push myself to become more confident, but she is patient with my growth and values me and my choices as a writer.*

JAZMYN TUBERVILLE

YEARS AS MENTOR: 2

OCCUPATION: Digital Supervisor, Horizon

BORN: Austin, TX

LIVES: New York, NY

MENTOR'S ANECDOTE: *Nyasia's journey to becoming a more confident writer has been truly inspirational to witness. When I first met Nyasia, she shared that she wanted to become a journalist one day and would like to go on to do profile writing in her professional career. Over our time together this program year, I've watched a shy, sweet girl from Manhattan blossom into a fearless young woman ready to take her place in history. I'm so proud and excited for Nyasia's beautiful and truly "from-the-heart" work to make its debut in the Girls Write Now anthology and into the world!*

TALE OF AN UNSUNG WRITER

NYASIA BAILEY

I decided the best way to approach this year's broad theme centered on history was to show how I can change the trajectory of my own story by being honest about my passions.

First grade

I became a writer at six years old. My career began with a series that told the tale of two brothers, pencil and paper (derivative of their appearance). The idea for their epic tale actualized when I got bored during first-grade social studies and decided to entertain myself by using my school supplies as dolls. Stirring up stories and reenacting them through writing and objects helped pass the monotony of the long day at school. Even at family functions, I'd dig in my grandmother's bag, animating her makeup as my made-up characters. But my elementary years came and went like the ebb and flow of an ocean tide. At the end of fourth grade, my classmates and I were given superlatives based on our character and achievements over the past four years. I was given the award in scripted print saying: "The most interesting stories." Winning this award provided proof of my ability to tell interesting stories and made me feel valued. Aside from these few memories, I do not remember much from elementary school but that I often felt neglected. Thus, I turned my attention to the safety and comfort of my imagination. Going into middle school, I took being a naturally born writer in stride and hoped to receive the same recognition. A younger me held so much excitement for the new wave of change to come.

Seventh grade

No one told me middle school would suck. The stress of balancing grades, family, and friends left little time to dream—no time to casually read a book or immerse myself in my favorite adventure cartoons. Everything became exhausting. I continued to write but found myself unable to fully free myself from life's complications. My writing took a rather peculiar shape: I'd rant about everything and aggressively scribble lyrics from 2000s emo songs in my notebook (songs from Paramore's album *Brand New Eyes* stayed on repeat in my iPod during this time). Writing remained my cure and gave me comfort in the face of the unknown. Then, one fateful spring day, mid-year superlatives came once again, bringing the hope of renewed validation from the faculty and my peers. In my head, I thought some teacher who was secretly a shaman had been watching me from afar and decided to conspicuously nominate me as the best writer. Another girl won the award as "The Aspiring Novelist." In my heart, I wished I was accepting the certificate for that award. Just as I felt my body go cold, my name was called for the very last award for mathematics. Once again, I found myself receiving praise for an achievement I unknowingly made. From that day on to my first year in high school, I decided to familiarize myself with "Nyasia, the Mathematician."

Eleventh grade

To be frank, I hate math. People say it's a perfectionist's paradise because there's usually only one correct answer to any math problem. I won't lie and say I'm not a perfectionist, but I simply value the freedom of being able to have my own answer. Despite the feeling that the people around me were trying to contort my ideas, writing let me express them freely, without judgment. In retrospect, school has always set me up to believe I'm not good at something until I'm told. In my first two years of high school, I continued to pursue STEAM because everyone around me pushed me in that direction without asking if that's what I wanted. On the rare occasion I was asked, the simplest answer was "yes," since it is the twenty-first century and people empower women by suggesting they pursue male-dominated careers. Because I haven't been honest with myself I became caught up in other people's expectations. Beginning to write again feels like too much exposure and a tedious task. Because of the ubiquitous toxicity and pressure of school, I've realized that comparing myself to my peers has impacted how my external identity shape-shifted throughout the years. Nothing I've done has ever been for myself, but has been in search of validation from others.

Now I know I never needed it, but yes, I still care what people think. Like the sun lying along the edge of a horizon, honesty is the beginning of my revolution. A small step is the beginning of an unsung writer's story.

SIERRA BLANCO

YEARS AS MENTEE: 2

GRADE: Junior

BORN: New York, NY

LIVES: New York, NY

PUBLICATIONS AND RECOGNITIONS: *The New York Times, Tapestry, Ellipses*; Interlochen Fine Arts Scholarship; Stephen Sondheim National Young Playwrights Winner, Michael Perelstein Scholarship; Scholastic Art & Writing Awards: Gold Key, Silver Key, Honorable Mention

MENTEE'S ANECDOTE: *I always love meeting up with Abigail for good tea and discussion. Abigail is especially encouraging to me when gearing up for entering competitions like Scholastic! She gives really insightful feedback on all my pieces and has an interesting perspective on details in my pieces. Moreover, the intriguing activities Abigail comes up with are incredibly fun! It was also absolutely amazing to have her at the third (staged) reading of my musical,* Farewell Chris Yee!

ABIGAIL KEEL

YEARS AS MENTOR: 1

OCCUPATION: Podcast Producer

BORN: Saint Louis, MO

LIVES: Brooklyn, NY

MENTOR'S ANECDOTE: *Sierra and I meet every week at Argo Tea. Every time she walks in and I ask how she's doing or how her week has been, she replies "Epic!" or "Splendiferous!" or "Awesome!" It always puts a smile on my face to see her embrace school, life, and writing with so much enthusiasm. It's infectious. And watching the staged reading of her original musical this winter was definitely "epic."*

THE CRASH

SIERRA BLANCO

It is not a boom It is not a ba-ba-bang It is not even a pft It is the sound of division typed into a four-function calculator One divided by four divided by three divided by two divided by one divided by infinity Because infinity plugs into a four-function calculator just like four or pi or number x Because x is a number that means everything And everything is nothing And nothing is truth And I am a liar, so I plug that in as well The broken solar-paneled four-function calculator That will now someday run out of battery Because there was a battery of the battery and soon there will be no sun Strong enough to charge a broken solar panel Just enough to charge a sentiment-less machination for a second So I shall plug that in along with biochemistry and clocks that run fast and closets and cores But since it can't code, I need to plug it into a graphing calculator One of the ancient ones you get off eBay for three bucks Because nobody sane wants to use plus-plus-Polish entry on their chemistry test So they buy the twenty-dollar ones at Staples, or the pricier ones wherever else And they plug in the price in their new graphing calculator and it graphs a 100 Which they put on their test, and it gets marked down to an 85 because nobody sane Can actually get an 85 without trying. And it comes with a bang And a boom And a pft Because it is the crash and it is the sound Of one girl sitting and staring at the ceiling While her parents are a whirlwind around her A tornado, a tidal wave, an unstoppable Tsunami Is-adore, like alternating rhythms in music class Like trying to ignore how there are names for fragments of herself The tidal wave of laundry and fix the sink and new shower curtain and love Because there is no boom big enough, No punctuation or onomatopoeia to explain The self-fulfilled prophecy of someday of ignoring of impossible She feels at home where she fails and at home where she exceeds And she is not I is not an i because i is an imaginary number, and she wants to use her four-function That will die before the end of the year, so she wants to make it feel useful and loved Because she loves her calculator and she loves her tidal wave and she loves her life

And she knows she has run out of time, but her heart is too stubborn to accept life True life, like the lives on reality tv, that know what normal is Because normal is not a function on a four-function calculator There are only four, and she is only interested in the divide symbol Which really looks like a percent symbol from the side, when you tilt your head right And it's rather important she remember ⅓ as a decimal and .142857 repeating as a fraction Necessary like her remembering how to spell necessary Which she rarely does, like she spells which wish sometimes Perfectly necessary typos and terms and hopes and dreams and lies But she is not a liar anymore Because she forgot that lies are only graphed on the z plane And she's only supposed to do trigonometry and calculus next year And she prefers to pretend she knows nothing of a subject until she needs it Like memorizing the 7th fractions as decimals and never mentioning it until eleventh grade. She remembers it, almost everything she wants to really Because she is a ninja in her sleep, her sleep is self-defense and stealth attacks She is a warrior with her sleep, showing opinions she is brave enough to never say awake She lies in her sleep, she steals in her sleep, she creates and destroys gods in her sleep Her sleep is deadly, but not half as deadly as a shard from a broken solar panel Like the one on her four-function calculator That was probably stabbed with a protractor, but it was also stabbed with sleep Because sleep means dreaming and the girl forgets how not to dream And in the wake of her forgetting how to not, sleep surrounds her Sleep engulfs her, builds walls around her like a princess in a tower And the tower is made of the best and favorite books and worlds and movies And spans for centuries and centuries above the ground, too far for any prince to climb And the dragon that guards her is friendly and her best friend But that does not fit in a four-function calculator, not even on a graphing calculator So the girl knows her name means everything and nothing And it ends without a boom Without a ba-ba-bang Without even a pft

KINAH BRITTON

YEARS AS MENTEE: 1

GRADE: Freshman

BORN: Gulfport, MS

LIVES: New York, NY

MENTEE'S ANECDOTE: *My relationship with my Girls Write Now mentor is PERFECT! We always meet at 3:45 p.m. at the latest and sometimes she helps me with my homework, and then we both work on our Girls Write Now projects. I absolutely love hanging out with her. She makes me feel comfortable, safe, and happy. Even though I have known her for only a little while, I would like to say that she is the most AMAZING mentor I have ever had!*

CASEY CORNELIUS

YEARS AS MENTOR: 1

OCCUPATION: Head of Content and Client Services, CredSpark

BORN: Delmar, NY

LIVES: New York, NY

MENTOR'S ANECDOTE: *Kinah is so talented! She is a singer and an actor and I am so proud of how hard she works at her art. She is also a thoughtful and insightful writer and I love seeing her develop her own voice and confidence on the page. I always look forward to our meetings and especially her big, generous hugs.*

SCARS

KINAH BRITTON

This story is about how I claim my own face.

When I look in the mirror, all I see are scars. ACNE SCARS. Sometimes I think to myself, *Do I look pretty? Why can't I just have clear skin?*

I ask these questions and many more all the time. But the answer is always the same: "Do a morning and night routine, wash your face every day, and you'll see the difference."

The thing is, there is no difference. All of the products that I use don't even work. I do what they tell me all the time and nothing seems to work.

Sometimes I feel insecure about my facial appearance, especially when I go to school. One of the kids said that I look older than my age. WAY older. I didn't like the way that sounded. It made me feel ugly inside, like my face would never be the way it was before my scars.

But then I realized that my acne scars are not permanent. I'm going to love and embrace my face. And to all the girls who struggle with acne or any scar that makes you feel less than beautiful, don't let society dictate whether you're beautiful. We are ALL beautiful, just the way God made us.

JANEIN BROOKES

YEARS AS MENTEE: 4

GRADE: Senior

BORN: Brooklyn, NY

LIVES: New York, NY

MENTEE'S ANECDOTE: *Between me getting into Kenyon College and Emily traveling the world, sometimes our schedules were not compatible, but we made sure to always make a day to Skype, catch up, and choose a prompt. I came up with the idea for my piece through one of Emily's classic prompts about a text that we felt we had missed out on when we were young because I had read* Strange Case of Dr. Jekyll and Mr. Hyde *very early on in life and never got the chance to analyze it until now.*

EMILY MORRIS

YEARS AS MENTOR: 3

OCCUPATION: Strategic Planner, Zeno Group

BORN: Stamford, CT

LIVES: Brooklyn, NY

MENTOR'S ANECDOTE: *Over the past two years I've known Janein, I've watched her evolve into her own person and be accepted into her dream school, Kenyon College. Her creativity, perseverance, and strong work ethic have served her well throughout high school and will be qualities she can draw upon for the rest of her life. I'm so honored to have been able to witness her growth.*

HYDE YOURSELF IN ME

JANEIN BROOKES

My piece surrounds the text Strange Case of Dr. Jekyll and Mr. Hyde.
*I got inspired by the text because it is a classic and Emily and I have
been exploring classical texts through modern lenses.*

"They call it dissociative identity disorder."

Nyne stared at the multitude of diplomas and framed awards
behind Dr. Meyers's head and wondered if education was all it was
cracked up to be if the doctor himself couldn't recognize the symptoms of DID when he saw them. Nyne knew firsthand what DID
was, and he knew, without a shadow of a doubt, Malcolm didn't
have it. Malcolm was a nine-year-old with a bigger problem than
the voice in his head. The problem was that the voice was Malcolm's, just the part of Malcolm that had used his bare hands to kill
his class rabbit.

"With all due respect, Doctor," he started, almost amazed at his
steady voice, "my brother doesn't have dissociative identities."

The man across from him quirked a shedding brow, and Nyne,
not for the first time that night, was forced to cover his nose and
mouth from the pungent scent of cat piss that was coming from the
doctor's clothes. "Victims suffering from DID have distinct tells
and their behaviors can switch from identity to identity. It sounds
just like what Malcolm described."

Nyne wasn't aware that he was a "victim" or "suffering." None
of his other eight identities were particularly violent, at least from
what he could see from the aftermath or what Malcolm described
to him. He questioned for a second if Malcolm had repeated what
Nyne had explained to him after a particularly long visit from Blair
"Bai." Nyne had felt lucky that it was Bai, as Bai and Nyne were
two of the most similar of the identities, except that Bai's preferred

pronouns were "ze/zir" and often clicked ze's tongue whenever zir was annoyed. Nyne didn't know if he felt as lucky anymore.

"When can I see Malcolm?" Bringing him here was a mistake, but he didn't know what else to do. His own therapist, Dr. Athena, wasn't in today, having come down with a migraine earlier that morning. When he walked into her office, her secretary introduced him to Dr. Meyers, a balding man with crooked glasses and a crooked nose, who took up too much space behind Dr. Athena's extremely organized desk and insisted on biting the tops of her pens. Telling their mother probably would've led to an even worse result, as their mother was of the same opinion as Dr. Meyers: that Nyne was "suffering" and needed to be medicated at every twitch. He didn't want to know what she would do to her youngest son, given the same prognosis.

Dr. Meyers stacked some papers together and tapped them against the desk. The overhead light shone through them, making them translucent for a second, and Nyne could see that there was nothing written on them. Nothing but two names. The first was Malcolm's, but the second he recognized instantly.

Hyde.

Nyne paled.

Some people like him stated that they couldn't feel the transformation before it happened, most that they couldn't remember what had transpired when the other identities came into play. Nyne remembered everything Sin did. It was like Sin left his memories there for Nyne to watch through to declare that he wasn't ashamed of himself. That they might share a body and a brain, but Sin controlled his own emotions and actions.

Nyne could feel Sin first in his spine. He straightened in the chair, squared his shoulders back, and faced Dr. Meyers. Then Nyne felt Sin in his hips. Sin was agile and easily maneuvered Nyne's lean body as if to throw their weight forward at any given second.

"Wait." Nyne held back Sin with the plea.

Sin was calm unless provoked, not one for logic or reasoning and as quick with his hands as he was with his mouth. Nyne needed evidence and maintained fifty percent of the reasoning of all his identities, Ryder and Alexis dividing the other fifty percent.

"Dr. Meyers, where is my brother?" Nyne's voice had deepened into Sin's baritone voice, the space between each word making the question more of a demand. The doctor's eyes flinched to the door of the room that he had pulled Malcolm in, dimming the lights so Nyne couldn't see clearly through the one-way glass. "Where?" Nyne bit out, Sin rolling his neck back. His leg started to bounce, the energy in his body going into overdrive, but his head almost lolled to the side, as if his neck was too tired to support its weight, his consciousness fading in and out.

Dr. Meyers—*Was he even a real doctor?*—took off his glasses, folded them, and set them off to the side. He looked Nyne in the eyes even as they flickered. Nyne wasn't seeing him anymore. Instead he was looking at Sin's consciousness as it held his hand out to him, Sin's hand still covered red from the corpse of the bunny after Malcolm had snapped its neck.

"Take a load off, Eight." Sin spoke in his mind, the sound echoing as if his skull was nothing more than an empty space. He had always called Nyne "Eight," as a reminder that even as an identity of Nyne's, he would always be the one not included. Be his own person. "Let me be the best big brother. Again."

Even though Nyne hated his arrogance, he knew better. Sin was the only one that could understand Malcolm because he was just like him. Nyne was just like him. Because Sin wasn't just another identity.

Sin was Nyne.

Nyne was Sin.

Dr. Jekyll and Mr. Hyde.

"I sent him to Eden," Dr. Meyers announced, but it was no longer Nyne listening. Sin picked up his head, a wicked grin pulling his lips taut, and Dr. Meyers's brow furrowed in confusion at the new man sitting in front of him.

Pulling his knees up onto the chair, Sin was all smooth motions and long, controlled limbs, not awkward at all. "'If he be Mr. Hyde, I shall be Mr. Seek,'" Sin quoted, a warning.

And in the next second, he launched himself across the table.

SCARLETT BURWELL-PHAREL

YEARS AS MENTEE: 1

GRADE: Sophomore

BORN: Brooklyn, NY

LIVES: Brooklyn, NY

MENTEE'S ANECDOTE: *I enjoy the time Danielle and I spend together. She helps me realize the importance of poetry and how the poetry I write can influence other girls like me. She also helps me dream big, that my poetry will be as big as that of my favorite poets.*

DANIELLE CHÉRY

YEARS AS MENTOR: 1

OCCUPATION: Author and Teacher

BORN: Brooklyn, NY

LIVES: Brooklyn, NY

PUBLICATIONS AND RECOGNITIONS: *Peers, Cheers, and Volunteers* (GP's Honey Tomes LLC, 2013)

MENTOR'S ANECDOTE: *I always order a small black coffee, and she likes to get peppermint tea. The cafés change, but our preferences remain the same. We chat and sip our hot beverages. Oftentimes, we'd sit at a table inside of the café, but that one time in Brooklyn during the brisk of February winter, it happened to be sunny and too small of a space inside, so we sat on a bench outside of Hungry Ghost, hot beverages in one hand and a draft of her poem in the other. It was windy. The papers almost flew away, but we sat, unbothered. I'd suggest an edit. She'd agree. We'd bond over our love for poetry. We both like Rupi Kaur. I told her one day, she'll have published books of poems, just like Rupi. She read her poem out loud, and it beautifully depicted the promise of a silver lining. Scarlett has evolved to a state of mind where she recognizes herself as God, and it's inspiring.*

I MET GOD HERSELF, AND SHE WAS BEAUTIFUL

SCARLETT BURWELL-PHAREL

I wrote my poem after my ex-boyfriend and I broke up; we were on and off for three years and when we got together it was very toxic. The day after we broke up I wrote this poem because I felt uplifted after the breakup, and I felt like God.

I met God Herself, and She was beautiful

She was tall and strong.
Taller than I imagined.
She was as strong as ten men.

Her beautiful caramel skin glistened in the sun,
Her ancestors' spirit shining through the sun.

I met God Herself, She was powerful.
Her long locks flowed in the air, a symbol of Her ancestors'
    resilience.

I met God Herself,
Her long beautiful arms, a symbol of all the pain and struggle
    She gracefully overcame.

I met God Herself as I was crying about why he won't love me.
And God Herself told me She loved me.
And that was the best love I've ever truly experienced.

I MET GOD HERSELF, INSIDE ME

JOANNE CAI

YEARS AS MENTEE: 1

GRADE: Senior

BORN: New York, NY

LIVES: New York, NY

MENTEE'S ANECDOTE: *Over Starbucks coffee from the Barnes & Noble in TriBeCa, Leela and I dove into conversation about everything from my impending transition to college (!) to the Trump era to world news. Leela pushed me to be a better writer and thinker, encouraging me to dig deep into my emotions and interests to enrich my writing. With her, I've written my college essays, reflected upon my heritage, and wrote about my greatest passion: the environment. I am so grateful for Leela's advice, wisdom, and insight; she has made me more aware of the power of my voice and ability to make an impact.*

LEELA DEO

YEARS AS MENTOR: 1

OCCUPATION: Freelance Writer and Editor

BORN: Philadelphia, PA

LIVES: Brooklyn, NY

PUBLICATIONS AND RECOGNITIONS: Reuters

MENTOR'S ANECDOTE: *When I first met Joanne I was immediately struck by her confidence, passion, and ambition. As a senior, she was very focused on applying to college. A scientist at heart, with a deep appreciation for biology, nature, and animals, I am certain Joanne will chart an impressive path forward to put her stamp on the world. We both enjoyed the poetry workshop, which we explored further in our pair writing sessions. We had so much fun playing around with skinny poems and lunes.*

THIS SACRED EARTH

JOANNE CAI

Growing up in Midtown Manhattan, spending the weekends at tree-filled Central Park instilled in me a love for nature, leading me to reflect upon our treatment of the environment.

THIS SACRED EARTH

From the grass that sways gently Azaleas kissed shades of pink
A sunset so graceful
The sky lit red and gold
Breathing life inside our lungs
Nature untouched, beauty before brutality
Before the trees disappear
And the birds vanish

I wonder what air would look like If it would lend itself to our
    eyes
I wonder if it would drift by gently Or rush, forcefully gusting
    past

I imagine gentle breezes of yellow As I stop to admire wildflowers
I imagine shades of green
As I lay on freshly mowed grass
I imagine explosions of blue
As my toes sink into sand Watching the waves
Return to the sea

This sacred earth, beauty and glory Emblazoned with history

Life, living in harmony
Streams flowing through jungles Mountains hidden underwater
  Towering above clouds
Grassy green flatlands
Tranquility
Before humans

FIRE INTO WATER

Clear, blue
Calm, serene
Flowing free
Quiet power
Until angered
Stormy, gray
Littered, blackened Controlled, unwillingly
No longer home

Beautiful, calm fire
Enflamed, enraged, out of control Ravaging the world

AMANDA CASTILLO

YEARS AS MENTEE: 2

GRADE: Senior

BORN: New York, NY

LIVES: Bronx, NY

PUBLICATIONS AND RECOGNITIONS: Scholastic Art & Writing Awards: Honorable Mentions; Recognition from Day One Youth Voices Network

MENTEE'S ANECDOTE: *The two years I've spent with my mentor have been nothing short of wonderful. Words can't express the amount of support and love and overall laughs I've shared with her. To Miden, thank you. Thank you for helping me further my craft, and thank you for being that person that I cry on and trust wholeheartedly. We both started this crazy journey together, and I hope wherever we end up, we never forget each other.*

MIDEN WOOD

YEARS AS MENTOR: 2

OCCUPATION: Television Writer

BORN: Great Falls, VA

LIVES: Brooklyn, NY

PUBLICATIONS AND RECOGNITIONS: Wrote and developed an original animated short with Sesame Street's Sesame Studios, to debut on YouTube this year.

MENTOR'S ANECDOTE: *This might sound kind of goofy, but one of my favorite parts of this year was when Amanda would text me asking for help trimming a piece of writing to meet a word limit. We'd take to Google Docs and prune college essays or fiction pieces together. I loved the teamwork and the feeling of victory when we finally cut the very last word—and I loved that this task showcased how much Amanda loves words! It's so cool to see her passion for putting ideas to paper (or G-Docs), and I can't wait for her to write many word-limitless novels.*

OPPIDUM EXSPIRAVIT

AMANDA CASTILLO

The inevitability of death orbits in the very fabric of your existence from the moment you're born to the day death comes. History proves time and time again how precious our actions are and that it's up to us to take our place before our time runs out.

The morgue creaked all the time. Sometimes it creaked because the pipes were old, or loitering kids broke in, creeping around trying to become the next paranormal investigators.

Working as a medical examiner there, I didn't expect anything odd to occur. Granted, that should've been my first thought. Dead bodies are practically the pinnacle of horror movies, right? But real life is real life, those are just stories that keep wimps up at night. Besides, I'd been working here for months and there was nothing that fazed me. Bodies were locked up and the only thing that remotely bothered me was the one light on the sixteenth floor that no one would dare change.

So when the morgue creaked one night, it didn't catch my interest. I could probably attribute the sound to a pipe or the heater—which I'd asked to be turned on hours ago. But then followed a loud bang, a crawling on the walls, like someone dying to get in. If I'd had half a brain at the time I wouldn't have been bothered. It could've been kids breaking in, playing some prank. I mean, just last week I'd scared off some kids that tried to "hold a séance." This would've been nothing new.

A body lay in front of me, ready to be autopsied. The other bodies were lined up and locked behind metal doors. I opened the door; peered down the hall. Nothing, as expected. I laughed out loud to myself, amused that I, for a quick second, truly believed something was out there.

Within the hour I'd finished excavating the man's body and had samples ready to be tested. As I stitched the body up with a tight seal, another creak flooded my ears.

I put the body away as soon as I finished—there were still more bodies to go. The mother and her two kids. I'd put sheets on them so I could work on one body at a time. This is until I noticed one of the sheets resting flat on the table.

The mother was missing.

Now, I don't want to brag, but I'm great at my job. I'm meticulous and make sure to keep track of everything I do, so as to not make the slightest mistake. Maybe I'd forgotten to bring the mother after all. I moved on to the children, making small incisions. I tried not to stare for too long. I mean, they were kids, damn it. They didn't deserve to die so young.

Just as I'd moved on to the second child, I heard the creaking. But this one, it was right behind me. I turned around.

The mother stood before me. In all of her naked, uncut glory. Her skin was pale, only tinted with purples and reds where blood pooled. Her face drooped, flesh loosened by pallor mortis. A smear of red stained her lips and she cocked her head to one side, inspecting me like fresh meat.

I held my tongue and gripped the scalpel tightly in my hand. She leaned in, her mouth emitting a foul stench. Her vocal cords were shot, but the air that left her body came out as a low groan. Her pearly white eyes looked between me and the kids, then widened.

Her mouth hinged open. The snap of her jaw detaching made me almost defecate as a shrill, inhuman scream escaped her body. Her bony hands wrapped around my neck before I could scream in reply. Her body had probably dropped only a couple of degrees, considering I held the bodies for well past seven hours. But it felt like dry ice, latching on to my skin.

I struggled against the weight of the . . . thing as her eyes bore into mine, a soulless expression behind them. She leaned in, to eat me, it seemed, but in a turn of events she didn't. She hurled me across the room.

In between trying to place whose blood was which, I can vaguely remember the dead mother sinking her teeth into her own child, blood spraying everywhere and organs spilling out, like something from a horror movie. I then thought, *I have to be dreaming, because things like this don't just freaking happen. Right?*

Snapping out of my daze only to find myself holding the last stitch of the man I'd just put away—the mother and her two kids lying right beside him—meant I was dreaming, right?

I stitched up the man and shoved him into his respective box at lightning speed. It was worth a damn award.

I ran to the bathroom and hurled up everything in my stomach; it wasn't really a lot. I didn't eat before I worked, for more reasons than one. I couldn't begin to comprehend what transpired, let alone if any of it was real. It couldn't have been.

Yet as I rose from the floor, I finally got a glimpse of myself in the mirror.

A ring of purple around my neck, and a line of blood trickling from the corner of my head. Now I believe. There's something completely off with the place.

SAONY CASTILLO

YEARS AS MENTEE: 3

GRADE: Senior

BORN: New York, NY

LIVES: New York, NY

MENTEE'S ANECDOTE: *Lauren and I met through Girls Write Now and were able to share our perspectives and views with each other, although under no other circumstances would we have been able to meet and be friends. There's a sort of division when it comes to our generations, and it becomes hard to be able to have conversations and make friendships, but when you actually get to know each other you can see how alike you are, and you've gone through similar situations. Lauren and I are constantly learning new things from each other and it's always fun working together.*

LAUREN KIEL

YEARS AS MENTOR: 2

OCCUPATION: General Manager for Climate and Sustainability Initiatives, Bloomberg News

BORN: Wilmington, NC

LIVES: New York, NY

MENTOR'S ANECDOTE: *I'm so grateful to Girls Write Now for bringing Saony and me together. I really enjoy our wide-ranging life conversations over coffee, and I have her to thank for teaching me about BTS and K-pop and fan fiction, and for being my cohost for my first podcast! Her creativity inspires me, and I can't wait to see her apply that creativity to her film studies in college and in her future career.*

GOODNIGHT

SAONY CASTILLO

My mind tends to wander when it's dark and I'm alone; this is a sort of letter to myself, to the part of me that keeps me up at night.

My chest feels heavy.
My red bloodshot eyes stare back at me. Right now, in this moment, do I exist?
If I do, then why does it hurt so bad?

Why are you hurting me for breathing?

Why do you only appear when I'm all alone?

Why do you mask yourself in the presence of others?

Please let me sleep, I'm tired.
Go away.
I want to sleep.
Stop invading all my thoughts and dreams. I gave you no permission.
Let me sleep.
I can live without you, but you can't say the same. If it's you or me, then I'll go.
I'm going to sleep now.
Stay away.
Goodnight.

DOMINIQUE DE CASTRO

YEARS AS MENTEE: 1

GRADE: Junior

BORN: Queens, NY

LIVES: Queens, NY

MENTEE'S ANECDOTE: *Sweets, books, and giggles—those are the three words that come to mind when I think of my relationship with Courtney. In the little time we have been together, she has bought me cake, given me a library of books, and laughed at many of my bad jokes. I feel like I've found a person as quirky and silly as me in her. I feel free to experiment with new types and styles of writing around her, and I'm insanely lucky to have her as both a friend and a mentor.*

COURTNEY STEVENSON

YEARS AS MENTOR: 1

OCCUPATION: Assistant Editor, HarperCollins Children's Books

BORN: Greenwich, CT

LIVES: Brooklyn, NY

MENTOR'S ANECDOTE: *From the very first time we met, I've been constantly amazed and impressed by how Dominique thinks about the world—she's one of the smartest, most curious people I know. We've gotten to share lots of laughs, lots of books, and one large cake (she's got a big sweet tooth!). I'm so excited to see what other pieces (and stories, and worlds, and jokes) her magnificent brain will come up with!*

INTO THE UNDERWORLD

DOMINIQUE DE CASTRO

This is the first chapter of a novel I've been developing for about six months. It is set in a future where humanity is divided by pollution, class, and race and the world order is on the brink of total upheaval by two very spunky girls and a suction tube.

As the tongues of fire licked my face, I thought, *Oh, shit! I'm gonna die!*

I could see my fate in the eyes of my assailant, too. The fire danced in them, illuminating the malice and anticipation hidden behind those dark irises. *Crack.* She snapped her fire whip, flicking more flames as the whip returned to its owner like an obedient dog.

I flitted my eyes across the scene, but the brown glow of day had long disappeared from the sky. The only light in the underground market came from the dust-covered fluorescent bulbs strung across the tents. Shadows of fights happening around me danced along the ground. I could hear the grunts of my brothers in the distance. Screams were chased by the whoosh of bats cutting through the air.

"What's wrong, Marisha?" my assailant asked, as she stepped further out of the shadows. *Crack!* A fruit stand exploded in fire and rotting oranges behind me. I ducked as sour smelling pulp flew across my back. The burning hot liquid seeped into my shirt. *That's going to leave a stain,* I thought.

Black boots stepped into view just under my nose, disturbing the dirt as they filled my nose with the sharp smell of shoe polish. The gleam of the silver buckles taunted me. They were emblazoned with the symbol of a snake spitting fire. *She's a part of the damn Cobras.*

"Go ahead. Lick my boots. It'll probably be the most expensive thing you'll ever taste." I glared down at those buckles and clenched my jaw. *No time to think. Just move.*

My mind went blank. I felt my muscles tense as I lunged forward, arms outstretched, launching myself into my attacker's stomach. My face collided with buttons and leather as I tackled her. *Let's see how you like the taste of dirt.* Her arms flailed as she stumbled backward. In a desperate attempt to remain upright, she lashed her whip out at another helpless market stand.

Crack! A stand once covered in intricate, though no doubt counterfeit, designer rugs was engulfed in flames.

"Nice try," she whispered. For just a moment, I was distracted by the explosion and she decided to strike. Her hand reached out for my elbow and yanked me in a full circle, finally releasing me just beyond the reach of the flames now surrounding this corner of the marketplace.

My eyes watered. Smoke choked my lungs. I could feel the heat cooking my skin. *Who would've thought it'd end like this? The only witnesses to my death will be rotting fruit and burning rugs.*

Somewhere to my left, a tent pole buckled. The canvas stretching over it was engulfed in flame. The fabric appeared to float as it fell to the ground. Around me, I could hear the creaking and moaning of the other poles. To my left, another pole snapped. I watched as the burning tent fell slowly toward the ground.

A burst of hot air blew over me, whipping the flames out as a shadow flew across my vision. *Crash!* The shadow ripped the canvas out of the air mid-flight. I lifted my head and turned toward the burning crates behind me—or, at least, they had been burning a second before. Now they were dark charred masses cradling the ashen remnants of the tent. I crawled toward the smoking pile, coughing and sputtering into the dirt. Something was moving under the cloth.

Cough! "That was not a soft landing!"

A girl with straight black hair poked her head out of the ashes. She stared back at me with bright green eyes that glowed through the ash smudged across her face.

"Don't you look wretched!" she said with a cheeky smile. She rubbed her hands over her face, covering it with more soot. "Well, come on, then. We can't stay in this smoking wreck forever!"

She reached out for my arm and pulled me up. Her grip was like iron as she dragged me through charred stalls and darkened dirt pathways. Too weak to fight back, I stumbled helplessly behind her.

As we ran in and out of dimly lit stalls, I caught glimpses of her clothes. She wore a flowy silk dress and emerald bracelets jingled on her wrists. Her heels were studded with gold that clicked against the rocks on the ground. *Could you be any more loud?* I thought, rolling my eyes as she stopped to fix one of her heels.

"My name's Stephanie, by the way. What's yours?" she asked, as she stomped her heel in the dirt. I eyed the gold on the heel. *That could buy dinner for my family for a week. If I don't steal it, someone else will,* I thought.

"None of your business," I said. I shoved my body into her back. As she fell, I grabbed her legs and pulled her shoes out from under her.

"Help! Help me!" she screamed into the dirt.

"Sorry, but you wouldn't have survived here long anyway." I left her there, crying in the dark as I ran out of the market and into the night.

AMINA ROSA CASTRONOVO

YEARS AS MENTEE: 1

GRADE: Sophomore

BORN: New York, NY

LIVES: New York, NY

PUBLICATIONS AND RECOGNITIONS: *The Broadsheet, E—The Environmental Magazine, Beacon High School Literary Magazine*

MENTEE'S ANECDOTE: *As soon as Angelica stepped through the door to the New-York Historical Society the first day, I knew she was my mentor. It was the type of face, the type of energy, that was so familiar. I felt that I had known her forever, and ever since our conversations have never proven otherwise. On the first day after we both shared our love for zodiac signs, Angelica took us across Central Park to a French library with a ceiling of the constellations. This, combined with my favorite language, spoke to my soul and I was confident that Angelica understood.*

ANGELICA PUZIO

YEARS AS MENTOR: 1

OCCUPATION: Psychologist and Researcher

BORN: Charlottesville, VA

LIVES: Brooklyn, NY

PUBLICATIONS AND RECOGNITIONS: *Gender & Culture*, chapter in *The Oxford Handbook of Culture & Psychology;* The Judith Gibbons Award

MENTOR'S ANECDOTE: *When I first sat down next to Amina, the first thing she asked me was my zodiac sign. When I told her I was a Capricorn, she told me, "Oh, I already guessed that." We immediately shot into a conversation on astrology, where I learned that Tauruses, her sign, are emotionally attuned, stubborn, and deeply passionate. Amina has held true to these traits while I've gotten to know her, but now I know she's more than her sign could ever capture about her. If you're lucky enough to be let into her life, you'll find a girl who is taking her place in the world.*

EVERY SHADE OF BLUE

AMINA ROSA CASTRONOVO

Don't be afraid to get in touch with the deepest of your emotions, even the heartbreaking ones. There are oceans in you if you learn how to swim.

I only lied to you once.
You looked me in the eyes from across the room and asked me
If my favorite color was still blue.
I told you no.
That I had moved on,
I am vibrating a different color without you now.

I pleaded with you to stop asking me if I ever loved the color
    blue,
What are colors,
Do I see them the same as you?
I scream at you to stop talking so I can remind myself
That I feel like a deep twilight around you.

You are an old memory,
Skipping down the sidewalk to my house
Reminding me of the whispering in my conscience that we met in
    another life,
A life that left behind a residue of crushed soot on chimney brick,
The thick dust staining my fingers with
How my soul recalls kissing in the streets,
Speaking in poetry,
And a dozen dainty, ultramarine roses every day.

Your question catches me by surprise; it muffles turquoise secrets
I know but am not allowed to utter.

This silence paints me a Persian blue,
Brushing me with the strokes of knowledge that I can't just
     pretend
You aren't there,
How does one ignore the first chirp of the bluebird in the spring?
Just as March is sure to storm after the first burst of a bud,
With every new love you linger like a parade of snow on lilies,
Flinging open our window to let the aqua rain fly in,
Drenching our clothes in the celeste ink of love.

I am soaked with our small universe
That is as light as crystal blue rivers and
As dark as the depths of the ocean—
Because where the sun hits has never mattered to us.

I shine this light on you
When I say that you are everything:
The first bellflower popping out of the earth,
Waves lapping against the shore,
A new blanket of snow resting on evergreens during sunset,
And the periwinkle moon we dance under
To the melody the color of the sky

If you listen closely your voice is the background music to my
     heart,
The sound projecting a glow of bittersweet nostalgia
Just like the Eiffel Tower's light rains down onto the Parisian
     streets at night, and
Every time I turn to you I prance down another avenue
That leads me to a navy solitude
Echoing your baby-blue voice that is bursting with the seas and
     skies
Of which the water you want to hide from
In a world that prefers dry deserts,
And so you run from me because
When our eyes meet I wear you like a sapphire ring around my
     heart

As you send electric-blue currents into me and
The way you look at me when the world cries
Is as if you are seeing
The color blue for the first time.

Alas, colors are fading away.
You are not blind or deaf to me, I know you see them vanishing
    too,
Is it too late to say that the waves on your chromatic spectrum
Are the only hues my light can capture?
This state of being demands, commands me to sew your lapis
    heart onto my sleeve
Because I know you will always be my coolest primary color,
Embodying a royal blue wedding gown in a musty antique shop,
But I won't breathe in this confining dress.
I can't be until you come to me.

Why must you swim away like a fish, yet be the king of the
    jungle?
I don't expect you to be
A fairytale horse galloping into the teal sunset,
Or even Prince Charming,
But now you have disguised yourself in the cloak of the unknown
    and
Offered me an icy blue apple.
How did you know that
Even if love was labeled poison
I would drink it if it meant a breath of you?
Taking a sip will force my poor heart to ache,
So please don't leave quite yet, now I know
It's always been you
The world could be every shade of blue.

GENESIS CESPEDES

YEARS AS MENTEE: 2

GRADE: Senior

BORN: Santo Domingo, Dominican Republic

LIVES: Bronx, NY

MENTEE'S ANECDOTE: *Whenever Katy and I meet at the Bean Coffee and sit down to write stuff, I get stuck. So Katy came up with a technique where she would search up a word and we would free-write for ten minutes regarding the word. It was funny because I learned big words that I used with my friends and they looked confused. Overall, these two years with Katy were great because she pushed me to think outside the box and my writing became more fun and creative. She became my friend and I was excited to have a friend in her twenties.*

KATERINA ALLEN-KEFALINOS

YEARS AS MENTOR: 2

OCCUPATION: Personal Assistant for Film Writer

BORN: Miami, FL

LIVES: New York, NY

MENTOR'S ANECDOTE: *This year was Genesis's senior year of high school. This year was also the year I started a new job. We both had full plates, to say the least, and spent the first half of our meetings catching up. Our conversations revolved around nostalgia for the present moment, mixed with anxiety about the future. Although I am at a different stage in life, I could totally relate. Women can be havens of safety and validation for each other, no matter the age difference. Genesis lifts me up whenever I see her, and I hope I do the same for her!*

BEAUTY

GENESIS CESPEDES

This poem emphasizes the beauty of tomorrow's uncertainty. Anything could happen tomorrow, so we might as well just do whatever our hearts desire and enjoy the ride until it lasts!

The future holds the unknown in a crystal ball
Beautiful sorrowful nights that I can't recall
How can I stay miserable when there's so much beauty in the
    world?

Time elapses like a violent waterfall
Whatever happens tomorrow we've had today, after all
The future holds the unknown in a crystal ball

The golden waves driven to the shore
The little kids as happy as the sun
How can I be miserable when there's so much beauty in the
    world?

The unknown is daunting, but never knowing is even worse
The clock is ticking, I better make this second worth
The future holds the unknown in a crystal ball

I swim through the wildly beautiful waters of life
It's all in the sky, the rain, the air, the love
How can I stay miserable when there's so much beauty in the
    world?

Tomorrow's uncertainty is one of life's thrills
I urge to make the days count, time won't be still
Because the future holds the unknown in a crystal ball
So how can I stay miserable when there's so much beauty in the
world?

JORDAN CHE

YEARS AS MENTEE: 3

GRADE: Senior

BORN: Queens, NY

LIVES: Queens, NY

PUBLICATIONS AND RECOGNITIONS: Scholastic Art & Writing Awards: Silver Keys and Honorable Mentions

MENTEE'S ANECDOTE: *These past three years with Maria have proved that she is more than just a mentor—she's a friend like no other, who has supported me with every decision I've made. From picking what restaurant has the best mac and cheese to ironically giving in when I choose not to write during a pair session, Maria knows me probably better than I know myself. She orchestrated meet-ups during the summer, she nearly brought me to her high school reunion, and even after I graduate, I know she'll continue to stay by my side no matter what.*

MARIA WHELAN

YEARS AS MENTOR: 3

OCCUPATION: Literary Agent

BORN: Dublin, Ireland

LIVES: Brooklyn, NY

MENTOR'S ANECDOTE: *For Jordan and I, it started out small. We'd have bubble tea while writing at Queens Crossing mall. The more I got to know her, I knew my mentee was a winner, so our sessions evolved into dinner. Over mac and cheese or omurice, we'd chat about mutually loved TV shows, dogs, and life; somehow we'd even write. Jordan's imagination is extraordinary and writing strong, yet it didn't take me three years to figure her brilliance out. It was clear all along! Skillfully, she depicts everything from burger rivals to the lives of doomed toys. Topics that I most enjoy!*

VALENTINE'S DAY

JORDAN CHE

Each year I become a victim to the elaborate scheme that is Valentine's Day propaganda, getting unreasonably self-conscious when the day never goes as planned. But my friends have made me realize that I can be loved without romance involved.

A few years ago, candygrams had your entire eighth-grade class buzzing with unconcealed excitement the moment an upper-termer would walk through the door with a plastic bag. A spotlight was cast on your teacher as she would reveal the names of the lucky students excruciatingly slowly, like a host at the Grammys. Your classmates teased and cooed at the chosen ones, who would brush them off with a sheepish yet prideful grin, rereading the few sentences written by their prepubescent suitors. You left empty-handed, too busy laughing fondly at your seatmate in global studies, who had just been asked to "hang out during lunch" by her longtime crush, to worry about yourself. But once your homeroom class split up for their respective foreign language classes, you wondered if you would ever get the chance to own a personal message scrawled beneath a piece of Starburst.

Each passing year made candygrams seem less exciting and more childish. If someone had something to say to their significant other or a confession to make to a crush, they took to Facebook Messenger like normal people. The one candygram you ever got was in tenth grade, one out of a total of five in the entire bag. It was a premeditated decision by you and two other friends, who had planned to participate in the event at least once for the sake of friendship. The message was one word, affectionately dubbing you a "fatty." It had no signature on it, but you knew who it came from—you sent him one back with the same phrase on it. When your name was called, you scanned the room for reactions, as if assessing everyone else's faces was more important than the candygram itself. Nobody seemed surprised, like they were thinking, *Finally she gets what she deserves after all these years of being empty-handed!* Not a single person seemed vindictive or jealous, like a secret admirer worried that someone had gotten to you before they had the chance to make a move. You hid the card and its platonic message in your folder, choosing to bite down on the enclosed butterscotch droplet while watching the other four people in the room receive their own candygrams. It was bittersweet.

You know better than to expect a candygram, especially as a senior. But like tradition, you can't help but get your hopes up for no reason. Maybe somehow your secret admirer, who had stayed hidden for the past five years, realized that he had to take advantage of the last Valentine's Day we would have as high school students before it would be too late. Your teacher would call your name and everyone in the room is suddenly paying attention, mouths dropped and eyes wide. "Who gave her a candygram? Her?" But you float back to your seat, walking on air as it sinks in. Someone gave you a candygram. You. "Meet me on the roof at 3 p.m." There's no signature. "You should go!" Your best friend eggs you on, even prouder than you are about finally getting the romantic validation that you had been waiting for. *But I have ninth period,* you think for a split second, until you realize. You're graduating in four months, screw ninth period, you have a Valentine. You skip class to meet your Unidentified Lover on the roof and he confesses like the Peter Kavinsky to your Lara Jean, complete with a single red rose and the sky is unnaturally blue even during the middle of February because you have a Valentine, why wouldn't it be nice outside, too? And you forget to actually respond to your now Identified Lover because you're too busy thinking *Holy shit, yes, I'll be your Valentine,* so you say it out loud and the two of you hold hands on the 6 train but you have to let go because he probably doesn't take the N to transfer to the 7 (you know everyone who does well enough to know that they probably aren't your Lover). You still feel the warmth on your hands as you bury them into your pockets and they're still warm when you text the rest of your friends how your candygram adventure went and why you weren't in class during ninth period.

You're so deep in your daydream that you barely notice the pink cardstock heart being handed to somebody that isn't you. It's given to some boy on the math team, who, after opening it, immediately punches his friend, who punches him back. The term council member leaves with an empty bag. Your friend is already out the door, one hand scrolling through Instagram and the other hand outstretched behind her, waiting for yours. She doesn't look back because she expects you to sidle up behind her. You do exactly that, still riding on the high of your fantasy. Both of you are distracted for different reasons. It isn't until you reach the second floor that you snap out of it. But your hands are still warm.

CHELSEA CHINEDO

YEARS AS MENTEE: 1

GRADE: Sophomore

BORN: Westchester County, NY

LIVES: Bronx, NY

MENTEE'S ANECDOTE: *Olivia and I connect on a variety of different levels. We share a lot of the same views and are very interested in each other's lives. Her laugh makes me laugh and she always encourages me to try my best. She never fails to remind me how proud she is of me and how proud I should be of myself. She's positive and we have such an optimistic relationship. She isn't too pushy and isn't too quiet, she's just right. I appreciate our bonding over our love of food, especially that chocolate-chip cookie we get at Culture Espresso every week.*

OLIVIA JANE SMITH

YEARS AS MENTOR: 4

OCCUPATION: Senior Editor, NYU Langone Health

BORN: United States

LIVES: Brooklyn, NY

PUBLICATIONS AND RECOGNITIONS: Ragan Communications award

MENTOR'S ANECDOTE: *Chelsea and I have come together from different generations and geographies: from her family's roots in Nigeria and mine in western New York State; her current home in the Bronx and mine in Brooklyn; and her as a high school sophomore and me a mid-career professional. We share so much more than the chocolate-chip cookies at our pair meetings. We talk about friendships, fitting in, the writing we aspire to do, and the writing we are doing together.*

MORE THAN 71 INCHES

CHELSEA CHINEDO

Yes, we are all either short, average, or tall, but there is more to us than height. It's about who we are on the inside. Look into the interior and less at the exterior. We are all perfect the way we are. We are never too this or that.

I love being tall
I would hate to be small
I'm tall like a tree but hey that's me
I know I'm tall but no, I don't play ball
I don't care for this conversation all

I know I'm five eleven,
I see myself twenty four seven
But my height isn't really that relevant
What matters is that I'm intelligent and my height
is only part of my development,
I'm like a chemical element,
My unique qualities are evident

Being tall is not the only thing that defines
me when I hear it all the time it stings like a bee,
I wish they would see that there's more to me

If people could see beyond my height
they would realize that I'm bright
not because I'm high but I'm full of light,
I see things from a different sight but that doesn't mean
that I'm uptight

I'd appreciate it if you didn't look at me
like a hermaphrodite

Girls come in many different sizes and when everyone
realizes we will be undivided if anything reunited
Being tall doesn't make me any less feminine, in fact
I benefit because I look elegant
and no, I'm not a gentleman

For the last time! I'm not too tall! Do I need to install
that into your brain
because you don't seem to recall, not at all
And while this has been fun, I really should run because
this conversation is too overdone

How's the weather up there you asked?
It's about negative two degrees maxed and while we both
listen to the same weather cast, I'll leave you with that thought
because it's the only one that I've got

ATIQA CHOWDHURY

YEARS AS MENTEE: 1

GRADE: Junior

BORN: Dhaka, Bangladesh

LIVES: Brooklyn, NY

PUBLICATIONS AND RECOGNITIONS: *But Then I Grew Up* by the New York Writers Coalition

MENTEE'S ANECDOTE: *Once a week, Nandita and I would meet in a cozy little bakery in the city. In the midst of the gesticulating college students, focused typers, lonesome eaters, and first dates, Nandita and I would talk about our weeks and appreciate the solace of writing. I always look forward to our sessions because they allow me to expand on what I already love. I'm so glad to have had you as my mentor, Nandita, and I can't wait to see what you teach me next!*

NANDITA RAGHURAM

YEARS AS MENTOR: 4

OCCUPATION: Editor

BORN: Buffalo Grove, IL

LIVES: Brooklyn, NY

PUBLICATIONS AND RECOGNITIONS: *Vice* magazine, *Vox, Mashable, The Village Voice, Bustle, Refinery29, Chicago Reader,* and more

MENTOR'S ANECDOTE: *Atiqa and I meet once a week in a bakery in Manhattan. I've had several wonderful moments with her and we've written a bunch together, but the moments that I love are when we just sit there, chatting like old friends. She tells me about her week, and I tell her about mine. I love to hear about what's going on with school and her personal life. I'm so excited to watch her grow as both a writer and a person as she takes her place in history.*

BELOVED

ATIQA CHOWDHURY

This piece was an exploration of different relationships: friendship, familial, romantic, and self. I hope to make other women want to take a reflective look inside themselves and the way they interact with others. Honesty is the best way to take your place within your own history.

She sat cross-legged across from Priya on the gym floor's bright yellow planks. They hid behind columns, their eyes darting boldly around the room, staring at the mass of teenage bodies that filled it. V thought she could see each specific sweat droplet form on her classmate's pale skin and make its wretched descent toward the very floor they sat on. The room's stagnant musk hung heavy around Priya as she spoke to V about her weekend, eyes never fully meeting V's intense gaze. V lent Priya her ear, as she always did, becoming more aware of the amount of bodies and lack of space in the gym.

Priya described staying at her dad's apartment last weekend to V, whose eyes were now glued to a spot on the floor near Priya. She talked about the Polaroids she took with her friends at the park and her new love for flared jeans. What she didn't mention is everything else: How his usual pile of crusty dishes filled the sink, and mounds of dirty clothes littered the floor. How his presence was no longer a presence. How he wasn't a person who needed food, water, and air. How he didn't laugh at her jokes or greet her at the door. To Priya, her father was now like a painting: a still life with smooth brushstrokes of cool grays and muted blues. His lonely silhouette, painted with rough brushstrokes of charcoal black, left the imprints of swirls on the canvas.

V stared at Priya, taking in her stories. But even as V held her ear in cupped palms, she couldn't help but feel her bones aching, shoulders sagging, eyes glossing over, and mouth filling with yawn after yawn. Priya was the last to notice V's exhaustion. V had already prepared herself for the usual tap on the shoulder, soft empathetic eyes, whispering voice. Maybe they'd pull her aside and talk to her individually this time. It is always the same: Are you all right?

And she answered the same answer every time: Yes, of course, eyebrows always scrunching, voice becoming a little higher, as if it was such an out-of-bounds suggestion, for V to not be all right. V forced herself to come back here, next to Priya, so she could soak up as much of her as possible. V had been doing this for as long as she'd known Priya, saving Priya in little jam jars: one for the morning, one for the night, one for lunch, and one for the rides on the bus. V always had just enough of Priya left to last throughout her weekend.

V smiled, listening to all of Priya's sentences under the harsh lighting of the gym, letting the swishing of air from Priya's gesticulating arms kiss her face. All the while, V thought about how she would describe this moment to her mother. *Yes,* she thought, *this is exactly what I'll say.* A smile played on V's lips as she sat there examining Priya. *Her fingers are long and thin, they belong on a piano,* she'll say to her mother. Pieces of hair fall out of V's low ponytail, tickling the apples of her cheek, sticking to her thick lashes.

Priya paused her conversation midway through with a wave of her hand. She reached over with those long, thin fingers, and tucked that piece of hair behind V's ear. A soft sigh escaped Priya's lips and the vapor of her breath hung in the three feet that separated them, Priya's finger still tucked behind V's ear.

The sweat-soaked wood planks were the only thing keeping V from falling into an abyss of warmth. Priya's hand was a lifeline, keeping her from melting into a puddle.

Hours later, as V tells her mother about the Suspended Moment, she twirls her mother's coiled hair in her fingers. She glosses over the moment, instead talking about the other parts of her day. She sits cross-legged across from her mother on the carpet of the living room floor. She knows. V says to her mother, "We intersect, we feel we live, we exist." I see us often. I think us often I feel us often and there's no life that I can miss. That night, Priya dreams about V: She talks and talks and talks, V listens and listens and listens until V and Priya are like honey and sugar melting into one another, making one sweet drop.

JAYLI MILAN CHRISTOPHER

YEARS AS MENTEE: 2

GRADE: Sophomore

BORN: Brooklyn, NY

LIVES: Brooklyn, NY

PUBLICATIONS AND RECOGNITIONS: The School of *The New York Times* Summer Academy Alumni 2019 and 2020, Scholastic Art & Writing Awards: Honorable Mention and Gold Key

MENTEE'S ANECDOTE: *When I met Isabel I discovered what true listening and pointed feedback sounded like . . . Isabel has become my confidante, my fellow wearer of the flyest petty boots.*

ISABEL STANISH

YEARS AS MENTOR: 2

OCCUPATION: Creative Strategist, true[X]

BORN: Philadelphia, PA

LIVES: Brooklyn, NY

MENTOR'S ANECDOTE: *As soon as I met Jayli, and saw she was taller than me and rocking Doc Martens that almost reached her knee, I knew we'd get along. She's only continued to impress me with her confidence, creativity, and incredible G-Cal skills (sometimes I question who's the mentor and who's the mentee!). She shows the kind of insight and patience with new ideas and the habits of humanity that usually come from a much older person. I am so proud to call Jayli my mentee.*

MY FIRST REJECTION

JAYLI MILAN CHRISTOPHER

My first rejection was serendipitous. While a relationship seemed appropriate at the time, the universe didn't agree. I devoted my time to writing and painting many works. I thank that event for giving me the precious time to make history.

My first rejection
Upon reflection
a deflection
An interaction of which he probably has no recollection
Something that I loathed with the greatest conviction
It irked my very soul
Explained but still inexplicable
My anger lit more of a passion in me than the prospect of I
    and he

My first rejection
Made me look at my reflection
I saw nothing but perfection
I still don't understand

I am grateful for the graceful bow
Teenagers. Boys.
I'm sure he was just cowed

Curtain call
Roll call
I'll find a new male lead
Someone to fill the role until I reach the Apollo
A new script for a new age

My rejection, fodder, fuel for the engine of my brain
Spurring me to write a new page
He simply wasn't for this stage

I now have very little recollection
My lack of recall, a reflection of our petty connection
Alas, no summer flirtation,
Yet still, I'm glad
What wasn't meant to be never came to fruition,
My first Rejection

LAUREN CICHON

YEARS AS MENTEE: 2

GRADE: Junior

BORN: New York, NY

LIVES: Brooklyn, NY

PUBLICATIONS AND RECOGNITIONS: Scholastic Art & Writing Awards: Gold Key, Silver Key; school newspaper publications

MENTEE'S ANECDOTE: *Kara and I tend to meet on Sunday afternoons for coffee or pie in Brooklyn. These outings have started becoming a comfort to me throughout the chaos that has been seventeen. Although our lives are so different, I'm so grateful to have a constant in an ever-changing world. This is us, marking our moment in history. However different our moments may be, we come together and share them through our art.*

KARA STILES

YEARS AS MENTOR: 2

OCCUPATION: Senior Editor, *Forbes*

BORN: New York, NY

LIVES: Brooklyn, NY

PUBLICATIONS AND RECOGNITIONS: *Forbes*, *Tablet Magazine*, msnbc .com

MENTOR'S ANECDOTE: *What I adore most about Lauren as a developing writer is that she's so many other things, too. Like the women in history we revere, her varied and dynamic strengths inspire and anchor her art. She's an activist, a photographer, a documenter of city streets and subway characters, a curious listener, a skilled people-watcher, and more. Her many crafts are reflected in storytelling that's complex, honest, and in touch with the world around her. Separately, I'll add one of my most cherished moments as Lauren's mentor: When we realized we share the same Myers-Briggs score. Good work pairing us, Girls Write Now!*

GREEN TEA. HOT. MINT WITH HONEY.

LAUREN CICHON

My piece, "Green Tea. Hot. Mint with Honey.," is a reflective personal narrative about a specific vulnerable period of time in my young life.

I've been so conscious of the rise and fall of my chest lately. When my anxiety is worse, I feel the strain on my breath. I hate that I feel this stress in a normally comfortable place: my summer camp upstate. A year ago, I developed a lot of distrust toward people in my life and became skilled at distancing myself. I struggled to open up, and if I ever did, I'd feel guilty about letting my guard down. I wanted to escape. Normally, camp was that escape—I could breathe because the air was fresher and more familiar.

In the crisp air, I tried to find calm in the burnt tongues of caffeine-addicted teens. Tongues touching other tongues, warm with tea. We loved green tea and mint with honey. We tried to keep the heat in our mouths because summer nights are so cold in the mountains. So cold when you're on the top bunk, even with three sweatshirts.

I remember seeing you on the first day of camp that year. I was drawn to you. Everything you did or said was so effortless and gentle. Now, five days in, we wore our unwashed, fleece-lined sweatshirts and held our greasy braids over our ears as a guard from the chill. Greasy braids and body odor mixed with the faint smells of Old Spice deodorant and Victoria's Secret Sweet & Flirty perfume.

I couldn't see anything and neither could you. I knew this because you were holding my hand, clutching it. We were in the back of the group without flashlights. Both of us were simply guided by a soft glow from the people in front of us. As tree roots became hurdles and branches barbed wire, I fell over my own feet.

"Where are you?" you asked me, as I escaped into my wandering brain.

"I'm sorry. I like putting myself in other places, like mentally."

"Stay here," you said.

You told me to look up and I could feel my legs shaking, which can happen when I feel a loss of control. You didn't put your hand on top of my kneecap to make them stop, like some friends did. I felt connected to you. There were so many stars, and even though it felt cliché, I was enchanted by them. That's what you wanted me to see: the thousands of stars.

I was back in our cabin with the other girls, unhooking push-up bras and sighing out of relief because we no longer had straps cutting into our backs. I popped a piece of Juicy Fruit gum into my mouth and chewed it for a minute before spitting it out, grabbing my flashlight, sliding on Blistex, and heading outside to see you on top of the hill. There, you'd been waiting.

Then, we began *star-tripping*. I handed you my flashlight and started spinning, focusing on one star while you made sure I didn't stumble over myself. You shined the flashlight in my eyes and I collapsed, laughing hysterically. You fell on top of me and we glanced up again to avoid looking at each other. The sky was a blur of yellow stars. You were the color yellow, too. The color of pencil shavings and lemon zest.

"Stay outside," you said with a grin. I nodded as you ran back to the cabin. My heartbeat quickened and usually, I'd want to run away. But I wasn't frozen like I'd been before. I wanted to be near you. It was a different tension, more like butterflies.

You returned with your comforter and we fell on top of it, separated from the wet grass. My leg was violently shaking as I tried so hard to let everything go and be in the moment. *Stop shaking,* I told myself. The universe was spinning so fast.

"It's okay, I'll move over," you said. We moved two feet apart, but still felt close.

We were quiet, even though everything in my head was so loud. I was coping. I was okay. No hair tie snapping against my wrist and no nausea. We were safe. My universe was spinning slower. I'd never fallen asleep under the sky.

SUNEI CLARKE

YEARS AS MENTEE: 1

GRADE: Senior

BORN: Charlotte, NC

LIVES: Brooklyn, NY

MENTEE'S ANECDOTE: *A good mentor is hard to find. Thankfully, I lucked out. My favorite thing about my relationship with Caitlin is I have someone to talk to about anything I want. Our conversations are quite fluid and I am never afraid to be open and honest about my feelings on even the most controversial topics.*

CAITLIN CHASE

YEARS AS MENTOR: 3

OCCUPATION: Creative and Content Strategy Consultant

BORN: Syracuse, NY

LIVES: Brooklyn, NY

MENTOR'S ANECDOTE: *Sunei is—in a word—tenacious. She doesn't just plan to go to college, she wants to go to college in Spain. She doesn't just wish to be a doctor, she intends to be a doctor in the military. She doesn't just love to travel, she endeavors to explore the world. When I first met Sunei last fall, I was struck by her curiosity, confidence, and determination. She is eager to engage with the world in all its complexity. We've had conversations about feminism, eugenics, and racism, to name just a few. Sunei—I am certain—is ready to take her place in history.*

RELATING TO, DERIVED FROM, OR CONSISTING OF MATTER: HAVING REAL IMPORTANCE OR GREAT CONSEQUENCES

SUNEI CLARKE

In honor of Black History Month, I have written a piece that reflects on everyday reminders of slavery. I draw an unconventional parallel between my life and the experience of an enslaved woman.

glass

A few months ago, I heard that drinking a glass of water first thing in the morning helps reset the body. True or not, it's a ritual I will always keep. The glass is always the same—the tallest clear cup with six ridges.

The first ping was when they all knew to start moving. By the time the spoon hit the glass again, they were to be standing in front of her, waiting for an order. It didn't matter the time of day.

cotton

At the beginning of my night the sheets always cover the four corners of my bed. By the time I wake up the smooth cotton sheets are no longer there. All that is left is the itchy stitching of the mattress beneath me.

It seemed like the loudest sound in the field. Her heart beat faster, harder. She moved with the wind. Each step she took, she felt the stems scratching at her legs. No longer did they blister her fingers.

water

Clothes off. Hair up. Shower on. Pink bar, white bar, or body wash? My face wash is always in the same spot, perched on the window ledge. My towel hangs, stuck between the sliding door. Shower off. Towel dry. Day starts.

Sack secure. Dark sky. Head down. Knees bowed. Ready. As tired as she was, the brush of the crisp water against her bruised feet gave her instant relief. She waded through the water in the opposite direction, finding it harder to keep herself afloat. Another step. Don't stop. Keep going.

BRIANNA CLARKE-ARIAS

YEARS AS MENTEE: 3

GRADE: Junior

BORN: New York, NY

LIVES: Bronx, NY

PUBLICATIONS AND RECOGNITIONS: Scholastic Art & Writing Awards: Silver Key

MENTEE'S ANECDOTE: *Rachel has played no small part in my writing evolution. She has been my mentor for almost three years, and throughout my shifts in style and my confusing thoughts about the world, she supports my voice. She helps me realize my strengths in my writing when I'm blind to them, and it makes me feel like her comments about what I share with her come from a place of real understanding. I can't share with someone who I don't believe understands my words, but Rachel makes that her priority first and the emotional content of my work is handled carefully.*

RACHEL SHOPE

YEARS AS MENTOR: 3

OCCUPATION: Senior Editor, CB Insights

BORN: Chapel Hill, NC

LIVES: New York, NY

MENTOR'S ANECDOTE: *Brianna and I have worked together for three years now and it has truly been an honor to watch her grow. She is brilliant, talented, and so much wiser than her sixteen years. Her writing is so unique and smart—I feel so privileged every time I get to read a new piece that she's written. I believe in Brianna and her voice, and I believe in this program. I'm so thrilled to be a part of it.*

VERB: TO SEE

BRIANNA CLARKE-ARIAS

This piece is about the process of reconnecting with our past selves and how the way we see things changes as we age.

The rain falls into Object's thin hair, across the faint pale scar on their cheek, and down the curve of their head before it continues down the hill. A bus waits in the dark, the white of its hood bright under the streetlights. Object continues forward, gravel of the street pressed into the soles of their shoes. Their face is slick with water, but pulled taut as if by tears. They feel the headlights of the bus against the side of their face and a low rumbling that vibrates into their ears.

Water is pooling in the dirt patch beside the sidewalk and Object tracks it into the bus. At the top of the steps, they lie across a pair of seats as the wheels release and start forward. Object rocks with the movement and the fibers of the seat pull in the wetness and the salt until the pungent smell of the sea wafts throughout the aisles. The bus is steady against the sounds of cars skidding outside, and the prickling of the streetlights into Object's corneas.

The bus continues on into the city until it reaches the large stone structure of the Forty-Second Street Library. Object steps down into the street. Their clothes are covered in a stale wetness until the rain bursts out again and the activity outside resumes. They wait in a glass bus stop across from the library. A small girl waits beside them, her hair long and pulled tightly into high pigtails, dressed completely in a tart pink that looks sweet and tastes bitter and strong. She turns to Object. "Are you hungry?" Her eyes are curious, large with what Object does not think is innocence, but something more perceptive. The rest of her is abrasive: She has lost several teeth recently and the gaps that sit in her gums make her look younger but sore. She's young and vibrating with color like a molecule of light.

"I'm cold," Object replies, and sits still, save for their hands flexing and their eyes darting about. The neon yellow of their sweater has soaked through and become translucent. The color sticks to their body and spreads up their neck.

"I want to eat." The color still creeps up.

"You should have eaten dinner." Object can feel the brightness flood their cheeks and wave up their temples.

"I hate to eat meals. And I hate so many foods. I have to go to the biggest place where I can find exactly what I want."

"You're a picky eater." The neon pulses in Object's eyes. They close them. "I'm selective because I'm too sensitive."

"I'll eat, but only to see how hungry I am. What's your name?"

"Macula. My mom named me Macular Pigment."

"What's that, a muscle?"

"It's in your eyes." Object looks around at the sharp yellow that filters the night and supposes that they are right. They walk with the girl toward the library.

Everything about the library is large: its doors, its ceilings, its echoes. The girl takes Object's hand and leads them down the stone stairs. They are sturdy, but under her feet Object can feel the floor shake and the walls rumble very softly. She reminds them nothing of themself. Object supposes they should go home, caught in the feeling that they should leave early enough to go home, but they want to sleep in this dark building, a small crook in a large empty space. The feeling of being outside is half the sensation and half the memory that they will return to after leaving, even as it forms between their eyes and their brain.

At the foot of the stairs, in a basement, Macula brings them into a children's library and, despite looking so young, Object feels them stick out sorely. The pink of her clothes is bright and girly and should make her fit in among the concealing and innocent children's books, but instead she seems too strong, too demanding. Her hair seems shorter, but the pink brighter. She picks a book from the shelf in earnest and Object is curious. They pad slowly over and look over Macula's shoulder. The cover looks familiar.

They open the book and Object brings it closer to their eyes. The language is incomprehensible.

"   "

Macula speaks clearly. It feels just like rumbling.

"That was my favorite book," Object says. Macula's face turns up at that, the neon of Object's vision bringing out the scar on her cheek. They had not noticed that before. At the dip in her skin across her cheek, Object notices the brightness of the room becoming darker with shadow.

Object takes the book and moves to the corner. They flip through the pages; they cannot make out a word. Macula must be reciting the story, but it sounds alien.

"How come you can read it—" Object starts. "How come you can read it and I can't?" They know the story, they do, but they cannot remember it. They look into Macula's big eyes and see themself refracted in their irises; Macula sits in the reflection. The room is sharp with neon highlights but for Macula's dark eyes. As Object moves their mouth, they see the image of Macula move its mouth as well.

"That was mine."

BLAKE CONIGLIO

YEARS AS MENTEE: 4

GRADE: Senior

BORN: Bronx, NY

LIVES: Bronx, NY

PUBLICATIONS AND RECOGNITIONS: Scholastic Art & Writing Awards: Silver Key

MENTEE'S ANECDOTE: *Jude and I are local public menaces. To Buunni Coffee and Go! Go! Curry. If we didn't pay them, they'd surely kick us out. But that's okay, we had fun anyway. We get along like peas in a pod—we share ridiculous memes and laugh over nonsense, and I trust her the most with my writing and my struggles. Jude is a wonderful and phenomenal rock in the hurricane of my life and I am incredibly thankful she's stuck with me throughout our four years together. Girls Write Now may end for us, but Jackie is forever.*

JUDE WETHERELL

YEARS AS MENTOR: 4

OCCUPATION: Program and Development Coordinator, Intersections International

BORN: Brooklyn, NY

LIVES: Brooklyn, NY

PUBLICATIONS AND RECOGNITIONS: *Reckoning* magazine; amateur podcast on *Cats*, the musical movie

MENTOR'S ANECDOTE: *Blake and I have been meeting on Sundays at a coffee shop on 207th and Broadway for so long that said coffee shop actually changed ownership seemingly while we were sitting there in the corner, cackling among ourselves and eating pastries. (And writing.) These four years have been a complete blessing, and I feel so lucky that I got to witness Blake grow as an artist—and that I can call them my friend. It may be the end of our coffee shop reign, but it's the beginning of something new; I can't wait to see what Blake's future holds.*

SORORICIDE

BLAKE CONIGLIO

For class, I had the task of writing a monologue. But as an avid horror fan, I went off the rails. That's how sororicide happened. Writing horror serves as an outlet for me, to create a world where this fictional horror is the only scary thing in the world.

I am alone at my twin sister's funeral.

My parents remain at the other end of the aisle, weeping silent tears. And behind me, a sea of my twin's coworkers, friends, our family—rising and falling like a sea of black. The church is seeped in rays of colored light.

The casket is open. Her face is peaceful and still—in perfect symmetry, like an angel ripped from her own little heaven and framed. Tucked beneath a lace blanket, like a child. She even has her ribbon, still tied perfectly in her hair. A gift from our parents.

I hated her.

She was the pinnacle of it all—perfect daughter, straight A's throughout her education, a well-respected member of her field. All the charity work in the world beneath her belt. Even the most brutish of people couldn't hate her. I watched her worm her way into people's lives like an infection, a plague of false smiles and pearly white rows of fangs.

And then there's me—college dropout and unpaid intern. I was always nothing next to her. She loomed over my life, a shadow of everything I could never be. I left a trail of failure in my wake, sticky on my shoes. But all she had to do was exist. Every single word was what they wanted to hear, her every breath never wasted. My lungs were filled with heavy nonsense, a chokehold on my throat before I could utter anything.

But now, I can't even breathe—the knowledge in the pit of my stomach, wasting away on the tip of my tongue—and rotting me from the inside out.

That she died because of my mistakes.

I bet you're wondering, *What the hell does that mean?* Then ask her. Blame her for jumping right in front of that truck, taking the blow meant for me. I was supposed to die, I was supposed to make it right—nobody ever wanted me, it was all her, her, her, her, her, her, her, her—like the fucking universe was carved and shaped for her.

How could I live if nobody gave me life in the first place?

And here we are. Sitting in a church, staring at her as if that fourteen-wheeler didn't tear her apart into a mangled abomination of roadkill—innocent lace hiding her perfect head that was decapitated by the first tire that hit her. Now I'm left with what she left behind. Which is nothing but a world torn from its light, its hope—judging by the crowd.

Out of the corner of my eye, I see people begin to approach my parents, quiet murmurs and mumbles of condolences.

Nobody gives a shit about me.

And who would? I'm what's left behind, the ugly reject, something made in the shape of her. When we were younger, we'd do that twin thing. Swap clothes, share a hairstyle—and act like our parents could still tell us apart. I was her, she was me—and nothing could take that from us.

It felt so nice to be her. To be loved like she was. And is that so wrong to ask? All my life, I've been kicked, discarded, invisible, thrown around like bottom-of-the-barrel shit. Maybe I just want to be loved. What gave her the right? To be the golden child, flawless in anything and everything. Maybe I wanted to be the golden child. To be loved, to be priceless.

She knew what love was—she was treated like a national treasure, perfect little darling from day one. Every single facet of her life gave her admiration, respect, love, attention.

And she can give it to me, one last gift from my sister dearest.

It's time I take what's rightfully mine.

I am alone at my twin sister's funeral.

The pews are empty. The church is dark. The casket has been

closed and fastened. The body within is stripped of its life, its rights, its definition.

The ribbon in my hair is mine.

It's always been mine.

All I had to do was take it.

DALYA CORDEIRO

YEARS AS MENTEE: 1

GRADE: Junior

BORN: Curitiba, Brazil

LIVES: Queens, NY

MENTEE'S ANECDOTE: *My mentor is Paige and she's more than I had ever hoped for. I knew going in that I would want a mentor whose attitude and spirit matched my own, and Paige not only fits that criteria, she flies far beyond it. Armed with a kind hand and a quick wit, Paige has been a superb teacher and a lovely companion. The Starbucks by Queens Plaza South will never be the same after we've spent so many Tuesday nights huddling inside it. I'm incredibly grateful for her edits, her laughter, and her constant support of myself and my writing.*

PAIGE CARLOTTI

YEARS AS MENTOR: 2

OCCUPATION: Marketing Manager at UNTUCKit

BORN: Erie, PA

LIVES: New York, NY

MENTOR'S ANECDOTE: *I feel strange being Dalya's mentor, as she has far more to teach than I do. I was stunned to find out that English is her second language, given the command she demonstrates and maturity in which she writes. Many girls can be talented writers—which she is, no doubt—but she also has the drive to do something great with this gift. Despite our age difference, our senses of humor are identical (unsure what that says about me . . .), so meeting up at a Starbucks in Long Island City on Tuesdays always feels more like a privilege and less like an obligation.*

THE BRIGHTER SUN

DALYA CORDEIRO

This piece unintentionally secured itself a special place in my heart. It reflects my feelings, my aspirations, and my hope that this new country will allow me to embrace my new place in history.

Where you're from, the summers are incandescent. They're scorching sun on blazing sidewalk, and they're light glistening off colorful cars. They're skin baking in the heat and hair plastered to forehead and sweat high on your brows. They're condensating water bottles against your face. They're the hiss of a new can of soda and the gentle clinking of ice. The summers are women in cangas and men in havaianas and children precariously clutching on to ice-cream cones, licking sticky fingers and smiling sticky smiles.

Where you're from, the winters are cutting. They're frigid winds and icy rain and hailstorms. They're hand-knitted scarves and woolen tights and snug sweaters. They're dark hardwood and cold granite and comfy bedspreads. They're stiff fingers and red noses and chattering teeth. The winters are brief conversations and distant acknowledgments—half-hearted pleasantries before everyone scurries back to their rooms, where it's nice and warm and safe.

Where you're from, fall and spring are tantamount. They're the strange parts, the spaces in between, where everything's blurring together and every day feels as dispiriting as the last. They're waiting rooms, or limbo, or purgatory. The flowery ipê trees lining the streets are either blooming or sagging, but regardless, there are petals carpeting the sidewalks and a subtle breeze in the air. Feels less like a season and more like a well of untapped potential and anticipatory anxiety. Feels like something should be happening but isn't.

Where you're from, the people are friendly. They're kind and approachable and genial, but always busy, and always with some-where to go. They're preoccupied yet disposed, generous with di-rections and advice and witty quips at everyone's expense, especially their own. Their banter's always rich with laughter, even if only to hold back tears.

You miss it, sometimes—that feeling of "forever." That stomach-churning, goose bump–raising feeling of permanence that comes with comfort and, ultimately, complacency. You hate change—but you hate forever even more.

Things are different, now.

You don't really know when your life became a whirlwind, but it suddenly feels like there's so much more to worry about than there'd ever been. You suffer overwhelming feelings of displace-ment, like you'd been uprooted and hastily planted into new soil before you could wither away entirely. The soil feels the same and looks the same—rife with noisy urban life, with forgettable faces, with your mother's grounding presence—but now you're perpetu-ally wondering when you're going to be ripped from it and depos-ited someplace else.

That's how you live, now. You wonder and wonder and wonder, but you don't hope too much and don't wish too hard. Wishes have no business here. This soil caters to doers, not dreamers. You try very hard to be the former, and yet all your effort just feels like more dreaming—useless and irrelevant.

At certain points, you weigh trying against giving up, and it's rarely more appealing. It just becomes a matter of pride now, per-haps even resignation. *I didn't ask for any of this, but now here I am so I'll make the best of it, come out of it all just good enough to make the naysayers eat their words. That oughta make everything worth it.* You cling on to that as hard as you can, because some days it's the only thing that still feels solid—still feels true. The only thing worth really trying for.

That's what you do, now.

You wonder, you try, you cling, and at all times, you stop your-self from hoping and dreaming and wishing. You savor the sunlight and endure the rain and don't thread roots into foreign soil.

If any petals droop, well. That's no one's business but your own.

CHENICIA CUMMINGS

YEARS AS MENTEE: 1

GRADE: Junior

BORN: Georgetown, Guyana

LIVES: Brooklyn, NY

MENTEE'S ANECDOTE: *This was me and my mentor's first year in the program. Working with my mentor has been great. Despite our busy schedules, we made completing this project work. Jennifer has given me the tools to improve my writing. I'm happy that I had the chance to be her mentee this year.*

JENNIFER FORD

YEARS AS MENTOR: 1

OCCUPATION: Associate Beauty Editor, *Essence*

BORN: Philadelphia, PA

LIVES: Brooklyn, NY

PUBLICATIONS AND RECOGNITIONS: *Essence*

MENTOR'S ANECDOTE: *I enjoyed working with Chenicia. She loves reading romance novels, so I was a bit surprised and excited to see that she chose to write a memoir on topics that aren't so romantic: death and teenage pregnancy. Chenicia challenged herself this year by exploring different genres and multimedia, and I'm glad that I could be here to support her throughout the journey.*

DARK CLOUDS WITH A SILVER LINING

CHENICIA CUMMINGS

I wrote this piece because I know how difficult it can be to succeed when dealing with unfortunate circumstances, like death or teenage pregnancy. It's assumed that these events are setbacks. I want people to know that despite hardship and difficulties, they can achieve anything.

It all started on the day Erica was born. Life changed drastically. I gave birth to my child at the vulnerable age of seventeen. Erica came into my life, and it forced me to take on the roles and responsibilities of motherhood. My dreams, goals, and aspirations of becoming a social worker felt impossible to achieve with a baby. I struggled with being a teenager, and a parent to her.

So much happened after Erica was born. My body physically changed. I lost friends, and my grades dropped. I went from being a student who received A's and B's to a student who could barely pass any of her classes. I felt as if I wasn't good at anything anymore, and as if my life would never get better. It felt as if one negative thing occurred after another.

My senior year in high school was somewhat of a turning point. I brought my grades up and came to the realization that there was hope for me to achieve my goal of becoming a social worker after all. I was also accepted into college. I had joy.

I am from a low-income family, and I always thought it would be impossible for me to make it out of my neighborhood. Few people have. There were many times throughout my four years at Rider University where I felt like dropping out. I worried about caring for my daughter. I struggled with giving in to my family's expectation to fail. Hardly anyone ever makes it from where I'm from.

College was just too hard, or at least that's the excuse they'd always give. I didn't want to be like them. I wanted to be better, for me, and for my daughter.

Erica helped me to stay in college, and she showed me that despite having her, I was still capable of making something out of myself.

While traveling home for Thanksgiving break, every college student's favorite time of the year, I got into a car accident that injured me and killed my daughter. The loss left me lost for words. I felt I had no reason to live. My daughter was gone.

I came to a crossroads: Stay in college or drop out. I wanted to do the latter. The pain of losing my daughter was too much, but I also knew that she wouldn't want me to give up, especially during my last year in school, so I stayed.

Being in college after losing my daughter was even harder than being there and taking care of her. I knew I had to be the first one in my family to finish, and that I also had to be an inspiration for the other children in my community. I wanted them to know that you can make it out of the hood and accomplish something for yourself. And despite what I had been through, I pushed myself to graduation. I did what no one in my family and community had done. I know I made Erica proud.

As I delivered my valedictorian speech, I told everyone in the room, "If I can do it, then you can do it, too." I never thought that I would get to achieve my dreams having had a teenage pregnancy. Having my daughter ensured that I did. No matter what has happened in your past, you can accomplish anything you put your mind to.

FAITH DESTINY CUMMINGS

YEARS AS MENTEE: 1

GRADE: Senior

BORN: Brooklyn, NY

LIVES: Brooklyn, NY

MENTEE'S ANECDOTE: *Katy is like my big sister—in every sense of the word. Not only does she develop my talents as a writer, but she also listens to my problems. She understands my anger if something had upset me in the past week, but, unlike my friends, is able to give me clear, coherent advice. She's relatable and listens to all of my crazy writing ideas, and helps me bring many of them to life. Katy is beyond talented and anyone would be lucky to have a mentor as compassionate, talented, and thoughtful as she is.*

KATHRYN CARDIN

YEARS AS MENTOR: 1

OCCUPATION: Freelance Writer and Editor

BORN: Springfield, MO

LIVES: Brooklyn, NY

MENTOR'S ANECDOTE: *Returning to high school can seem nightmarish to many, but if I could go back and befriend Faith at age seventeen I would. Poetry is not my first language (or second), but Faith's writing has opened my eyes to the genre. She is self-aware, honest, and adroit— the embodiment of a good and thoughtful writer. Our meetings have been cathartic, and our talks the highlight of my week. I can't wait to see what she chooses to do with her future, and I hope to be a part of it.*

THE ART OF SELF LOVE

FAITH DESTINY CUMMINGS

This poem follows a girl who, similar to any other teenage girl, has a hard time in her own skin. As she gets older she learns how to navigate being a young adult and finds herself—she overwhelms a callous world with light.

she stared with sullen eyes at the vending machine overflowing
    with snacks;
she already had a bagel today. more food would only make her
    fatter.
she squeezed at her dimensions as she eyed the candy bar
like a bittersweet prize resting on a nest of regret.
she sulked as the emotions rose in her like

vomit. that was what she did when she got home later that day,
gripping the toilet bowl as the half-slice of greasy pizza revisited
    the surface.
she had stuck her finger so far down her throat that it felt raw and
    disgusting.
her heart had the potential to do nothing but

ache. her muscles ached and groaned as she lay sobbing in her
    bed begging for a brighter day.
her throat was scratchy and begging for water, but she couldn't
    bring herself to get

up. she sat up on the kitchen counter, pulling at a banana.
    nothing tasted right.
everything tasted like calories, fat and grease. it had been a while
    since she felt

full. the voice message box of the person you are trying to reach
 is full.
please try calling again at a—she ended the call before the
 automation could finish.
the tears cascaded as she called for people who cared less than she
 thought,
hoping their opinion would change if she didn't feel so

large. the hole in her heart gaped as the razor blade sliced
 against her skin.
her heart sank lower and lower
past her stomach as the drops of gooey blood left her arms.
thick and

red. her face was flushed crimson. her brain rattled
with rumors that were "true" about her;
she had never known these things. she didn't know people could
 be so

fake. how is it possible to post something to social media and
 make a fake thing look so real?
plastic-covered barbies are better than the velmas these days she
 guessed.
instagram was simply more important than real

life. what was the meaning of it? she could go on and on with her
 questions
but as she got older and façades faded all she realized was that life
 was too short
to worry about what people said about her body. too short to get
 caught up in the

superficial. she is beautiful. now more than ever. now she knows
 it, but it is exterior.
still shallow. looks are unimportant to her now. appearances fall
 at her feet. queen.

she has a meaning for life. for her life. everyone has a different
    one. hers is making her

mark. sure, their words, bitter and angry had left a couple.
but her kindness and art cover the callouses.
she is okay with herself, the pain fuels her to enjoy her real
a r t.

CHEYENNE CUTHBERTSON

YEARS AS MENTEE: 1

GRADE: Senior

BORN: Staten Island, NY

LIVES: Staten Island, NY

MENTEE'S ANECDOTE: *All the memories you have are historical! Having a mentor and meeting weekly is historical because of the impact they have on your life. Girls Write Now has reached out to girls and women to connect the generations. The program and the people in it help us, teenagers, develop a deeper understanding and experience with writing and what it can do in your life. One of my favorite memories with my mentor is meeting up on a Saturday and getting bagels; on that Saturday we caught up and wrote.*

KAYE WEINSTEIN

YEARS AS MENTOR: 1

OCCUPATION: Copy Lead, Centron

BORN: Mountain Lakes, NJ

LIVES: New York, NY

MENTOR'S ANECDOTE: *From the moment we first met at the New-York Historical Society, Cheyenne has lifted me up with her enthusiasm, joy, and curiosity toward everything and everyone around her. Since then, we've visited what might be every café in the Financial District, exchanged countless cute animal photos, and shared many laughs over swapped writing prompts. I've watched Cheyenne develop into a wonderful poet, mentee, and soon-to-be college student and I am so proud of all her accomplishments!*

THE INSIDE WHIRL

CHEYENNE CUTHBERTSON

I write all my pieces about something that affects me in life. This one is about Emotions and how they feel.

To live with yourself
        Is like living with
            A thousand people
The swirl and whirl of
        thoughts
            Racing through your mind
                Racing down the track
        Down the streets
of Manhattan
Emotions are those people
They surround you
        They are everywhere and nowhere
            Your friends and your enemies
              They keep your secrets
        Alone and isolated in your head
            Cold but warm at
            the same time
              Happy and scared
              and fearful
        The outcome alone.

MARTA DAVILA-LOMAS

YEARS AS MENTEE: 1

GRADE: Junior

BORN: Union, PA

LIVES: New York, NY

MENTEE'S ANECDOTE: *Since the first time I met Valentina, we instantly clicked. I remember when I asked her if she liked to watch any TV shows, because unfortunately watching TV is a big part of my life. She told me she loves novelas, especially* Jane the Virgin, *which is my favorite show! After that, I looked forward to seeing her and talking with her because she is so kind and inspiring and we always have a great time together. Honestly, Valentina is such an amazing person. I mean, she moved here when she was only sixteen years old and I don't think I could do that.*

VALENTINA ESPAÑA

YEARS AS MENTOR: 1

OCCUPATION: Senior Copywriter, Anthem, Inc.

BORN: Anaco, Venezuela

LIVES: Weehawken, NJ

PUBLICATIONS AND RECOGNITIONS: *Yellow Arrow Journal*

MENTOR'S ANECDOTE: *Every week, Marta and I are taking over the New York City streets drinking horchata lattes, matcha lemonades, and catching a movie (hello,* Little Women*!). She's outgoing, mega-smart, passionate about her endless list of hobbies—dance, art, writing, fashion, music, travel, and, yes, watching lots of shows—and her attitude is contagious. Marta always goes for what's fun and challenging. For one prompt we decided to channel the energy of accessories into a character. She brought me a tiara and a pair of cat-eye sunglasses that made me feel like a rock star.*

HER FIRST DAY

MARTA DAVILA-LOMAS

I'm tired of stories about girls falling in love with others, so I wrote, inspired by the meaning of self-love, how I realized I love myself. I define self-love as the regard for one's own well-being and happiness. I wanted to portray a snippet of the journey that I made.

Switching schools has never been easy for me. I remember crying on the last day of elementary school because I was leaving the friends that I had known since kindergarten. In eighth grade, leaving felt even worse, I was separated from friends who had begun to feel like family. Looking back, I think I was being dramatic, but it was painful. Except now it was high school! I was excited because of, you know, John Hughes's *Sixteen Candles*. I looked at my phone and realized that I was going to be late. I left my apartment, walked to the corner to catch the bus. Sitting in the first seat I could find, I looked at my shoes, which I had just gotten a week ago. They were blue and white high-top sneakers. I had chosen to get these because they could go with anything and are trendy but not basic, but glancing at them, I began to worry that everyone else would have them, too. I laughed at myself, got my headphones, and shuffled the playlist my best friend Natalie made for me the last time I saw her.

The song that played was "Why Try" by Ariana Grande, which she claimed reminded her of me. It was one of those songs that makes you feel like you're in a coming-of-age movie, riding in a car on a summer evening with your friend after just having broken up with your boyfriend even though you're still in love with him. Honestly, I didn't really know what that felt like because no one ever even thought of me like that for some reason. But no, I have a fresh start now, maybe I'll finally experience what it feels to be in love, because everyone always seems so happy in a relationship.

I looked up from my seat and saw I was at my stop and got up. I noticed two other girls also got off the bus and I wondered if they were going to my new school, too. I walked toward the building when one of them came up to me, and asked if I was wearing the Jordan 1 Obsidians. I turned down my music and said yes while getting a good look at her. She was wearing black leggings and white Converse shoes, with a Brandy Melville crop top: in other words, the most basic outfit ever. She even had the classic Fjällräven Kånken, however you say it, in yellow, and she had clear hazel eyes and a scrunchie in her brown hair. She began telling me about how excited she was to start high school as we walked with her friend up the stairs, and after what felt like a million years of her going on and on about her summer vacation, she asked me for my name. Without missing a beat I told her the nickname I had been called my whole life, Bella, but then I remembered I was going by my first name instead so I corrected myself and said Isabella and asked for hers. She looked at me, smirking while saying Emma, and then proceeded to tell me she knew someone who was "a total bitch to her," named Isabella. I scrunch my eyebrows together, confused as to what that implied about me, then I looked down at my shoes as I replied "Oh," and said I had to get to my first class but it was nice to meet her. As I walked away I heard her say to her friend that I was just as bad as "Izzy" and that I didn't know how to dress. *Wow, that was harsh,* I thought to myself as I turned the corner and bumped into a girl holding an iced coffee, which somehow she managed to keep from spilling. I told her I was so sorry and that I hadn't seen her, to which she smiled and said it was fine because it wasn't my fault. She asked me my name and complimented my makeup, to which I responded with "Isabella." She told me her name is Ashley and that she had math in room 313, which happened to be the same class I was in.

She smelled like vanilla and had the same pink top that Natalie had gotten when we went shopping for back-to-school clothes. She smiled at me genuinely when I told her and we laughed together as we walked into the geometry class. I took a seat and settled down for the long day of ice-breakers that teachers insist on doing and the quizzical stares from girls and boys alike. I felt at home with Ashley, as if everything was going to be okay just like Natalie had said to me last night over the phone. I could imagine myself, Ashley, and Natalie becoming the best of friends, and that was worth more to me than the judgmental remarks I had gotten from Emma. All I wanted was to surround myself with kind, compassionate people who would accept me for who I am . . .

KRISTINA DAWOUD

YEARS AS MENTEE: 1

GRADE: Senior

BORN: Queens, NY

LIVES: Queens, NY

MENTEE'S ANECDOTE: *Working with Jordan has definitely been an amazing experience. She allows me to write however I wish, allows me to speak my mind and put thoughts onto the page. She also encourages me to be free with my writing. Aside from this, we have a lot of bonding time such as going to the museum, getting coffee together while talking about our caffeine addiction, making our relationship grow stronger and stronger. Jordan has made me more confident in showcasing my written works. I couldn't be more thankful to have her as my mentor.*

JORDAN GASS-POORE'

YEARS AS MENTOR: 1

OCCUPATION: Podcast Producer and Investigative Journalist

BORN: San Marcos, TX

LIVES: Queens, NY

PUBLICATIONS AND RECOGNITIONS: *Bloomberg, Mother Jones*

MENTOR'S ANECDOTE: *Kristina reminds me a lot of myself when I was seventeen, despite growing up in different states. She's taught me about growing up and going to school in New York City (and why I need to buy a monthly MetroCard). We both enjoy writing creatively and teaching others. She wants to major in education; I have a teacher's certification. (And our reasons for wanting to pursue this noble profession are the same. If interested in our reasons, please feel free to ask.)*

A PLACE IN HISTORY

KRISTINA DAWOUD

This memoir is about realizing a place in history is out there, you just have to find it.

A place in history. That phrase has lingered in my ears and has stayed in my head for a long time. It's such a weird thing to think about, how one is able to have a place in history, much like a stamp on an envelope.

Having a place in history is so strange to me. I should be excited: I say an opinion about something I believe in and then it gets documented. That's supposed to be a good thing. But when I say something, I feel like no words come out. I feel as though I'm trapped. My throat is clogged, I'm suffocating, gasping for air by the second, but no one is noticing.

It's like I'm fighting for my place in history and that's what makes the whole concept so bizarre. And, of course, many people in history have rightfully earned their stamp and now have a legacy that sets a reminder to aspiring young people who wish to move forward.

But with all the empowerment that fills the atmosphere I walk in, I still feel stuck. I feel lost like a puppy trying to find its way back home. I hear all these great things about kids my age doing something successful with their lives and I'm just sedentary, not moving a muscle.

I feel like I want to do something, but my feet are glued to the pavement. The pavement that someone who made history might've walked on. The pavement our relatives may have walked on. The pavement we walk every day to school to learn something. To become something. To have a place in history.

But achieving this takes courage, takes practice, takes a lot of patience that I know I'm not ready for just yet. A place in history reminds me of a placemark on a map. A destination, a goal. And I don't really have a set direction on what I want to do and where I want to go. And thus, my place in history remains ambiguous, continuously asking myself *Why?* and *What if?*

What if I am on the right track? For example, I'm part of the Leaders program at my high school. This program has taught me leadership skills by being a teacher's assistant for a gym class. I joined the program on the recommendation of my gym teacher sophomore year. She saw potential in me that I never saw in myself. I signed up, but I didn't know what I was getting myself into. Junior year came along and other kids who were interested in the program were all placed in a class called Leaders in Training. The class rules were discussed and my interest was piqued. I wanted to be in the Leaders program and so I pushed. I pushed and pushed until the trainer told me I wasn't fit. I grew mad, ranted to my friends, and proved him wrong until, finally, I earned a spot.

Being in the Leaders program has made me grow as a person. Leaders gave me the opportunity to be confident in speaking. I never used to say what was on my mind; now people consider me to be talkative. I also gained confidence in being a part of the student body. Many teachers throughout the years have told me to be more involved in extracurricular activities and I always brushed them off. At the time, my daily routine consisted of going to school and coming home to finish homework. Now I participate in different school activities, such as International Food Festival, competitions from the sports teams my school offers, and being part of the school's choir. The Leaders program has shaped me into a better person, into the person I am proud to be.

I lead by example. Throughout history, there have been women like me who have questioned their leadership abilities and have had to overcome adversity. One of these historical figures is Coco Chanel. I first learned about her from a paper I wrote in middle school. Women's fashion always interested me, and learning about how she made herself known when everyone turned her down really motivated me to want to do something along those lines. Up until my junior year of high school, I wanted to be a stylist. I would plan out different outfits on myself as well as my friends. But I soon learned there was a difference between doing something you love and having that as a job. In psychology, they call this intrinsic motivation and extrinsic motivation. While I still love beauty and fashion, I wouldn't want that to be a profession I want to take on in the future. It would make me feel unmotivated if I did something I love as a profession because I'm doing it for a reward and not because I genuinely like it. For a long time, I didn't know what I wanted to do in the future, but because of my time in Leaders, I gained confidence in my abilities. And I can confidently say I want to be a writer and an educator. Through these professions, I will have a positive impact on people and will find my place in history.

LORENA DE LA ROSA

YEARS AS MENTEE: 2

GRADE: Senior

BORN: New York, NY

LIVES: Bronx, NY

MENTEE'S ANECDOTE: *My mentor Judy and I share a strong bond of friendship and a love of the Met Museum period rooms, avocados, and scary movies. During the time we spend together at weekly pair sessions we laugh a lot and share everything about our lives while we do free-writes, thanks to the random word generator. My life and my writing are infinitely better since joining Girls Write Now, and I'll miss the program when I start college in the fall. But I've already told my mentor that she will be my roommate freshman year!*

JUDITH ROLAND

YEARS AS MENTOR: 6

OCCUPATION: Ghostwriter

BORN: Oceanside, NY

LIVES: New York, NY

MENTOR'S ANECDOTE: *I greatly admire my mentee Lorena for so many things. She's one of the kindest, most considerate people I've ever known, and she's a great, loyal friend. Beyond that, she pushes herself to continually improve her writing and challenge herself. She never lets fear get in the way; to the contrary, she channels it to push beyond her comfort zone and achieve what she never thought possible. She dreams big and is capable of accomplishing anything she sets her mind to. I have no doubt that she will take her place in history!*

FEAR = FEARLESS

LORENA DE LA ROSA

Girls Write Now and my mentor have helped me change from fearful to (almost) fearless. I still get scared, but I've learned to push past my fear.

I try to walk, but my feet are CEMENTED to the pavement
I try to talk but my lips are GLUED together
I try to open my eyes but all I see is the darkness I have drowned
    myself into
Fear, Fear, Fear
Get up, Lorena! Stop being such a baby! It's not a big deal!
For you it isn't a big deal, you who have never gone through what
    I've been through, you who make EVERYTHING seem so
    damn easy
If it was so easy, I would've been up on that stage already. My lips
    moving confidently and my body language so well
    CONTROLLED no one would know I was nervous
It's not that easy
I want to scream but somehow screaming makes me angry as if
    I'm betraying myself, letting myself fall down once again
You got this! Get up! You know you can do it!
I know I can, but you don't understand that I'm scared
That the fear rips at my insides and tries to shred my heart
Lub-dub, Lub-Dub, LUB-DUB
I start to move, but something within me tells me to stop, "How
    dare you be confident," it says
I shake my head, just breathe, Lorena!
You are fearless, didn't you know
Doing the things that scare you just shows how strong you really
    are

It's okay to be scared but never let it consume you

The GLUE from my lips slowly turns into honey and my feet start moving on their own

I make it to the stage, I feel the stares of many burning through me, but I don't dare look at them just yet

I grab the microphone, take a deep breath, look at the crowd and with UNWAVERING confidence I speak about the thing I'm MOST passionate about

Fighting for justice

JAIDA DENT

YEARS AS MENTEE: 1

GRADE: Sophomore

BORN: Brooklyn, NY

LIVES: Brooklyn, NY

PUBLICATIONS AND RECOGNITIONS: Scholastic Art & Writing Awards: Gold Keys

MENTEE'S ANECDOTE: *When I first met Jalisa, it was shockingly scary how alike we were. We both have a love for poetry and had similar views and interests. As much as I loved the creativity she brought, she brought some practicality to my reality. I always knew I needed to get serious about my life and seeing someone with similar passions opened my eyes. Through spending time with Jalisa, I've realized that I have more options than I thought I had and I can express my writing in tons of different ways.*

JALISA WRIGHT

YEARS AS MENTOR: 1

OCCUPATION: Educator; Creative and Technical Writer

BORN: Brooklyn, NY

LIVES: Brooklyn, NY

PUBLICATIONS AND RECOGNITIONS: Every Girl Deserves to Blossom Writing Competition; Brooklyn Lit Match Teen Writing

MENTOR'S ANECDOTE: *I believe God has an interesting way of bringing two people together. This is too true for the mentee relationship I have with Jaida. Working with Jaida is like working with my fifteen-year-old self (only Jaida is a far better writer/human than I was at this age). Believe it or not, she has taught me a thing or two about being, and I hope I've taught her a thing or two about emerging.*

TOO FAST

JAIDA DENT

It is hard being a teenager in this day and age. Layla is constantly pestered with questions about what she wants to do with her life and is it going to make her money. However, she just wants the freedom to be happy in her career path.

> To get to a place where you could love anything you chose—not
> to need permission for desire—well now, that was freedom.
>
> **—TONI MORRISON**

Sitting up in her bed, jerking forward quickly, escaping these stressful thoughts that have bothered her for the past few months. She is reading over "Sweetness" for a third time today with scattered pieces of paper on her bed. Layla wants to be like her, for her words to have an effect on people. Yet sadly, that is not the way the world works. The world requires you to have a good job, make money, and provide for yourself or an entire family.

Don't get me wrong, I want to do that, but doing that means that I probably can't live my dream. What is my dream, you ask? To write, that's what it is. To be able to live a life where I can write endlessly for days, talking about the things people want to hear and saying the things that need to be said. To be able to write under my own name and be satisfied with the work I Produce.

Her parents are a different story. For the last few weeks, her parents have been pestering her with questions Layla asks herself.

"Layla, you have got to start thinking about what you want to do with your life. College applications are around the corner and you have to know what you will spend your four years on," her mother had commented a couple of weeks ago.

Her father added, "Your mother is right. We don't have time to waste thousands of dollars for you to work a subpar job. You need a career that is going to put you somewhere in Life."

"Layla, you are never too young to think about what you want to do with your life. The sooner you know, the more likely you'll be able to accomplish it." A statement said far too often for the young girl.

"But what if I want to be somewhere in history, not just life?"

In silence, she sits.

Her mother had walked around the mahogany dinner table and sat next to Layla. She saw the disappointment in her daughter's eyes, knowing that they had stepped on her dreams like it was nothing. The woman hugged her daughter, bringing warmth in a cold conversation.

"We want you to be different, better than us. We want you to be able to be happy, but also financially supported no matter what."

"But why can't I be both happy and financially supported in writing?"

She nods.

"We're only saying these things because we love you and we know you can do amazing Things."

"I know, Mom," she said dejectedly.

She sighs. With a foggy vision, she remembered back to when she had time. No deadline, no due date, nothing to stress over. There used to be a time when she had freedom. Now everything seems like it's about doing things for your future. Yet, it's at the cost of killing your Present.

What if I get so far, but barely scrape success? What if my dream is never meant to be chased? What if everyone was right? What if it was time to get practical?

With no resolution to her problem, she was overwhelmed. No one seemed to give her the answer she needs, or at least the one she wants to hear. At times like this, she turned to her brother: an eleven-year-old wise beyond his years was somehow a solution for all her problems. He ran from his room on the second floor into the dining room, to be faced only with gloom etched on his older sister's face.

"You seem stressed. What's got you down?" His brown eyes had pierced into her Playfully.

"You wouldn't understand. It's too mature for you."

"When has that ever stopped me from helping you?"

She laughed.

"I'm having a problem figuring out what I want to do with my life, Aiden. Mom and Dad want me to have a job that's boring and is just good for money when I want to have a job that is fun and makes me happy."

"Why can't you have both? Who said there isn't a fun job that makes you money?"

She knew her baby brother was smart, but not this smart. The dinner table was always a place for serious, gut-wrenching conversations. Yet, the carefree answer her brother gave her opened up what else could be talked about here.

Laying back into her bed, she breathed. Forgot everything in the world and took a moment to live. She took in the feeling of the bed beneath her. The way the pillows cradled her head, the way the sheets hugged her body. She calmed her raging thoughts and finally felt some Peace.

Yesterday is yesterday, today is tomorrow, and I am growing up too fast.

MARIAMA DIALLO

YEARS AS MENTEE: 1

GRADE: Junior

BORN: Harlem, NY

LIVES: New York, NY

MENTEE'S ANECDOTE: *When first seeing Angela, I was so nervous because I had never opened up to or really kept in touch with an adult other than a direct family member. The thing I appreciate more than anything is her ability to listen. Half the time I was just ranting about social issues, hot topics, and my past week without any interruption. It was kind of like a therapy session. She shared some of her story, which made me feel open to new ideas as well as get a better sense of who she is. Junior year is stressful and these meetings are such a refresher, thanks to Angela.*

ANGELA DORN

YEARS AS MENTOR: 1

OCCUPATION: Chief Operating Officer and GC of Youth INC

BORN: Chicago, IL

LIVES: New York, NY

PUBLICATIONS AND RECOGNITIONS: *BlackHer; Forbes*

MENTOR'S ANECDOTE: *Mariama enjoys writing poetry. I have read several of her poems and she is a great and creative poet. I write articles and interviews. We both write about race and racism, among other things. When we worked on the "Tribute" prompt in a Girls Write Now workshop, we wrote about two black women artists who lived pre– and post–Civil Rights Movement, with similar life experiences: Billie Holiday and Whitney Houston. It was interesting to discover our common empathy and admiration for these artists.*

THE ILLUSION OF INCLUSION

MARIAMA DIALLO

I believe that as a leader you can do two things: either dig people deeper into their illusions and create false hope or free them of their social standards and stereotypes to reach their fullest potential.

We are often told if you turn your frown upside down
Put on the right gown
You will win that crown but when you're black they shoot down
Strip you of your gown and take your crown
Then tape your lips shut so you cannot make a sound
There was a time period where they didn't want us to stand for
  red, white, and blue
We see injustice and we kneel but they had a problem with that
  too
But let's get to the roots of the issue
Back when I was young I couldn't be myself
Walking into stores and seeing images of everyone else on the
  shelf
Selling us a fantasy knowing that most of us will not live to
  accumulate that amount of wealth
Because there was a strategic system put in place
Ages ago so my people would never be able to be in "your"
  spaces.
Yet you have people talking about coming together as a human
  race
But how can that be the case when the issues pertaining to one
  race are consistently overlooked
Generations of people being mistreated but that somehow being
  justified under a holy book

But forgive me for complaining about issues we face in our
    present day
Because our ancestors went through so much more
And we should instead raise our hands and thank God
That at last we have made it through
But I still feel guilty knowing that while I swim in these oceans
    of blue
Beneath my feet lie the DNA and decomposed bodies of my
    ancestors
Would they be proud to see that I am swimming happily in these
    same bodies of water that transported them from their homes
    to hell
That transported them from being the kings and queens of the
    motherland to being treated worse than dogs
Would they be proud to see that I am not fighting as hard for
    them as they were willing to do for me
Which ultimately were the actions that set all of us free
Would they be proud to claim our lack of loyalty to one another
That we have become so wrapped up in consumerism that we
    can't see the true value in each other
We can only blame those in power for so long
Because they've trained us to believe we are not strong
Part of the reason we can't get along
But at the end of the day we must stop our carelessness and it is
    up to us to create the melody to our own song

MANAR DIHYEM

YEARS AS MENTEE: 3

GRADE: Senior

BORN: New Rochelle, NY

LIVES: Queens, NY

MENTEE'S ANECDOTE: *Getting to know Jaime for who she really is has been nothing but honoring. She is one of the brightest and most talented women I have ever met. We've learned from each other that encouragement is vital in any relationship. I pray that our bond never breaks, as she has become not only my writing mentor and my friend, but my mentor for life.*

JAIME FULLER

YEARS AS MENTOR: 3

OCCUPATION: Editor

BORN: Glens Falls, NY

LIVES: Brooklyn, NY

MENTOR'S ANECDOTE: *The speech that Manar decided to include in this anthology—her last Girls Write Now publication before graduating—shows off how impressive she is, and how much this writer and thinker and activist has grown over her time in the program. It's not just in the words on the page; picture her giving this speech, with immense verve and excellent timing, in front of her school. She's a confident person who has read her work at the New-York Historical Society and been the lead in the school musical. She is an expert at reading and singing words she cares about in front of a crowd. And, a coda for the speech we worked on during our pair sessions—she won the election!*

BECOMING MANAR THE STAR

MANAR DIHYEM

I walked into Dunkin' for one of our pair sessions, and I told Jaime that I wanted to run for school senate. But I needed a speech. Thus, the speech below is a result of our collaboration. This speech motivates me to pursue my dreams.

Growing up, I wasn't used to seeing many Muslim leaders in my community, on TV, or in pop culture. But now I see public figures beginning to rise to represent the Muslim community: everyone from civil rights leaders like model Halima Aden to political leaders like Representative Ilhan Omar. Finally having people who look like me taking big steps like being part of Congress inspires me beyond what words can describe. It makes me want to take leadership, wink-wink. I have more hope and faith in the world when I look out and see leaders I can connect with. My life and my background and what I see when I look at the world have given me plenty of ideas that I think could benefit everyone at my school.

I believe that creativity should never be taken away but treasured. I believe that fashion is creativity. With that being said, dress codes eliminate students' sense of freedom through the way they dress, their ability to figure out who they are. This is the reasoning behind my plan to eliminate the dress code. I believe that if the school allows students the ability to choose how they want to dress, then students are more likely to follow other, more important rules, like even showing up to school on time. Students stress about what they're going to wear on a daily basis already and dress codes only make things worse by bombarding them with guidelines that their outfit must meet. School leaders should instead be stressing how their *grades* are looking, not their hemlines, because while appropriate dress code is important, education is even more vital.

A student's voice is also crucially valuable. I find that maintaining one's mental health is extremely difficult when you're a teenager. We tend to feel obligated to deal with the world's obstacles. As minorities, we struggle to deal with never-ending brutal racism and stereotypes. As teenagers, we struggle to deal with the idea of self-identification. As scholars, we have piles and piles of work laid before us and we are told to "do it." How are we expected to manage all of that while we are only human?

Last Ramadan, I didn't have a good place to pray in school. So I proposed the idea of opening a prayer room. I told the principal that I believed it was a First Amendment issue. And, lo and behold, the first prayer room at the school was opened for business. I decorated it with my dear friend. We felt heard and respected. I will always stand and try to better what is wrong. It doesn't matter if it affects one student or the whole school. We are to be heard—never silenced. I'm here for you.

LAILA DOLA

YEARS AS MENTEE: 3

GRADE: Senior

BORN: Noapara, Jessore, Bangladesh

LIVES: Queens, NY

MENTEE'S ANECDOTE: *Sometimes God crosses our path with certain people to teach us to continue to move forward in our own lives. Those people nourish us, they push us, and they teach us to believe in ourselves. For me, my mentor Jill is that gift, and I have been extremely lucky to have her in my life. She always amazes me with her open-mindedness and her knowledge of every little thing in the world. I greatly appreciate her presence in my life.*

JILL KAMINSKY

YEARS AS MENTOR: 2

OCCUPATION: Freelance Writer

BORN: Cocoa Beach, FL

LIVES: New York, NY

PUBLICATIONS AND RECOGNITIONS: *The Washington Post*, Davenport Theatrical

MENTOR'S ANECDOTE: *When I joined Girls Write Now as a mentor two years ago, I had the self-aggrandizing belief that I would be a shining example of wisdom to a young woman. I would be the envy of all the other mentors. What I didn't know is that I would be paired with Laila, the most wise and compassionate person that I know. Every time I meet with Laila, I walk away with some new insight, something new to think about, something to consider in my own life. She is the mentor. I am the mentee.*

A PACKAGE OF COOKIES

LAILA DOLA

This piece is about my relationship with my father, and my appreciation toward him for bringing our family to the United States. His sacrifice has given me the opportunity for a better future.

My family is everything to me. I realized this while sharing with them a package of cookies.

My two younger sisters, Shaila and Nila, were five and two and I was nine years old. We had emigrated from Bangladesh to the United States just a few months prior, knowing little to no English.

One day, my father decided to take us out for a walk. My father has a habit of spontaneously coming up with crazy activities for us, so we didn't question the fact that it was windy and bitterly cold outside. We stepped out into the frigid air.

After walking three blocks, my father stopped at a small grocery store. He walked straight to the cookie aisle, with the three of us following, like good little ducklings. He said to us, "Pick one."

That's when the negotiations began. Shaila wanted chocolate cookies. Nila wanted vanilla cookies. And I didn't care which cookies. After a few minutes, which felt like hours, no decision had been made. My father picked up a small package of cookies and declared, "Let's get this one."

At the cash register, I watched my father count out the change, while my sisters were giggling with each other. That's when it hit me. It was a sacrifice for my father to buy those cookies. At the time, he was working day and night as a delivery man. I suppose I already knew how difficult it was for him. But that package of cookies made me fully appreciate what he was doing for our family. To give us a better life in our new home country.

We stepped back outside into the freezing cold wind. My father stopped, turned to us, and ripped open the box. My sisters were like a pack of ravenous wolves. They grabbed a few cookies each. When my father put the cookies in front of me, I noticed he was not taking one for himself. I also saw that my sisters were ready for more, and there were only a few left. I told my father, "No thank you, I am full."

My father smiled at me. I smiled back. It was a smile that spoke so many words. Words that cannot be communicated verbally, but only through a look of understanding.

In that moment, at nine years old, I decided that I would do whatever I can within my ability, and work hard toward a better future for me and my family.

KIMBERLY DOMINGUEZ

YEARS AS MENTEE: 3

GRADE: Senior

BORN: Queens, NY

LIVES: Queens, NY

MENTEE'S ANECDOTE: *I am very grateful and fortunate to have spent three years with Liz as my mentor. She instantly became one of my favorite people and I cannot fully express how much her guidance and friendship have meant to me. Liz has always been there to help me with whatever I needed, whether it was some wise advice or proofreading a paper. I am always incredibly impressed by her discipline and the way she acts on her interests, always talking about them enthusiastically. I am very excited to see what she'll accomplish next!*

ELIZABETH THOMAS

YEARS AS MENTOR: 3

OCCUPATION: AVP of Communications, New York Law School

BORN: Norfolk, VA

LIVES: Queens, NY

MENTOR'S ANECDOTE: *I'm so grateful that Kimberly and I have worked together for the last three years. From the first time I met her, I've been amazed by her openness, creativity, talent, and resourcefulness. Our conversations have touched on everything from art history, Disney movies, and the personal shortcomings of famous musicians to dystopian novels, socialism, Marie Antoinette, the Beatniks, and meditation. Kimberly is a gifted journalist, poet, and thinker. No matter what career she pursues, she will impact many people and will take an important place in history.*

MISS MANNERS' GUIDE TO PREVENTING TRAGEDY

KIMBERLY DOMINGUEZ

I have always loved learning about different historical figures and trying to relate their experiences to my life, often with little success, as I am not at a point in my life where I am a founding father or queen of any country; this piece is the fruit of that.

DEAR MISS MANNERS,

I had this old friend, Mr. Burr, with whom I recently had a falling-out. It's stupid, really. All I did was tell a newspaper a slight indiscretion. Then suddenly I am challenged to a duel! I think he is overreacting. My inquiry is, what is the proper way to approach this? Is a DM too informal?

Alexander Hamilton

GENTLE READER,

Miss Manners means no disrespect to the classical tradition of the duel; however, she does believe in the civilized manner of solving disputes over an iced chai latte.

P.S. Good luck!

DEAR MISS MANNERS,

I was recently in New York City working on a new fresco for the Rockefellers. Unfortunately, this did not go as planned as my Commie friends started circulating nasty memes (something about selling out). Because I was scared of getting canceled on Twitter, I drew a big fat Vladimir Lenin in the middle of my fresco. The next day, after stopping for a bacon, egg, and cheese,

I walked into work to find some fools chipping my art off the wall! What do you think would be the best form of retaliation?

Diego Rivera

GENTLE READER,

While Miss Manners would not like to disclose her personal politics, she suggests bribing members of Congress to impose a wealth tax.

DEAR MISS MANNERS,

I had just posted a picture of my mid-afternoon cake with the caption "#blessed #cheatdayeveryday" when I received an onslaught of angry DMs from peasants with private profiles claiming I was insensitive since they didn't have bread. The next thing I know, I get a GIF of a guillotine! Would it be impertinent to post a picture of my newly renovated palace?

Marie Antoinette

GENTLE READER,

Miss Manners suggests taking a break from Instagram. She also suggests volunteering at a soup kitchen; remember to call the *Daily Mail* and TMZ in advance.

MADOLLEY DONZO

YEARS AS MENTEE: 1

GRADE: Senior

BORN: Monrovia, Liberia

LIVES: Queens, NY

MENTEE'S ANECDOTE: *I have had so much fun these last few months getting to know my mentor Annie. We usually meet in cafés around Queens and contemplate what it's like to live in New York City. When I talk to Annie, I feel as if I'm talking to a friend because she is understanding and she always guides me in the right direction. I'm glad I was given this opportunity to develop my voice through writing while sharing my thoughts about everything from school to life with someone who's as interesting and vibrant as Annie is.*

ANNIE BRYAN

YEARS AS MENTOR: 2

OCCUPATION: Associate Creative Strategist, *Time*

BORN: United States

LIVES: Queens, NY

PUBLICATIONS AND RECOGNITIONS: *Off White, Macbeth in the Basement*; Society of Professional Journalists Mark of Excellence

MENTOR'S ANECDOTE: *Madolley is one of the most bright, intuitive, wise, joyful, and effusive people I've ever met. She takes her place in history every day by taking constant strides toward her goals of entering psychology and helping others. It has been an absolute pleasure working through senior year with her and witnessing her take her place in history!*

A FALSE HOME

MADOLLEY DONZO

We tend to cling to our past and the sense of familiarity because it reminds us of home. This prevents many of us from ever actually trying something new or finding who we're meant to be. My story takes you on the journey of discovering why home isn't always home.

The blinds were down and the curtains pulled shut. The lights were off, but in the moonlight, the room glowed. Four walls and a single door. There was a chair in the middle of the room and a lamp on a nightstand in the far corner. I strode toward it, realizing that there was no way to turn the lamp on only once I stood right in front of it. I walked toward the heater to check if it was on. It was, but somehow I still shivered in my dark cashmere sweater.

I sat in the chair in this dark and cold room and thought to myself, *Could this be home?* There was a burning smell, almost that of popcorn that had been left in the microwave too long. Yet, somehow, it was the only indication that this room was home. Growing tired of just sitting in the chair, I stood up and walked toward the window. I drew open one of the curtains and looked out into the night. In the dark of the night, all I could make out were the tall, spindly trees with sickly branches that grabbed for the moon. There was a long animalistic howl in the distance that begged me to concede that "Yes! This was home, all right."

I closed the curtain and walked toward the door. I turned the knob to the right, then the left, but nothing happened. The door wouldn't budge. But how could it be locked? How could my *home* not let me leave? I went back to the chair, but instead of sitting on it, I decided to lay on the cold, wood floor. I couldn't help but wonder, "Could this overwhelming darkness be a product of my lost dreams? Or could I just be reveling in the joy of finally being *home?*" I shut my eyes because the darkness was almost blinding. And that's when I realized that this—whatever this was—wasn't home.

I quickly sat up and looked around the room again, more frantic than ever. As I became aware that this room wasn't home, I was finally able to see the pictures on the walls. Those pictures depicted moments in history, moments that we sometimes overlook or forget entirely. Realizing that this room was a shrine to the past, I jumped to my feet and walked toward the lamp again. Unlike before, the lamp had a small switch. I flicked it on and the room became dimly lit. I looked up to the ceiling and saw someone looking down back at me.

"Go out into this world and make history. The kind of history that people will want to read. Leave your mark on this world and never look back." That's what the person in the ceiling mirror mouthed to me. And though I understood what she was asking of me, I wasn't sure I could do it. But I pushed my fear down, squared my shoulders, lifted my head and walked toward the door. I turned the knob and this time I heard the lock click. I opened the door slowly and stood before the bright lights of the hallway. This threshold between the darkness of the past and the light of the future is what encouraged me to take the step toward something new.

As I stepped into the hall, I didn't look back at the room I believed to be my "home." And even now as I write this, I don't miss the burnt popcorn. Or the cold, staleness of the air. I don't miss the howls to the moon and surely don't miss the crippling darkness. Because I found a new home on the pages of my journal and I found my voice within the ink stains of my pen.

ILANA DRAKE

YEARS AS MENTEE: 2

GRADE: Junior

BORN: New York, NY

LIVES: New York, NY

PUBLICATIONS AND RECOGNITIONS: Scholastic Art & Writing Awards: Gold Key, Honorable Mention; Rising Voices Fellow 2019–2020

MENTEE'S ANECDOTE: *I know that I say this over and over, but Erica wins the award for "best mentor in the world." Throughout the past two years, Erica has helped me to find my footing and my voice, and I can honestly say that she is the best thing that happened to me during high school. Erica's smile fills up any room, and every time she says the word "interesting," we both burst into laughter because we use that word way too often! Erica is a "Renaissance Woman," and I can't wait for her to finish her novel in progress!*

ERICA DRENNAN

YEARS AS MENTOR: 2

OCCUPATION: Ph.D. Candidate, Columbia University

BORN: New York, NY

LIVES: Brooklyn, NY

MENTOR'S ANECDOTE: *Ilana is the most enthusiastic person I have ever met! Her smile and laugh are infectious and our pair sessions are the highlight of my week. She is always excited and ready to write, no matter how busy she is with school. At our first meeting this fall, Ilana started writing about her summer in Germany. I remember getting chills hearing about her experiences confronting anti-Semitism. It's been an incredible privilege to watch her process that experience and powerfully put it into words. With this piece, Ilana is keeping history alive and taking her place in it.*

75 YEARS

ILANA DRAKE

I wrote this piece after visiting the Dachau Concentration Camp Memorial Site last summer and attending the United Nations Holocaust Memorial Ceremony on January 27, 2020. Seventy-five years have passed since the liberation of Auschwitz.

On January 27, 2020, we held up signs near the gate to the United Nations. Our hands were cold, and we were mentally preparing for the morning. When my grandmother and I sat down together in the auditorium, I realized that everyone in this room was affected by the Holocaust. I saw elderly men with military badges on their jackets, people wearing the infamous yellow star with "Juden" written on it, and I heard people speaking many languages. As I brought the earpiece to my ear to listen to the speeches, I wondered how the people in Bad Reichenhall were commemorating the day.

Last summer, I participated in a homestay program in southern Germany. When I arrived, I was shocked to realize that I was the only Jewish person in the town. I decided to go to church to try to fit in and observe the culture. The first time I went to church, I didn't take the Eucharist. People gave me weird looks as I stood alone in the pew. I felt uncomfortable and different. The next time, I took the Eucharist. I prayed on my knees and took the cookie from the altar without knowing what I was saying or doing or even what the cookie was called. It tasted like chalk. At home, I think through the pros and cons of every decision I make, but now I was just following the pack. Is this what it means to be complicit?

I asked my host mother if we could visit Dachau, and on my last full day in Germany, I traveled there with my host family. The bus ride through the town of Dachau gave my spine chills. It was a functioning town with Italian restaurants where people lived and had families. I could not process the idea that people lived in the same town as a concentration camp.

While my host family and I waited for our tour, we sat at a picnic table outside in the middle of the visitors' center and I looked around. There was a café that sold refreshments and ice cream. I always thought ice cream was for happy occasions, for normal summer days. I would never have guessed I would see ice cream in a place where so many people perished.

My tour guide bragged about giving Mike Pence a tour, and he barely mentioned the Jewish people who were sent to Dachau. He told us about political prisoners and the different color triangles given to specific groups. At one point, we were free to explore part of the memorial site on our own and I learned about some of the people who ended up in Dachau. Seeing the manicured grounds made me feel like I wasn't in a place built for extermination. The pebbles on the ground made it seem like this wasn't real, like nothing could have happened here. As the tour guide rambled on about political prisoners, I came up with the courage to ask about the Jewish people who had entered the gates. He dismissed my question. I knew that was wrong.

The rain started to fall as we walked to the multicultural centers and I felt splattered with so many emotions. My mom visited Auschwitz a few years ago and came back changed at the age of forty-seven. I was sixteen and scared. I was in a foreign country with no Jewish friends and no one to understand how this experience had woken me up. The history I had read about in memoirs and books had become a reality. When we passed the "Arbeit Macht Frei" sign at the entrance to the camp, all I wanted to do was cry. I had seen photos of this slogan but now I wasn't looking at it through a screen. This was real.

Sitting in the chair next to my grandmother at the United Nations, I listened to speeches from Holocaust survivors about anti-Semitism. I didn't know most of the other people in the room, but we were united that day. This was my community.

That morning, Fred Heyman, a Holocaust survivor, gave me a card about being an upstander. An upstander is someone who acts when they see injustice. When I travel, I will discuss my religion, even if it is uncomfortable. I will not tolerate anti-Semitic remarks. I will not pretend that everything is okay. I will speak up and try to never allow an event like this to happen again. Irene Shashar, another survivor who spoke at the U.N., ended her speech with the words: "Don't let Hitler ever, ever win."

Before the U.N. commemoration, I stood up at the podium and looked out over the huge auditorium. I was overwhelmed looking out at the crowd. In ten years, there may be no Holocaust survivors left. We must carry on their stories. Otherwise, their stories will fade and the Nazis will win.

YADYVIC ESTRELLA BATISTA

YEARS AS MENTEE: 2

GRADE: Senior

BORN: Bronx, NY

LIVES: Bronx, NY

PUBLICATIONS AND RECOGNITIONS: Scholastic Art & Writing Awards: Gold Key, Silver Key, Honorable Mentions

MENTEE'S ANECDOTE: *It is crazy to think that Kimberly and I met just a few months ago. Whether it be at the Girls Write Now workshops or during our own weekly sessions, I know I am in for a good time. I believe that Kimberly has helped me further mature my writing and has expanded the way I think. I know that I can rely on her for an understanding mind, a listening ear, and amazing feedback. Thank you, Kimberly, for everything. I hope we can stay close even when I graduate from Girls Write Now and continue to take our places in history.*

KIMBERLY JACOBS

YEARS AS MENTOR: 3

OCCUPATION: Executive Assistant, Rockefeller Group Business Center

BORN: Los Angeles, CA

LIVES: New York, NY

PUBLICATIONS AND RECOGNITIONS: *Parade*

MENTOR'S ANECDOTE: *Every Tuesday evening Yadyvic and I meet at the Lit. Bar bookstore. It's been a quaint and exciting place to write, as we're surrounded by so many interesting books and blaring music that somehow puts us in the perfect mood to share and write. Yadyvic's stories are always very interesting because she includes subtle yet beautiful aspects of her culture and her love for science, animals, and the outdoors. I know she will go on to do great things in her life because of her ability to combine creativity with science and technology.*

SEREIN: EN VIDA Y EN MUERTE

YADYVIC ESTRELLA BATISTA

This piece was inspired by a story my grandfather told me when I was younger about shape-shifting beasts in my home country of the Dominican Republic. I introduce you to both his world and a retelling of Mulan as we reach for a way to make our ancestors proud.

My mother's father trained me ever since I was seven years old. While the thought of hunting beasts excites me, my mother never really approved. My mom, who holds the mundane above all else, has never held any interest in being my grandfather's successor. The family duty then falls to the next in line, my elder sister—though she, much like our mother, has not one adventurous bone in her body. Now there's me, trying to uphold the legacy that rests upon me.

In a faraway place deep in my mind, I dreamed of having a Galipote-hunting family. It wasn't so much about the hunting, it was more so about doing something together. However, taking into consideration that the sightings of Galipotes have become scarce, that dream died long before it became anything other than a daydream. *God forbid it became an all-consuming fantasy*; at least I like to tell myself that.

The very first time I heard about Galipotes was when I was four. It was already dark. The cool-ish wind was a refreshing contrast against the all-year summer in the tropical island. My cousins and I were surrounding our grandpa like he was our only sense of warmth during a winter night. He didn't much like the close proximity, but his concern passed unvoiced. He was telling his favorite story set in a starry night just like this one.

My papá was walking home with one of his cousins, Marianela. She had decided it would be fun to sneak out and go visit her other cousin in the club. They mindlessly chat as they walk through the night. It was a quiet night, not even the stray cats dared meow.

From far away, it seemed like a big dog was planted in the middle of the road. As they drew closer, Marianela froze.

This was no ordinary dog—this was no dog at all. There, in the middle of the road, was a Galipote. Galipotes are monsters of the night. It's said that they're human during the day and feed on the flesh of those who dare go outside during the night. Everyone here knew about the beasts but few have encountered one firsthand.

Slowly, the beast advanced toward them. Something you have to know about my papá is that he is fearless—the only thing that remotely stirs fear in his stomach is the angry face of his then girlfriend and future mother of his kids. The only noise that could be heard is the beast's heavy breathing, saliva dripping from his bared mouth and sharp teeth.

"Nela, I swear to God, do . . . not . . . move." The young girl whimpered in response, scared for her life. Though the man's body is as still as a mannequin, his eyes searched his surroundings for something to defend themselves with. To his left, he saw a multitude of rocks. He figured they would be able to do some damage. "Okay, get behind me in one . . . two . . . three!"

Marianela runs behind her cousin. The beast sprints toward them, growling and snarking. Papá quickly grabs a medium-sized rock and waits for the beast to come closer. He aims at the beast's hind leg. He throws, hitting the beast at command. Maybe throwing rocks at mango trees does help for something. He doesn't wait. In seconds, he throws another rock, then another, then another. He stops only when the beast whimpers, falling down to the dirt.

Papá and Nela don't wait for the beast to get up. Nela sprints; she will only be safe when she gets home. Papá follows her, but he spares a backward look at the beast. He sees as the beast limps in the opposite direction, struggling to move.

The next morning, he gets up bright and early to follow his daily routine in the field. Though on his way, he sees Alejandro, a man who had moved to the village a few weeks prior. The man was limping.

Papá's eyes train after him, even when the man refuses to make eye contact. Then, he is sure, Alejandro is the Galipote he and his cousin had encountered the night before, and he had confronted the man that same day.

Grandpa's fearlessness is what got him killed. His reckless and stubborn need to protect those around him, putting himself right in the unforgiving hands of death. Every hunter is to die proudly, to know they fought well, and that their inevitable death by beasts was worth it for the lives they saved.

The beast that killed him was too strong, even for Papá, who had years of experience.

Even when the warm days turn into cold nights and the wind blows harshly against my neck, my fingers stoned, my limbs heavy with exhaustion and my stomach growling with spite, I will not give up my search. My mind nor my heart will be at peace until I find the beast and make sure it does not try to kill anyone else. I will not let the beast walk freely in the land Papá died protecting. I will not let my grandfather's death be in vain.

I will avenge my grandfather's death by any means necessary.

AMOYA EVANS

YEARS AS MENTEE: 1

GRADE: Freshman

BORN: New York, NY

LIVES: New York, NY

MENTEE'S ANECDOTE: *When I met my new mentor I was excited to work with her and her enthusiasm encouraged me.*

REBECCA SANANES

YEARS AS MENTOR: 1

OCCUPATION: Journalist and Podcast Producer

BORN: New Haven, CT

LIVES: Brooklyn, NY

MENTOR'S ANECDOTE: *The first thing I noticed about Amoya is how committed and engaged she is. Those qualities will get her anywhere she wants to go.*

WEEKENDS/WEEKDAYS

AMOYA EVANS

I awake to my upstairs neighbors yelling and my mom shuffling to get my sister out the door for school. It's 6:00 a.m. and my mom is shouting my name. I jump out of bed. My body isn't ready to go but my brain is telling me to move. The black skirt I put out the night before is sitting on my dresser, waiting for me to wear. Not having to choose what I wear in the morning makes it faster for me to get ready. Even though it's not in the dress code, I put any shirt on and toss my "York Prep" hoodie over. Finally, I'm ready and my mom and I are walking out the door.

I walk down the block, shivering, to the Ninety-sixth Street train station. It's quiet on the street, but once I get underground it's a different environment. The smell of rust from the cars fills the air. Uptown and downtown trains pass by rumbling. People on the platform zone are into their phones. Once the train approaches the platform, I prepare myself to get on the train. When boarding the 1 train, I'm aware of my surroundings. There are so many different people and different moods. People in a hurry, or not. I put on my study tunes playlist that contains mellow and soft songs and tune out the rest of the world. As the train continues downtown, I begin to think about when I'm getting off and what's my first-period class.

Once I get off the train at the Sixty-sixth Street/Lincoln Center station and start walking to school, I ease back into the world and realize that I'm walking into a school environment. When I see ABC News, Lincoln Center, and Columbus Circle, I know I'm walking toward my school. I start to think about my work, what assignments are due, and tests and quizzes I need to take. Suddenly, my music dims and my school thoughts come back.

On weekends, I wake up to my dog licking me and I notice that my mom has left for work. I get breakfast—Honey Nut Cheerios from my kitchen. Unlike weekdays, I get ready in the afternoon. I look on Snapchat to see my twenty unread messages from a group chat. One of my friends is suggesting for us to meet up at Starbucks. It's our typical meeting place in the center of our homes. It takes a while for everyone to read the messages, but we all agree and we meet up.

My life on weekdays and weekends is very different. On weekdays I care about my work and I make it a top priority to complete all my homework the night before. My schedule is different. I wake up and try to get out the door as quick as possible and I get breakfast elsewhere. On the weekends I wake up naturally and eat breakfast at home, typically oatmeal. On weekends, I really have to choose my clothes, compared to weekdays, when I wear my uniform. Overall, my weekday schedule and routines are completely different from each other.

SIARRA FRANCOIS

YEARS AS MENTEE: 2

GRADE: Senior

BORN: Brooklyn, NY

LIVES: Brooklyn, NY

MENTEE'S ANECDOTE: *Throughout the writing program, Ashley and I were able to bond and learn a lot about each other, whether it be through workshops or meet-ups. Meeting Ashley through this program has allowed me to open up and interact with someone in a circumstance that I probably would not have put myself in otherwise. Throughout the program, we have been able to learn new interests about each other and things that we have in common.*

ASHLEY WELCH

YEARS AS MENTOR: 2

OCCUPATION: Senior Media Relations Specialist, NYU Langone Health

BORN: Yonkers, NY

LIVES: Queens, NY

MENTOR'S ANECDOTE: *Siarra and I have worked to hone many of her written skills over the past two years, from switching from the passive to active voice, to making her work more descriptive by "showing, not telling," to multiple rewrites. When she showed me the story she wanted to submit to the Girls Write Now anthology this year, I was absolutely floored. With so much emotion and insight, the words jump right off the page and into your heart where they leave an indelible mark. Siarra has grown so much as a writer and a person and I am so incredibly proud of her.*

BROWN SUGAR

SIARRA FRANCOIS

This piece is a fictional short story that tells the tale of a young African American girl who comes to the realization of who she is and what it means to her.

Jasmine lifted her collar and threw the sweater vest over her button-down shirt. "Pacific Poly Prep," she whispered to herself while looking in the mirror. She quickly put her headband on her head, grabbed her bag, and rushed out of the room. While checking the time on her Apple Watch, she slid on her shoes and grabbed a banana from the fruit basket and her keys to her 2019 Mercedes-Benz. As she pulled out of the driveway and waited for the security to open the gates, she noticed the sun beaming, highlighting her hazel eyes, and turned on the new Ariana Grande album. Jasmine was one out of the three black people that attended her prestigious private school in Garden Hills. If you asked her where she was from, she would never forget to tell you she was black but she would always mention that her great-great-grandparents were Irish and Polish.

As she pulled into the parking lot of her school she threw on some lip gloss, fluffed her puff full of kinky curls, and grabbed her bag. She walked into the school hallways and met up with her best friend Rebecca Clinton (yes, the granddaughter of Bill Clinton). "Today's the day! Are you ready?" Rebecca excitedly asked her best friend. Jasmine was finally going to ask her crush, Brady Thornton, captain of the lacrosse team, out on a date. "Of course I am. How could he say no to me? I'm captain of the debate team and class president." Jasmine grabbed her book and closed her locker, ready to ask Brady to the homecoming dance, which was the following week. "Hey, Brady," Jasmine nervously said while sitting down in the seat next to him. Brady looked up quickly while pushing his blond locks out of his face and gave Jasmine a nod while turning back to his phone. "So, are you going to the dance next Friday?" she asked him while opening her book, trying to make it all seem casual. "Not sure yet," he said, still refusing to look up from his phone. "Well . . . I was wondering if you'd want to be my date to the dance?" Brady finally looked up from his phone and his pale cheeks turned rosy. "Look, Jasmine, I think you're a great girl," Brady nervously said while scratching his neck, "but I don't think us going to the dance together would be such a great idea." Jasmine's face dropped and all she could muster up was a quiet "Why not?" "Because, you know . . ." he said while rubbing his hand. "Maybe you should ask Justin Thompson . . ." Brady said, giving her a smile. Unironically, Justin was the only black boy in school.

Jasmine raised her hand and asked to be excused to the bathroom. She opened the door and looked at herself in the mirror. "What does that even mean?" she whispered to herself. "I'm smart, friends with everyone, and I know my looks aren't the reason for him saying no," Jasmine thought out loud. Then it dawned on her as her brown hands ran through her hair, removing the scrunchie and letting her kinky curls loose. He wouldn't go to the dance with her because she was black. Jasmine had never experienced something like that in her life. Her skin color had never got in the way with any of her interactions because of her status in life. As she splashed cold water over her face, she noticed the features that made her different. Of course she spent all of her life around white people, so she never really realized that she was any different. She ran her fingers against her plump lips and grazed her slightly bigger nose before walking out of the bathroom. "Psst, psst," she said in front of Rebecca's class, signaling for her to come outside. "So did he say yes? What color are you guys gonna wear? I was thinking . . ." "He said no," Jasmine said flatly, knowing that if she did not cut her friend off then that she would continue to ramble on. Rebecca turned red and pushed back her blonde hair. "What? Why?" she said with her blue glassy eyes. Rebecca knew how much her friend wanted this and hearing those words crushed her. "He said it's be-cause I'm black, Beck," Jasmine said, still in shock. Rebecca quickly wrapped her lanky arms around her best friend and began to walk down the hall. "And beautiful," she said, reassuring her best friend as they walked down the halls.

LIZBETH FUENTES ASCENCIO

YEARS AS MENTEE: 1

GRADE: Senior

BORN: Queens, NY

LIVES: Bronx, NY

PUBLICATIONS AND RECOGNITIONS: Scholastic Art & Writing Awards: Silver Key

MENTEE'S ANECDOTE: *Coming into this program, I was very anxious but ready to take a step and give a voice to my writing. At first, the thought of having a mentor scared me. I had many insecurities about my writing and if I would be understood. However, I've lost that fear with Deiona. When I first met Deiona, I was greeted with a big smile. She helped me feel more comfortable expressing myself, and every week she highly motivates me to be successful. She empowers me to make decisions and overall makes me want to be a better version of myself.*

DEIONA MONROE

YEARS AS MENTOR: 1

OCCUPATION: Development Fellow, Newark Opportunity Youth Network

BORN: Harlem, NY

LIVES: New York, NY

PUBLICATIONS AND RECOGNITIONS: Scholastic Art & Writing Awards: Gold Key, Silver Key

MENTOR'S ANECDOTE: *As a first-year mentor, I was terrified but felt led to give back—specifically to our girls. I was a Girls Write Now mentee in 2007/2008 and, I must say, it planted a seed in my life. And when I met Lizbeth, I wanted to keep planting those seeds. At first, she was very reserved—as was I when I was a mentee—yet she was willing to open up to me. Now our space is much warmer. She's a phenomenal young lady, growing into an even more amazing woman. Through her, I'm watching more seeds get planted and marks being made in history.*

DEAR FRIEND

LIZBETH FUENTES ASCENCIO

This piece is dedicated to my younger self, who deserves the recognition for keeping her head high through all the downfalls presented through-out her life. With all my faults and mistakes, yesterday's me is still me.

Dear Lizbeth,

How are you? You probably don't know, but you're a very big person now. Ha! These past years have been like a kick in the butt, but unfortunately I must deliver to you the news that you must face all those things to get to where you are now. Honestly, you didn't do so well, but the many struggles and events you faced made you grow. You managed to get back up and start building a castle out of the bricks thrown at you. I just want you to know how proud I am of you. People say you're too cold because you keep your dis-tance, but in all honesty we know that you've learned to no longer let yourself be a fool or let yourself be stomped down. We're too grown and too great for that.

Not to get too emotional in this letter, but as I'm writing this, we're in the middle of becoming an adult. I'm glad you got to have special teenage memories that you'll forever cherish, even though the storm was still going on. Your world must've been gray for the most part, but it finally started sprouting colors when at fifteen you discovered BTS. I could see how the world lightened up within your eyes and grew to have a purpose—however, I must say you're still in the process. The process to loving yourself never stops; it's a continuous road that you must take until you're satisfied with where you are.

BTS, however, wiped away your sadness and loneliness with their music and love. They've helped you come to the realization that we deserve better; loving ourselves comes with many challenges and tears, but that's the beauty in it. You must love yourself for who you are and for how far you've come.

Don't let things that hurt you haunt you. Try and focus on what's good in your life. Little by little, hurt fades and the void is filled with goodness. Just as BTS genuinely cares about their music's impact and uses their platform to remind and send love to their fans, I encourage you to push forward a change in the world that really needs it. Just as the lyrics in the BTS song "Love Myself" say:

Loving myself might be harder
Than loving someone else

Therefore, look into the future. The grind ain't over. You're about to go to college and life will take you on another long rollercoaster ride. Let's keep going together—for a long time—into the future.

GABRIELLE GALCHEN

YEARS AS MENTEE: 2

GRADE: Junior

BORN: New York, NY

LIVES: New York, NY

PUBLICATIONS AND RECOGNITIONS: Scholastic Art & Writing Awards: Silver Keys

MENTEE'S ANECDOTE: *At the beginning of junior year only one adjective could describe me: stressed. In a STEM-based society, I was addicted to creative writing but had no idea how to fit what I loved into a feasible reality. I knew Emily could sense how I was feeling. She reassured me that writers can take many different paths in life, pursuing it full-time or as a secondary job, but first and foremost I would always be a writer. Such an integral part of my life could never be removed from me, and time would only help unveil more of who I was. I am grateful that my mentor understood me in a way no one else could.*

EMILY BARASCH

YEARS AS MENTOR: 4

OCCUPATION: Writer (Creative and Branded Content)

BORN: New York, NY

LIVES: Brooklyn, NY

MENTOR'S ANECDOTE: *If working together with Gabi in Girls Write Now last year was about finding her voice, this year has been about her exploring new, complex, and unique ways of expressing it. From playwriting to poetry to podcasting, Gabi has challenged herself and come out on the other side with brilliant work, tenacity, and wisdom that surpasses her years. I particularly revel in the way her work can emotionally move me, from a genuinely terrifying (and riveting) play to more candid and heartfelt work.*

WITHIN LIMITS

GABRIELLE GALCHEN

To take our place in history, we must also take a place within ourselves by being conscious of how we feel. Mental health is one of the least discussed yet most prevalent parts of our past, present, and future, as our mentality about ourselves and about the world defines us.

Note: Names have been changed.

It was in those days of such similarity that they could all be Mondays or Wednesdays—or whatever pointless label clumsily attached to it—that I wished that the lab paper I was writing on would be scalding hot, just so all paper wouldn't monotonously mirror itself by being all smooth, happy, and white. Maybe then I would finally believe in the space between "every day" as a noun and "everyday" as an adjective, would not believe the latter to merely describe— define, rather—the first.

But one lab day, a girl who always worked alone suddenly turned to me and started crying. I quickly went to hug her and stared into the distance as she cried, looking around to see who had taken notice. No one seemed to.

But I was that "nice girl" in my grade and who I wanted to be. I was one of the few who was still civil to Lana after she had returned to school from a mental health institution. I was one of the few who she could even call a friend, because after months of trying to alleviate her of her alcoholic and self-harm habits prior to hospitalization, her friends had decided that they could no longer emotionally handle taking care of her. I was one of the few and I knew I was satisfied with how I treated her. But that past week, she had sought me out every day to help her get through a crying fit or panic attack, and I didn't know if I still wanted to be.

Depression and bipolar disorder affect approximately 14 percent of youth aged thirteen to seventeen. Of this 14 percent, about one in three teens will abuse substances as a coping mechanism.

Before she was institutionalized, it quickly became a well-known fact that Lana was drinking stolen alcohol from an opaque water bottle during school. When Lana vomited in the middle of English class and had to be physically assisted to the nurse's office, everyone in her class went out of their way to spread the story. Though multiple versions were presented, the look of haunted disgust upon remembering the vomit was almost comically mirrored in everyone's expression.

Teenage girls are twice as likely to experience depression than boys, due to varying concentrations of sex hormone receptors in brain regions affected by depression. The female vulnerability to intense emotions is inherently linked to sexism, as women are generally regarded as more irrational.

Lana's name quickly degenerated from "Lana" to "crazy." Everyone regarded her cautiously as one would a rabid animal. In turn, she came to school in thirty-degree weather in just a sports bra and leggings, started messaging old men on dating apps, and stopped showering for days on end. When she finally left school, she had for all intents and purposes become who she was said to be until it was all that she had left to define her.

At my generally far-left liberal school, I had seen many openly cry. It was common for kids to joke, "I want to kill myself," or say, "I'm so depressed," whenever something slightly negative happened.

Yet when Lana returned to school, no one acknowledged her, and all her friends refused to interact with her. I was shocked by the hypocrisy of my grade, at how they alleged themselves to be so accepting and inclusive until they actually had to be.

Like any ignorant person, I thought I knew everything. Yet even though Lana's mental illness debilitated her just as a broken leg would an athlete, the situation ran deep and convoluted within the recesses of her mind. And when she wanted help, she was not simply asking for someone to carry her backpack or open a door.

Later, her former friends opened up to me about how she had texted them repeatedly, threatening to and then proceeding to do something to herself if they did not answer.

When all she started talking about with me was how her life was harder than mine and how her week was going terribly, instead of responding, I laughed. I laughed with all my heart, because happiness could easily be like a soap, beautiful and cleansing, yet slipping away from my greedy hands all too quickly. I hated her for assuming that she knew me, for always telling me how "sweet" and "happy" I was, when she of all people should have known how no one is how they identify, how one's presentation is who they want to be as opposed to who they actually are.

Sixty-seven percent of Americans believe that there are insufficient existing services for people with mental illness, and they are undoubtedly right. People who are mentally ill will never have enough treatment to overcome whatever demons plague them simply because no one's mind can be fully understood.

But it is a universal fact that all human beings will ultimately prioritize themselves: The very function of humanity is to survive. And though it varies subjectively, every individual's maximum limit for empathy, like an inevitable stain on their soul, remains.

JYOTI GANDHI LAVERACK

YEARS AS MENTEE: 2

GRADE: Junior

BORN: Brooklyn, NY

LIVES: Brooklyn, NY

MENTEE'S ANECDOTE: *I always look forward to meeting in our sunny coffee shop. Both Ashley and I are quiet observers of human behavior, and we love observing dynamics and interactions in our favorite Brooklyn café and making up bizarre and far-fetched backstories for everyone who orders a cup of coffee! Despite my initial timidness in my writing, Ashley's support and kindness have helped me push myself to document aspects of my own history that would have made me squirm even a few months ago.*

ASHLEY MANNETTA

YEARS AS MENTOR: 1

OCCUPATION: Educational Game Designer

BORN: Boston, MA

LIVES: Brooklyn, NY

MENTOR'S ANECDOTE: *Jyoti and I meet in a sunny coffee shop every week. When we have the time, we'll look around at the other sleepy brunchers, eavesdrop on their arguments, observe their flights of feeling. Then we'll take a few minutes and write down a story about one of them. I think about how writers define history by what they choose to write about and how. There are so many stories yet to be told. The potential of a writer like Jyoti—so curious about those around her and observant of every detail—to document untold experiences and perspectives thrills me.*

DISORIENT

JYOTI GANDHI LAVERACK

This story is an excerpt from a larger coming-of-age piece involving themes of friendship, sisterhood, and romance.

After a long drive from the city, Brian's mom parked the car and suggested the teenagers go for a hike. The five of them walked in a single-file line through a thin, sequestered pathway in the woods. Bright greens, fresh raspberries, and dew-drenched forsythia hung in their faces. Camille requested something other than the cliché romantic Top 40 music that Brian and Ophelia loved. Instead, Camille and Tyler took over the music: Gambino, Chance, and Tyler the Creator. Camille enjoyed bonding with Tyler, even over something so customary as music taste, hating to admit that she sought any excuse to watch his dimples appear, for his eyes to meet hers for just a moment.

"Bertha!" Camille called to her best friend as she held Brian's hand, snapping a picture of the two of them as their palms touched in the alcove of the early spring flowers. With the soundtrack, Camille felt as if she were in the final scenes of a two-and-a-half-star high school movie. Their coquettish friend, Ophelia, whom Camille had often asked for unsuccessful flirting advice, was suddenly lustful, leaning into Tyler with a giggle. Ophelia tossed her sun-soaked mane of wavy black hair and grinned from ear to ear with her tanned, freckled cheeks, looking between the two guys. As she walked, she almost seemed to be imitating Bertha, swaying back and forth in a black sundress and swirling her hair into a huge messy bun.

Camille, stranded at the back of the single-file line behind Tyler, analyzed her own walk. She didn't sway or toss her hair; Camille walked into herself. There was nothing sensual about the way she moved. Her stride was lanky, like a fish out of water or an animal finally released from her cage—attempting to navigate a body in a world that was foreign to her. Camille hadn't mastered the art of looking effortless, or even that of feeling at home enough in her own body. Bertha and Ophelia had grown to act romantic even in the way they moved, with the way they twirled their hair—burgeoning sensuality oozed from the way they confidently flaunted their low-cut shirts and batted their eyelashes.

The kids finally approached the water. Tyler smoothly pulled off his loose, burgundy-ink printed button-down, the cotton sliding seamlessly off of the arc of his sunlit back. Brian, preemptively shirtless, wiped the grease from his nose with his shirt and flexed his chest. Camille tightly twisted her hair into a small, prudish bun, tentatively pulling off her long, thrifted skirt to reveal her '20s flapper body in broad daylight. She sucked in her stomach and pulled down the high legs of her bathing suit.

The beautiful beach lasted for hours. The teenagers sat in a sun-lit alcove reserved for only them—a capsule moment of perfection that a picture might capture, but that failed to represent the many feelings and thoughts that coursed through Camille's body. Camille grappled with feeling happy for her best friend—laughing one minute, leaning on her shoulder the next. But the same feeling pressed that Bertha was in another world. Bertha was in another world that Camille could not understand. Bertha was in another world that felt more important in this moment, no matter how much she loved Camille. Camille couldn't blame Bertha, yet she also was at a loss of what to do with herself. Her eyes scanned for Ophelia, who lay, stretched out sexy as she tanned on a towel, asking everyone to take pictures for Instagram. Camille had tried to tan and look pretty for pictures, but after seeing one or two, she felt self-conscious next to the other girls.

Camille, as loved as her friends could make her feel, felt like she was in the bubble of a misunderstood, lonely world. Tyler sat on a rock, boring his eyes into the sand rushing between his toes with the waves. Camille found herself, almost in desperation, absorbing the details of Tyler's appearance, attempting to find solace in the familiarity of their repartee. Lost in the self-consciousness, loneliness, and insufficiency that washed over her, Camille found herself reliant on his attention. Tyler suddenly, as if reading Camille's mind, leaned in to say:

"In this thick, copious greenery, I wish that my girlfriend was here to *caresse avec*."

"French class showoff," Camille teased. Yet she was again, for the second time in the past day, enveloped in a foreign desire for the same thing. The deliciously delirious, movie-like sensation she craved was so intertwined with the jealousy and bitterness she had toward being left behind.

Camille was at the point where she almost couldn't pull the two apart.

VICTORIA GAO

YEARS AS MENTEE: 2

GRADE: Junior

BORN: New York, NY

LIVES: Queens, NY

PUBLICATIONS AND RECOGNITIONS: Scholastic Art & Writing Awards: Honorable Mention

MENTEE'S ANECDOTE: *Throughout this school year, Soyolmaa and I have experimented with genres like science fiction, journalism, and erasure poetry. It was exciting to combine elements from different genres into a fictional short story about climate change leading to the destruction of the world. Editing with Soyolmaa is always an eye-opening experience when we add in clarifying details and cut redundant phrases. A memorable moment was editing a rough draft with erasure poetry to home in on key ideas.*

SOYOLMAA LKHAGVADORJ

YEARS AS MENTOR: 1

OCCUPATION: Assistant Editor, HarperCollins Publishers

BORN: Ulaanbaatar, Mongolia

LIVES: Brooklyn, NY

MENTOR'S ANECDOTE: *Victoria is truly the hardest-working sixteen-year-old I've ever met. I have no idea how she juggles schoolwork, extracurricular activities, hobbies, and writing! She inspires me to make the most out of my day (and planner). It's been a pleasure getting to know her over the past year and watching her grow more comfortable with her writing. I was so excited when she told me she wanted to incorporate her interests in both coding and advocating for climate change into her story. I can't wait to see her writing develop even more in the future!*

EPIPHANY

VICTORIA GAO

Taking our place in history means making contributions to solve societal problems and being accountable for one's actions.

Sunlight shines through the reflective windows of Helen's workspace in the late afternoon. A group of software engineers separated by gray cubicles is coding on their computers, hoping to finish the tasks allotted to them by their manager, Mr. Bob Monaine. Helen sighs as she runs her code: Error messages in small, red font keep popping up. When she shares her progress with Monaine, he listens half-heartedly. Without looking up from his computer, he reminds her of her assignment: Write code that creates animations that will feature the latest products and applications on a pharmaceutical company's new website. All the features must work before they present to potential clients in three days.

As the late afternoon darkens to early dusk, Helen writes code for a tree that expands outward when users click the node at the end of each branch. Afterward, she adjusts the size of the branches and the color scheme so the text is easier to read. When it's time for the daily standup, Helen shows the team her tree and says, "I finally got the tree's data structure to work, and the next step is to upload the text for each branch." The other engineers nod, and they move on to what they've accomplished for the day. Monaine compliments the men for their work but pulls Helen aside.

He asks, "Can you stay later to add text and create the webpages your tree will link to?"

"But I finished my tasks for the day and have a . . ."

"The presentation is in three days. It's your choice to stay or leave the office, but the webpages better be made by tomorrow morning."

Helen keeps a straight face as she nods and barely gets out the words "See you tomorrow" before he walks away. She can feel the weight piling up on her shoulders with the assignment of more busywork. For the first time that day, Helen leaves the office. A light breeze wafts through the cool summer evening, keeping Helen's mind off of her menial tasks and upcoming deadlines. The refreshing smell of pine trees brings Helen back to when she hiked the Adirondack Region with her college classmates. They collected plant samples and analyzed data to measure the effect of pollution on the environment. She enjoyed contributing to the greater good and working with people who shared her interest in ecology.

Back then, she would often spend time dreaming of her life after college. Would she be a doctor, engineer, or teacher? The uncertainty of the future thrilled her younger self because the possibilities felt endless. As she approached the end of college, she spent grueling hours applying to job after job with few prospects. Her heart sank every time she saw emails starting with "Thank you" instead of "Congratulations."

Finally, Mr. Monaine from Western Pharmaceuticals got back to her. The luxurious office building and Mr. Monaine's mentorship reeled her in, but the façade wore off quickly. After the first week, she found out that her job was to create websites selling expensive products she'd never heard of. The descriptions portrayed the products as supplements to maintain good health, but none of them had been approved by the Food and Drug Administration (FDA).

She promised to stay at Western Pharmaceuticals until she found her dream job. That was three years ago, and she's still hesitant to quit before her student loans are paid off. Her disappointed younger self would think she had sold out.

That's when Helen realizes what she truly wants: a job where she can actually make a positive impact on people's lives, learn as she works on more complicated projects, and even have time for hobbies and socializing. She vows to look for job opportunities tomorrow, and reluctantly completes her assignment.

The next morning, Helen scours the internet for any job that might fit her criteria. She notices an advertisement from a company, the Environmentalist Foundation, that works toward reducing waste and manufacturing eco-friendly products: "Looking for full-time Senior Software Developers." As Helen scrolls, her heart beats faster as she checks off the requirements she meets: a bachelor's degree in computer science, three to five years of experience in software engineering, and a deep understanding of databases. It sounds almost too good to be true—she rushes to complete the application and submits it with fingers crossed.

Two days later, Monaine presents the work that his team created for their clients. It's a hit. But none of the software engineers are credited. Clients rush to shake Monaine's hand, bid on products, and place huge orders. Helen's phone buzzes with an email notification. The director of the Environmentalist Foundation, Dr. Ada Kent, has written, "I'm really impressed by your experience and passion for protecting the environment. I hope to speak with you about your interests and projects my lab is working on. Do you have time to meet tomorrow?" Helen is giddy with excitement and can't stop smiling. As she stands up to leave the auditorium, she feels a sense of freedom. She knows leaving the profit-oriented corporation is just the beginning of a new career path.

AALIYANA GARCIA

YEARS AS MENTEE: 1

GRADE: Sophomore

BORN: Valhalla, NY

LIVES: New York, NY

MENTEE'S ANECDOTE: *Lauren and I have a lot in common. We're both very close with our mothers. We both are oldest children who roll our eyes at our younger siblings' shenanigans. We are also both true '90s kids (even though Lauren is actually the only one born in the '90s). We often talk about pop culture from back then. Fun fact—Ariel is both of our favorite Disney princess!*

LAUREN McDERMOTT

YEARS AS MENTOR: 1

OCCUPATION: Marketing and Business Development Associate

BORN: Greenwich, CT

LIVES: New York, NY

MENTOR'S ANECDOTE: *Aali has been an absolute joy to work with. She always shows up to our pair sessions with a big smile on her face, excited to start working on different writing ideas she's come up with or chat about her day. Creativity, grit, and open-mindedness come naturally to Aali. Although I am the mentor, I admire Aali's can-do-it attitude and have learned SO MUCH from her ingenuity. I cannot wait to see the pieces that Aali creates in the future— everybody should be on the lookout for her writing!*

¡DAVID!

AALIYANA GARCIA

"Heyyy, where's the bacon?" Don't get me wrong, I like fruit and pancakes, but lately I haven't been able to eat anything but fruit.

"Rapunzel, we've talked about this, you know he doesn't like when you start to gain weight." Of course he doesn't. I rolled my eyes, hoping she would see, but she just shrugged it off; I plopped myself in the chair and began devouring the meal in front of me. She looked at me with disgust, but then again it is her fault for starving me for this long. I was done with the meal and I was still hungrier than ever.

I ran back upstairs, knowing that I had only about thirty minutes to fix and curl my hair, do my makeup, and get dressed. I pulled open my drawer and ripped through my clothes as if I were a tornado. I selected the pink miniskirt and the white tube top to match it. I threw on my pink jean jacket but made sure that my shoulders were still showing, even after all these years. I quickly threw my hair in a braid that lay down my back and began my simple but extensive makeup process. After the long, tedious, and agonizing process, I took my hair out of the braid and looked at myself in the mirror. I turned to look at my crimped hair from the braid and shrugged at it; I pulled my hair behind my ears but let a few strands loose. I stood up and ran toward my black mini-bookbag and my white sneakers. Loopty-loop then pull. I was finally ready. I checked the mirror one more time. I looked closely at myself, and it was almost as if I could see a timid little girl in a pink sweetheart neckline dress clinging on to her jacket for dear life. I shook my head, trying to get that bad memory out of my head, and snatched the gold locket from my dresser before heading downstairs.

"Rapunzel, dear, where are—oh, hello, my dear. He is going to be here in ten minutes." She leaned in close and took a whiff; soon after, she spritzed me in whatever the hell she was holding and then shoved me out the door.

"Go on now, dear." That same black limo from all those years ago was now sitting on my lawn, but why should I be surprised, it was here every Sunday. He doesn't even bother to come out anymore; I couldn't tell whether it was because he's gotten bigger or because he simply doesn't care anymore. Is he now realizing that I was replaceable? Was I too old? No, that was just wishful thinking; of course I'm still trapped here. I climbed into the back seat of the limo and greeted David with a quick kiss on the cheek.

"Is that all I get?" he squealed. He grabbed my face roughly and gave me a big wet kiss. He reeked of alcohol—this was going to be fun. He quickly flipped me over on my back so that he was now lying on me. I had put baby powder on my legs so that it would be easier to move around. I had a plan and I needed to act on it now; it was now or never. I had some regrets, being that this was the only place that I had ever known, but this wasn't right. It never had been. He began unbuckling his belt rapidly. I counted to three before I would make my first move. One. Two. Three. I unlocked the limo door and rolled out of the car. I stood up and ran as fast as I could. I knew there was limited time before he would tell the driver to step on it.

I ran through the forest, pushing and breaking my way through all the vines and leaves. I tripped over a tree stump and felt a sharp pain right on my knee. I looked down to see my knee completely covered in blood. I limped as fast as I could to a tree and took a seat. That was the worst decision I had made that day. I heard tires screeching in the distance. Then silence. Leaves were crunching before I had heard a whistling sound. I recognized this so clearly. This was the tune that he would sing to me before dropping me off every time. It was burned into my memory. I couldn't help but weep; I don't know why, but in this moment I felt so alone and vulnerable. I covered my mouth, scared that he would hear me breathing. I heard his footsteps get closer. I was terrified. I had no idea what he was capable of. I picked up a rock near my foot and chucked it as far as I could. Footsteps, and then he was gone.

I limped all the way until I saw a road, and just a few feet ahead was a village. Children were laughing, people were singing. It was nothing but joy. I looked up to see a beautiful white castle ahead. So this is what it felt like to be free. I was finally free.

CLAIRE GIANNOSA

YEARS AS MENTEE: 1

GRADE: Senior

BORN: New York, NY

LIVES: New York, NY

MENTEE'S ANECDOTE: *I always look forward to my Friday-night meetings with my mentor Anna at Think Coffee. The rickety stairway, faint music, and coffee grinding in the background (if we're lucky we can find a table) provide the perfect ambiance for an evening of writing. Not only has she taught me how to look closely at my writing, been a brilliant editor, and helped me to cut down my rambling work, we've also bonded over Taylor Swift, romance, and so much more. I am so happy I have Anna to share my writing adventures with.*

ANNA HUMPHREY

YEARS AS MENTOR: 2

OCCUPATION: Speechwriter

BORN: Lexington, KY

LIVES: New York, NY

MENTOR'S ANECDOTE: *In many ways, Claire and I have a lot in common: our birthdays are a day apart, we both dream of someday writing a novel, we're both suckers for boys with dimples. There's a key difference, though: Claire knows her own voice much better than I know mine. She has a keen sense of who she is as a writer, and it's been a privilege and a joy to watch her develop that even further this year. I can't wait to see her words in print—both in this anthology and in another book someday.*

DISTORTED ATMOSPHERE

CLAIRE GIANNOSA

This poem tumbled out of me on a night when I felt lost and confused in my own mind. This is a compilation of my insecurities and social anxieties; I wanted to write this piece for anyone who needs a reminder that they are not alone.

I feel like I have lost my sense of place.
I used to know where I stood—or at least where I wanted to
    stand,
In terms of what I wanted to give to this earth—
But every day it gets more and more unclear.
More and more murky,
Like a puddle of rain sitting on the New York City sidewalk for
    too long.
Everything about myself,
Used to be so *easy*.
I don't know, it was just that I understood myself.
Like every day I would look into the bathroom mirror and say hi
    to the reflection.
As if I knew that person, and accepted who they were supposed
    to be.
But now,
Now I face a distorted black mirror.
With cracks and scratches like a big piece of marble.

Something is rotting in my gut.
I'm on the verge of throwing up, but then my body pushes it
    back inside.
This moldy, rotting thing is growing in my stomach, the roots
    too thick and too strong for it to ever be pulled out.

My face twists up like I used some strange photo booth filter.
And I feel like I can't do anything.
My hands shake as I try to grab a pencil and a piece of paper,
But nothing good comes out.
My entire being, my entire existence, my only hope,
Has dried out. Sucked out of me.
And I'm floating in an eternal darkness, too cold for me to even
    be in the atmosphere.
Too dark for it to be space because, where are all the stars?
And—did I fall down a black hole? Because this is *not* where I'm
    supposed to be, I'm—

A writer. I'm supposed to be a writer.
But—
What if that's not good enough, what if I'm not good enough?
What if I wake up one day, and
My family is sitting rigid in the dining room chairs, fingers
    interlocked, all stiff, all cold.
And my words are sitting on the table, crumpled up—
"Weren't you supposed to be the good writer?"
And—
How do I even respond to such a question? Such a violation of
    my soul that I want to crumple up just like the paper so I will
    never have to look at a blank page again—

And—
I'm sorry.
That I'm so unaware, and so—
Unexciting and not fun at all, and so, *bland.*
I seem like the type of person who has got it all together, and
    doesn't need help, and is too bothered with her own needs to
    help anyone . . .
I'm sorry.
That I don't always say the right thing, or the necessary thing,
And I stumble over my words,
And I seem to freak out over everything,
And I never fully say what I mean,

And I have terrible advice,
And never know what to say to comfort someone,
All I know is that I want to be there for them.
I want to hug them and let them know I'm there.
I want to show myself.
But I never show myself.
I'm very good at hiding.
So good—
That I lose myself in the depths of my never-silencing thoughts,
In the echo of my brain.
That when I try to speak—
Try to scrape out a word or a vowel from the hollowed out
    tunnels of my mind,
I am nothing but an empty void, ringing with an eternal silence.

And—
How can I even be mad?
When I look into the distorted black glass—
All I can see is myself,
The marble rolling over and over again in my crumbling hands,
I am the enemy.
I am the queen sitting on my high-backed throne—
The black velvet and gleam of silver gems
Signifying my viciousness,
Like in a fairy tale.
Like ancient history.
What about my history?
Her-story
How am I supposed to go anywhere with a stone wall
    surrounding my heart? My brain? My thoughts? My words?
As blank as the stone used to make it.
But I keep chipping at it.
Little by little,
Stone by stone,
Each and every day,
With the hope that eventually, a speck of starlight will shine
    through.

ISABEL GOLIGHTLY

YEARS AS MENTEE: 2

GRADE: Senior

BORN: New York, NY

LIVES: Brooklyn, NY

MENTEE'S ANECDOTE: *Anna and I had to work quickly to catch up on deadlines. Her positive and supportive attitude has made her enjoyable to work with. I am so glad to have someone to support me with my pieces and I am looking forward to the many opportunities we will have to work together throughout the year.*

ANNA PERLING

YEARS AS MENTOR: 1

OCCUPATION: Writer, *Wirecutter*

BORN: Atlanta, GA

LIVES: Brooklyn, NY

PUBLICATIONS AND RECOGNITIONS: *Wirecutter, The New York Times*

MENTOR'S ANECDOTE: *Isabel and I were paired together halfway through the year. I've been blown away by her candor and willingness to jump into workshopping her creative pieces. She says that she writes to figure stuff out and situate herself in the world. Well, Isabel, I think you've got a lot figured out—your strong voice joins the chorus of women poets, writers, and speakers.*

FREEDOM

ISABEL GOLIGHTLY

A big part of women "taking their place in history" involves them stepping outside their comfort zones and being free to express themselves in a patriarchal society. My poem explores this freedom and the mixed emotions that come with this feminist evolution.

Cool air captivates her senses.

She wonders
Is she up too high?

Her wings beat harder
never clipped but
Folded

soon
gliding along peaceful skyline
thoughts evaporate
like rain

She soars
higher
testing the limits,
Herself

She laughs
her voice
dipped in honey

She is
unbreakable

Abrupt like thunder claps
she laughs again

she is free.

RUBY GOWER

YEARS AS MENTEE: 1

GRADE: Sophomore

BORN: London, England

LIVES: Brooklyn, NY

MENTEE'S ANECDOTE: *Janice and I recently took a trip to the Met Cloisters to get imagery for the medieval-style novel I'm working on. We met two of her friends there, who were both writers and were really supportive of my book. I got a lot of ideas from seeing the architecture of the old Cloisters, like the high ceilings and the frequent arches. We went outside to look at the courtyard, because there's an important scene in my book featuring one, and even though it was wrapped away for winter, I had a really great time and learned a lot.*

JANICE NIMURA

YEARS AS MENTOR: 1

OCCUPATION: Writer

BORN: New York, NY

LIVES: New York, NY

PUBLICATIONS AND RECOGNITIONS: *Daughters of the Samurai: A Journey from East to West and Back;* Public Scholar grant from the National Endowment from the Humanities (2017)

MENTOR'S ANECDOTE: *Ruby's fictional world is full of the material culture of medieval Europe, so we arranged to meet at the Cloisters for inspiration. I almost didn't recognize her when she arrived: The night before, Ruby had shaved her head. We spent the afternoon time-traveling: a girl of the future, a curious elder, and the splendors of the Middle Ages. We were surrounded by stories told not just in ink but in silk and gold and glass and stone, and I couldn't wait to see all of it reflected in Ruby's writing.*

FLOWER CROWNS

RUBY GOWER

This is a scene from a novel that I've been working on forever. Anna is saying goodbye to her best friend—who has died trying to save her—and learning about grief and the past from an older woman.

Now that Ela was dead, she had to let her go down the river, but first she would make a flower crown for her. Herminia braided the stalks expertly, and Anna realized with a pang that she must have done it many times before.

"I made one for my father," she said suddenly, as if she had read Anna's mind.

"Oh. What was he like? I've never had a father."

"I never saw him much. Always out working. He died when I was seventeen. I had just gotten married."

Anna leaned in, fascinated.

"It hurt for a while, even though I barely knew him. He would cook for us sometimes, even though the village said it was a woman's job. But I healed eventually."

Herminia shot her a meaningful glance from over the stems she was twisting together.

"And my sister died from rabies when I was four. She was my first flower crown. Not these sort of flowers, of course."

Anna bit her lip.

"I'm sorry, Herminia."

"Don't be. It's not your fault. Many village children died that year, in one way or another. There was a sickness going around."

Anna's stomach shifted. She could tell with her eyes closed where they were going next.

"But not the Queen, of course. Your mother. She was nine."

"I—"

"She was walled away for the longest time. Came out a different girl."

"Do you know—"

"That she's dead? Yes. I didn't know if you did."

Anna couldn't bring herself to tell her what she had done, so she just shrugged.

"Here's your crown. You ready?"

"I think so. But I'd rather do it alone, if you don't mind."

"Of course. You just have to let go. It all gets easier after that, I promise."

She would have to let Ela wash away down the river. A pain went through her stomach.

"Can't I bury her?"

"You can. But you'll never find your peace that way."

Anna nodded. She was right. Of course she was.

"Come on," Herminia said gently.

Anna took the flower crown and held it as gently as she could as they trudged back up the slope. It was beautiful, the pinks and whites and blues somehow woven like fabric together. It would be heartbreaking to float it away.

"You do need to float her away at some point. Shadowchildren are meant to run, even in death. She'll do well as a river spirit."

"I know. Tomorrow?"

"Perfect, Anna. You're doing great, you know that?"

* * *

So this was it. The final goodbye. She looked down at Ela's peaceful face, finally at rest after so many brave deeds done in her name. She traced her cheekbones, already sallow from death, until they came to her mouth, her beautiful carob lips, shaped like a rose. She should have spent more time studying her face, appreciating every moment she got to spend with her.

But she hadn't. And now this was all she had left. All of a sudden, love and grief and pain overcame her and she dived down, kissing her hard, her tears dripping down onto her face. She sobbed into her closed lips, shaking her desperately, even though she knew the effort was futile.

She could have sworn that her lips were still warm as she broke apart from her. She wouldn't be able to let go. She couldn't. But she owed it to Ela. Far better to dissolve into the water and become a spirit of the river than to spend her death locked away in a casket.

So she had to let go. She rose up onto her knees to see Ela's whole body, to take one last picture in her mind to join all the frozen moments of Ela laughing and running she had stored in her head. Ela had never been more darkly beautiful than now.

And now it was time. The last time she would ever see her again in all her days. She secured the flower crown onto Ela's head and around her beautiful black hair. She wouldn't want her to lose it as she became a river spirit. On a whim, she gently pulled a pale pink petal from the weaving and put it gently into her dress pocket, careful not to damage it.

Then she took a shaky breath and stroked a stray piece of hair from Ela's unlined forehead (how young she was, too young to die).

And then, closing her eyes to hold back the tears ready to spill forth, she let go. The last she saw of her best friend was a dark shape floating down the river, distorted through the tears in her eyes. She rubbed desperately at them, trying to get one last clear image of her Shadow, but Ela was long gone by the time she pried them open.

SIARA GRECO

YEARS AS MENTEE: 1

GRADE: Senior

BORN: Staten Island, NY

LIVES: Staten Island, NY

MENTEE'S ANECDOTE: *As a first-year mentee, I was unsure of what to expect through Girls Write Now. I always wanted to improve my writing and find a genre that I truly enjoyed to write. In the first few months, my mentor Eleanor inspired me to combine my passion for science, writing, and multimedia through our shared love of science. Without Eleanor, I would have never been able to recognize my true passions and apply them to making a difference within my community.*

ELEANOR CUMMINS

YEARS AS MENTOR: 1

OCCUPATION: Freelance Journalist

BORN: Kennewick, WA

LIVES: Brooklyn, NY

PUBLICATIONS AND RECOGNITIONS: *Popular Science, The Verge, Wired, Slate, Atlas Obscura, The New Republic, SELF, Bright Wall/Dark Room, Ars Technica, Vox, The Outline, The Guardian, Gizmodo*

MENTOR'S ANECDOTE: *Siara and I connected over our shared love of science. I write about climate change and the environment, and she thinks she might want to become an environmental engineer. It's been wonderful to meet every week with someone who's thinking about the future of our planet—and wants to be an active part of the solution. (It's even better when that person is as fun and funny as Siara.) I can't wait to see what she accomplishes in college and beyond. I have a feeling it will benefit us all.*

THE JOURNEY

SIARA GRECO

My piece is about my journey traveling across the world to build my confidence in the science world. I was taught to make history in breaking the stereotypes of women in STEAM (Science, Technology, Engineering, Arts, and Math).

I am on a flight from Washington, D.C., to Germany with fourteen other girls from across the country. This is my first time traveling internationally and aboard a plane without a family member beside me. The seatbelt light begins to flash and I feel the plane drop along with the feeling of my heart sinking into my stomach. The three of us in our row instantly grab one another's hands as we head into the turbulence and simultaneously acknowledge the sisterhood we are already fostering at the start of this two-week journey. We are headed to Estonia for an opportunity to connect with girls from across Eastern Europe and to expand our interest in STEAM. I notice the same anxious feeling continues to linger as I exit the plane, but this time it is the doubt of not being smart enough to take part in the rigorous classes taught by Google, Intel, and NASA, as well as the overwhelming worry ruminating in my mind that I might not truly belong here. I felt as if I would not be smart enough to complete the assignments, and that my level of knowledge in science would not match the other girls'. Typically, I have always thought of men when I heard science. These stereotypes affected my confidence in believing that I could be a part of the STEAM world.

As this life-changing journey truly begins, I am introduced to new cultures and mediums of learning. My first assignment is announced: coding a doorbell system for the deaf community with the Google team. My heart once again drops to my stomach as I panic, while trying to instantly come up with an idea that would be deemed "good enough." However, I need to realize I am enough and so are my ideas. Through this larger assignment I am able to build my confidence and recognize that I have the knowledge to be successful in new tasks.

The feeling of doubt drifts away and a new feeling of joy takes over as I complete my first assignment with pride. I stand in front of my fellow campers and the Google staff and present my first-ever app. As I watch the classroom smile and clap, I know it is time for me to realize that I truly belong here. I am pushed to tap into my full potential within the science world. I never realized how far my passion in science could take me. I begin to code apps, drones, and robots, all of which I had never considered possible. I am able to explore science in a new hands-on way that I have never been exposed to in the traditional classroom setting. My growing confidence overpowers the doubt within me. One project has allowed me to recognize my worth in the science world and continues to build my confidence in pursuing my passion in engineering.

JAYLA GREENBERG

YEARS AS MENTEE: 2

GRADE: Senior

BORN: Brooklyn, NY

LIVES: Brooklyn, NY

MENTEE'S ANECDOTE: *For two years I've been opened up to a world of new experiences. And in that time I've been very lucky to learn through them with my mentor Caroline. There's always something new to expect when it comes to our meetings. From discussing the latest books we've read to working on writing and ideas, Caroline has definitely helped me find the author in me. If I have a problem, I know I can go to her for help. Not only do I work with a mentor, but with a great friend.*

CAROLINE K. FULFORD

YEARS AS MENTOR: 2

OCCUPATION: Information Specialist, The 4As

BORN: Westwood, NJ

LIVES: Brooklyn, NY

PUBLICATIONS AND RECOGNITIONS: 2019 Indiana Review Fiction Prize; 2019 Center for Fiction NYC Emerging Writers Fellowship

MENTOR'S ANECDOTE: *This is my second year with Jayla, and I can already see how much she has grown—not only as a writer, but as a person. Her growing interest and involvement in mock trial is the best example of her growth. As proud as I am that she writes and expresses herself with more courage, confidence, and fluidity than ever, it's bittersweet to see Jayla go off on her own, pursuing her interests and making new friends. However, I know that my role is to encourage and support her, and Jayla only ever needed the slightest encouragement to flourish.*

IT RUNS IN MY FAMILY

JAYLA GREENBERG

My family means everything to me, so I'm giving back to them when I succeed. This piece reflects me giving back by making them proud, and by rewriting the course of my family history.

Ever since grades had started to matter to my future, people held high expectations for me. It seemed a bit odd, considering that most of my family did not do well in school. I've been told that I was different, that I'd be the one to break the cycle of failure that seemed to run through my DNA. I couldn't see what they saw in me. But as I got older, I realized that I was different from my relatives.

From then on, it felt much more difficult to uphold my success, as I had so many people putting their faith in me. School had gotten harder, and every time I outdid myself I felt the overwhelming need to do better. It was as if the higher my average became, the higher the stakes got raised.

I started as a prodigy in elementary school, with perfect grades and a newfound passion for reading. But diving into middle school, tasks became more demanding and I fell off the ladder a bit. Seventh grade had not been a good year, and eighth grade followed suit. I started to lose faith in myself and struggled under the stress of making my family proud. After failing to get into any high schools of my choosing, I began to worry much more. I felt as if I were on track to spiral downward in life, just as my family always seemed to do.

For a while, I questioned how I wanted to proceed with my studies. I was more unsure than ever of the road I was on. I felt as if I had let my parents down and that I didn't try hard enough.

Ninth grade had given me some clarity on my high school goals.

I was back to the grades I'd been comfortable with and I felt more confident in myself. In addition, I loved my friends and my courses, especially my Intro to Law class. For a while, I was content. But toward the end of the school year, many problems arose, one after the other like dominoes. In short, I had to reevaluate my priorities. Over that summer I realized something felt missing the previous school year, but I couldn't be sure what it was. I figured, as long as I was a 90-and-above student, I was reaching my goal. Going into tenth grade, I assumed that I had a pretty decent plan for the year: Join a club, study, possibly get a job. But right from the first day, my plans were turned upside down.

One day, I found myself walking home from eighth period with my friends. The next, I had nine periods and I decided to join the girls' soccer team. I was far from my comfort zone. I'd never played soccer seriously and I barely knew the rules. I needed equipment. And practices were four days a week. It was a challenge.

From my first game to the very last, soccer sparked something in me. That feeling of competitiveness and being a part of an amazing team gave me a new sense of identity. On the field, I was shaking away the troubles of school. I was reborn.

Following the end of soccer, I was left wondering where I'd find my next adventure. And it just so happened that it found me. My friend had mentioned Moot Court/Mock Trial to me on the train one evening. It was a team I thought I'd never join due to the extremely demanding requirements. And that evening, on impulse, I joined.

The day I walked into that law firm and met the lawyers, I felt like I belonged. From the time I first presented my work, my fear turned into adrenaline. And to this day, I have not once regretted joining. Moot Court/Mock Trial is an experience that completely changed my high school life and that I'll continue until senior year. It so greatly fuels my passion for the law and criminal justice and I love to work with my peers, coach, and lawyers on the cases. When I compete, it is as if I've found my calling.

During the first semester of tenth grade, my grades had risen high above any expectation I set for myself. I was ecstatic. So many things had changed in the course of the year, and all for the better.

I used to believe that there was a good chance that I'd end up like many of the adults in my family, struggling to stay afloat in life. I was nervous with all the pressure I felt to do better. And most of all, I was constantly doubting myself. It was difficult to picture things any other way. But I miraculously found a path and stuck to it. And I've been making great strides since. Now I'm on my way to becoming one of the first in my family to graduate high school and go on to college. I'm in control of my life. And I will be one of the first of many.

ANIYA GREENE

YEARS AS MENTEE: 2

GRADE: Senior

BORN: Harlem, NY

LIVES: New York, NY

PUBLICATIONS AND RECOGNITIONS: Scholastic Art & Writing Awards: Gold Key, Silver Keys

MENTEE'S ANECDOTE: *We sit across from each other, pens in hand. She gives me a prompt, a scene, or a word, and instructs me to "just write." For ten minutes she says. I always stop to watch her somewhere in the interim. Her pen never stops flowing against the lines of her purple notebook. I look down at my page that always seems to hold less ink. When time is up, I share first, fearing my words aren't as good. My sentences won't flow like hers. Her words are stories, painted pictures, and memories that remind me to keep writing.*

ROBIN WILLIG

YEARS AS MENTOR: 5

OCCUPATION: Chief of Staff, Center for Reproductive Rights

BORN: Far Rockaway, NY

LIVES: Brooklyn, NY

MENTOR'S ANECDOTE: *I've had the privilege of mentoring Aniya for two years, meeting her every week in the public library where we both fear and love the librarian—the constant in the changing cast of characters there. Aniya is thoughtful, quiet, and caring: When I got stuck in a jacket with a broken zipper, she was reluctant to take off her coat so that I'd be comfortable. My favorite part of our meetings is when her shy smile appears as she recognizes she has written something beautiful, and sees her own power as a writer. She has so many smiles ahead of her.*

THINGS WE HOLD CLOSE

ANIYA GREENE

This piece reflects upon my relationship with my grandfather. His lasting presence in my life is a part of my personal history, one of the many things I hold close.

It is the same couch
but somehow different

Eleven years ago, I
Watched soap operas with Grandma
Your home was my jungle gym
Climbing on pipes
On summer mornings
Too early for you to walk me to the park

It is the same couch in new walls
Your one room farther west

We watch baseball now
I try my best to keep my eyes open
Halfway through the fourth inning
You share your Bible verse with me

You turn on that lamp
The one that formerly sat next
To your old recliner
Decorated with its gold shade
The pages of your Bible illuminated
By yellow light
Book of Psalms

Your most loved verse
The Lord is my shepherd
I shall not want

I think of you now as I ride the bus
Past 125th Street
Trips to Magic Johnson Theater
Movies of my youth that you
Shared with me
I pass 119th Street
Your home
Knowing I should
Be there with you
On that couch
Pass Marcus Garvey Park
To see the swings

You pushed me so high
Thinking back then
I could touch the clouds
You taught me to swing myself
To elevate
So that one day
I might fly high enough
To touch the clouds

What comfort you get from your Bible
You hold it close
Psalm 23
Proverbs 12
Those I may never know

You tell me stories, call out verses
Offer to accompany me to a Sunday service
I go when you ask, rarely on my own.
I go because we share time
Time on the couch

Watching baseball games
That seem to have no end
I go not because I pray before bed
Not because I have verses
Memorized
Although perhaps I should

It must be a sin
Not to love God
Like you
Disappointment
When you look at me
Pain in your heart I see
The prayers for me
Have they been wasted?
Nevertheless you keep praying
Reading your Bible verses
For me in case I decide
To set my heart free

But what comfort your voice brings me
Pained by the thought
That someday
I may no longer hear it
And like my grandmother's
I'll have no recollection
Of the sound

I save the voicemail messages
The mundane
"I'm just calling to check on you"
"Aniya, it's me"
Your voice takes room in my phone
I hold on to them for years
Like you hold your Bible
And in the meantime
Save our time on the couch

GYANA GUITY

YEARS AS MENTEE: 2

GRADE: Senior

BORN: Bronx, NY

LIVES: Bronx, NY

MENTEE'S ANECDOTE: *My relationship with Sarah has seriously grown over the past year. We have just gotten more comfortable with each other, and I feel like I have known her even longer than the two years we have spent together. Girls Write Now gave me the opportunity to meet such a special and amazing individual where I can't even imagine my high school experience being the same without Sarah in it. I talk to her about the smallest things, from my favorite BTS member to bigger and more serious topics like my friends and family. I love her more than anything, and I hope to know her for a long time, even after Girls Write Now.*

SARAH GOUDA

YEARS AS MENTOR: 2

OCCUPATION: Speechwriter

BORN: Cincinnati, OH

LIVES: Brooklyn, NY

MENTOR'S ANECDOTE: *Whereas I was an exceedingly timid teenager, Gyana is a force of nature. I'm so impressed by Gyana's fearlessness— she's always the first to raise her hand, volunteer to help, or offer up a wild idea. I love spending time together—whether we are seeing the latest anime movie or working through a draft of her college essay, we always manage to make whatever we're doing fun. She knows what she wants and she's secure in her voice—I've learned so much from her about speaking up and being an active member of my community.*

A GUIDE TO MAKING HISTORY

GYANA GUITY

Before I graduate from high school and move on to the next chapter of my life, I wanted to think back to my final year of high school and explain how I see myself, my future, and the idea of making history.

I spent my last few weeks trapped in a never-ending cycle. I woke up late in the afternoon, stared down at my phone screen, and let myself wither. I watched my passion for writing fade away, my social life dim, and thought that it was more important to watch reruns of old Disney shows instead of finding my voice again.

To keep it simple: I lost myself in 2019, and felt my insides breaking apart. I was standing alone on a battlefield, my grip on the world so frail and too weak, and it wasn't long before I was drowning in my own sea of guilt, fear, and zest.

In the distance, I saw the signs on Times Square: Gyana Guity . . . the new J. K. Rowling. Gyana Guity . . . more out of this world than Stephen King! I was in a place where my scripts weren't hidden anymore, my stories no longer a secret, and instead brought to life in the most beautiful of realities. I could see my dream. I could taste and touch it—practically dance with it. I was living my fantasy.

I don't know what went wrong. I couldn't even pick up a pen or a pencil, let alone type my thoughts in the notes of my iPhone. I was empty. Out of fuel. Lacking a heartbeat and a rhythm. Where was the Gyana everyone had such high hopes for? I didn't see her. I didn't feel her. Did I not have the same dream?

These negativities scared me more than anything. It felt like thunder knocking right at my door, and demanding that I come out and face the storm. The world was waiting for me, waiting for me to take my first big steps and walk down that road with signs that read HISTORY MADE THIS WAY.

But . . . what exactly was history? Was it what we read in our textbooks in school? Or was it about the women of color who stepped up and fought back against the inequality that attempted to suffocate them? Did I have to be the first to do something? The best to do something? Because when I asked myself these things, if I was truly ready to face the world, I felt like I was nowhere near ready for something as drastic as that. I felt small, and with this gloominess hovering over me like a cloud of rain, I felt smaller and smaller until I couldn't even recognize myself in my bathroom mirror.

Making history was just something I couldn't figure out. I didn't have the slightest idea about what was good enough or what was too lame—and never came close to knowing what would be accepted by those around me. I was worrying about everything else. Like trying to fill the shoes of famous writers like Toni Morrison and Victoria Aveyard, rather than worrying about what I liked and what made me happy.

I was looking at everything wrong. History didn't have to start after I surpassed someone, and it especially didn't have to be me doing something that was world-changing. History, to me, is going to college. I would be the first in my family to achieve a goal like this. History, to me, is being the first of my grandparents' grandchildren to graduate from high school. History, to me, starts right inside of my home, right inside of my family, and even right inside of my group of friends.

It seems hard to find—that hidden passageway that led you right into the shining, gold street that guides you into the unknown. That was what history was, what it still is: being brave enough to step out and chase something you don't even know yet. History is about finding yourself in a crowd of people who have gotten used to the norms of today. History is all about what you make it, and what you see in the distance when you step onto that pavement, spread your arms wide, and breathe in something completely new.

History, to me, is standing out in the smallest of places, and gaining attention when the people around you notice that you want to stand as tall as yourself, without the labels or standards or stereotypes. History, to me, is me. What I make it, what I see of it, and it doesn't stop with me. It continues with you, and all of the other history makers running down that beautiful, foreign road.

FRANCIS GUTIERREZ

YEARS AS MENTEE: 1

GRADE: Junior

BORN: New York, NY

LIVES: New York, NY

PUBLICATIONS AND RECOGNITIONS: Scholastic Art & Writing Awards: Silver Key

MENTEE'S ANECDOTE: *I remember being so nervous to meet Ashna, being so scared of whether or not she would like me. Now I can't even imagine where I would be without her. She pushes me past my limits when it comes to writing, and it has been so inspiring to be able to grow together and find comfort in each other. She is so easy to talk to and so encouraging. I couldn't have asked for a better mentor. I am truly grateful to have Ashna in my life. She has made me realize that there is more to life than succeeding; life is about being happy and finding your rightful place.*

ASHNA SHAH

YEARS AS MENTOR: 1

OCCUPATION: Senior Director Strategy, Albert.ai

BORN: Chicago, IL

LIVES: New York, NY

PUBLICATIONS AND RECOGNITIONS: Yale Alumni Award for English Excellence; Albert.ai Blog: The New Tenets of Digital Marketing

MENTOR'S ANECDOTE: *Don't underestimate this one; she packs a powerful punch. Francis thinks deeply and writes freely—honesty and bravery driving every word, every turn of phrase. When we first met, we were two introverts at a coffee shop, poring over writing techniques and partner goals. Today, we are two introverts at coffee shops, at book fairs, riding bumper cars. Giving time to the experiences that give us reason to write. I know Francis to be an incredible talent with a warm, magnetic personality. She lives heart-first, and watching her find her voice through writing has been a true joy.*

CRACKS OF SUNSHINE

FRANCIS GUTIERREZ

This piece is about my struggle with depression and mental health. I've learned that even some of the strongest, most influential people are struggling.

Tiny. An ant trapped at the feet of giants. Lost. Confused. Fragile. Scared to get stomped on, constantly trying to scurry away. It seems much of life has been spent this way, feeling so small. Feeling as though I would never be as big as the mob of giants above me, their heads towering over me from the clouds. At some point, I started feeling mentally fried, so much so that my body stopped complying. My world felt like it was crumbling around me, and I didn't even flinch. Instead, I lay in my ruins. I gave up. I didn't lift a finger. I stopped caring about anything that used to matter, yet I still had to put up a front. No one noticed. I lost my sense of purpose, and soon after, my friends. "Only babies cry" and "People who are depressed should just be happy." These were things I had heard for a lifetime. Instead of telling anyone how I felt, I cried myself to sleep every single night.

I was that tiny ant and no one understood. I grew up in a Hispanic household where no one spoke about what was going on in their minds or shared much. It didn't help that I was their golden girl, their angel, the way to success. I didn't want to let them down, so I swallowed my tears and held on to the pain. I tried to keep moving. That's the thing about depression, it eats you alive and spits you right back out. Numbness and pain at the very same time. I would look at the roof above my head and ask God why I was alive. I didn't understand how I was supposed to live like this. Truthfully, sometimes I still don't.

Even then, I was scared to admit I was alone. So I smiled and was the loudest laugh in the room. I became the girl who everyone associated with a ray of sun when in reality I was shadows. I needed help. It took me a while to admit I wasn't okay. My therapy sessions were hard and uncomfortable. Yet it felt so good to let it out. And that's when I discovered writing, I wasn't alone. I had my words and my thoughts.

When people finally found out they asked me, "Francis, why didn't you say anything?" I stayed silent. Why would I expose myself in that sense? It hurt so much to see my loved ones cry over me, to feel as though I hurt them. Because this couldn't be happening to their little girl. This couldn't be happening to the little girl who had a roof above her head, to the little girl who had a family and friends. To the one who had excelled, the one "destined" for great things. But it was happening, and it felt as though I had betrayed them. They loved me, and although this was all new to them, they stuck through it with me. I had support. I had just been too ashamed to ask for it, to go to them. I was too preoccupied with being perfect.

But here I am standing tall, on most days, at least. I let my passions in and let them consume me and slowly the sun started coming out again. Still, I am not always sunny, I have days where I turn into that same tiny ant scurrying away. Yet I force myself out of bed, and I tell myself it is time for another day. Another day where I can keep my mind tuned to all the things I love. Some might say it is shameful, and I remind myself it is where I came from. It is part of my past and may be even my future. That I have been able to break free from such a stigmatized illness reminds me that we are all stronger than we seem, that we can all rise.

GIANNY GUZMAN

YEARS AS MENTEE: 4

GRADE: Senior

BORN: Queens, NY

LIVES: Queens, NY

MENTEE'S ANECDOTE: *In my first year as a mentee, I placed Hermione on this golden pedestal. I looked up to her as this beacon of hope, knowledge, and wisdom. Four years later, she is my mentor and friend, and remains this beacon of light in my life. I may have taken her down from that pedestal, not because she let me down, but because she surpassed everything I ever thought of her. Her kindness and wisdom astonish me every day. I look to her for guidance, or even just for someone to have a conversation with. She is more than the pedestal I placed her on.*

HERMIONE HOBY

YEARS AS MENTOR: 4

OCCUPATION: Novelist

BORN: London, UK

LIVES: Brooklyn, NY

PUBLICATIONS AND RECOGNITIONS: *Virtue* (Riverhead Books, 2021); *Harper's;* Givenchy's '20 campaign film

MENTOR'S ANECDOTE: *Five years ago I met an effervescent teen who squealed upon meeting "a real Hermione." I remain a "real Hermione" and Gianny remains a real Harry Potter fan—these things have stayed the same—but when I recall the moment we met, I feel a vertigo of transformation. As in, how, in the space of just a few years, did that girl become this woman? Recently, she told me she wanted us to research political candidates together ahead of the 2020 election. Would that I'd had such a level of civic engagement at that age! I marvel at the person Gianny has become.*

A LETTER

GIANNY GUZMAN

This is a goodbye letter to all the relationships that shaped me as a person.

My dear,

It seems to me that so much has slipped my mind. But this is what I remember. This is my side of our truth.

We were young. The kind of young that flings you into life with blind eyes and bare hearts. The kind of young that made us claw our skins in desperation, too impatient to wait for the time of our metamorphosis. The kind of young that you can't blame because they didn't know any better, but we still bear the tattoo of guilt on our shoulders.

Oh, how foolish I think we were. But we just didn't know.

At the time we stood on a shore watching waves of our hopes, dreams, and promises, the tides too high for us to even try.

What we went through made me feel so small. It broke me down into grains of sand. But I couldn't stay small, it's just not what the world had in store for me. It wasn't in my parents' plan. With all the pressure of the world coming down on me from every angle of my life and the fire that fueled my soul, I became glass.

And you were broken down and small, too, but had no one to give you the pressure and your fire flickered far too much. So I lent you my fire and with the pressure of our friendship, we both became glass people.

People who are seen through because they haven't forged who they are. People who, instead, rely on the reflection of those around them to feel for a moment that they are more than they are.

If only we saw ourselves. If only you knew I could see you and you could see me.

But let's be honest, my dear. I was never going to be enough for you. And I could spend my whole life yelling at you about how you made me want to stay glass. I could blame you for every crack in that friendship made of glass.

I'm sure you blame me for sticking by you through it all. You never understood my unyielding loyalty. Not until I left you in the end.

We can spend our whole lives passing the torch of blame and guilt back and forth in an endless loop. But there comes a time where we must simply grow up.

Glass can break, that will never change. But I will burden the blame for what I did, and it may be heavy but it will strengthen me. And I will learn. I want to learn from it all.

We aren't meant to be a part of the others' life, we are the ones who turn each other into the grains of sand found at the shore of abandoned hopes.

It's time, my dear. As I say this final goodbye, I can remember now we had our beautiful times where we reflected the light into shimmers of laughter and smiles. But I'll be the first to say that I loved you, but without you by my side I found who I am. I am not glass. I am more than what we were.

In the end, I would not change anything at all.

LENA HABTU

YEARS AS MENTEE: 2

GRADE: Sophomore

BORN: Addis Ababa, Ethiopia

LIVES: New York, NY

PUBLICATIONS AND RECOGNITIONS: Scholastic Art & Writing Awards: Silver Key

MENTEE'S ANECDOTE: *Things just seem to click when I'm with Sammi, whether we saw each other last week or last month, it just works. This year, Sammi and I have been doing a lot of revisiting— old pieces, conversations, music, and memories. I love revisiting with Sammi, because it reminds me that we've built a home with each other to revisit. I'm so excited for the next few years with Sammi, and can't wait to create more experiences with her, and to revisit those with her someday.*

SAMMI LaBUE

YEARS AS MENTOR: 2

OCCUPATION: Founder and Leader, Fledgling Writing Workshops

BORN: Moorpark, CA

LIVES: Brooklyn, NY

PUBLICATIONS AND RECOGNITIONS: Second Prize in SMK Literary Competitions for an unpublished novel

MENTOR'S ANECDOTE: *In our second year together I can't help but feel Lena and I were always meant to be in each other's lives. Sometimes it seems like we could never have enough time to chat. Whether we're discussing our pop musician obsessions, sharing our social justice hopes with each other, or searching the city for the most chocolatey hot chocolate and the strongest cup of coffee, I always end our sessions smiling and further convinced that her voice will make the kind of waves in this world that will push us forward. And that she gives the best hugs.*

EXIST(ING)

LENA HABTU

My piece was inspired by an article in ZORA, *a publication by and for women of color, titled "Black Women Are Driving a New R&B Resistance" by Mary Retta. Black women's identities have been degraded for so long that in attempts to uplift us, we're portrayed as deities instead of human.*

to be black and to be woman is to be

we throw around words:
goddess, queen
those are inherent descriptors in being black and being woman
there is a special kind of magic in our resilience

but i want to shift the focus of the conversation
let black girls be normal
we exist beyond lazily constructed stereotypes and the pedestals
    of goddesses
there's not a duality to black women, there's multiplicity in
    transcending preconceived notions *we're human*

the coconut oil that glistens on our skin drizzles into our eyes
    sometimes
unadorned, unbothered
we create, we lay idle, we daydream
we laugh and laugh and laugh
and we'll be raw and honest and true
we're beautiful in our simplicity, stripped down to our truest,
    most uncomplicated selves

we lay in bed, stare at the ceiling, and dream up revolutions and
    melodies at the same time

let us normalize ourselves just being ourselves
we're simple beings
the notion that we're regular shouldn't be radical
amidst the trials and tribulations that accompany living as black
    and woman
it'd be nice if we could just
exist

NAOMI HABTU

YEARS AS MENTEE: 2

GRADE: Senior

BORN: Addis Ababa, Ethiopia

LIVES: New York, NY

PUBLICATIONS AND RECOGNITIONS: Scholastic Art & Writing Awards: Gold Key and Honorable Mentions

MENTEE'S ANECDOTE: *I am so grateful that Kristen decided to stay at Girls Write Now for another year. When she told me she might not be able to make the commitment, I held back tears. From the first day I met her, she has been incredibly supportive of not only my writing but all my endeavors. From short, timed free-writes to writing about random objects I observe, she has patiently pushed me to feel less intimidated by blank pages and more comfortable with slowly filling them up. I'm sad that this will be my last year at Girls Write Now, but I know my time with Kristen will be far from over.*

KRISTEN GAERLAN

YEARS AS MENTOR: 3

OCCUPATION: Associate Creative Director, Lippe Taylor

BORN: Bronx, NY

LIVES: Brooklyn, NY

PUBLICATIONS AND RECOGNITIONS: *Lessons in Language, Lunch Ticket, Pig on a Stick, The Rumpus, A Woman Like Me, The Dot*

MENTOR'S ANECDOTE: *The first time I tasked Naomi with a timed free-write, I was a bit nervous. I sensed her introverted nature and worried that I was pushing her too hard. However, not only did she craft something incredible, but she also asked for more timed free-writes. She wanted me to push her and her writing, so I did. Since then, I've watched her cultivate her talent and charge through senior year with both confidence and resilience. This year has been transformative for Naomi, and I feel so honored to simply be a part of it.*

EMBARKING

NAOMI HABTU

As my time in high school comes to an end, I am reflecting upon my strength during times of change. I choose to continue with the resilience I have developed and carry it onward while embarking on my new journey.

My mom was trying to push me in, but I didn't want to let go of her.

"You can do this. Your dad will be waiting for you." She said these words, attempting to make it easier for me, but I couldn't bear the idea of being alone without having anyone to protect me for what may happen. She nudged me in and told me to press the button for the floor just one level below us. As the doors closed, I stared at her waving, praying that this wouldn't be the last time I ever saw her.

I had no problem riding up and down elevators if I wasn't alone. However, my logic was that if it was just me, something really bad would happen. I always thought of the worst. *What if the "Emergency Call" button doesn't work? What if no one hears me repeatedly ringing the alarm? What if no one hears my screams?* I became so paranoid about the potential "what ifs" that I couldn't think rationally.

My mother knew of these fears, which was why she had my father meet me on the floor below. Without fail, he would be there for my landing. His presence would make my wildly beating heart slow back down to its normal pace.

Then, one day, he was no longer there. My father's passing marked a new timeline where I would begin high school while simultaneously dealing with loss. My mom sent me off to ninth grade, and as the doors closed, I entered a new stage of my life. One without my dad.

When he died I wanted someone to give me the answers: one ideal story about coming to terms with grief that would allow me do the same. I wanted that feeling of serenity, when the internal questions, the "what ifs," and the irrational fears would disappear. I wished that grief were an elevator that my mom could simply shove me into, a linear journey where I could witness my own landing. However, there isn't one eureka moment when everything falls into place. The gears of time keep turning. One of the hardest things about losing my dad was that I wanted time to stop, even if for a moment. I wanted to recollect and then continue.

There are many things that I've told myself I'll do eventually. Starting a daily journal, studying every day so I don't end up cramming, and drawing more. I promised myself I'll do them in a few minutes, then hours, then next week, after I submit college applications, after I graduate, when I finally have a break. I pressed pause on when I would begin truly enjoying life. I thought after I graduate, after I have come to terms with loss, I will be happy and content, and feel fulfilled. I will pursue my passion for traveling, I will have a job doing what I love, whatever that will be. I created some distant fantasy, that one day I will come to terms with my grief, and after that everything will be clear, I will be able to live the life I want to. But the truth is, this is it.

My grandma says, *"Yi koy malet, yi kir malet new."*

"Saying that you'll wait to do something means that you're not going to do it."

Month by month, then year by year, I have gotten through high school while coping with grief. From freshman to senior year, each grade proved to be its own level on an elevator. All I've been doing is simply continuing to be present. I now realize that, by doing so, I was pushing myself all along. Everything I do is an active choice. One that I used to take for granted, or one that most of my peers see as a given. I chose to get up, go to school, and be present every day. Knowing that I have survived these three years makes me even closer to achieving that internal peace. I have not only been able to take things day by day, but my challenges have also strengthened me.

I realize now that my mom was making me push myself when she pushed me into the elevator. I used to let my fears control me, but because of my parents a sense of resilience has been instilled within me. It's not always as easy as the day I was just put in the elevator and came out cured of my phobia. But, if anything, it made me stronger. Knowing that I have agency in my choices, I am choosing to overcome.

Now as I graduate high school, I am back on the top floor. My first-floor destination is embarking on a journey into independence. My mom isn't pushing me into the elevator this time, nor is my dad waiting in the lobby, but taking the first step has become muscle memory. There are times when I go on elevators and still think about pressing the emergency call button, but I stop myself and continue to ride with faith.

IRENE HAO

YEARS AS MENTEE: 2

GRADE: Junior

BORN: New York, NY

LIVES: Brooklyn, NY

MENTEE'S ANECDOTE: *Lauren this year in particular has been so lovely and patient, given my hectic schedule. As a freelance writer, she now has the freedom to creatively explore various writing mediums that have been the subjects of many of our weekly meetings. We have made great progress in our pair goals this school year, particularly in terms of making a habit of including writing exercises in our meetings. They're incredibly useful in keeping my creative juices flowing. When not working together and sharing our writing pieces, we are catching up on each other's lives, a persevering aspect of our meetings that I treasure.*

LAUREN VESPOLI

YEARS AS MENTOR: 2

OCCUPATION: Freelance Writer

BORN: New Haven, CT

LIVES: Brooklyn, NY

PUBLICATIONS AND RECOGNITIONS: *The New York Times, Atlas Obscura,* Amtrak's *The National*

MENTOR'S ANECDOTE: *I've loved watching Irene become more confident this year. When we started working together, she was finding her place at a new school. I've been so impressed with how she's balanced pursuing her passions and taking on new challenges. That spirit has carried over into Girls Write Now, as we've experimented with digital media like podcasts and stop-motion animation. Though she's new to these mediums, she brings the same ambitious creativity she expresses in her writing. I can't wait to see what she'll conquer next.*

FLICKER OUT

IRENE HAO

When I sat down one November evening and stared at the empty Google Doc on my laptop for fifteen minutes straight, I knew I was experiencing burnout. Drafting this piece was quite meta: I struggled to write about my struggle to write.

If passion were a flame, then it's flickered out
I've got a new candle ready
But my hands can't stop shivering from the cold wind
But I can't find the match to light it
I'm scraping the dried melted wax of the last flame
Where are the remnants of that candle?
If I collect the ashes, I should be able to see that flame again
If I collect the ashes, at least let me give this passion a proper
    burial

The lines in my notebook compel me to fill them
Letters, scribbles, patterns, sketches
Fill me, leave your imprints on me
Press the paper so hard you could trace the dents on the next page
And I do it, because I want to.
But how do I move my pen across the page
If nothing moves me anymore?

Writing—it's my thing
It's why I can face college essays unabashedly
It's how I introduce myself: I'm Irene, a writer
Expectant eyes, escapist essays, and empty lies
I'm a blank slate:
"You're good with words, so please write for me."

"You're a writer, so just do your thing."
Writing can't be my thing if the words I write aren't mine

I remember when I knew putting thoughts on paper,
Spinning ideas into words, words onto pages, would be my
    calling
I remember the A's, the praises, the excited gazes
Late-night conversations with parents, new friends, and a sense of
    pride
That I stood out from the crowd and that my future would be
    bright
I'll continue chasing after this flickering dream
When I fall, I know that I'll fall into my safety net: writing
But it feels like I'm falling for a lie instead

Writing—it's what got me here, standing proud
I should be proud, but I also should be writing this down
How I feel, what I say, what I think
Every word that spills from my mind
Could be left behind, so I craft a makeshift basket out of paper
And let the words ooze and bleed through
I'm a writer, so I should put something down

But how do I move my pen across the page
If nothing moves me anymore?

If writing were a flame, then this is burnout
That's right, it's writer's block, a plateau
It's a blank space, a blank line, a blank mind
Is writing even a passion when I don't feel passionate about it?

The pages in my notebook compel me to rip them
Tears, cuts, scrapes, and white-out
Cross me out. Erase me. There's nothing you want to write now.
Calm down, I tell myself. This will work itself out.
I toss the notebook against my bedroom wall
And I do it, because I want to

My mission is my passion: I love to create and imagine
I want my job to be my passion, the source of my excitement
And now I'm here. I'm making my way up, but
I'm scared of heights, and I want to climb back down
But I can't move. It's like the hardened wax from all the candles
    I've gone through
Has rooted me to the spot. I can't go back, but where should I
    go from here?
How do I move my pen across the page
If nothing moves me anymore?

NYLAH HARRIS

YEARS AS MENTEE: 3

GRADE: Senior

BORN: Brooklyn, NY

LIVES: Brooklyn, NY

PUBLICATIONS AND RECOGNITIONS: Scholastic Art & Writing Awards: Honorable Mentions

MENTEE'S ANECDOTE: *My mentorship with Kathleen, in our own love language, is as easy as solving the case at the end of a* Law & Order: SVU *episode. Now, to most that might seem weird and not quite understandable, but when there's a connection between two people, when are weird metaphors not a part of that? We build each other up creatively, offer a safe space, and, most important, support each other through the good and bad writing.*

KATHLEEN SCHEINER

YEARS AS MENTOR: 9

OCCUPATION: Senior Medical Editor at Havas Health Plus

BORN: Biloxi, MS

LIVES: Brooklyn, NY

MENTOR'S ANECDOTE: *When I first met Nylah in 2017, we bonded over our love of true crime and murder, and I found out that she wanted to study forensic science. We've written many pieces together full of blood and murder, poisonous plants, etc. Now, in 2020, Nylah has been accepted to Penn State, which has one of the best forensic science programs. And I expect to see Nylah soon as an expert witness on one of my favorite murder shows, like* Forensic Files *or* Cold Justice.

PERFECT WOMAN

NYLAH HARRIS

In correlation with the theme, this piece was written to show the roles women are often desired to play and to be in.

Scott knew that he had to create a wife any day now. His whole family kept pestering him with questions as to why he hadn't picked up a paintbrush to make his wife. Hell, he knew he could've just picked up some crayons and markers and drew her on printing paper. The only problem was, Scott wasn't sure how to design her. Three and half hours ago, he decided that tonight was the night he was finally going to go through it, but this was too much pressure. It's not like he had the option of accepting a woman as is. Frustrated with his lack of progress, he angrily turned off *The Fresh Prince of Bel-Air* and knocked over his bowl of Honey Nut Cheerios. His neighbor directly under him tapped his broom on the ceiling, a signal to stop all the commotion. With a groan, Scott flipped off his neighbor, thankful for the apartment walls surrounding him.

Heaving a sigh, Scott vigorously rubbed his hands against his face and forced himself to focus. He had known his whole life this day was coming. Actually, every male on the planet had the moment where he would have to settle down and make his soulmate to his liking. *It's normal,* he reminded himself; every male after twenty-five had to start thinking about this. *This process is so tedious,* he counterargued with himself. You first needed the perfect canvas and the right colors. Then you had to think long and hard about what you like and dislike. Should she be smaller than you? Do her breasts need to be full? Once you draw her with what you can live with for the rest of your life, the hardest part comes: personalities. The adjectives had to surround the frame in which you created, but forgetting one word could alter her altogether. You had to be extremely thoughtful and careful. It did help, though, that no matter your art skills, as long as you bought a wooden canvas, your dream woman would shine through. Wooden canvases allow you to project exactly what you want as your thoughts connect to your pen. It's too dangerous for women to use, as they are too fragile to handle the process, so men handle it. The only catch is you can have only one wooden canvas and it has to be passed on generation to generation. *That is so annoying,* Scott commented internally. Sometimes he wished so much power wasn't bestowed on his gender, but he took his responsibility in great, happy strides.

Shaking his head to clear his thoughts, Scott picked up the brush and started to create his woman. In one quick, swift motion, the pen went straight to the canvas. Her hair was thick and curly with light brown highlights. Her eyes were green like moss, which contrasted with her rich mocha skin. With one dimple, long legs with hips that had a slight dip in them, breasts full but *not that full,* and a small butt, she was absolutely breathtaking. Gasping in shock, he backed away as she started to walk out of the canvas. Standing in front of him was the literal woman of his dreams. Breathing in deeply, she fluttered her eyes for a second. As if she knew she needed a moment's peace for the purpose in which she was created for. Sharply, she opened her eyes and stared into his. For a second that's all she did, stare. Then, with a crooked smile so wide and her one dimple prominent, she spoke.

"Hi." . . .

LOLA HART

YEARS AS MENTEE: 2

GRADE: Senior

BORN: Queens, NY

LIVES: Queens, NY

MENTEE'S ANECDOTE: *My mentor and I have been in Girls Write Now together for two years. We started together and have grown an amazing bond since. My favorite time of us together is when we presented awards to honorees at the Agents of Change Awards, hosted by DVF in their New York City headquarters. From practicing together and then being there to showcase our amazing relationship for people to see, these are moments I'll never forget.*

DONNA HILL

YEARS AS MENTOR: 2

OCCUPATION: Assistant Professor of Professional Writing at Medgar Evers College

BORN: Brooklyn, NY

LIVES: Brooklyn, NY

PUBLICATIONS AND RECOGNITIONS: *A House Divided, Where the Heart Is, The Other Sister*

MENTOR'S ANECDOTE: *"We are dreaming great things and doing them!" Just when I think things are not going to work out in time, Lola puts on her Supergirl cape and pulls it off. She continues to amaze me! Sweet. Funny. Smart. Not one to be underestimated. I love her!*

5 YEARS FROM NOW

LOLA HART

This is what I imagine my life to be like in five years. The future makes me nervous because anything can happen, but I remain optimistic always.

5 years from now I will have graduated with my bachelor's degree. I'll be in medical school debt-free, learning how to professionally help people. I'll be surrounded by good friends who are all succeeding and doing good things with their lives. Kind, motivational, and extraordinary human beings.

5 years from now my heart will finally be healed. I'll have dealt with all the sadness and pain people have caused me. I will learn to forgive those who did me wrong even if they were not sorry. I will no longer accept less than what I deserve. No toxicity will be tolerated around me.

5 years from now I will have met the love of my life. A person who respects and loves me unconditionally. They will understand and value me completely. Communication will be our strongest suit. We will learn to apologize when we're wrong and not make silly mistakes to jeopardize our relationship.

5 years from now I'll have a nice little apartment in New York. A little job in my career field of psychiatry to pay the bills. I'll have a pet fish. Maybe even a roommate, who I'll grow an amazing bond with.

5 years from now I'll have started my first book. I'll write for it consistently. I'll attend writing workshops to keep me going and inspire me. Being in a book club would also be nice.

5 years from now I don't know where I'll be. But I will speak good things into existence. I said and it shall be.

MAY HATHAWAY

YEARS AS MENTEE: 1

GRADE: Junior

BORN: New York, NY

LIVES: New York, NY

PUBLICATIONS AND RECOGNITIONS: Scholastic Art & Writing Awards: Gold Keys

MENTEE'S ANECDOTE: *I feel so lucky to have Alena as my mentor! I've learned so much from her this past year, and I've really been able to grow as a writer with her guidance. Receiving her feedback on my work has made me more confident in my writing skills. She's incredibly kind and cool and funny, and I very much look forward to our pair sessions each week. I love every minute we spend together, whether we're writing poems, chatting about our weeks, or exchanging book recommendations. Being paired with Alena is the best gift I could possibly ask for.*

ALENA GRAEDON

YEARS AS MENTOR: 1

OCCUPATION: Novelist

BORN: Durham, NC

LIVES: Brooklyn, NY

PUBLICATIONS AND RECOGNITIONS: *The Word Exchange* (Doubleday, 2020); Lighthouse Works fellowship 2020; *Los Angeles Times; Vice*

MENTOR'S ANECDOTE: *The day I met May, she mentioned she'd built a data-analytics website. "You can build a data-analytics website?" I asked. She laughed and showed it to me. It analyzed debate team performances. "You also do debate and writing?" I said. I realized then that May is a force of nature. Clearly, she's brilliant—and funny, too. (The next week, she shared an opinion piece she'd published on the perils of bad Instagram poetry.) I'm not sure how I lucked into such a hypercompetent, fun, kind, and blazingly talented mentee, but I'm very grateful.*

HEREDITARY

MAY HATHAWAY

This poem is a reflection on what being multiracial means to me and how it impacts the space I occupy in the world.

When I am particularly sad
about not looking like anyone
I know, I convince myself
that the ocean belongs to me.
I am most comfortable
in the in-between, intersections,
crossroads. My inheritance is not
a continent. I separate land,
force my doppelgänger to
live in the unknown.

HERMEI HERMAN

YEARS AS MENTEE: 1

GRADE: Junior

BORN: Brooklyn, NY

LIVES: New York, NY

MENTEE'S ANECDOTE: *I did not know what to expect when I first signed up for Girls Write Now. But the experiences I've gained so far exceed any expectations I may have had. Even though this is a program about writing, I feel like I've learned so much more during my meetings with Eva. We talk a lot about the matters of life and it is truly an interesting experience, especially since it starts every time with "How was your day?" And from there, anything goes.*

EVA GREENHOLT

YEARS AS MENTOR: 1

OCCUPATION: Marketing Manager, nTopology

BORN: Wilmington, DE

LIVES: New York, NY

PUBLICATIONS AND RECOGNITIONS: Ghostwriter for *Next Level You* (SattvaMe, 2020) and *How to Win Clients & Influence People* (Tulip Media Group, 2018)

MENTOR'S ANECDOTE: *Entering into a pair writing relationship with a mentee was a new experience for me and I didn't know what to expect or what it was going to be like. Working with Hermei over the last couple of months has been incredible. She is a smart, witty young writer who is discovering who she is through storytelling. This has been a great experience.*

SALTY, WITH A HINT OF BITTERNESS

HERMEI HERMAN

This piece is about the two sides of love that many people shall experience in their life. Because no matter where you are, or who you may be, you'll be able to relate to the emotions displayed in the story.

The feeling that takes up a good amount of room in your heart and sometimes you feel it's all in your head. The feeling you see when your dad makes your mother a cup of tea in the morning before they drop you off for school. The feeling you smell when he approaches you by your locker before lunch, the air suddenly crisp with a light fragrance of detergent as he hands you a bag of freshly baked cookies with a mischievous grin on his face, and he hurries away before you're able to ask what they're for. The feeling you hear when he confesses, later on, saying he's liked you for a long time now, but you're always too dense to notice, floating about in your own world, your thoughts and insecurities building a wall, yet one he managed to break down. The feeling you feel when your cheeks heat up, burning with embarrassment as you try to find the right words to reply. The feeling you touch when you reach slowly to cup his handsome blushing face, glowing with anticipation, and you whisper, "I like you, too," and press his lips to your own. The feeling you taste when his tongue meets yours, tasting the cookies he made before, warm and sweet.

The feeling that leaves an enormous void in your heart when it's no longer there and the hole feels like it will never close, leaving you to bleed out. The feeling you see when your mother hurls a glass at your father in a fit of rage, trading insults that seem to drag on for ages. The feeling you smell when she struts past your locker, with her mix of perfume and shampoo, tainting the air with a horrid smell, and the poison erodes the very life from your lungs as she runs into his arms, laughing as he kisses her cheek. The feeling you hear when she whispers, loud enough for you to hear, "I love you so much." The feeling you feel when he says the same thing back and your heart clenches, unable to bear not being loved by the one it loved so deeply. The feeling you touch as you raise your hand to touch your lips where his once laid, the flesh slowly becoming cold, the cold your heart wishes it had so that it would be able to feel nothing at the things it saw. The feeling you taste as your tears spill down your cheeks, one by one, salty with a hint of bitterness.

TIFFANY HO

YEARS AS MENTEE: 1
GRADE: Senior
BORN: New York, NY
LIVES: Queens, NY

MENTEE'S ANECDOTE: *Meeting Katie was one of the best parts of Girls Write Now. I came into the relationship thinking I needed to impress, but her empathetic and uplifting personality made it easy for me to be myself. Our weekly coffee shop meetings quickly became the highlight of my week; together, we explored writing genres that I wouldn't have done by myself. She became someone that I trust, and she has guided me not just with my writing, but also through college applications and academic stress. I can't thank Katie enough for being an amazing mentor and making this such a positive experience.*

KATIE REILLY

YEARS AS MENTOR: 1
OCCUPATION: Reporter, *Time*
BORN: Boston, MA
LIVES: Brooklyn, NY

MENTOR'S ANECDOTE: *Whether we're meeting at the New York Public Library or in a coffee shop, I'm always surprised and impressed by the creative twists Tiffany incorporates into her writing. She has brought to life a dream-like subway encounter with a mysterious magician, the beauty of a lush backyard jungle hidden from the city, and a dystopian world wrestling with feminism. Every week, I look forward to our meeting and to the thoughtful, funny observations that continue to shine through Tiffany's work.*

FOR ALL THE CHOICES GIVEN TO THE ONE TAKEN

TIFFANY HO

I wrote this piece to emphasize the struggles of women in a male-dominated society. Throughout history, social justice leaders have fought both within the system and against it. In my piece, different women have to make a similar choice in how they choose to fight against discrimination.

The spraying sound was getting closer. Natalie was careful not to step on one of the white building's loose tiles, as she crept behind the gothic pillars leading to the courtroom. *A couple more steps,* she thought. She found it. The vandalizer stood on the judge's desk and, on the white wall behind, wrote, "Battle for Reproductive Fre—" Freedom. Natalie completed the unfinished graffiti in her mind. How fitting that the insurgence movement would choose to vandalize the Arkansas state judicial building left in disrepair. *Still, it's illegal,* Natalie thought, reaching into her back pocket for her gun. Her duty as a police officer was to uphold the law.

Natalie tracked her boss's every move. She looked around at her coworkers: black suits, balding heads, identical cubicles. In her five years at an insurance office, Natalie witnessed multiple colleagues rise from manager to administrator. Today, it would be her turn to be one of the first female leaders of the company. In the corner of her eye, she saw her boss walking toward her.

"Natalie, have you seen Andrew? I'm waiting to surprise him."

Natalie shook her head, and her boss went to talk with other employees. A surprise for Andrew? It was impossible. Her heart dropped and her hand slammed her keyboard. The chatter of her coworkers halted.

"Sorry, it wasn't working. Everything's fine!" She forced a smile.

Her coworkers snickered. "Women," one of them whispered.

Later that day, at a little table on the roof adorned with fairy lights and lavender, Natalie shared a drink with her boyfriend, Matt. The night sky glowed with the light from the distant city. If it were any other day, she would have been happy.

"I deserved that position. Andrew always leaves his work incomplete and he's only been in the office for three years. I'm much more qualified," Natalie seethed.

Matt patted her. "Don't worry so much. There's always two sides to a coin."

Natalie glared at him. All she wanted was empathy and someone to rant to. He was not about to play devil's advocate for men's role in leadership again.

Seeing the look on her face, Matt quickly added, "No, no, no. I respect women. After all, I'm dating you. I believe that you completely deserved that position, but maybe he's just a better fit in some aspects."

"Matt, you can't be serious."

"Really, Natalie? Don't be so irrational. Maybe this is why he got the job. Don't use gender discrimination to make up for your own pitfalls."

Natalie threw her arms in the air. "It is about gender. You don't see how isolated I feel when my mostly male coworkers laugh at me. You don't understand how many additional projects I took on, just so my boss would look at me with some respect, while the male interns easily gained it. You don't feel my inadequacy."

Matt looked at her and sighed. "You know what, maybe you're right, but let's just calm down and go back inside. You can't fix the way our society was built."

Matt closed the door to the roof behind him, leaving Natalie gazing at the city beyond. *I'll prove them wrong and I'll show them I can lead. I'll change this system from the inside, through its own laws.* She smiled to herself. *I'll become a police officer.*

Natalie took a deep breath and pointed her gun at the insurgent. "Stop right there."

The hooded figure whipped around. Dainty features lined her soft face, but her expression hardened when her eyes met Natalie's.

"You're a traitor," she screamed at Natalie, echoing the cries of the protests around the country. "You're following the law, but the law is unjust. We have to stick together."

No, Natalie thought. *I'm following the law to gain the respect and power to change our justice system for all women.* "Hands up," Natalie yelled, as she pointed her gun at the insurgent. Desperation flickered through the insurgent's eyes.

"Don't do this. Have you ever been shamed for being pregnant at eighteen?" The insurgent paused, fully turning to look at Natalie. "They say you'll be an embarrassment to the community, so then they send you away. But they won't let you end the pregnancy, either, because then you'll be a murderer. That was my life. Every choice I had and every piece of my dignity was stolen from me. We can't let this persist. Please."

Natalie released the breath she had been holding all this time. Behind the insurgent's defiant stance was brokenness. She genuinely wanted change, too, Natalie thought. But we won't get anything done by breaking the law. They'll just ignore our cries and silence us like they've done to the other insurgents.

The insurgent dropped the spray bottle and put her hands up. The echoes of the falling bottle reverberated through the whole chamber and the bottle rolled to Natalie's feet. The decision was hers. *What now,* she thought.

OLIVIA HOM

YEARS AS MENTEE: 2

GRADE: Senior

BORN: New York, NY

LIVES: New York, NY

MENTEE'S ANECDOTE: *My mentor Linda and I are always surprisingly productive whenever we meet up. I can say for sure that I've written some of my best work when I'm with her. Although I remember one time we were both feeling stressed and not willing to write so we just walked around Columbus Circle, window shopping and scrutinizing the clothes that were on display. It was fun and relaxing. It's important to take a break sometimes and just get lost in the wonders of New York City.*

LINDA CORMAN

YEARS AS MENTOR: 10

OCCUPATION: Freelance Editor and Writer

BORN: Newton, MA

LIVES: New York, NY

MENTOR'S ANECDOTE: *During a pair session, Olivia was describing feeling neither Chinese nor American in a college application essay. She'd recently learned that Chinese people had been very active in the Civil Rights Movement and in avant-garde art. This helped her to embrace her identity, because she had previously given credence to the stereotype that Chinese people were conforming. She was thrilled to learn that this stereotype was just that—a stereotype. I then recalled my own discomfort with stereotypes of my own Jewish ethnicity. We were definitely taking our places in history, and getting to know each other.*

THE DESERT

OLIVIA HOM

This poem is about a deeply personal experience I've had this year. It's about feeling bitter, betrayed, and abandoned. And no, it's not about a romantic relationship.

The glass of my iPhone shatters as it meets the wooden floor
There's a bitterness forming within me
The world stands still as if a pause button is pressed
I'm too numb to cry
I want to scream but my throat dried up
Suddenly all hope has disappeared
I glance at the small bowl made of multicolored radishes that
    rests on a shelf
Inside the bowl is a tiny clay bird painted in swirls of white, gray,
    and bronze
A message is tucked within a hole in the bird
The message is full of gratitude and well-wishes
I laugh bitterly
I could've had that same happiness
Were it not for you.

Now I'm trapped in a desert
There must be an oasis somewhere
But I can't reach it, no matter how hard I try
All that exists is myself and the wasteland around me
The wind grows in its intensity
The sand rises into the air and stings my eyes
I stumble around blindly
It feels like I'm aimlessly walking in circles
All I can think of is why

Why did this happen?
Why did you leave me?
Why did you blame me when it was all your fault?
The scorching heat of the desert begins to magnify my
    insecurities
It takes control of my mind and fills it with doubt
I am trapped within the eye of the sandstorm
The voices in my head grow louder and louder
They whisper poisonous words
You're not good enough you're the reason she left she never cared
    about helping you everything was all a lie
Suddenly I cry out in pain
The voices are silent
Slowly, the harsh winds sweep away the fiery anger,
Which cools into an aching sadness.

Time passes but the stinging bitterness within me still lingers
And I wonder when that feeling of betrayal will go away
Maybe someday I'll find a way out of the desert.

MAXINE HSIUNG

YEARS AS MENTEE: 1

GRADE: Senior

BORN: New York, NY

LIVES: New York, NY

MENTEE'S ANECDOTE: *I felt an instant connection with Emma from the day we first met at orientation. She has helped me through my entire college application process and has been there for me through a stressful school year. Emma understands me well, and helps me articulate my thoughts. I love catching up with her and laughing at our weekly pair sessions. I am incredibly lucky to be paired with such an inspiring, hardworking, genuine mentor.*

EMMA BAKER

YEARS AS MENTOR: 1

OCCUPATION: Freelance Writer

BORN: Los Angeles, CA

LIVES: Brooklyn, NY

PUBLICATIONS AND RECOGNITIONS: *Los Angeles Review of Books, Cosmopolitan, Bedford + Bowery*

MENTOR'S ANECDOTE: *This is not Maxine's first time around the sun. Within the first day of meeting her, I felt like I had known her all my life—but this effect is less of a testament to our connection than it is to her incisive emotional intelligence, thoughtfulness, and genuine curiosity about all that crosses her path. I've watched her navigate college applications, relationships, and the slog of high school with unyielding drive and grace. Despite formally being my "mentee," she has taught me so much about handling difficult situations and always sticking to your values. I'm honored to know her and so excited to see the woman she becomes. Undoubtedly, she will do great things.*

SERENDIPITY

MAXINE HSIUNG

This is a piece dedicated to some of the closest people of my life, all of whom I had never expected to be so crucial to my personal growth.

ser·en·dip·i·ty
/ˌserənˌdipədē/
the occurrence and development of events by chance in a happy or beneficial way

T,

Sixth grade: we walked out of math class, stunned at how terribly we did on the test. We looked at each other. *You, too?* We burst into laughter.

I never thought we would become best friends—you had your friends, and I had mine. Yet, I was drawn to your energy; you were always laughing. Through you, I learned how to color every aspect of my life with humor.

We would go to Chelsea Market during lunch and wander around through all the various shops and take in all the aromas. We discovered a shortcut—a narrow pathway full of loud, large air ducts—to our spot with our beloved Thai curry pot pie, and then struggled to find seats. After school, we would loiter around 16 Handles, sampling all the flavors and only occasionally actually purchasing our own cup.

Our adventures didn't stop after middle school. One summer day, we took a ferry to Governors Island and wanted to rent a surrey bike. We were both under eighteen, so we approached a random Asian lady, and by some miracle, I was able to use my clumsy

Chinese to convince her to pass off as our guardian. We took turns learning how to navigate the surrey bike and struggling to get it uphill while getting soaked by a fire hydrant.

Despite not being able to see each other much in person, we talk every day. We communicate through memes and random Snapchats. Even a Snapchat of just you sneezing will send me into a fit of laughter. Throughout the challenging school year, we FaceTime to motivate each other to work. Your presence alone gives me the energy and strength I need to get my work done.

Reflecting on everything about our friendship—from the chance way we met to how we've stayed close despite attending different schools—reminds me of the strength of our bond and the gratitude I have for you. You have made me more confident and outgoing: You know me completely and still accept me. You finish my sentences even when I can't articulate them, and you are always there for me. Seven years after our failed math test, I can't wait to celebrate the successes our lives have in store for us.

* * *

E,

Neither of us quite remember how it happened: After six years of loosely knowing each other, we found ourselves in a friendship. We go to the piers near Battery Park and let out whatever is on our mind while the sun sets. Intention sometimes gets lost in our texts, but our missed connections and endless inside jokes never fail to make me laugh. Every year, I look forward to updating our "progress doc" with our reflections and our hopes for the future. You are always there for me when I need to rant, and you always offer an insightful, fresh perspective.

You have continuously inspired me through your various passions—knitting, ukulele, violin—and optimistic mindset. I love how we cheer each other on, try new things together, and share opportunities with each other. In fact, I would not have been able to write this piece if it weren't for your creative mind and willingness for me to emulate your work. I'm grateful that we're there for each other, and I enjoy sharing new experiences with you.

L,

We met at a bus station in the Bronx on our way to our first 5K race. We made the usual small talk. We both were looking for a running buddy: Although I barely knew you, we exchanged numbers and planned to meet up every Saturday morning to run in Central Park. We didn't talk much when we ran, but being by each other's side pushed us to run farther. I often feel like stopping, but I continue since you keep going. I learned later on that you, too, felt like stopping but continued only because I did.

In January, five months after our weekly runs began, we finally ran the full loop without stopping. Running, like relationships, takes time to progress. Every time we meet, we build upon what we had. Despite not being a morning person, I now eagerly get out of bed on cold Saturday mornings to run and bask in the beauty of Central Park with you.

* * *

Relationships like these have shaped who I am today. By sheer chance, we meet people who have the potential to meaningfully impact our lives. It takes just one person to spark joy, passion, or motivation in you.

VICKY HUANG

YEARS AS MENTEE: 1

GRADE: Senior

BORN: Miaoli, Taiwan

LIVES: Queens, NY

MENTEE'S ANECDOTE: *When Neha first introduced herself, I immediately noticed the electric-blue eyeliner she rocked with her otherwise all-black outfit. I grew to admire her chill personality and passion for politics, and we bonded easily over the stress of applications and our love for Dum Dums. I am incredibly grateful to have met a mentor who always helped me with my writing judgment-free and made me feel more confident and comfortable as a writer.*

NEHA KULSH

YEARS AS MENTOR: 2

OCCUPATION: Manager, Global Creative, Clinique (The Estée Lauder Companies)

BORN: West Hollywood, CA

LIVES: Queens, NY

PUBLICATIONS AND RECOGNITIONS: *Bon Appétit; Architectural Digest*

MENTOR'S ANECDOTE: *When I first met Vicky I was sad she was a senior because it meant we'd get only one year together. We share a fondness for Awkwafina, all things Japanese, and the Pixar film* Bao. *We're also the product of no-nonsense immigrant households. No surprise, then, that Vicky is a powerful observer of culture and family dynamics. An economical writer, she writes effortlessly and without pretension—skills that eluded me at her age. I can't wait to see what she does next!*

MONOLID

VICKY HUANG

This piece describes my experience growing up with beauty standards. It highlights my first encounter with eyelid tape and the contrast between East Asian and Western notions of beauty.

I must've been no older than ten years old when I first saw my mom tape her eyelids. Every day was the same: She stood in front of the mirror, used a blade to cut off a slit of tape—no longer than two inches and much thinner than one millimeter—and I watched as she closed her eyes and pressed the tape against each eyelid. *It makes my eyes bigger,* she'd say. She did this for years until she gradually stopped—the constant artificial crease on her lids forced her original, natural monolids to change shape and, eventually, stay that way.

I never understood why she did it, and it wasn't until I entered high school that I really began to understand the concept of East Asian beauty standards. I had gotten into K-pop, and learned about how idols got plastic surgery to have eyes like Westerners and wore foundation multiple shades lighter than their skin tone to look whiter. Female idols like Bae Suzy or Krystal Jung, with their long hair, pale skin, and round eyes, were at the forefront of "feminine ideals," and a quick YouTube search would give you an abundance of tutorials on how to have makeup or hair *just like them.*

It suddenly started to make sense why my mom taped her eyelids every day for years. And why whenever she complimented my eyes, it would just be about the left one. 妳的雙眼皮今天好漂亮哦! *Your double eyelid looks so pretty today!*

Double eyelid. Singular.

Only my left eye had a double eyelid. And the other? A classic, East Asian monolid. I never saw anything wrong with my monolid.

But I *hated* my double eyelid. I hated the way it never folded all the way across my eye. How it seems to get stuck halfway, and how I'd feel it every time I blinked.

It was then that I realized the subjectivity of beauty.

I remember watching a video of a Western girl showing her viewers how she transforms her natural double eyelids into monolids to look like the "perfect Korean idol"—using *Elmer's Glue*. I watched, in shock, as she talked about dabbing glue onto her lids, pulling the double eyelid over the surface of her eye, and securing it in place—as if it were the most natural thing in the world! Why did East Asians work so hard to change their physical features in order to match those of Westerners, while Westerners were making tutorials on how to obtain the very same features that East Asians so strongly disliked?

Now, as I try to do my makeup in front of the mirror, the question remains unanswered. I know the black eyeliner won't show up on my right eye unless I draw a layer thick enough to go past my monolid, but I do it anyway. My eyes won't look as accentuated as Bae Suzy's, nor will the bright eyeshadow pop on my eyelid with barely any lid space—but I do it anyway.

FIKIRTE HUNT

YEARS AS MENTEE: 1

GRADE: Senior

BORN: Awasa, Ethiopia

LIVES: New York, NY

MENTEE'S ANECDOTE: *Every week Stephanie and I have met either at a mall giggling about life or in her podcast studio recording. Going into Girls Write Now, I had no idea what my relationship with her would end up being. All I knew is that we would become friends. Well, we've become best friends. We make jokes and have fun, but still manage to get work done. I feel like we can talk about anything and be sassy to each other. I am so grateful I have a wonderful mentor like Stephanie.*

STEPHANIE KARIUKI

YEARS AS MENTOR: 1

OCCUPATION: Senior Producer, Stitcher

BORN: Nairobi, Kenya

LIVES: Brooklyn, NY

MENTOR'S ANECDOTE: *When I came into Girls Write Now, I had no idea what kind of mentee I would have. All that I hoped is that we'd become friends. As soon as I met Fiki I knew that my expectation would become a reality. She is smart, kind, hilarious, and just an amazing energy to be around. She reminds me of the kind of young woman I wanted to be at eighteen. We spend our sessions getting things done while joking around. I've watched her grow a lot this year and am excited for her future. She is wholeheartedly herself in a way that many people my age are still trying to figure out and I can't wait to see what kind of woman she becomes.*

"YOU'RE TOO YOUNG, YOU WOULDN'T UNDERSTAND"

FIKIRTE HUNT

This is for anyone who has ever said or heard the words "you're too young." It's for the generation before me, after me, and, most of all— mine. It's for all my friends, who are frustrated daily by the adults in our lives, and for the adults in our lives who've forgotten what it's like to be young.

There has been a time in everyone's life when they heard the phrase "you're too young" or even said it. To me, there are two main issues with this phrase, the first pointing out my youth and second shutting me out of the conversation. Pointing out my youth establishes a barrier and implies that I am too inexperienced. In some cases that is true, but it also implies that someone my age would not understand or empathize with the situation. Wisdom and empathy do not necessarily come with age. We are all humans and have basic needs, wants, and emotions. Things are not the same as they were long ago.

Growing up now is not like it used to be. People my age are exposed to the horrors and dangers of life. From mass shootings to cancel culture to coping with severe mental health illnesses, we know a lot, have seen a lot, and have been through a lot. I am old enough to have my opinion and have it heard. The phrase "you're too young" also shuts me out of the conversation entirely without allowing a different perspective to be heard. At the end of the day, we were all young once. We experience things differently, but no matter the age, we should be heard.

For example, I love true crime podcasts. In many cases there are two sides to a story. The judge and jury have to hear all sides, no matter how outlandish the arguments are, to give a ruling. A fair trial means both sides are heard, even if the outcome is not what was wanted. I have a right to share my opinion, but that does not mean everyone has to agree with it; you just have to listen.

To all the adults: It's easy to forget what it feels like to be young, but it is not an excuse to ignore me. To anyone like me: the next time someone says, "You're too young," stop them in their tracks and say, "At least do the right thing and hear me out," because you never know . . . they just might have something insightful to say.

ELISABETH HYNES

YEARS AS MENTEE: 1

GRADE: Sophomore

BORN: Staten Island, NY

LIVES: Staten Island, NY

MENTEE'S ANECDOTE: *Jennifer allows me to express who I am and encourages me to keep on doing so. She has no problems about voicing her ideals to me and that is a quality that I admire. I think that people should stand up for what they believe in and Jenni does just that. With Jenni, I am able to be who I am in a world that wants to put me in a box. My writing has taken on a different meaning to me since we've been working together.*

JENNIFER MILTON

YEARS AS MENTOR: 1

OCCUPATION: Copy Supervisor, Grey, and Fiction Writer

BORN: Rochester, NY

LIVES: Brooklyn, NY

PUBLICATIONS AND RECOGNITIONS: Fiction Editor of *Faultline*; since then, I've published a couple of stories in *Juked* and have been hard at work on a novel

MENTOR'S ANECDOTE: *When I first met Elisabeth, we chatted about anything from religion to climate change to gender and sexuality. She is anything but shy about voicing her opinion, and I so admire that. She told me she was frustrated by people who felt the need to categorize everything. Why can't we just be who we are? That's a question that people seem to be asking now more than ever, when the basic rights of so many are being called into question. But Elisabeth is someone who lives and breathes her ideals. It's rare to meet someone who is so completely open and accepting of herself and others. I'm certain it's a quality I will continue to nurture, and what better way to do that than writing?*

WHERE AM I?

ELISABETH HYNES

A poem that questions if where you're from identifies who you are.

I am from told stories, and sage.
I'm from Dunkin' Donuts bags
From late-night fights
and Friday-night traditions
From chili and pierogies

Where I'm from is my mother's necklace
and Pop pop's ring.
Scoliosis bars turned coat rack
Where I'm from is Jack's lap
And late-night snacks

I'm from illegal fireworks
Neighborhood hot-boxers
Faint smells of weed
And hints of cinnamon and lavender
And fresh flowers

MEKKIAYAH JACOBS

YEARS AS MENTEE: 4

GRADE: Senior

BORN: Bronx, NY

LIVES: Bronx, NY

MENTEE'S ANECDOTE: *"Hey, how are you?"*
"I'm good, so let me tell you what happened in student government . . ." That is usually how my conversations with Brooke start: with my school drama that we both love. We always make sure to get something to eat. Sometimes I try to be fancy and get something new, but I usually go for avocado toast and a chai latte. Brooke and I are so close that we can literally talk for most of our time together and forget what we are there for. But we do get to work on my own project or Girls Write Now workshop projects.

BROOKE BOREL

YEARS AS MENTOR: 7

OCCUPATION: Journalist and author

BORN: Topeka, KS

LIVES: Brooklyn, NY

MENTOR'S ANECDOTE: *I am so happy to be Kiayah's mentor. We always have a mix of fun and writing at our weekly sessions, from gossiping about the latest drama in her student government group, to talking about our families, to working through edits on her latest poem or essay. I'm excited—and, selfishly, sad because I will miss seeing her every week!—for her to continue to take her place in history when she goes off to college next year.*

IN AND OUT OF THE STRUGGLE

MEKKIAYAH JACOBS

I tried to be different this year and not make a piece about me or my family, but I failed terribly. This piece shows how I am no different from anyone and how I can make my mark in my community by creating awareness of the issues in New York City.

The news really shocked me when the words came out of my mother's mouth. I wasn't angry and I wasn't sad. It just made me realize that anybody could be in this situation, no matter who you are. I was too young to remember that we were once homeless.

"There were times we went to places in Manhattan where it was like basements and we slept on bunk beds and I would lay our coats down so we could sleep," Mom remembers now. "But I could never sleep in those places."

My family's story of homelessness started in 2005 and continued until 2007. Throughout those three years we were in and out of homes across New York City, where the housing program placed us because we kept getting rejected for a voucher. When Mom finally got the news that they approved us, we were in a battered women's shelter in Queens. She was grateful and so happy that she didn't have to keep going back to the building where they processed the voucher applications and do the process over and over again.

"It was like the holding cell of a prison," she says.

They called the building Prevention Assistance and Temporary Housing (PATH). PATH is the citywide shelter intake center for homeless families with children with no other housing options available to them.

The process could take more than two days if you weren't early enough. There are many programs out there to help the homeless with food, clothing, and stationery, but this doesn't help the fact that the lack of affordable housing plays a big part in the system. For my mom, it was a very stressful process. She has a lot of patience and knew that it was either living on the street or waiting for acceptance for the voucher.

Our housing voucher was for $900 a month to cover rent. Not all landlords would accept the voucher, because at the time, the voucher program was new, but Mom found a studio apartment in the Bronx with a landlord that accepted that specific kind of voucher. We lived there for about two years, then we moved to Maryland.

But I didn't know my mom, my sister, and I were homeless until we moved back to New York a few years ago, which was when she decided to tell us. My mom explained why she thought that it was the best option for us to go through at the time, but something she wouldn't do again. The process for getting into housing when you are homeless is difficult.

We are hardly alone. There are many families that go through this process, and even more times than we did. So many people out there with no roof over their head. Being homeless is defined as a person without a home who is living on the streets. There are many causes for this, such as unemployment, lack of affordable housing, poverty, and drug abuse. And in New York City, the main cause is the lack of affordable housing. According to the online newsletter *The Bowery*, out of New York City's 8.4 million people, one in 125 are homeless. That's 70,000 men, women, and children. Every night, 4,000 people sleep in train stations and other public places.

So what does this say about what "affordable housing" means? This means that it's affordable to everyone except for the people who live in poverty, which is 19 percent of the population. So what is being done to combat this big problem? In *The New York Times* there was an article about what is being done by Mayor de Blasio. His plan is to preserve the affordability of 180,000 units and build 120,000 new ones. But the plan hasn't worked out, entirely. As a 2019 article on the website *Curbed* put it: "The mayor's housing plan has taken heat for building or preserving apartments that are mostly affordable to households with incomes at or above the average for a given neighborhood." Which is unfair, because the national definition of affordable housing is a household that can be obtained for 30 percent or less of its income. So, by this definition, a dwelling is considered "affordable" for low-income families if it costs less than 24 percent of the area median. De Blasio does not direct sources for the people that need housing.

People out in our city need our help, no matter what form it is in. The smallest penny to the largest bill. To half our lunch to all of our lunch. No one should be left out in the street with no guidance and help. My grandfather helped my mom out in any way he could and it meant the world to my mother and now to me. Do something to help in your city today.

SHEYLA JAVIER

YEARS AS MENTEE: 1

GRADE: Junior

BORN: Queens, NY

LIVES: Queens, NY

MENTEE'S ANECDOTE: *The first pieces of writing I shared with Shannon were a collection of poems I wrote freshman year. Little did I know I would be submitting them into the Scholastic Art & Writing Awards and later sharing them for other people to hear. I thank her for helping me find my voice through writing. Shannon encourages me to do my best when it comes to reaching deadlines, sharing my pieces, and really anything in general. She's always listening to the stories I share with her about school, my childhood, and what makes up the kind of person I am.*

SHANNON CARLIN

YEARS AS MENTOR: 5

OCCUPATION: Journalist

BORN: Ronkonkoma, NY

LIVES: Brooklyn, NY

PUBLICATIONS AND RECOGNITIONS:
Refinery29, Pitchfork, The Lily

MENTOR'S ANECDOTE: *Sheyla loves naps, which as someone who can't sleep once the sun comes up, I thoroughly respect. What I also respect is just how hard Sheyla pushes herself. Maybe it's because she was a competitive gymnast (!!!), but I believe it's just who she is. She's always striving to do better. Not only in her writing but everything. She set a goal to read her poetry out loud, and midway through the year, she did it. I'm so excited to see what else she accomplishes in the future. Who knows, she might even convince me to love naps, too.*

TWO SIDES

SHEYLA JAVIER

My inspiration for this piece came after having a deep conversation with someone I trust. I came to the realization that there are two different sides to everyone—including myself.

They say there are two sides to every story
The same goes for yourself
You have the side that everyone
Sees, knows, and perceives
The mask you unconsciously wear
The walls you hide behind
That cause you to
Hold your breath and bite your tongue
You have moments where you
Laugh with tears in your eyes
You're distracted
Psyched out
Your smile comes off so genuine
Yet you feel like it's forced
Even if it's just for a second
You also have the side that only you
See, know, and understand
The side that is
Completely unfiltered, raw, and real
You have
Flaws, insecurities, habits, quirks
You can't seem to get rid of
But you stand up to them like a
Gust of wind
At full force

In the middle of fall
Yet the bar is set so high
Expectations seem out of reach
The weight
Pressing down on you
This is the side that has you
Wrapped around its finger
Constantly lurking in the back of your mind
One second you seem to be
Soaring way above the clouds
The next
Underwater gasping for air
Your inner voice
Constantly torn between the two sides
Your conscious says it's okay to be
Double-sided.

JESSICA JIANG

YEARS AS MENTEE: 1

GRADE: Junior

BORN: Brooklyn, NY

LIVES: Brooklyn, NY

PUBLICATIONS AND RECOGNITIONS: Ned Vizzini Teen Writing Contest: Finalist; Scholastic Art & Awards: Silver Key, Honorable Mention

MENTEE'S ANECDOTE: *I don't believe in God, but I can believe, honestly, truly, that someone out there must be looking out for me, because Kelly has pulled me through my hardest times. From obsessing over chocolate-chip cookies to serious (Should we make eye contact? Awkwardddd, no thanks) conversations about family, Kelly has become more a friend than a mentor. Beside her, I can feel myself grow not only as a writer but also as a person as we shuffle through our childhood and as she (silently) judges me for not using a planner. As I plow through the world in the years to come, I'll always remember her motto: "SUGAR IS KEY!!!"*

KELLY MOFFITT

YEARS AS MENTOR: 1

OCCUPATION: Content Manager, Columbia University

BORN: St. Louis, MO

LIVES: Brooklyn, NY

PUBLICATIONS AND RECOGNITIONS: Producer, StoryCorps stories

MENTOR'S ANECDOTE: *I knew Jessica and I would get along the moment we met and geeked out over the Throne of Glass series and its tough-as-nails heroine, Celaena Sardothien. What I didn't realize is that over the hours we'd meet each week at the Center for Fiction, I'd find a true friend in such a singular writer. Jessica constantly surprises me with her candor, specificity, and vulnerability. Turns out Jessica is tough as nails too, yet her writing cuts to the soft, beating heart of a generation.*

THROMBOCYTOPENIA

JESSICA JIANG

"Thrombocytopenia" is a semiautobiographical poem that details the struggles of a health condition exacerbated by America's broken health-care system. Through the conglomeration of a child's worst fears, I hope to spur the need for change.

I see shadows on the back of my legs,
on the width of my arm and length of my body.
If I get lucky they blossom yellow,
but now they stay blue like the eyes of my doctor
when he tells me about treatments that don't really treat.
I prayed for the first time behind hospital walls that
isn't exactly a church but people find God here sometimes,
but why couldn't I? How can I live when all I see these days are
1.   white pills in orange bottles
2.   red blood in plastic tubes
3.   blue gloves covering steady hands
"It's okay close your eyes it'll be over soon I promise it'll be over"

just a little longer is a lie

"Immune thrombocytopenia is a genetic disease."
My mom looks at my dad, but my dad stares at the ground:
I can already hear the divorce papers being drawn.
"Do any of your family members have a history of low platelets?"
Grandparents were called and accusations assigned.
I see shadows behind his eyes and on the back of her thighs.
"We should begin talking about treatment plans."
I smell remnants of cigarette smoke even though he gave up
    smoking

when I was born. I guess my life is no longer worth that much.

"Though costly, your daughter would be given the best care
possible."

There are half-crescent indentations on the palms of his hands as
he runs

through the numbers in his bank account. He feels his wallet. It
is thin.

"NEXT TIME YOU START BLEEDING AND IT DOESN'T
STOP, CALL 911"

My mother pleads with the doctor for other options. Does the
hospital offer some

financial coverage? Are there other treatments that are less
expensive than this?

"MA'AM, YOU CAN NOT ATTACH DOLLAR SIGNS TO
YOUR DAUGHTER'S LIFE"

my life used to be worth more than this

"It's an autoimmune disorder" is ironic because it means
that my body decided to commit suicide even before I knew
just how badly life sucked if you:
1.   live in america
2.   don't have insurance
3.   don't have insurance and live in america
When the tax collectors came, my dad left but the bruises stayed
and so did the hospital bills and the bottles of antidepressants.
There are some things that a child should never get to hear like
the sobs
of my mother when she got down on her knees to beg him to
stay.
There are some things that a child should never get to see like the
eyes of my
father when he lies or the light of a late ambulance before
everything flickers out

MARIBEL JIMENEZ

YEARS AS MENTEE: 1

GRADE: Senior

BORN: Brooklyn, NY

LIVES: Bronx, NY

PUBLICATIONS AND RECOGNITIONS: Student, International Center of Photography's THE POINT

MENTEE'S ANECDOTE: *Meeting Meghan was exciting because I never had a mentor who is close to me and has seen the journey of my process of my photography and school. She taught me how to be open when it comes to writing. Being with her I learn so much, like how to edit my video for Girls Write Now and going to different places where I need to take the train. I was afraid to take the F, M, or Q, but I made it there on time and home safe. But now I'm not afraid anymore, because Meghan taught me to be strong and be open.*

MEGHAN McDONOUGH

YEARS AS MENTOR: 1

OCCUPATION: Video Journalist, *Quartz*

BORN: Stamford, CT

LIVES: Brooklyn, NY

PUBLICATIONS AND RECOGNITIONS: Producer, *RISK*, a 3-part video series for *Quartz*

MENTOR'S ANECDOTE: *The first time we met, Maribel showed me a portrait she took of a woman she met on the street and told me that photography basically allows her to travel the world without leaving her city. I'm so impressed by Maribel's openness and generosity of spirit. I've gotten to see firsthand how her creative work is the perfect vehicle for it, by allowing her to document the stories of the people she passes and capture the beauty she sees. This passion motivates me to see the world the same way, wherever I am.*

LET'S PLAY AROUND: A GAME OF SLEEP PARALYSIS

MARIBEL JIMENEZ

Sleep paralysis has been envisioned in art since as early as the 1700s, when it was described as a demonic visitation. But the fear it represents cannot play with women, because we are powerful and control our own dreams.

It's time to go to sleep.
Our dreams become nightmares, living in a bubble with fear
fear loves to play around and you're scared to see the reality
dreams are the longest two minutes of your life.

Now your body is half asleep and half awake
there is a hand wrapping around your neck
but you don't notice;
you are out of breath

People don't know if it is real or just a dream
blood covers your hand,
it's dripping, the blood
and the taste of blood is chili sauce

There is a gun in a hand with fear
It sparkles through the body;
the body becomes jello when you touch it.
Is it real or is the devil trying to play mind games?

Being afraid of the dark
it starts as a child

and humans think there is a shallow
and we go crazy.

The body is fighting to wake up
but it triggered your mind,
and when you wake up nothing happened.

Nightmares love to play with you

JADAH JONES

YEARS AS MENTEE: 1

GRADE: Senior

BORN: Lincoln, NE

LIVES: Bronx, NY

MENTEE'S ANECDOTE: *Girls Write Now is a great program that I would recommend everyone to join. My mentor Nikki is just as amazing a person as she is a writer. She has made an impact on me in my senior year of high school, helping me set deadlines and manage my time better (something I'm not amazing at) as I prepare for college. Recently, Nikki texted me, "Hey, sometimes, instead of making excuses, you can just do the work," and that has become my new mantra. Girls Write Now has made me better as a writer and a person.*

NIKKI PALUMBO

YEARS AS MENTOR: 4

OCCUPATION: Comedian and TV Writer

BORN: Union, NJ

LIVES: New York, NY

PUBLICATIONS AND RECOGNITIONS: *The New Yorker, McSweeney's, Reductress*

MENTOR'S ANECDOTE: *You'll know the second you read something written by Jadah. Her personality's all over it. It's effortless, raw, stream-of-consciousness, thoughtful, and impossible to predict. So our writing relationship has naturally followed that. Jadah lets the words fall out of her, and I stack them into an order that makes sense for the rest of us.*

NOT ANYMORE

JADAH JONES

*Women in the past fought for the rights we have now in our present.
And we'll continue that fight for the future. I wrote this poem to reflect
on the progress we've made.*

If only my ancestors could see me now
they'd smile and be proud
of me and my ability to think and work
outside the boundaries
men have built for us.

Empowered to push the limit
break the ceiling
shatter expectations
and not stand for anything
but everything
and run for something.
President?
"That's a man's job"
Not anymore.
Choosing a spouse?
"That's your father's decision"
Not anymore.
Be quiet?
"This is none of your business"
Not anymore.

Ruling our lives
one inch at a time

no one can take that away,
tomorrow, yesterday, today.

Our previous places in history:
humiliated
ignored
silenced
torn down
overlooked
rejected
yet
Not anymore.

RACHEL KELLY

YEARS AS MENTEE: 1

GRADE: Freshman

BORN: New York, NY

LIVES: Brooklyn, NY

PUBLICATIONS AND RECOGNITIONS: Eleanor Roosevelt Center at Val-Kill, Girls' Leadership Worldwide; Girl Scouts of Greater NY Leadership Institute

MENTEE'S ANECDOTE: *Lauren has transitioned to a new job, and even with increased social responsibilities, she still has made time to meet. We have FaceTimed and met in person. We always meet at least once a week. She loves to share her knowledge of how to build a story and often stops me from jumping too far ahead. She is also very easy to contact and always messages back. Thank you, Lauren, for being an awesome mentor!*

LAUREN THOMPSON

YEARS AS MENTOR: 1

OCCUPATION: Director; Executive Producer at *National Geographic*

BORN: Abington, PA

LIVES: Brooklyn, NY

PUBLICATIONS AND RECOGNITIONS: Emmy, *CNN*'s "United Shades of America" (Co–EP/Director), Telly Award, *This Is Happening* (EP)

MENTOR'S ANECDOTE: *Working with Rachel this year has been a true pleasure. We usually meet at Park Slope Public Library in Brooklyn for our weekly sessions. It's great because there are always new faces and lots of energy to get us going. Rachel is a joy to be around. She is a kind soul, a free spirit, and has a genuine laugh that bubbles to the surface. I really enjoyed learning about podcasting together and cocreating funny haiku. We also had fun collaborating on her multimedia piece about her favorite activity: ice-skating. I can't wait to see her creativity soar!*

A SNAPSHOT IN TIME

RACHEL KELLY

"A Snapshot in Time" is a story about June, a teenager who bonds with her grandmother and learns how far her love reaches.

It's Thanksgiving morning, and I flip through the musty old photo album in my grandmother's study. I admire the pictures of my mom and four aunties, but I admire the pictures of my grandmama the most. It's funny how we look so much alike. Seeing these photos, I sometimes feel like I'm seeing myself. Looking through these photo albums is one of my favorite things to do. Every time I look at them, I'm transported back in time.

I see a photo of my grandmama sleeping with hair curlers (the style in the '70s); another one of her picking up a telephone that was wired to the wall; and my favorite in this album, a photo of the bright red front door closing and Grandmama's favorite pair of blue spool high heels peeking out. These were photos taken by my mom and her sister Suzie when they got a hold of the prized Instamatic family camera. My mom told me that Grandmama got really angry at them after that, because developing the film was expensive.

I'm alone in the study room while Grandmama is cooking, and Tom, my older brother, is helping Mom clean up before everyone arrives for Thanksgiving dinner. I'm supposed to be doing homework, but I can never help looking at the photo albums whenever I'm in this room.

My favorite album is the one of their trip to Washington, D.C., where they marched for women's equality. I get out of my chair and am on my tiptoes, almost touching the album. I reach as far as I can for it and sit back down. I slowly open the album, and that's when I see my grandmama peek through the study door. I gasp and hold the album tight.

My grandmama walks into the room. "I didn't know you were interested in old photos." She sits down in the chair next to me. "You like the photos of the march?"

I nod.

"That day was so historic," she remarks. "Your mom, her sisters, and I went all the way to D.C. to be there. I even took them out of school. Their teachers thought I was crazy, but your grandpa and I knew it was the right thing to do."

"Wow, did Grandpa go? How come I don't see him in any of the pictures?" I ask.

"Oh, he wanted to go so badly, but right before we were going, he broke his leg. I wanted to stay with him in New York, but he made us go. His mom thankfully took care of him, since she also knew the significance of us going to the march."

"I thought you didn't drive?" I ask.

"No, I still don't," she replies sadly.

"How did you—"

She cuts me off. "We took a bus from New York with other people in the march. There were buses with loads of people going— but enough with this book. You see it all the time, and you've heard this story at least twenty times! I want to show you my favorite album." She proudly picks up a thin book all the way at the end. "Have you ever looked at this one?"

I shake my head no. I hadn't noticed it before because it was so small.

"I thought so. Here are the photos of you and your cousins. Memories from each time you came to visit. Look, this section is all photos of you, June."

I gasp at the sight of me holding up the poster that is the same poster in the photos of Grandmama at the march.

"When was that taken?" I ask.

"When you were two. Somehow you found it all on your own from under the couch."

"I thought you didn't have the poster anymore?"

"I don't." She sighs. She turns the page, and you could see Tom in the next photo ripping the poster into pieces while I was crying.

Then, the photo after that shows Tom and me in a full-blown tug-of-war for the poster.

"At a young age, you were always curious and stood up for your rights." Grandmama smiles. "It's so appropriate that you are carrying around that sign. I am so proud of how you have become such a strong-willed young lady and for all of the opportunities you will have, compared to the time of the march in D.C. I see a lot of me in you and hope that you will forge ahead in whatever you want to do, and not to let anything—or anyone—get in your way."

That Thanksgiving, I gave thanks to my grandmother, all of her stories, and all of the women before me who have paved the way for me to be all that I can be. Today, I realize that my grandmama is thankful for me, too—and all of the future girls who will stand up for gender equality and for themselves.

NORA KNOEPFLMACHER

YEARS AS MENTEE: 2

GRADE: Senior

BORN: New York, NY

LIVES: New York, NY

PUBLICATIONS AND RECOGNITIONS: Scholastic Art & Writing Awards: Silver Keys and Honorable Mentions

MENTEE'S ANECDOTE: *On Mondays, I'm most likely sitting across from Natalie at The Wing or any café we happen to find ourselves in. There's such a level of comfort and joy I feel whenever we meet. Although it's our first year as a pair, we have developed familiarity and ease with each other. Whether we're walking to the subway together, strolling through a gallery at MoMA, discussing a* Sex Education *episode, or I'm teaching her how to send effects on iMessage, there are always smiles. I am so thankful to be paired with her for my final year of high school!*

NATALIE DAHER

YEARS AS MENTOR: 2

OCCUPATION: Multiplatform Editor, *NowThis News*

BORN: Philadelphia, PA

LIVES: Brooklyn, NY

PUBLICATIONS AND RECOGNITIONS: *HuffPost, Lapham's Quarterly*, and *The Week*

MENTOR'S ANECDOTE: *Nora has been such a joy to work with this year and a very special part of my Mondays. She is beaming with creativity and a fountain of ideas, and she makes the writing process look easy. She's incredibly curious about the world around her, and I enjoyed being able to share experiences at MoMA, K-Town cafés, The Wing, slam poetry salon, and more. Nora shows the type of commitment and openness that it takes to thrive as a writer, and I can't wait to watch where she goes in college and beyond. :)*

THOSE WHO CAME BEFORE

NORA KNOEPFLMACHER

This short story is inspired by Mohsin Hamid's novel Exit West. *For Lana, the protagonist, taking her place in history means being the person who studies and gives a voice to the stories of those silenced.*

Her process had begun slowly. One day, while locking up, Lana searched the library stationery closet for a paper clip. Defeated and frustrated, she shut the door, unable to find the small piece of metal to secure the stack of attendance sheets together. As she leaned against the closing door, her eyes darted toward the locked closet. It always felt strange that the closet was seemingly ignored by the library faculty. The head librarian hadn't even mentioned its existence to Lana during her very thorough orientation. Lana jabbed each key on her keychain into the lock, convincing herself that this late-night scavenging was in desperate pursuit of a paper clip. The fourth and final key granted her access to the closet, and she obliged. A thin layer of dust coated the file cabinets that lined the narrow space. She pulled at one of the cabinets, surprised to feel it graze her leg and accept her invitation. What began as a harmless endeavor that night became a monthly, then weekly, and, finally, daily ritual.

In the dark room, she discovered a collection from the past. Specifically, sixty years ago—a past that not even her teacher Ms. Zee liked to discuss, a past that whispered Lana's name. This past told the story of war, of chaos, and of uncertainty. The government censored any remaining trace of this past, attempting to free Lana's country of the pain that once seeped through the sidewalk cracks. With each image, social media archive, and newspaper clipping, Lana grew closer to the silenced secrets of her ancestors.

Lana wasn't particularly fond of school, for she often felt out of place in one way or another. She began to notice this isolation and general social discomfort more as she grew older, departing from the yellow jubilance of youth that characterized her grade school years. She especially noticed the feeling now, in a classroom of chancellors' children, secured by their inherited safety net of trust funds and workless lives. Sometimes her peers could sense her lack of financial security, as if she were forced to wear a neon T-shirt every day adorned with the term "scholarship kid." Some days, her lack of wealth was plastered across her body—her fellow students' eyes lasering holes into her cardigan. But, other days, she felt like she could go hours without someone acknowledging her presence, as if she were submerged beneath an opaque haze.

History class was the only place in school where she did not contemplate other people's perceptions. In class, she became consumed by the stories of the past that Ms. Zee shared. Sometimes Lana felt as if she were the only student in the room who felt such overwhelming joy during Ms. Zee's lectures, which led her to believe that perhaps the class wasn't what she loved so passionately, but rather the study of history itself.

As a library assistant, she now devotes her weeks to the vast library that she once timidly walked through, dragging her fingers lightly across an endless row of dusty books. Now she has found friendship in the librarians—at first demure, but then animated— carpeted floors, and red wood tables. She has grown accustomed to the decrepit computer system and the faint kissing sounds of couples lingering in corners. She spends her breaks under the tickling warmth of the sunlit windows while dissecting collections of historical journals, textbooks, and sources, armed with her gold pen. She craves the moments spent long after closing hours where she huddles over the cabinets' contents. There, in the closet, she dedicates time to her self-designed project's aim of preserving and amplifying the voices enclosed in her country's history.

One image in particular brought her closer to this goal: a flimsy newspaper clipping with a blurred image of a man and a woman. She discovered the photograph during one of her early explorations of the closet's files, yet always returned to it. The pair in the photo sat unaware, huddled on a stoop under an apocalyptic sky. She would remove the clipped image from a stained manila folder, holding its corners tightly with her thumb and index fingers. Lana would study each pixel, forming a bond with the scrap of paper and the lives enclosed within it.

In her notebook, she observed the bravery wrapped in the black folds of the woman's robe or the man beside her, with his creased forehead, seeming to tell the story of a different place. Lana longed to understand these people, for they embodied lifetimes washed away by the fears of today. These people looked to Lana through the old photograph, requesting her assistance in ensuring that their story escaped from the borders of the tiny image, and she accepted.

ELI KOWAR

YEARS AS MENTEE: 1

GRADE: Senior

BORN: Bronx, NY

LIVES: Bronx, NY

PUBLICATIONS AND RECOGNITIONS: Scholastic Art & Writing Awards: Honorable Mention

MENTEE'S ANECDOTE: *When I first met Rachel, I was terrified we'd have nothing in common, but twenty minutes into our first pair meet, we just clicked. Whether it was me running late to our meets, or us making bad jokes, getting chased down by a security guard at the Met, arguing over* Star Wars, *and twinning for our pair photo, I've learned so much and grew from our pair relationship. I can't wait to use this experience to grow my writing, and I hope to maintain this beautiful friendship in the near future.*

RACHEL LUDWIG

YEARS AS MENTOR: 1

OCCUPATION: Literary Agent Assistant

BORN: Cincinnati, Ohio

LIVES: New York, NY

MENTOR'S ANECDOTE: *When I first met Eli, it was Halloween and he was dressed up as his favorite pro wrestler, Orange Cassidy: shades indoors and full light-washed denim. My first thought was that this was a person worth knowing! From writing poems about Icarus to laughing our way through the galleries of the Met to catching up over a spicy McChicken and Sprite, it's been my privilege to spend time with this young artist. I am incredibly excited to see where his poetic talents will lead him and how his writing will continue to develop.*

ICARUS ASCENDING

ELI KOWAR

I've always been fascinated by the story of Icarus and how his fall has been portrayed, comparing him to myself. I wanted to showcase my point of view, along with a side of the story no one's really considered.

They call me Icarus
And tell me my story was doomed from the start
When I was young,
I heard whispers of the one,
Who almost flew higher than the sun.

I heard of how his wings of wax
Melted, dripping like gold down his back
How he gasped for air
During his dying fall
How he grasped for the feathers
As they drifted down
How he struggled to float
As the tide swallowed him whole
How he drowned in the clear water
As the waves glittered, and he sunk down
Forever lost, now one with the sea.

They forget who he was,
Before he fell.
They forget his crooked smiles
And his sun-kissed hair
His gleaming eyes,
And his dream to fly.
They forget that he was brilliant

Much like his father.
They forget what he once could have been,
That he was once flesh and blood,
Now he lies forgotten, a lesson on mortality.

Icarus was just a boy,
But I am so much more
I am a legacy of the gods
Who once walked the earth.
And if I fall, I'll be glad,
I have no fear,
For I'll relish the fall
It means I once flew.
My name will be branded in the clouds
And will burn me into history.

Icarus was just a myth,
But I will be a legend.
He was admired by the gods
But I'll be treasured by the world
With golden wings and starry eyes.
He will no longer suffer,
I've come to take his place.
I will fall, as all things must,
I'll rewrite the end of this story.
No one will fly higher than me.

ALICE KRESBERG

YEARS AS MENTEE: 1

GRADE: Sophomore

BORN: Seoul, South Korea

LIVES: Queens, NY

MENTEE'S ANECDOTE: *Amelia, my mentor, and I always meet at this one coffee shop in Williamsburg, Brooklyn. It's always a struggle to find a table and pick something to eat. Our conversations about writing can be a bit weird, such as this one conversation we had about an octopus who was a librarian. The customers sitting next to us probably think we're crazy and usually give us some side eyes.*

AMELIA POSSANZA

YEARS AS MENTOR: 1

OCCUPATION: Publicist

BORN: Bryn Mawr, PA

LIVES: Brooklyn, NY

MENTOR'S ANECDOTE: *Alice and I first connected over her cats. She has two—Lola and Charlie—and I've got one. As we continued to meet for our writing sessions, though, I quickly realized that we also share a love of sitting quietly to write (often while eating brownies!) and playfully building on each other's prompts. Alice's imagination is quick to leap into other worlds, whether she's casually describing her mother as an eight-armed librarian in conversation or writing a story about a girl who can speak, not just to wolves, but to every animal in the kingdom. Yet her writing is always grounded in this world and shows us our surroundings in a new light. Hers is a voice that we all need to hear.*

THE GIRL WHO SPEAKS MILLIONS OF LANGUAGES

ALICE KRESBERG

This piece is about a girl who can talk to animals and is meant to show how she struggles to find her identity.

MIRA'S POV

Seven years ago, she wandered from the woods and stood curiously in front of my house. Today, she had just turned nine years old.

She'd walked out of the forest wearing just a dirty rag. She wasn't injured, however. I figured maybe she had wandered from her own home, so I called the police about a missing child. They said no missing child fit her description. Knowing she had wandered from the woods, I decided to look around in the woods a few days after that call. Weirdly, I found no sign of human life. I gave up on trying to find anything out about Arden's life after that. When I asked what her name was, she didn't respond. So I decided to call her Arden.

It took her a while to start speaking. She didn't know any English. The first year she stayed with us, she was silent most of the time. I had a few stray cats at the time and two of the most energetic dogs, who made a huge racket throughout the night as they fought and chased each other around the house. One night, I found the dogs and cats all curled up, fast asleep, around Arden. Astounded, I took a photo to remember the weird occurrence. I had a younger daughter, Lena, at the time, but Arden paid no attention to her.

Arden came downstairs with her hair all frizzy. Not far behind her, the Saint Bernards Arvis and Arti followed her.

"Ms. Mira, Avis is hungry and so is Nora," she announced. Nora was one of my cats who wasn't the most fit cat in the world. Recently, I'd actually put her on a diet. Avis stared at me with puppy eyes.

"No more. I fed you just an hour ago," I told Avis. Avis trudged away and collapsed on a couch.

"Arden, come here. I have something for you," I whispered to her excitedly. She followed me to the backyard, where I had left her gift. Her eyes glistened as she ran to the big animal and gave it a huge hug. I'd gotten her a horse, knowing the most important things to her were animals.

"You can play with her later, Arden. Come inside and let's eat," I said, opening the back door. She followed me inside the house, and we sat around the small wooden table.

"Happy birthday, Sis!" Lena said to Arden, who smiled and thanked her quietly.

After breakfast, Arden dashed upstairs before running back out to her horse.

"I'll be back later, Ms. Mira!" she called out, halfway out the back door. The door closed with a painful squeak.

ARDEN'S POV

There was no time to waste. I had waited for this moment for so long. Walking on foot had never got me anywhere close to it, even when I had Avis and Arti with me. Now I had the opportunity to search the whole area. *What's your name?* I asked the horse. *Faye,* she responded. *Okay, Faye, let's go fast,* I commanded. Faye galloped through the woods. I didn't know if our meeting spot was gone or not. Flames had taken over the forest when I'd left.

I reached the stream, which was now clogged with leaves and tree branches. The rock was still there. I hopped off of Faye's back and climbed onto the rock. *Wait for me here, Faye,* I told the horse. I left the meeting spot and searched for any living creature. A few rabbits rustled in the distance. *Excuse me, have you seen any wolves around here?* I called out to them. *Yes, but they're caged up,* one of them told me. I asked them where they were caged up and quickly returned to Faye.

We arrived at the site where the wolves were. I saw Cody, Nora, Aspen, and Atlas behind the wired fence. They didn't seem to be in pain, but they all had bandages on them. Cody's hind leg was wrapped up, and Nora had a huge wrap on her torso. Someone was missing, however. Lexi was nowhere to be seen. *Cody, where is Lexi and what are you all doing there?* I asked him. His ears twitched, and he turned to look at me slowly. *Lexi isn't with us. We got split up when she was carrying you through the fire,* he explained. I stood there in shock. Cody and the rest of the wolves had come to the fence to speak with me. Suddenly, a lady appeared. *Go,* Cody told me, urgently. I climbed onto Faye's back and galloped off.

MIRA'S POV

I don't think I was surprised when I found out that Arden could talk to animals. I simply asked her, and she had said *yes.* News sure spreads fast, though. Almost everyone in this small area knows about Arden's ability. Some lady reported seeing Arden talking to wolves she was taking care of. Arden is sixteen now, and slowly, she is becoming known as the girl who can speak millions of languages.

CAITLIN LEVY

YEARS AS MENTEE: 1

GRADE: Sophomore

BORN: New York, NY

LIVES: New York, NY

MENTEE'S ANECDOTE: *I still remember how excited I was when I first met Celia! I saw that she was my mentor, and I ran up to her and gave her a big hug. I was just so grateful to have her. It still feels like that when I see her every week. I feel so privileged to have someone who is not only so kind and giving but also someone to look up to, as a woman who's carved out such an amazing path for herself. She is a mentor in every sense of the word. I can't explain how magical it is to have someone who believes in the beauty of your dreams. She encourages me to believe in myself and point my eyes to the stars. I'm so lucky to have her.*

CELIA ALICATA

YEARS AS MENTOR: 1

OCCUPATION: Founder, BrighterGood

BORN: Hartland, CT

LIVES: New York, NY

MENTOR'S ANECDOTE: *I warmly recall first meeting Caitlin. Her enthusiasm was simply infectious. Whether we're poring over our favorite works or sharing personal updates from our different lives, there's a common quest for meaning, purpose, and individuality that we share. Caitlin is steadfast in the belief that her generation is unencumbered by societal pressures for women. With the strength of character that she possesses, Caitlin will flourish—in her writing and in life.*

BROKEN GLASS/NOT YET FORMED

CAITLIN LEVY

I've been thinking a lot lately about being myself—and what that means for me as a young woman. I wanted to write something that reflected being free in my ability to dream and imagine any life for myself as a girl in the twenty-first century.

She stumbled through cobblestone streets of baskets of citrus, ripe with spring and the gentle touch of strangers, streets of green and gold from small-town trees, and the urban lights that peek through. Her whole body gasped at the familiarity of it all, like she had always meant to be in this rural pocket of America, but the feeling never quite passed through some white blood cell deep down. It was the summer before ninth grade. From the ages of four through eight, she had imagined, quite vividly, that she was destined to stay as a *city girl*, that she would pursue some career sentencing criminals and climb to positions far higher than that ladder given to small children. Pieces of broken glass surrounded her. They gleamed from the smiles of her nana, from politicians who came before her, and from young women who had sought to shatter something above. She wanted to pick them up and fit the pieces, each little curve and ridge of glass, into each other. They could make a mosaic, one of stone and color, and make her reflection clear.

It was this little interlude of sea salt and sleep in which she teetered on the edge of high school and wondered if this life she imagined belonged to her. She began to dream of something that may be different. Maybe a life that felt right in her hands and feet. She thought about helping people who struggle with sadness. She wanted to lift people from the rubble of ceilings that were crashing down. She dreamed of mothering guinea pigs. She wanted to smell piles and piles of tattered books and pages that she could write all over. She thought of dancing and karaoke at little bars down the street until her hair was clouds of gray. The girl swam in loose-leaf homework, stories in pencil of young women who were property. She had been told, as a child, of women cramped in spheres of influence and worlds not made for them. Her eyes were also alight with stories in the news of women who fluttered to heights, like blue jays and swallows of a broken country. Politicians and paramedics, women who could finally pursue the ancient prophecy of the American Dream. Their hearts beat collectively to the song of their ambition. But she knew she was not exactly these women. Their minds were unalike, as unique as eyebrows and insects and planets. She was not an expectation. The world belonged to her, and no one would pickpocket her life away. This, to her, was some flower in a dark forest, a bit of rain in a barren place. It was the twenty-first century, and in any weird and wonderful way she liked, she could individually dream.

MAI LISTOKIN

YEARS AS MENTEE: 1

GRADE: Junior

BORN: New York, NY

LIVES: New York, NY

MENTEE'S ANECDOTE: *My mentor Emily and I have been contemplating some exciting manifestations of my emerging voice through the exploration of historical fiction and poetry. Emily is a constant inspiration to me, and one of the reasons we clicked right from the start is her incredible ability to unearth and refine my message with her experience as a published author. We navigate through a vast ocean of abstract and visual concepts, humor and pathos, hope and despair, and the ability to traverse between safe ground and literary courage. I am so glad that we have found a creative shore where we can sit and dream together.*

EMILY NEUBERGER

YEARS AS MENTOR: 1

OCCUPATION: Writer

BORN: Long Island, NY

LIVES: Brooklyn, NY

PUBLICATIONS AND RECOGNITIONS: *A Tender Thing* (Putnam, 2020)

MENTOR'S ANECDOTE: *Mai and I meet every week at Girls Write Now, and she consistently inspires me as she balances a heavy school workload, a job, her family, and many friendships—all while turning out beautiful work every time she writes. She has such a kind demeanor and, despite lots of stressful obligations, approaches her challenges with positivity. We both enjoy writing and reading historical fiction.*

GOODBYE BERLIN

MAI LISTOKIN

My family's suffering in Russia, Poland, and Germany during World War II prompted me to reflect on the values of courage, perseverance, hope, and the price of war. My great-grandmother's ordeal in occupied Russia during the Battle of Stalingrad inspired this story, about a single mother's sacrifice amid the inferno of war.

The months rolled on, and Berlin's Jewish-owned shops, which had once bubbled with the chatter of customers, had closed, the little bells on the doors never to be heard again. Slander and insults against the Jews were painted across the wooden doors and windows. A blanket of invisible hatred was building, and an early winter seemed to engulf Berlin in a frozen feast of silence. By mid-August, Germany's Nuremberg synagogue was destroyed by the Nazis, and Max's little kitchen table radio kept on spewing dreadful news. In early November, his mother, Emma, a hardworking single mother and chemist by profession, came home with a strange fabric yellow star declaring "Jude." She told Max he would have to wear it to school every day, pinned to his shirt.

On the chilly night of November 10, as Max was doing his homework, the loud noise of men shouting and explosions firing suddenly filled the air. Against his mother's orders, he climbed the narrow staircase to the roof of their building and gazed out at his city. A cold, harsh light glowed from the glittering sea of broken glass. Up and down the dark alleys people were rushing in every possible direction, casting rocks and metal rods against the windows of the storefronts. His mouth dropped when he saw the kosher butcher's store being crashed and shamelessly broken into—someone was painting a red swastika on the wooden door. Close to midnight, Max's mother rushed through the door, sweating profusely, horrified as she cradled her son in her arms. "Max, are you okay?" It was only the next day that Max and his mom learned of the full extent of that tragic night. They would smell the heavy smoke hovering over their city and feel the disturbing pain of broken glass underfoot for days to come. He sensed that his youth had abruptly come to a halt, the honey color of his fond childhood memories fading into gray.

As it happens in life, the solution for Max arrived from an unexpected angle. It was Ingrid, Emma's friend and lab coworker, who hatched a careful plan to help spare Max. Ingrid, whose own son, Hans, had passed away of typhoid a few months before, had found solace in the idea that she would help her friend's son escape. She had requested transit papers for her and Hans under the pretense of seeking medical help for her ailing son in England. Once she received the papers and train tickets, she masterfully altered Hans's picture to resemble Max's photo. Together, Ingrid and Max would make their way to England, where she would deliver her friend's son, now Hans Schmidt, to his uncle in Liverpool.

The dreadful day of departure had finally arrived. Ingrid, dressed for the journey and carrying a worn suitcase, met Emma and Max at their house. Emma had been helping Max practice his new identity as "Hans" for the past month. To avoid the smallest suspicion during the journey to England, he was to speak only if approached and spoken to by the German authorities.

Emma impulsively decided to follow Ingrid and Max to the busy Friedrichstrasse Station. But now, after an intense month of planning, when the moment to let Max go had arrived, a terrifying fear engulfed Emma. What if Ingrid and Max were exposed and arrested? All of a sudden, as she watched Ingrid holding her son's hand as they approached the platform, her heart skipped a beat—what if Ingrid simply stole her son and raised him as her own? But then she felt a sharp pang of guilt for even questioning the noble intentions of her longtime friend. Max seemed nervous and suddenly so small and vulnerable; her heart ached. From the corner of the ticket office, Emma observed Ingrid handing her transit papers to the policeman by the train tracks. She drew her breath in sharply as she noticed how the policeman gazed intently at Max's face, matching it to his forged passport picture, and back to her son's sweaty face. She mumbled a silent prayer, but Ingrid was calm and assertive, and was finally signaled to move forward and enter the train. Ingrid and Max climbed into the train car. Max's eyes searched frantically for his mom through the dusty windows. Their eyes locked in relief just as the long and doleful sound of the horn echoed into the coming evening. Max planted a final kiss on the window, his small palms open in despair on both sides of his face, which was pressed against the glass. Was he crying? She couldn't tell from the distance, but she could swear he was mumbling "Mama" again and again, like a sweet promise, or a prayer. He waved sadly behind the glass as the train pulled out of the station. Max was no longer able to see his mother through the hazy smoke, hovering like a cloud over the ruins of a burning city, his train snaking along the tracks through a burning Berlin.

GIFTBELLE LOMOTEY

YEARS AS MENTEE: 1

GRADE: Senior

BORN: Bronx, NY

LIVES: Bronx, NY

MENTEE'S ANECDOTE: *There is a saying that goes "Good things come in small packages." I did not give much attention to the saying until I met my mentor. But I now think of it every time I see my mentor. Since the day we met, she has filled my life with light. Bad days are not so bad because I know that I will be in her presence. I have the great honor of calling her my mentor but the even greater honor of calling her my friend. Our spoken words may have helped build the first connection, but our connection grew deeper from the many words we have written in texts, in emails, and, most important, on paper.*

JORDANA NARIN

YEARS AS MENTOR: 1

OCCUPATION: Speech Writer, West Wing Writers

BORN: Los Angeles, CA

LIVES: New York, NY

PUBLICATIONS AND RECOGNITIONS: *The New York Times*

MENTOR'S ANECDOTE: *I can't help but feel like I'm boasting when I tell people that Gifty is my mentee. She's a ray of sunshine, a standout soul, a once-in-a-generation fount of wisdom who makes me better for knowing her. In Gifty, I've gotten not just a little sister but a lifelong friend. I'm ever grateful to Girls Write Now for introducing us, and immensely excited to see where the next stage of life takes her.*

WHERE I'M FROM

GIFTBELLE LOMOTEY

In this piece you are about to read, I am telling you more about who I am and exploring all the layers of my identity. I use the words "I am" to highlight the different places, physical and emotional, that have made me who I am today.

I am from countless early mornings and late nights
Waking up every day to be better than who I was yesterday
Working every day, to put myself in a position to be successful
    and succeed
Working every day just to be better

I am my parents' greatest accomplishment
Who would have thought their union would have made blood
    run through the body of a Queen?
Who would have thought their by-product would be a young
    Queen?
Who would have thought they would create such a Powerful and
    Beautiful being?

I am from Ghana and Nigeria, the land of the original creators
    and inhabiters of the earth
I am from a land filled with beautiful brown bodies, a culture so
    rich
If culture was currency I would need no money to survive
I am from a place where my people take care of each other, even
    at the cost of our own lives
I am from royalty
I have enough power in my veins to make the earth shake and
    bow before me

I am also from the South Bronx, and here's a few things I can tell
  you
In my Bronx we cannot see the stars at night
To remind us of how far we can go and what we can achieve
In my Bronx most people are bunched up in 5x5 containers

Oops! I really meant apartments
In my Bronx living in a roach- and rodent-infested home is a
  norm
But
Let me tilt your head the other way
In my Bronx you can travel to the other side of the world without
  having a passport
All you have to do is knock on your neighbor's door and say
  "Hello"
But be careful, this is still New York.
In my Bronx people move their tongues in so many different ways
You would think we have three tongues
In my Bronx people Hustle like they know they're dying
  tomorrow
Hard work is a must and we value life like it is a Treasure
I am from hard work and many prayers
I bent my knees many nights and kneeled over my bed
And prayed for everything I have now
And to be everything I am now
I am from the hardest parts of my childhood
And the most beautiful parts of my surroundings
I ultimately and favorably am from me.

JADE LOZADA

YEARS AS MENTEE: 3

GRADE: Senior

BORN: New York, NY

LIVES: New York, NY

PUBLICATIONS AND RECOGNITIONS: Scholastic Art & Writing Awards: Gold Key; American Voices Nominee; 2019 Climate Speaks Spoken Word Finalist; *Gotham Gazette*

MENTEE'S ANECDOTE: *I will always be grateful to have Carol as my mentor. Our relationship over the last three years has grown into more than writing. Carol's listening ear and advice empower me to seize opportunities and risk my comfort for growth. I will miss our Thursday afternoons at Cafe Lalo, but I will never lose the confidence and ambition she inspired in me.*

CAROL HYMOWITZ

YEARS AS MENTOR: 3

OCCUPATION: Journalist, Author, Fellow at Stanford Longevity Center, Mentor-Editor at The OpEd Project

BORN: New York, NY

LIVES: New York, NY

PUBLICATIONS AND RECOGNITIONS: *The Wall Street Journal; Bloomberg*

MENTOR'S ANECDOTE: *I'm so proud of all Jade has achieved. She has grown enormously as a poet, essayist, and journalist, and written deeply about such themes as bridging her Latina roots and American upbringing and the effect of climate change on minority communities. Jade has performed her poetry at the Apollo Theater, published in* Medium, *and become a leader in the climate movement. I'm going to miss our coffee dates (hot chocolate for her, latte for me), but I'll continue to be inspired by Jade's risk-taking, her talents, and her caring for others.*

THE CLIMATE CRISIS NEEDS A STORY

JADE LOZADA

I first joined the New York City Youth Climate Strike Coalition in July 2019. In the company of such impassioned, optimistic youth activists, I quickly realized that the climate crisis is not about numbers. It is a human story, with a human solution.

I sat facing a blindingly blank-white computer screen at midnight. This was not a particular point of concern for me; all of my best writing began with this standoff between my mind, silently grappling with competing imagery and the nuances of style, and an untitled Google Document daring me to commit to any one expression of my thoughts. Anxiety-inducing images of wildfires, hurricanes, and doomsday newscasts flashed through my head. All of them related to the climate crisis, the theme of the spoken-word poetry competition to which I was applying, but none of them illuminated its personal toll. Staring at my screen, I realized that the climate crisis was comprehensible to me only when I was confronted with a victim's story, and that is what I could compel an audience with. Storytelling transformed my writing into activism.

I wrote my poem about a girl of color who comes to realize that the climate crisis is subtly intertwined in her own life. Pollution has given her asthma, and extreme heat has burned down blocks of her city neighborhood. "Babygirl" is a story of the disproportionate effects of climate change on communities of color, and climate change's significant consequences in my own life.

In retrospect, my first undertaking in climate activism began with this midnight poetic appeal to myself. I could read dozens of news articles and scientific studies detailing the crisis, but no expiration date on my Earth empowered me. A story answered how I could take action, rather than wait for change—or disaster—to arrive on my doorstep. Months later, in July, I said as much at my first New York City climate organizing meeting with Fridays for Future, the global school strike movement for climate action. I was invited to join the Core Committee of fifteen youth organizers as a representative of the Arts Committee. In the race to plan New York City's Global Climate Strike on September 20, I confronted the challenges of a grassroots movement with storytelling.

As difficult as it was for me to comprehend a permanent alteration to the global food supply or seismic change in my city's weather, it was harder to convince a potential striker that their actions could change the outcome. The climate crisis was perceived as a threat looming on the horizon, and our September strike needed personal investment in the lives of those already affected. The Core Committee invited members of frontline communities to speak at our rallies, from a survivor of both Hurricanes Sandy *and* Maria to indigenous activists whose Ecuadorian village faced deforestation. We told our own stories, too: the indigenous activist who moved to New York after her village in Mexico was flooded; the activist whose asthmatic lungs could not withstand the California Camp Fire smoke; and me, the activist who did not plan on being an activist a few months ago.

I learned from my fellow activists, as well as my own poetry, that we can rewrite the narrative of a crisis. The young are victims of climate inaction until we portray ourselves differently, and climate change will destroy our way of life until we paint it as an opportunity to reform society. In many ways, the narrative is all a youth activist has. I am not a voter, nor a decision-maker in the institutions from which I demand transition. However, I can shape my message to my listener. Stories inspire radical change by finding what resonates within each bystander. For me, it was the climate injustice suffered by low-income, often minority communities through environmentally damaging projects. For my audience, there is no telling. Yet whatever our climate stories may be, they possess untapped potential to realize the goals of the movement.

PILAR LU-HEDA

YEARS AS MENTEE: 2

GRADE: Sophomore

BORN: New York, NY

LIVES: Brooklyn, NY

MENTEE'S ANECDOTE: *This is my second year at Girl Write Now and writing with my mentor. I was so scared at the beginning of last year that I wasn't going to fit in well in the community or with my mentor. With that said, I feel so lucky to have a mentor like Catherine, who understands me and supports all of my creative choices. There's never been a week where I don't look forward to our meeting, which is usually over cookies and filled with laughter. She helps me feel reassured about my writing, which always feels stronger after her patient help. I'm certain my place in history will be secured by how I've grown within the two years I've been in the Girls Write Now community.*

CATHERINE SANTINO

YEARS AS MENTOR: 2

OCCUPATION: Freelance Writer

BORN: Albany, NY

LIVES: New York, NY

PUBLICATIONS AND RECOGNITIONS: *Ladygunn, Glam*

MENTOR'S ANECDOTE: *Over the past two years, I've had the privilege of watching Pilar grow and explore her incredible creativity. She's far more mature, well spoken, and wise than I was as a fifteen-year-old, and I know she has an incredibly bright future ahead of her. I'm proud to be her mentor, and I'm proud of all the work she's done this year, including this print anthology piece.*

A GATHERING STORM

PILAR LU-HEDA

I wrote this piece as a 200-word exercise but ended up liking it enough to continue it. Like it or not, here goes:

We made fairy houses out of cardboard when the world was shiny and new. Rain boots sunk into freshly dewy grass and fingertips grazed the mellow May breeze. Gates swung and smiled upon our eager faces. The world was our stage. We found happiness in simpler things. Promises and tree houses. Melting ice cream and friendship bracelets. Woven with much more than craft strings and plastic charms, they held our pasts and what we wished our futures would be. But threads do not stay bound forever and frays turn to rips. Now we sit under the willow, the sunlight dappled through the branches. All is forgiven. The wind and birds sing together in our moment, weaving in and out of harmony. They sing an old song. I know the tune but not the words. The notes creep into my mind, erasing all other thoughts. I feel panic rise in my chest. Why can't I think? The breeze shushes my mind, reprimanding it for not remaining idle and letting the light soak into my body. The air smells like fresh earth. A newly placed bracelet glints softly in the splatters of light. When was the last time I was outside like this? Somehow I don't care to find the details in the back of my mind. Am I awake? We are blissfully unaware of the storm lurking and threatening to swallow our world until it arrives. The flowers between my fingers curl away, shrinking into dust. A hand tugs mine and we run. To what? I can't remember. The dust swirls around us, like a sick tornado, chasing me and diving away. I try to swat it away but it circles my head. The tune grows stronger. I look up but the swirl of dust attacks me as the tune surges to a pulsing ring. The bracelet rips and flutters into the dust. I reach out. Where are you?

The tears don't have time to fall. The ringing subsides. Silence. I'm awake. The clock above the window ticks on, dragging out the minutes. The room is remarkably quiet; the only noises are the clock's steady ticking and the drowsy drizzle of rain sliding down the roof. As if I don't already know the answer, I pull my wrist from the tangle of covers. No bracelet.

LORENA MACA GARCIA

YEARS AS MENTEE: 2

GRADE: Junior

BORN: Bronx, NY

LIVES: Bronx, NY

MENTEE'S ANECDOTE: *Meeting with Candace on Fridays is always something I look forward to, especially our many fun conversations and varied shared interests that make up the majority of our meeting time. She is my number-one cheerleader and I know she will always come through when I need her because I trust her, I can count on her. She understood what I went through when there were some tough times during my home life this year. I am forever thankful for whoever paired Candace and I together, because they made such a perfect match.*

CANDACE CUNARD

YEARS AS MENTOR: 2

OCCUPATION: High School English Teacher, Little Red School House and Elisabeth Irwin High School

BORN: Laguna Beach, CA

LIVES: New York, NY

MENTOR'S ANECDOTE: *My Friday afternoons with Lorena are a highlight of my week. Whether we're meeting at our usual café in the South Bronx, or venturing out in search of specialty pens or Japanese bookstores, I know our conversations will range as far and wide as our meeting locations. Even in a difficult year, Lorena's confidence in her voice continues to grow. As she told me: "I don't write because I think I'm going to be a professional published writer someday. I write because I don't want to fall apart . . . Also, I'm really good at it." (And, yeah, she is!)*

RUNAWAY GIRL

LORENA MACA GARCIA

Writing this piece was an outlet for my internal and external struggles when things were at a low point in my home life. I figuratively escaped by writing something that closely resonated with what I was feeling at that time.

Runaway. Run away from this lifeless body beneath me, stranded on this deserted yet not really deserted island, especially when surrounded by a vast collection of blue crystals, shadows lurking in the dark. Unknown tales that corner the very air around me, while I jog toward the confusing pathways that present themselves in my line of sight. Entering an endless maze in my own thoughts, drowning the forsaken visions of the past. Feeling the wind respond to my inkling of a correct makeshift road that has never been touched, yet I know deep within it's the correct choice. The littering of rocks and pebbles underneath my feet stab me as I hastily walk, hoping as I have always done to be rid of the fear that is the embodiment of me—once again afraid of those shadows that are always in alliance with the dark coming to life, and what's beneath them. Letting go of reason, or more likely losing grasp of anything that is left of my sanity. I run. I run toward the crystal-blue gems that lay about with no care, just being in tune with the tranquility of the sky, having no fear to reach the outskirts of their larger collection of bodies across the globe. Feeling the wind cutting through my raggedy hair where it once was silky smooth, where anyone could slip their fingers in and go straight through like it was never there. Having been so desirable, each strand reached the end of my slim waist and the beginning of my small portions of flesh that I had always been ashamed of. Now my hair is cut down to the tips of my ears, being starved to where the ends of my bones look unsightly.

Stripping my face of any grain of dirt I once had while lying on the ground, emotionless for the duration of hours as the only sort of warmth came from the earth itself. Recalling the Earth as she once brought me tremendous comfort, for she shielded me, offered me the fruits of her hard yet natural labor in edible leaves and berries. She was my own mother and the animals that were her children were my siblings. Having the need for knowledge and hunger driving the base of my mindset, I learned from my brothers and sisters. They did not think of me as an outsider, for they accepted me. Intellectuals would jump to the conclusion that my siblings were dangerous since they were animals with no morals, no customs, but I knew better. I recalled the skills I have gained along my path to salvation regardless of whether the end destination was Death herself. As I continue, the rocky road transforms while easing its way toward a bark-covered road and letting the leaves of old, the forest of ancients, climb down from above. Letting themselves be free, just to have a tangible taste of feeling as if they were flying. However, when they do land there is no celebration from up above or down below, only the feet of many pressing on them as I do now. If you were to ever murder such a tremendous giant, only those with no soul, count the rims; they are the only ones that surpass the shackles of time. Scaling over broken pillars of strength as I jump over logs, even if my bones jump back with such ferocity as I continue. The smaller, carved-out logs covered in moss that house many living things including myself at one point in time, during the not-knowing.

Not knowing how this bleak tale ends, this story of mine. Known to the world as just a runaway girl. Yet in some strange shape or form I'm free in every possible being. Connected to the trees, connected to the earth, the wind, and the waters, my form of reality has changed perspective. I go back to what I thought I was meant to be, just a normal girl, walking the streets with her too-naïve eyes, her too-big heart. Yet now I prosper as many have done in the past, and will continue to do so in this near future.

Having her dreams shattered yet never deterred from her wayward path as so many have done and seem to do. I say a little prayer for those who have truly loved me to seek comfort and protect against the judgment in this world I have encountered too early in this short life.

LYLA MALCOMSON

YEARS AS MENTEE: 1

GRADE: Junior

BORN: Queens, NY

LIVES: Queens, NY

MENTEE'S ANECDOTE: *Alikay and I hit it off the first day we met! She is so lively and bright every time we hang out, and we both have the same sarcastic tone that I love. I am so fascinated by her career and her college experience, which she never fails to give me amazing advice about. She is an inspiration to me: a strong woman who is always determined to improve her writing. From bonding over coffee and croissants to discovering a new café every week, I am so grateful for her help in this journey of mine. I can't wait to call her up in ten years and fill her in on my life!*

ALIKAY WOOD

YEARS AS MENTOR: 3

OCCUPATION: Digital Editor, *Guideposts*

BORN: Sacramento, CA

LIVES: Queens, NY

MENTOR'S ANECDOTE: *My first thought when I met Lyla was: This person is way too cool to hang out with me. Spending every Sunday morning caffeinating together has only confirmed that Lyla has the confidence and drive I dreamed of as a teenager. I'm consistently impressed with her intelligence, curiosity, and honesty. She pushes herself to participate in workshops, challenge herself in her writing, and to dream big about her future. I'm so proud of how much she's grown in these past few months and can't wait to see her take over the world.*

THE DAY I FELL IN LOVE

LYLA MALCOMSON

This is dedicated to my boyfriend, who helped me overcome something I didn't know I could get over: my insecurities. It's also dedicated to myself, as I am slowly learning to love myself more and more every day.

The day I fell in love. It was a gorgeous, sunny day in November. While the weather was perfect, my mood was the opposite. I was extremely self-conscious that day, more than normal. At school, I could feel every single pair of eyes staring at my face—at my breakouts. This might not be a big deal to some, but for me, I have to hide my face. I've gotten pretty good at perfectly covering my face with my hair, turning to the side slightly so no one notices it. And that day, my skin was at its lowest point. All I wanted was to just go home so no one would see it. Although I'd never dare tell anyone I feel this way, because it's embarrassing.

Well, that day my mom was taking me to the dermatologist. She picked me up in front of the school. My boyfriend walked me to the car, greeted my mother, and kissed me goodbye. He knew I was upset, and my mood was off, but I wouldn't tell him why. But as we were about to drive off, he asked, "Do you mind if I come with?" I wasn't so sure. I knew the dermatologist would take off my face makeup and pick at my skin. He would see my skin bare naked, all red and gross. I just couldn't let him see that. But on the other hand, I thought he would make me feel better. His presence was all I needed for my mood to lighten. So I hesitantly said sure, and he jumped in the car.

When the doctor called me in, my mom and I walked in and they did what they usually do. Once they finished up, I walked outside. I saw him smile that big smile of his. But I looked away. I tried to hide my face using my hair. He took my hand, and we walked to the car. He didn't let go of my hand the entire car ride. I couldn't believe it. He just saw my skin like this, with no makeup, and he really didn't care? I started to worry less; at one point I forgot why I was even upset. He was next to me, there to protect me.

When we got to my house, he sat next to me and just held me in his arms. He picked up my face, his hand cupping my chin. I couldn't bear to make eye contact with him, up close. But I saw his big, brown eyes and I swear, as corny as it sounds, nothing else around me mattered. And as I finally looked up, he told me how beautiful he thought I was. He told me my acne doesn't change how he feels. I just blushed. I was speechless, this warm feeling in my heart took over my entire body. He cared enough to look me in the eyes and tell me I'm beautiful. I truly started to forget about my skin. I didn't feel like his eyes were looking at my skin; instead they were looking right into me. And in that moment, I knew that warm feeling in my heart. I knew it was love. I was in love. How could I not be? I felt like I was worth something despite my flaws. When I realized that he looked past my not-so-perfect skin and still thought I was beautiful, I started to love myself more and more. He taught me that I am more than my acne, more than my insecurities. And to me, that is love.

MARY MASSAQUOI

YEARS AS MENTEE: 1

GRADE: Senior

BORN: Staten Island, NY

LIVES: Staten Island, NY

MENTEE'S ANECDOTE: *When I was accepted to Girls Write Now I remember thinking to myself,* I would like someone to look up to. *Meeting my mentor proved to fulfill my wishes. Every week we met I became more grateful for this program because of my mentor and the opportunities it held. One thing that brought us close was meeting at a poetry slam. The event combined both of the things we loved: music and writing. From that day I realized we were extremely similar, though we were in two different places in life.*

ARRIEL VINSON

YEARS AS MENTOR: 1

OCCUPATION: Development and Marketing Assistant, *Poets & Writers*

BORN: Indianapolis, IN

LIVES: Brooklyn, NY

PUBLICATIONS AND RECOGNITIONS: *Shondaland, Catapult,* and *BOOTH*

MENTOR'S ANECDOTE: *My mentee and I are so alike it's almost scary. One of my favorite parts about our sessions is that we can talk about music and TV shows and movies. We read the work of black women together. Somehow, there's a lineage being created. Then we read each other's work. That's where we take our place in history. We learn from the women before us, and write in their tradition.*

THE SHORTCUT

MARY MASSAQUOI

I was inspired to write this story because it is a common fear/nightmare that women have and I wanted to write a story in which the woman was victorious in the end.

When I was younger, I wasn't allowed to go out late by myself. My younger brother could go wherever he wanted whenever, and that always irked me. Younger me was a feminist. I told myself that when I left for college, I would do whatever I wanted because I would be free of my mother's tight hold, finally.

It was a Thursday night during my sophomore year of college—moon full and gentle. I walked to a frat party in a skimpy black dress. My roommate and I were supposed to go together, but she decided last minute to go with girls from a sorority she wanted to get into. Derek, a guy in my psychology class, invited us. With his curly hair and caramel skin, I couldn't say yes fast enough. I was flattered, and couldn't wait to tell all the girls in my suite.

Halfway to the party, I felt like I was being watched. I turned around. No one was there, so I kept going. Derek texted me to check in, and I smiled at my phone without thinking about anything else.

The street was empty except for someone across the street. When I looked at him, he put his head down. My pace quickened.

"There's no way he's following me," I said. When I looked again, he had come to my side. My heart pumped. I examined him. He was tall and lanky, wearing black, with a cap on. I realized he was also stealing glances. I raised my phone to my ear and had a fake conversation, because I had read that works if you're being followed.

There was a dark, wooded area I had to pass to get to the party. My throat got dry. As I walked through the shortcut, he got closer and I started to run. He was fast. He would eventually catch up, so I needed to figure out something. My mother raised me to fight, and fight was what I was gonna do.

My chest burned, so I slowed my pace, then felt his hand on my shoulder. He whispered, words slurred, "You look *nice*." The sharpness of "nice" turned my stomach. The vodka on his breath and whiff of his cologne were pungent. His grip on me was tight, but I turned and jabbed my keys above his eyes. He screamed in pain but still got ahold of my dress. I kicked him, kicking up dirt. He groaned and released me.

I finally understood what my mother meant. I was vulnerable, prone to being attacked if I walked around late. If this was freedom, this isn't what I asked for.

"Stop. Stop. I just want to—" he heaved as he crouched over. I didn't let him finish. I sprinted out of the woods and to the frat house, out of breath. Party music blasted from the windows. Derek found me as I stomped into the kitchen.

"Are you all right?"

I explained everything, falling over my words.

Derek took me back to my dorm. My dress was ripped, boots dirty. Shaking, I told Derek how familiar he seemed. His smell, his voice. As I stood there, Derek took hold of my wrist, his eyes sympathetic.

"Breathe, you're okay now. Why don't you shower and change out of these clothes? I'll wait."

After scrubbing my body and disposing of those clothes, we sat on my bed talking until my adrenaline fell. My hands stilled and fatigue kicked in. But once Derek left, I couldn't sleep.

* * *

In class one week later, packing up my things, I heard the same deep voice. It was a guy talking to Derek and his frat brothers. He stopped when he saw me staring and guilt crept up his face. I noticed a scar above his left eye. *What if that's the guy who attacked me?* I shuffled out of class and a waft blew past me. The same cologne. I finally realized—it was Jason. He lived in my dorm, a few hallways down. Earlier this year, he had asked me out. I'd laughed it off.

Something told me to go back. I approached him so quickly it's like I flew.

"Who do you think you are?" I screamed. He turned to me, startled, then pulled me to a corner.

"I'm sorry."

"Why?" I asked over and over again. I couldn't help myself.

"I don't know. I was drunk." This wasn't a conversation that would resolve what happened. So I stopped having it.

"I'm reporting you!"

His eyes grew with fear, alarm all over his face.

"Please, no, I . . . I . . ." He didn't finish his sentence. I walked away, passing the group of guys, avoiding their confused stares. I glanced at Derek, hoping he would understand. Later that day, I reported him. My mother's precaution came with reason. She was trying to protect me.

Afterward, I felt fearless. I was not only standing up for myself, but for other girls who might experience this. At the end of the week, I walked past his dorm and the door was wide open. I caught a glimpse of his empty bed.

ALICIA MAXWELL

YEARS AS MENTEE: 1

GRADE: Senior

BORN: Brooklyn, NY

LIVES: Brooklyn, NY

MENTEE'S ANECDOTE: *My mentor happens to be a beautiful woman who is going to go far one day. That day being every day. Rebecca is a woman that has built a life off of her pain. A pain she could've kept hidden, but decided to share with the world. She lives her life to the fullest, not letting nothing stop her. As I've gotten to know her this past year, she's become like a big sister. Giving me her love, kindness, and ICE CREAM.*

REBECCA LOUISE MILLER

YEARS AS MENTOR: 1

OCCUPATION: Writer and Performer

BORN: Santa Rosa, CA

LIVES: Brooklyn, NY

PUBLICATIONS AND RECOGNITIONS: 2020 Town Stages Sokoloff Arts Fellow; short film *One Day Home*; short play *Spent Hens*

MENTOR'S ANECDOTE: *Our culture is starved for truth-tellers. I came into Girls Write Now expecting to help a young girl muster the courage to share her deepest truths. Instead, I was matched with Alicia, whose fearless honesty and integrity have made her a role model to me. Those qualities also make her a brilliant observer and writer: one who's kind but doesn't suffer fools, who cracks amazing jokes, who eats deadlines for breakfast. Alicia, I hope you know you can always turn to me if you need someone to cheer you on, or just to share a laugh and some ice cream.*

BEHIND ELEVATOR DOORS

ALICIA MAXWELL

This short horror piece, based on the Elevator Game, is just another tale that shows women can tell beautiful stories, but also show the world something dark.

I still have nightmares about that day.

I can still see the woman standing outside my house with that creepy smile stretching across her face.

I still hear the elevator sound; it haunts me in my dreams. That day, before I even pressed the button, I felt the chills run down my body. Now I know it was a warning sign. It's too late anyway.

I already played the game.

"Can you press six for me, please, darling?"

The voice of an elegant woman disturbed my thoughts and nervous chills ran down my body. Breathing out, I kept my eyes closed and leaned to my right, pressing six. My shaking finger steadied against the cold buttons.

The elevator moved up.

"Ding."

I felt a shift in the elevator.

"Oh! And one more thing."

I opened my eyes, turning to face her.

The woman was tall and heavy, with loose, dark hair curtaining the sides of her chubby, dark chocolate face.

Her head was tilted in a way that made it look detached. Blood started to drip from her mouth, pooling at her feet.

"Don't be scared, darling. You can talk to me."

What the fuck.

She seemed to fill up the room, and it wasn't just because of her weight. The air started to feel heavy and suffocating. Tears pricked at the corners of my eyes and my breathing got quicker. I stepped back, circling around her.

Shit, I should've just stayed home.

Sweat built from the roots of my dark hair down to the tiny kisses of my pink lips. I felt the oxygen being sucked out of my body. Her face lit up in excitement, as if she just sniffed crack. Her pupils went wide and her body expanded. I fell to my knees, clutching my throat, trying to draw back air into my body. Tears clouded my vision. My body shook uncontrollably. I was losing strength in my limbs. I saw my reflection on the elevator door.

Don't go out like this.

Get up. RUN.

Scared for my life, I gathered all the energy I could. Pushing off on my heels, I reached for the elevator button. The doors closed in her face.

Whew.

Feeling luck siding with me for the first time that night, I let my body relax against the steel elevator walls and gulped in air. *I just want to get back to my room.*

"Ding."

Eyes wide open, I threw myself against the middle wall. Her eyes were bloodshot and bull-like. Her body heaved an angry radiation that filled the closed-in space. I felt whatever strength I had in me before evaporating. A hand dug into my hair, lifting my body off the ground like a rag doll. We stared in competition, my eyes shadowed by fear.

I felt a wind whip against my face as a painful pressure slammed me up against the frozen, silver elevator walls. With the metal railing pressing hard into my stomach, a scream clawed itself up from my throat before being shoved back down by a hard blow to the left side of my head.

Why is she doing this to me? Why the hell would anyone ever want to play this damn game? Sinking to the floor, my head fell in my lap and my eyes rolled back. I felt myself losing consciousness.

A piercing scream escaped her lips, threatened to shatter my skull and break through the metal walls. I covered my ears and shut

my eyes tight, but the scream still seeped through the space between my hands and ears, forcing me to suffer even more.

"Ding."

ELEVATOR GAME

Ten accessible floors

Enter on the first floor. If anyone else gets on with you, you must
    get off and wait.

On the first floor, press four. Stay on.

Press two, stay on.

Press six, stay on.

Press two again. If you hear someone call your name, do not
    answer and do not get off.

Press ten, stay on.

Press five. A lady might walk on and start a conversation with
    you. Do not answer and do not look at her but stay on.

Press one, the elevator will shift to the tenth floor.

From there you are on your own.

CIARA McKAY

YEARS AS MENTEE: 3

GRADE: Senior

BORN: Brooklyn, NY

LIVES: Brooklyn, NY

PUBLICATIONS AND RECOGNITIONS: Scholastic Art & Writing Awards: Gold Key

MENTEE'S ANECDOTE: *I have a lot of things to thank Hannah for (like helping me get into my dream school with her dope editing skills), but the biggest thing is for always being there, and being understanding. From our first session editing my college essay over tea to our latest FaceTime call, our meetings have always felt warm and safe. Our tea and Edna St. Vincent Millay–filled sessions are totally unforgettable.*

HANNAH WORBY

YEARS AS MENTOR: 1

OCCUPATION: Donor Services Coordinator, Planned Parenthood Federation

BORN: New York, NY

LIVES: Brooklyn, NY

MENTOR'S ANECDOTE: *A hot cup of tea, Edna St. Vincent Millay, and laughter. Like slumber parties for poets, meetings with Ciara were silly and comfortable, evenings that we spent smiling and making fun of ourselves and finding new things to laugh about and new stanzas to pore over. Her writing, though, brings a maturity and a resolution that press beyond those bubbly evenings. For all her cozy silliness, Ciara is strength. Composure. Her writing grounds you in a reality all her own, yet firmly accessible. She inspires me, and I am so grateful to have sat across a café table with her all those tea-, Millay-, and giggle-filled nights. Ciara is everything!*

EVERYTHING THAT EVER HAUNTED US

CIARA McKAY

I wrote this poem while thinking about two of my favorite poets—Edna St. Vincent Millay and Elizabeth Bishop, and the imagery they use. In this piece I hoped to follow in their footprints and create something within their styles.

The azure sea trapped us here,
A cruel and ruthless master
A pocket watch, long broken and your mother's ring
Our only tools for survival.
The lightbulb flickers, and there you are
You and I,
The lighthouse,
And everything that ever haunted us.

The waves crash over the decrepit sea wall
We stare, hopelessly at the briny expanse.
The lighthouse, once bright red,
Stalks us, the bulb turning and flashing.
I wonder who you were before
You and I,
The lighthouse,
And everything that ever haunted us.

You swear to me that you've seen ghosts,
The men that were here before.
You grip your mother's ring, and pray.
Breathless chanting, ritualistic.

I ask if they answer you.
You and I,
The lighthouse,
And everything that ever haunted us.

The empty island, the stormy sea,
The lighthouse, with its blinking eye.
We hold our talismans
Chant breathlessly
And pray
You and I,
The lighthouse,
And everything that ever haunted us.

ODALIS MENDEZ

YEARS AS MENTEE: 1

GRADE: Senior

BORN: Puebla, Mexico

LIVES: Bronx, NY

PUBLICATIONS AND RECOGNITIONS: "Long Live Misery!" in the LEAP OnStage anthology, published by Samuel French

MENTEE'S ANECDOTE: *Meeting Rachel has changed my perception of writing. She taught me how to appreciate writing and how it contributes to our everyday lives. Our weekly meetings have become something I always look forward to. I am glad that we bonded quickly on our first meeting over our common interests. She has inspired me to share my story and to speak out. Rachel has allowed me to believe that I can make history by inspiring others to speak as well. Not only has Rachel become my mentor, but she has become a friend I hold close to my heart.*

RACHEL PRATER

YEARS AS MENTOR: 1

OCCUPATION: Production Editor, Scholastic

BORN: Miamisburg, Ohio

LIVES: New York, NY

MENTOR'S ANECDOTE: *Girls Write Now has changed my life. I am incredibly proud of Odalis and am grateful for our quick bond. It helps that we have a lot in common (ghost stories, music, entertainment, and love for our family)! But she has taught me more than she knows and inspired me to be a better woman and writer. She is the first generation in her family and the first female to graduate, then attend college. Because of this, I've been more encouraged than ever to support the stories of immigrants. Everyone's journey is important as we take our place in history.*

THE JOURNEY WE TAKE

ODALIS MENDEZ

All of our stories deserve to be heard, which is why I decided to share mine. This experience has been the motivation that pushes me to demonstrate to others, and myself, what I am capable of. .

I have no memory of my journey. I hear countless stories about it, but not once can I recall the experience.

I always try to imagine how it all happened. To imagine the emotions my parents felt at the thought of me coming alone without them. My papá left when I was only two months old and my mamá soon followed eight months later. Me? My abuela wouldn't let my mamá take me with her and her request was for me to stay with her for one year. No more, no less. From what I have heard, my abuela loved me more than I can imagine. However, the only memories I have of her are those taken by the click of a camera. My abuela was able to complete her promise before she passed away on that cold fall day of November 3. My mamá tells me that this became the deciding factor in finally reuniting with me.

Some would feel shame at the thought of mentioning this. Maybe it isn't because they are ashamed. Maybe it's because of . . . fear. Fear of losing what they have now. Fear of being separated from their *familia*. Fear of not being able to have an *educación*. Fear of not being accepted by society. It sounds like we turn it into a big deal. The truth is that it is—at least to the ones who have gone through it. I like to think that this experience is something one should take pride in. It's a journey not everybody can speak about. Many say it's a risky journey toward *la muerte*. I say it's a journey toward *oportunidad*.

I've been living as an immigrant in this country for almost my entire life. I came from Mexico when I was about two years old.

My mamá tells me that I arrived in Los Angeles and stayed there for about a month with my tías, until we got tickets for our flight to New York. I am proud to say that the Bronx has been my *hogar*, regardless of how I arrived.

I can't speak for everyone, but I speak for myself when I say that this journey was meant to happen to my *familia* and me. I was given the chance to excel and succeed. All my parents ever want for me is to do my best in school and find my passion. Yes, I did have obstacles growing up, but never obstacles that deprived me of being proud of who I am. It is the obstacles I face today that let me know the reality I am a part of. However, I know that I am not alone, because there are so many wonderful personas I have met. Each and every one of them support me in whatever they can.

I can't say that I took this journey alone, or that this journey has ended. It's something meant for me to tell and to learn from, and it becomes a concept others want to learn about as well. In the end, it's not the journey I take, he takes, or she takes—it becomes a journey we ALL take.

ANAEE MERO

YEARS AS MENTEE: 1

GRADE: Junior

BORN: Portoviejo, Ecuador

LIVES: New York, NY

MENTEE'S ANECDOTE: *Getting to talk about things in our sessions every week that really excite me and introduce them to Laura—things like my favorite music (yay BTS!) and my closest friends and my plans for the summer—and to see that she was truly interested and enthusiastic and wanted to know more, that means a lot.*

LAURA LITWIN

YEARS AS MENTOR: 1

OCCUPATION: Author and Editor for Educational Publishing

BORN: Chicago, IL

LIVES: New York, NY

MENTOR'S ANECDOTE: *When Anaee comes bounding into our coffee shop talking a mile a minute, her phone in her hand, already shuffling through the pictures she wants me to see that illustrate her week's news, there's nothing better. It was easy for us to figure out how her writing would jibe with Girls Write Now's theme this year. Anaee is staking her own place in history, heart, eyes, and arms wide open!*

DREAMS, HOPES, FORWARD, FORWARD

ANAEE MERO

I want to dedicate this piece to the person I am becoming. The way forward for me feels inspiring and optimistic!

You'll be okay.

You won't believe me now, but you'll come to understand one day. You're still growing up, after all.

I know right now you're feeling very lonely and scared. I know that right now you don't feel like you have anyone to turn to—not your family, and not your current friends. It should not have been that way for you. You were so vulnerable and naïve and still learning left from right. Like every other kid, you had to go to school, but you carried extra weight on your back. Things were way difficult for you, in and out of school. You shouldn't have stayed up all night because you didn't know how to catch up with your thoughts. Thoughts that were running a mile a minute. You didn't have to depend on your parents' relationship to be happy. But you did, because that's all you knew how to do. You should've spent your days being a kid, not this. Yet despite all of it, you stood your ground. I'm proud of you for that.

But life moves forward and so will you. In the next couple of years, you come to learn how to stay strong in situations that would have knocked others down with one blow. You acknowledge that you're not perfect and you give yourself time to improve. You don't give up so easily anymore and you learn to appreciate life, no matter how shitty it gets sometimes. You no longer see black when you imagine your future. Rather, you smile brightly at the thought of it and assure yourself that, no matter what, you'll be the person you see in your mind because that's what will make you happy.

Not only that, but you meet the most important people! You come across a group of folks who shelter you from the bad days and motivate you to do better on the good ones. You meet friends who listen to you and your troubles and tell you that you're a good person when your silly brain tries to convince you that you are not. You meet someone very like you and you are so happy about it that it's really all you ever talk about on some days, but deep down we understand why this person is special. You will no longer wander alone on earth, because you have so many people to lean on and you have a mindset and a will that shields you from thoughts that might lead you down a dark path. You look for ways to avoid that dark place, but I'd be a liar if I did not confess that occasionally you do go back there. No matter, though, you always end up back home.

The best thing is that there's more to come! More good days, more time to work on yourself. More time to plan a trip to California and maybe meet your bestest friend in the world. More time to plan your outfit for the next concert, more time to plan the layout of your own apartment.

More time to do So Much More. Unfortunately, you also have a lot of school days left, but there's not much we can do about that one. Although that doesn't seem fun, in the end, all of this just means more days to learn and to love and to feel with every part of yourself.

You will get fucked over many, many times—everyone does— but I have faith you'll be okay, because you always are. And besides, I know you're beyond ready to go out and kick life's ass.

TATIANA MEZITIS

YEARS AS MENTEE: 2

GRADE: Senior

BORN: New York, NY

LIVES: New York, NY

PUBLICATIONS AND RECOGNITIONS: "Where Summer Went" (independent publication of my art and poetry), Scholastic Art & Writing Awards: Gold Key, Silver Key, Honorable Mention

MENTEE'S ANECDOTE: *From discovering the beauty of Sappho's writing to giggling in the Girls Write Now kitchen while we cooked eggs and recorded our podcast, Caroline and I have made nothing but good memories this past year. Her ability to patiently read through my writing and provide honest, helpful feedback never fails to inspire me, and I feel that I've grown to be a better writer because of her. I'm looking forward to continuing our exploration of the writing world during the next few months. :)*

CAROLINE SYDNEY

YEARS AS MENTOR: 2

OCCUPATION: Assistant Editor

BORN: Dallas, TX

LIVES: Brooklyn, NY

MENTOR'S ANECDOTE: *That first day at the New-York Historical Society, Tatiana and I were handed folders with portraits of Sappho on the cover. A few weeks later, huddled over a copy of Anne Carson's* If Not, Winter *at a table in a buzzing coffee shop, we read a selection of the more complete poems. To reanimate/reclaim/reinterpret Sappho's place in history, we recast her lines into poems of our own. In this way, we could enter her story while she became a part of ours.*

OUR SOULS WILL RISE

TATIANA MEZITIS

Inspired by Sappho's fragmentary poems, "Our Souls Will Rise" describes the sensation of being trapped in a condition that is beautiful yet simultaneously confining love's attempt to transcend distance.

two februarys pass through a
pensive mind, a head
shrouded white
with lace

as a single lilac

and it is all at once
marble, too
transfixed and bowed to rest
in temples which stand here, awash in sunlight,
while our casts rest solid

awaiting the two-toned press of night.
we, sentries, watch for a sign
that there will come an after
that we will exist someplace beyond

this

oh, to kneel at your altar!
as clouds pass behind your head
it will feel summer again
every bit as cotton and dust and dollar bills
as july in your arms was

oh, to sing your praises to a hillside deaf
and to blow an eyelash away
with the wish that it'll rise, taking our souls
to coast on a golden summer wind
for miles of lake and light

HADIA MIAH

YEARS AS MENTEE: 1

GRADE: Senior

BORN: Bronx, NY

LIVES: Bronx, NY

MENTEE'S ANECDOTE: *Monique and I bonded over food, music, and our journey with the STEM field and writing. I came to see how smart and cool she is and became instantly comfortable with her. She has been such a great help when it came to my college applications and really pushed me to become a more confident writer. She helped me navigate through my problems and was always ready to listen to my very long rants about anything. Having Monique as my mentor was an honor and I am looking forward to her meeting her goals and expanding on her passion for writing.*

MONIQUE HALL

YEARS AS MENTOR: 1

OCCUPATION: Associate Magazine Editor, *Scholastic*

BORN: Hackensack, NJ

LIVES: Paterson, NJ

PUBLICATIONS AND RECOGNITIONS: Sesame Street Writer's Room Fellow

MENTOR'S ANECDOTE: *Hadia is one of the most thoughtful and self-aware teens I've ever had the privilege of knowing. She bustles into our sessions every week with a story to tell, a question to ask, or a problem to solve that she's been puzzling over. Hadia is someone who lets her passion for social and political awareness shine through, while also being equally passionate about K-pop, technology, and makeup. I'm honored to have had Hadia as my first mentee and I can't wait to see not if, but how she cements her place in history!*

PERSONAL STATEMENT

HADIA MIAH

This is my college personal statement. As a senior, I spent a lot of time at Girls Write Now with my mentor working on this essay along with my other supplemental essays for college applications. This essay demonstrates my passion for technology and activism while also showcasing my growth.

Discuss an accomplishment event or realization that sparked a period of personal growth and a new understanding of yourself or others.

A white man walks into a mosque and is greeted warmly by an elderly man. The elderly man extends his hand to invite this new man in, and within seconds, he is shot point-blank. In the blink of an eye, a life is taken onscreen in what is the start of a killing spree seen around the world. How does one react to such a video?

On March 15, 2019, my perspective changed when a livestream of a shooting at a mosque in Christchurch, New Zealand, circled around social media. Upon watching the video, I wept hysterically while my friends rushed to console me. My family and I could have been a victim of this terrorist attack. We live in an apartment on the top floor of the West Bronx Jame Masjid in Bronx, New York, and attend services regularly.

Prior to watching that video, I was apathetic to the number of rapes, mass murders, and injustices happening around the world, as they seemed not to affect me directly. Instead of engaging with controversial events and ideas, I turned a blind eye, no matter their significance. However, after watching the video, I wanted nothing more than to spread awareness about the terrorist attack. Despite constantly requesting my friends to attend vigils and protests against white supremacy and Islamophobia—the very ideas that fueled the terrorist attack—not many people showed up. That's when I realized that I needed to do more.

In response to the Christchurch terrorist attacks and the lack of social justice awareness in my school, I cofounded the Political Awareness Club (PAC). Through weekly meetings, the club members share information and exchange ideas about current political events through stimulating student debates and "thought talks" in a no-judgment, comfortable space. As the president, I've engaged members in discussions on topics such as the Rodney Reed case and the dangers of fake news. Recently, we ran a campaign to encourage seniors in our school to register to vote and sign petitions against the Chinese concentration camps. For the remainder of the school year, we are planning fundraisers, protests, a women's panel, and workshops that non-members can also attend to discuss politics. In addition, we plan to attend the Women's March this January and conduct mock elections. Last week, we added our tenth member, and we hope to continue growing as the new year progresses.

While increasing political awareness through PAC, I consistently questioned the role of technology giants such as Facebook, YouTube, and so forth in propagating violence and xenophobic actions. The fact that it took Facebook nearly twenty-four hours to remove 1.5 million videos of the Christchurch livestream forced me to ask the question, "Could these tech companies have developed responsible artificial intelligence to flag the videos before they became viral?" This question prompted me to participate in Girls Who Code, a highly competitive summer immersion program for students interested in computer programming. As part of the program, I led a group of peers to build a website that aimed to bring awareness about the US Immigration System in response to the Trump administration's "zero-tolerance" policy. Over the course of the year, my teammates and I have been meeting regularly to continue working on our website called "Build a Wall Against Discrimination." Our vision is to create a one-stop shop for immigrants, such as my parents, to access immigration-related information and resources on demand.

My experience with Girls Who Code taught me that technology, if leveraged correctly, has the power to accelerate political activism and fuel awareness campaigns. As I stay up late nights to finish sets of source code for the website, I am reminded of the people whose lives were taken during the Christchurch shooting. I know I cannot bring them back, but I promise to work hard to ensure innocent lives are not lost due to misinformation and xenophobia again.

ANGELY MOREL

YEARS AS MENTEE: 3

GRADE: Senior

BORN: New York, NY

LIVES: New York, NY

MENTEE'S ANECDOTE: *Kate has become more than a mentor; she is a lifelong friend. We both have so much in common, and loving ramen is definitely one of those things. We both also start a brief conversation that lasts thirty minutes because we love to update each other on everything! It has truly been a ride—a fun ride. Kate is confident, strong, and authentic. I have learned so much about her that has inspired me to be myself. It's been more than just a digital and writing experience, but also a time of personal growth for the both of us.*

KATE JACOBS

YEARS AS MENTOR: 8

OCCUPATION: Editor, Macmillan

BORN: Grand Rapids, MI

LIVES: Brooklyn, NY

MENTOR'S ANECDOTE: *Angely is five feet tall and has a sweet voice and a warm smile. When I met her three years ago, I thought I would have to draw her out of her shell. I couldn't have been more wrong. Angely sees the world with razor-sharp clarity. She stands up for herself, knows when teachers are unfair, and she experiences discrimination. She is determined to be successful and show the world the richness of Dominican culture. She is on her way to greatness, on her way to taking her very own place in history. I will never underestimate her again.*

A LIFE-LONG TAXI RIDE

ANGELY MOREL

Growing up, I was raised in a very cultured and loving community. However, when I began to interact with the world outside my community, I became aware of the many issues people like me face daily.

I waved my hand to hail down the vibrant green taxi, rushed in, and proudly said, "Bendicion, papi!" All my life I've been driven around by my dad's green taxi. This taxi has transported me from one place to another and from opportunity to accomplishment. This car gives me and my family the freedom to experience new things, like visiting different states and attending events around the city. It's a representation of my family's sacrifices. As an immigrant family, it has granted us the opportunity to have an income to support one another and our dreams.

On the day of my cousin's graduation, my family approached the parking lot in our taxi. The white man in charge demanded that we park down the street. Sadly, we complied, but afterward we noticed that he let in every other car after us. I could feel that something wasn't right. My parents were discussing the situation in the front seat and I could tell by their body language and their scrunched brows that they were upset. My sister and I looked at each other in silence, bothered at the situation. As the youngest person in the car, I couldn't understand why everyone wasn't doing anything about it, and why it all seemed normal to them. I asked, "Why didn't we say anything to him?" They replied with excuses that failed to justify why we didn't stick up for ourselves. My family told me to just leave it alone, but instead I got out of the car to confront the parking assistant. As I angrily walked toward him, I imagined humiliating him as he did my family. I clenched my fists, took a deep breath, and instead I asked him, "If there was no available space for my family, why did you allow five other cars to access the parking lot after us?" Not once in that conversation did he look at me, and all he said was, "That was my first instinct." As a woman of color, I felt extremely disrespected by the gatekeepers' actions toward us. Those words enraged me, and I expressed to him that it was not a coincidence that his first instinct was to refuse to admit a Hispanic family who can't afford a regular car. The tension thickened as he dismissed the issue I presented him with; he looked down in silence.

I walked back into the car and my family stared at me with disappointment, as if there was no point in doing anything. They silently continued to act as if nothing happened and started unpacking the gifts. The man slowly approached us and looked me directly in the eye and said, "Ma'am, we have one more spot for your family." The parking space wasn't the lesson in this situation. Instead, it was for the white man to be aware of his biases and to respect everyone, regardless of their situation. For my family, it was to take up space as marginalized individuals. After this, a similar situation happened with getting into my sister's university in our taxi, but this time it was my dad who rolled down his window. It was rewarding to witness my family speak up. Situations like this are why immigrants and minorities stay silent and are satisfied with so little, even when they deserve so much.

After this incident, I felt I had a new voice that needed to be amplified and a story to share. I want other immigrant families to learn that it's not okay to be discriminated against and to stand up for themselves in an educated and nonviolent way. I now recognize how powerful my voice is when standing up for what is right. Whether it is on a podium or on the streets holding up a banner, I know I want to continue to speak out, continue to learn, and help others to advocate for themselves.

ALEXIS MORGAN

YEARS AS MENTEE: 2

GRADE: Senior

BORN: Brooklyn, NY

LIVES: Brooklyn, NY

MENTEE'S ANECDOTE: *I think that writing with Victoria has always been a way to prepare for my time of actually taking my place in history. I would love to be remembered for my work, not only in writing, but also in music and theater. I didn't know where to start—that is, until Girls Write Now and my mentor Victoria. She gives me amazing constructive criticism on all of my pieces, and helps me in fun ways, not only with academics, but also with personal issues. I love how much our relationship has grown, as well as how we've grown individually.*

VICTORIA CHOW

YEARS AS MENTOR: 2

OCCUPATION: Consumer Communications Manager, Reddit

BORN: Brooklyn, NY

LIVES: New York, NY

MENTOR'S ANECDOTE: *As Alexis's mentor, I've watched her grow from a high school junior trying to find her voice in the world to a college-bound young woman who's bold, self-assured, and excited for what's ahead. From the day we met, I've been in awe of Alexis's diverse skills, from sci-fi writing to playing five instruments to loving plants and biology. It's been an honor to work alongside her, in our local Starbucks, free-writing over coffee, marshmallow bars, and the very best company. I'm so excited for her next adventure, and to stay in touch along the way.*

WANTED FOOD, BUT I HAD HOMEWORK

ALEXIS MORGAN

This all started out with a six-word prompt written by a classmate of mine, "wanted food, but I had homework." I ended up turning it into something special to myself, and something relatable to everyone in high school.

I hadn't eaten a good meal in so long. All I wanted was a cornucopia of delicacies, a supreme pizza, a box of a dozen Krispy Kreme donuts, something, anything! My stomach turned from a content, peaceful being into a ferocious beast with each and every growl. There was only one thing holding me back: homework.

I stared at the endless textbook pages, the blank notebooks. Every question blew a dusty fog in my brain, which left my mouth parched and in need of some crisp, ice-cold refreshment, like a nice cold glass of lemonade.

But then I started to think of what I *really* craved. Was I jeopardizing my chance of improving my skills because of greed, because of thoughts of cheeseburger deluxes and a giant cup of Sprite? I wanted something so much that I forgot what I truly needed to crave: an education. **I wanted food, but I had**—and needed—**homework.**

MAISHA NABILA

YEARS AS MENTEE: 2

GRADE: Junior

BORN: Dhaka, Bangladesh

LIVES: Queens, NY

PUBLICATIONS AND RECOGNITIONS: Scholastic Art & Writing Awards: Honorable Mention

MENTEE'S ANECDOTE: *Working with my mentor has helped me open up about my writing more, which in turn has helped me open up more emotionally as well. Additionally, I've become more confident in my abilities. My mentor is a lot more organized than I am, and she has helped me become more organized and better at communicating as well.*

ALEXANDRA OSSOLA

YEARS AS MENTOR: 4

OCCUPATION: Chief Editor, *Quartz*

BORN: Washington, D.C.

LIVES: New York, NY

MENTOR'S ANECDOTE: *For the past two years, I've looked forward to my weekly meet-ups with Maisha to hear her take on recent events, either in her own life or in the world at large. She almost always surprises me. She is bold and determined, with a fantastic appreciation for irony—one day this year, after a particularly enjoyable pair writing session, I told her that I thought she would make a great boss someday, and she laughed and laughed, mostly (I think) because she knew it was true. In her writing she channels the force of her personality, her curiosity, and her brilliance. This piece is no exception.*

THE TONIGHT SHOW WITH JIMMY AND CHERRI

MAISHA NABILA

Gorillaz is a virtual band consisting of four cartoon characters created by Damon Albarn and Jamie Hewlett. Their albums have a backdrop of the character's personal "lives," which are often ridiculous, violent, and as cartoonish as the band itself. This "interview" is a tribute to Gorillaz's nonsensical ingenuity.

JIMMY FALLON: There have been a lot of stars rising from Gotham City these days, and our first guest tonight is one of them. Ladies and gentlemen, please welcome . . . Cherri!

(Audience cheers. A young woman with red hair in pigtails steps onto the stage.) **CHERRI:** Hey, everyone!

JIMMY: So, Cherri, last month you released your debut album and within a week your single, "Cherribomb," climbed to the Top 10 on the charts.

CHERRI: Yeah. It's exciting, but . . . also kinda disappointing, too.

JIMMY: Disappointing?

CHERRI: Yeah. I don't think "Cherribomb" is the best song in the album. My favorite is "Iron Bars," but I don't think people like it! Like, I went on Spotify and, you know the little bars next to the song?

JIMMY: Yeah, the ones that show you the song's popularity.

CHERRI: Yeah, those. "Cherribomb" has full bars, obviously, but "Iron Bars" only has, like, two or something. That's kinda unfortunate, given the story behind the song. Can I share it?

JIMMY: Um . . . we did agree on a script, but we don't have to stick by it one hundred percent.

CHERRI: Cool, cuz I don't wanna talk about "Cherribomb."

(muttering from audience)

CHERRI: So, as many of you know, I finished my jail time recently for an assassination attempt on the president of Mexico.

JIMMY: Ah, yes, that got us a lotta backlash for having you here. (nervous laughter)

CHERRI: Please, don't tell me that after years of hosting this show, *now* you care about the haters.

JIMMY: No, but—

CHERRI: This wouldn't be the first time you interviewed a supervillain on this show.

JIMMY: Well I'm not sure how much of a *super*villian the Joker was—

CHERRI: Woah, woah, so you're endorsing the Joker but not—

JIMMY: I'm not saying the Joker isn't a villain. I'm just saying he's not a super one. You can mind-control seagulls. He can't do anything. Joker is just like Batman. He can't do anything by himself, so he's a hero but not a *super*hero.

(audience mutters angrily)

JIMMY: We are getting incredibly off-track here. You were saying . . . ?

CHERRI: Yeah, yeah. So I got thrown in that nasty-ass jail cell where the tastiest thing they would offer me was the toothpaste. And guess who was running the prison!

JIMMY: Murdoc Niccals.

CHERRI: No, Murdoc Niccals! I was baffled, but then it hit me. Obviously Murdoc was running the prison, it's the type of thing someone who tricked the devil would manage to do! He was locked up himself, you know.

JIMMY: But . . . how would that happen?

CHERRI: Sometimes it's best not to ask? Anyway, he told me that if I could, and I quote, "Entertain him in this abysmal human bird-cage," then he'd lemme go.

JIMMY (shifts in his chair): So you . . . *entertained* him?

CHERRI: Yes, with the miniature keyboard I keep in my pocket.

JIMMY: Oh, I—never mind.

CHERRI: I played something that sounded fun, made you want to get up and mutiny. He was so impressed that he got knocked unconscious by my unbridled talent. Although . . . that may have been the guard who hit him over the head with a shovel.

JIMMY: What?

CHERRI: Apparently, after Murdoc overthrew the old authority, some dissenters were there? Anyway, while the guard was distracted by Murdoc, I threw my keyboard at his head and knocked him out. I played varsity softball in college, so I had a lotta training in using small objects as weapons. So, what I did—this is what I did.

JIMMY: (leans in)

CHERRI: I dragged Murdoc in my direction, unhooked the keys from his belt, and opened the cell door. I got him outside with me, where I called an Uber.

JIMMY: That's crazy. How did you feel?

CHERRI: Oh, I don't know . . .

JIMMY: You don't know!

CHERRI: Well, I know, but like . . . I feel like I should have been overwhelmed by some, some euphoric freedom, but the thing I played for Murdoc just kept pinging around my head like the DVD logo.

JIMMY: (laughs)

CHERRI: So when I got us two quaint motel rooms, I pulled out my phone and, using Garageband, added to the keyboard rendition I played for Murdoc. I've always been influenced by Gorillaz's music, their mixing of an ever-changing, experimental style with that signature, drawling funk. I wanted "Iron Bars" to be a tribute to that. And when Murdoc woke up and heard the music, he barged in and insisted on playing bass.

JIMMY: Where'd he get the bass?

CHERRI: I have no idea. Sometimes it's best not to ask.

ASHLEY NUÑEZ

YEARS AS MENTEE: 1

GRADE: Senior

BORN: Flushing, NY

LIVES: Queens, NY

MENTEE'S ANECDOTE: *The Girls Write Now pairing skills are truly unmatched! Amber is the coolest and cheekiest rascal. No words can truly describe our "pair writing relationship"; we work so well because we connect on a spiritual level (not a joke). From pikelets to 5Ks. Or games of "Guess who I'm writing about?" Or counting out syllables for our haiku. Amber and I have been the funniest, most interesting team imaginable.*

AMBER JAMIESON

YEARS AS MENTOR: 1

OCCUPATION: Breaking news reporter at *BuzzFeed News*

BORN: Canberra, Australia

LIVES: Brooklyn, NY

PUBLICATIONS AND RECOGNITIONS: Founder of *Better Have My Money*; cohost of *Get Money*

MENTOR'S ANECDOTE: *From the first day we met, and she mocked me for not knowing how to pronounce Rego Park, I felt very lucky to be matched with Ashley. I love our weekly Court Square diner catch-ups, where we write about customers, hope that our favorite server is working, and tell each other long and meandering stories about our lives. Ashley is kind, overwhelmingly thoughtful, and has an innate sense of justice. Plus, she's really funny. I'm so thrilled that she's going to study journalism at Stony Brook University, because she's exactly what our industry needs.*

GIRL (THE BEATLES)

ASHLEY NUÑEZ

This poem is meant to take you on a relatable musical journey. The songs were chosen based on my feelings sometimes, but they are mostly a reflection of a made-up character (loosely based on Napoleon Dynamite).

I'm Not a Girl, Not Yet a Woman (Britney Spears) I'm Just a Kid (Simple Plan) What's My Age Again? (Blink 182) We Are Young (Fun. featuring Janelle Monáe) I Don't Want to Miss a Thing (Aerosmith) I Don't Want to Be (Gavin DeGraw) Human (The Human League) I Fall Apart (Post Malone) I Do [Wanna Get Close to You] (3LW) I'm Like a Bird (Nelly Furtado) Wind Beneath My Wings (Bette Midler) Frail (Jars of Clay)

Remember the Days of the Old Schoolyard (Yusuf Islam/Cat Stevens) The Nicest Kids in Town (James Marsden) Good Girls (5 Seconds of Summer) Work Hard, Play Hard (Wiz Khalifa) TiK ToK (Ke$ha) American Idiot (Green Day) [You Drive Me] Crazy (Britney Spears) Friday on My Mind (The Easybeats)

Money, Money, Money (ABBA) I Hate My Job (Cam'ron) Work Bitch (Britney Spears) She Works Hard for the Money (Donna Summer) Que Calor (Major Lazer featuring J Balvin) fake smile (Ariana Grande) Por un Segundo (Aventura) Over It (Summer Walker) Blah Blah Blah (Ke$ha) Bitch Better Have My Money (Rihanna) $$$ (XXXTentacion)

New Person, Same Old Mistakes (Tame Impala) In a Dream (Rockell) I'm Strong (Robert Owens) It's So Nice [To See Old Friends] (Minnie Riperton) Stronger (Britney Spears) The Final

Countdown (Europe) Graduation [Friends Forever] (Vitamin C)
Good Riddance [Time of Your Life] (Green Day)

Who Will I Be? (Demi Lovato) What Am I Going to Do With
Myself? (Al Green) Time After Time (Cyndi Lauper) Girls Just
Wanna Have Fun (Cyndi Lauper) Fun, Fun, Fun (The Beach
Boys) Are You Bored Yet? (Wallows featuring Clairo) All Girls
Are the Same (Juice WRLD) Independent Women, Pt. 1
(Destiny's Child) I Got It from My Mama (will.i.am)

YAMILET ORTEGA

YEARS AS MENTEE: 2

GRADE: Senior

BORN: New York, NY

LIVES: New York, NY

PUBLICATIONS AND RECOGNITIONS: Psychology Award for Excellence and English Award for Excellence at Harvest Collegiate High School

MENTEE'S ANECDOTE: *Heather and I wrap our last year together at Girls Write Now with a bond that I will always hold dear to me. We grew closer during these past two years and I thank her for everything and every piece of advice she gave me. I will remember our afternoons at random cafés, drinking coffee and spending hours just talking. Those were the best. The gallery walks, scones, ceramic paintings, and writing we did together will always hold a special place in my heart because of you. I hope we remain close even after Girls Write Now!*

HEATHER STRICKLAND

YEARS AS MENTOR: 2

OCCUPATION: Playwright

BORN: Philadelphia, PA

LIVES: Brooklyn, NY

MENTOR'S ANECDOTE: *Yamilet and I are a lot alike. We are both on the quiet side when you first meet us, which means that it took a while for us to bond. But two years later we are so close. I am incredibly proud of how much she has grown as a writer and as a person, and I will always hold our relationship close to my heart. Sharing coffee, watching movies, walking the High Line, painting ceramics—so many memories, made so much better, thanks to our bond. I can't wait to see what's next for her, and us!*

BLOOMING

YAMILET ORTEGA

Growing up in a conservative and religious Hispanic household, certain things I went through were never explained to me. This piece speaks about my thoughts and feelings as I bloomed and went through big changes alone.

She watched herself become a woman. Her waist forms dips; she is unsure of what to call them. The dips hug her hips tightly. And below her hips are the thighs that had grown bigger. Chunky, chunky, they are. Leaving no space on the chair she sat on during dinner. Hair covered them, a knitted blanket on the coldest day of winter.

They stick close to each other on the hottest days, and snuggle up to her chest on the coldest. They are hers.

Her face has small red bumps. She questions their existence. Squeezing them only makes it worse.

That she learned quickly.

She doesn't recognize anything.

Her chest forms cushions she had only seen women on TV have.

The cushions pushed down her stomach rolls, she now grew more aware of.

Different. She knows she is.

Weird. A word used to describe the aroma of caldo de panza her mom cooked on the coldest nights.

Was now being used to describe herself.

It amazed her that the word hurt her so much.

Every night, she stayed up all night, Googling "What's wrong with my body" only to grow insecure of it all.

She cradled herself to bed at night.

Her mother watched the girl, struggling to find answers.

Her father noticed her move away.

But they remained silent. Because even they didn't know how to explain it all.

Hurting. Hurting I was.

GABI PALERMO

YEARS AS MENTEE: 3

GRADE: Senior

BORN: New York, NY

LIVES: New York, NY

MENTEE'S ANECDOTE: *Kate has been my mentor for the past three years and I could not have asked for a better mentor. This year has been very stressful because I have been applying to colleges, but Kate has been there with me to help me through this process. I feel like our relationship has become stronger throughout this past year and we have made really great memories with each other. One moment that really stands out to me was when Kate and I went to see* The Cher Show *on Broadway last year. I feel like this experience was really great for us because we got to have a fun experience with each other and become closer. Kate has been such an amazing person to have in my life, and even as I leave Girls Write Now, I know that I will always stay in touch with Kate.*

KATE MULLEY

YEARS AS MENTOR: 5

OCCUPATION: Playwright

BORN: Boston, MA

LIVES: New York, NY

PUBLICATIONS AND RECOGNITIONS:
Razorhurst, Hayes Theatre Company, Sydney, Australia

MENTOR'S ANECDOTE: *It has been an absolute joy to spend time with Gabi as she has grown as a writer, advocate, and activist over the last three years. While I'm thrilled to see her go off to her top-choice college in the fall, I know I'll miss our weekly meetings. I can only hope that at the very least she'll continue to text me to let me know what new music I should be listening to.*

MAYBE YOU KNOW

GABI PALERMO

My piece is about meeting my half brother who does not know that I exist. I created this piece after writing my college essay about the other half of my family that I know nothing about.

Maybe you know about me, maybe you don't
Have you ever wondered about me?
What I look like,
What I care about
How I'm doing?
Standing in the back of this dark venue,
Watching you perform
I don't know how to feel about you I hate that I know about you.
Knowing about you just hurts me even more
It hurts me to see that you're actually talented
If you were a loser maybe I wouldn't have this desire to meet you
On stage, you're rapping about all of the pain you have gone
    through
Maybe we can find comfort in each other's traumas.
Lights reflect off of my eyes and all I can see is you
You look so much like your dad
I don't know if that's a good or bad thing
I can tell so badly that you want to be a musician
I can tell that you hate your job just by how much passion you
    have on stage
The concert ends and I'm left in the dark
What do I do now?
What's the point of going up to you?
How will you react?
This isn't good for my anxiety

I'm just making things worse
My palms, sweaty and shaky
I go up to you to congratulate you on your performance
In the back of my mind all I'm thinking is,
Why are you lying?
You've been erased for so long and it's not fair to do this to
    yourself anymore.
He deserves to know who you are

Without even thinking I just blurt out
I'm your sister.

LESLIE PANTALEON

YEARS AS MENTEE: 4

GRADE: Senior

BORN: Brooklyn, NY

LIVES: Brooklyn, NY

MENTEE'S ANECDOTE: *Losing the café that we started at this year was a sentimental event that I think other pairs can empathize with. For Lauren and me specifically, it was an opportunity to reflect on our favorite memories there and together. Graduating feels a lot like the same process; Little Skips was never what made our mentor/mentee pair relationship special and neither was Girls Write Now, although both were important facilitators. Lauren and I made our time together special. I'm grateful to have had a mentor who allowed me the agency to make our time our own.*

LAUREN HESSE

YEARS AS MENTOR: 7

OCCUPATION: Social Media Director, Little, Brown and Company

BORN: Albany, NY

LIVES: Brooklyn, NY

MENTOR'S ANECDOTE: *A few weeks ago, I sat across from Leslie, talking about what mentoring will look like for me next year, after she graduates. When we met, Leslie was at a new high school with all new students. Even then, Leslie was thoughtful, kind, and driven. I've seen her grow into a young woman with passion, conviction, grace, and an intelligence beyond compare. I am so thankful for Leslie; she is one of the most important people in my life and it has been an honor to be her mentor.*

METAMORPHOSIS

LESLIE PANTALEON

Starting the program in my freshman year of high school meant I grew up with Girls Write Now. Although saying goodbye is difficult, it brings me great joy to present our history.

YEAR 1: 2016–2017

At orientation, I am introduced to my mentor, a kind woman named Lauren with warm eyes. She walks me to the library after our first Girls Write Now orientation and meets my mom. On the way there, we talk about Upton Sinclair and the tragic misunderstandings that occur between the public and a writer's work.

At orientation, I am introduced to my mentee, a thoughtful young woman named Leslie with a kind smile. I ask if it's okay to meet Leslie's mom, with whom she shares a deep bond. On the way, Leslie talks to me about Upton Sinclair and I jokingly text my mentor friend: "My mentee is smarter than me."

I walk into Little Skips for the first time and the grungy adult atmosphere disturbs me. I will not summon the courage to order anything for the first time until at least a year from now. Lauren and I play getting-to-know-you games with Skittles and M&M's. I become less nervous about sharing my writing with a stranger.

I am a little nervous that the café I picked will scare my mentee. When I get there, I ask if she wants anything. A fast "No, thanks," makes me think that, with time, she will let me treat her; after four years, no such chance. I bring candy with me for a fun icebreaker game I hope will make her feel more comfortable.

YEAR 2: 2017–2018

My great-grandmother dies suddenly, and I visit Mexico for the first time for her funeral. In the small rural village where my grandmother grew up, there is only a dial-up computer that I email and coordinate Girls Write Now anthology deadlines with Lauren from. She sends me love and support, and understands when I tell her I won't be able to use proper grammar because the keyboard has only Spanish characters.

I receive a beautiful but grammatically off email from Leslie, who I send love to during this time of mourning for her and her family. We are both inspired by these events, especially as I begin to think more about how we as humans grieve.

Lauren experiences a career change. She starts taking on more, and seems more stressed than usual. I am inspired by her grace and tranquility during this time in her life.

My transition into nonprofit work takes a strain on my mental health, which I notice during my pair sessions with Leslie. I try to be more conscious of curbing my distraction when we're together, but I am grateful for her patience and understanding while I take this leap during my career.

YEAR 3: 2018–2019

Lauren is "mean" to a tourist outside the Whitney who is confused about why it is so packed on a sunny Sunday afternoon following the opening of its Andy Warhol exhibition. I am reminded of Lauren's intrinsic conscientious ability toward thoughtfulness and kindness.

I feel a little bit guilty after snapping at an innocent question from a nice woman who probably didn't know any better. I feel worse that it was in front of Leslie, who I fear is less impressionable than judgmental at this age, despite her protests that I did nothing wrong.

Lauren joins my mom and me for our yearly dinner at the Shake Shack up the block from the New-York Historical Society, where they team up in their loving attempts to get me to sleep more. My favorite story about Lauren occurs: When someone offers to take her tray for her, she exclaims, "Amazing!"

I have dinner with Leslie and her mom at their annual Post-Girls Write Now Shake Shack. While we discuss Leslie's terrible sleeping habits over fries, I think about how proud I am of Leslie, who is officially one year from graduating.

YEAR 4: 2019–2020

Lauren and I establish a routine that cements an internal writing clock for me, even when we don't meet. Sunday mornings are impressed with her presence. Not writing on Sunday mornings disturbs my week; it feels incomplete.

A free-write at the beginning of every session helps us both focus as we settle into our coffee cups and check-ins about the week. The session, always thought-provoking, follows an easygoing pattern, from my subtle-not-so-subtle cue "What do you want to work on today?" to our weekly agenda planning for deadlines and other program requirements.

As Lauren and I prepare end-of-year deadlines and I reflect on our dynamic relationship and most significant moments, I cannot begin to express the deep and meaningful effect she has had on my life and the kind of woman I want to be in the future.

Our connection has been one that was special from the beginning. Like each other, it will continue to grow and evolve.

RIA PARKER

YEARS AS MENTEE: 3

GRADE: Senior

BORN: New York, NY

LIVES: New York, NY

PUBLICATIONS AND RECOGNITIONS: Scholastic Art & Writing Awards: Gold Key and Silver Keys

MENTEE'S ANECDOTE: *For the three years I've spent with Amy, all of them have been my favorite because all were memorable, like seeing a tribute for Toni Morrison or just meeting up at Irving Farm. Amy has inspired me to continuously take my place in history, whether it be when I was in eleventh grade and I joined the New York Civil Liberties Union Teen Activist Project or in the first year as a pair, when I first showed my vulnerability in writing. Now, in my senior year, Amy is still inspiring me to take my place in history through my future career goals.*

AMY FLYNTZ

YEARS AS MENTOR: 8

OCCUPATION: Founder, Amy Flyntz Copywriting LLC

BORN: Bridgeport, CT

LIVES: Brooklyn, NY

MENTOR'S ANECDOTE: *Since meeting Ria three years ago, I've had the pleasure of watching her grow into a confident, unstoppable force of a woman who continues to inspire me every week. Ria has a clear vision of the world she wants to create—and I have no doubt she will mold it as such through her writing, activism, and empathy. It has been an honor to witness Ria's incredible multiple successes, from summer programs at Ivy League schools and multiple Scholastic awards to full-ride scholarships at several universities. I can't wait to live in the world as Ria creates it.*

A TRIBUTE TO MYSELF

RIA PARKER

This piece was inspired by the Natalie Douglas tributes workshop, along with 2020 being a new decade filled with emotions. Additionally, since I am graduating this year, this decade will be filled with me taking my place in history.

There are so many people who have made a big impact on the world, whether because they stood up for change or you saw yourself represented in them. Whether because they loved you when you believed you weren't lovable or they taught you the biggest lessons you'd learn in your life. They can be celebrities, family members, friends, mentors, heroes, even fictional characters.

And with death being a never-ending occurrence, feeling like an end of an era, your childhood, you give tributes to these people. You give tribute to those people in different ways and because of these tributes you make yourself a part of their history.

A tribute is defined as an act, statement, or gift that is intended to show gratitude, respect, or admiration to a person. But a tribute isn't only for the deceased, it is also for the living, for those who still manage to give contribution or service, doing remarkable things, and still inspire and influence others. That's why I decided to write a tribute to myself.

A Tribute to Myself: If I were to die tomorrow, I hope I am remembered by:

1) My love for my family and friends
2) My love for learning
3) My love for science fiction and afrofuturism

4) My love for Michael Jackson and wanting to fight for his innocence and blackness that the world fails to see
5) My need to put my best in everything
6) My love for children: the ones who haven't been robbed of their joy and innocence; the ones who have been robbed of their childhoods because of a cruel world that sees them as voiceless; both groups are equally important and worthy of real love
7) My activism for all in terms of sexuality, disability, gender, race, class, ethnicity, all intersectionalities—even if mine is already at the bottom
8) My ambition, passion, and risk
9) My drive to change the world for the better
10) Saving you when you felt alone and something I wrote was able to transcend you to my soul and connect us both as if I am whispering "I love you" in your ear constantly
11) My introversion, my sensitivity, my blackness, my womanhood—all of which I define on my own terms

A Tribute to Myself: For now and all the things I hope to accomplish in my lifetime:

1) Everything I mentioned above
2) Being a screenwriter, where I am securing seats at the table for me and others like me
3) Owning my own production company, a place where everybody is accepted within good means and where everybody is represented truthfully because I for one know how it feels to not be
4) My fight for the incarcerated, for those whose souls leave their bodies due to living in a world that has done them wrong with an unjust justice system
5) My fight for the innocent, the ones proven innocent and the ones still fighting, who are trying to be treated like human beings and not criminals, because you are worth the fight

6) Giving those who aren't given a second chance by society that chance
7) Opening up a school where nobody is pressured to a certain field and where creativity and thinking for one's self isn't suppressed, a school that teaches REAL and ALL history and is inclusive and informative on ALL topics
8) Opening up a children's hospital in dedication to my role model AND children of the world
9) Many more failures and successes that will come in all due time

If I were to die tomorrow and somebody were to give a tribute to me, I'd want it to go something like this:

Ria Parker couldn't move all 100 billion galaxies, but she moved ours, with just her writing as it spilled out her words, her thoughts, and everything that made her vulnerable; with her words that could make fire freeze and death question itself. She was an introvert, but the notebook was her voice. She wanted to change the world for the better, and though there were people who had doubts because of her age, gender, race, and elsewhat, she managed to do that.

And this is how I, Ria Parker, am taking and will take my place in history.

LILLY PEREZ

YEARS AS MENTEE: 1

GRADE: Senior

BORN: Bronx, NY

LIVES: Bronx, NY

MENTEE'S ANECDOTE: *I'm really happy I met someone like Kiki, because even though we have our ups and downs, she still brings with her this aura of positive energy that never fails to brighten my day, and she's also helped me a lot, not only with writing but also my confidence and some pretty valuable life advice. I couldn't ask for a better mentor.*

KIKI T.

YEARS AS MENTOR: 1

OCCUPATION: Author, Columnist, Writer, Astrosexologist

BORN: New York, NY

LIVES: New York, NY

PUBLICATIONS AND RECOGNITIONS: TheFrisky.com, *Teen Vogue, New York Post Page Six,* and more; *Angst: Teen Verses from The Edge* (Workman Publishing, 2001) and *The Celestial Sexpot's Handbook* (Grand Central Press, 2007)

MENTOR'S ANECDOTE: *When Lilly gives herself the chance, incredible things happen. Her heart is that of an artist, and creating brings out her best, happiest, and most honest self. As expected from a cautious Capricorn and persistent Scorpio pairing, it did take time to build the right momentum, consistency, and foundation to bring her artistic inspirations to life, but once the ball got rolling, there was no stopping her. We even had sessions when I had to only sit back and watch. Those were proud moments. Capricorns—they love to surprise, by revealing their magic a little at a time.*

SCULPT-APOCALYPSE

LILLY PEREZ

"Sculpt-apocalypse" is about this postapocalyptic world that's overrun by the oppressive Aluminum Regime, which seeks to eradicate clay in favor of aluminum, but a young clay boy by the name of Goob forms and leads a resistance against them called The Uglies in order to avenge his people.

Scouring through the oversaturated gray wasteland that was once the land of Sculpticipica, two hooded figures were trying to find survivors from the Aluminum Regime's previous cleansing.

"Goob, how much longer are we going to look?" asked Cy.

"For however long we need to, Cy," Goob replied, scanning every square inch of gravel and rubble in his vicinity with the infrared setting on his mask. "Until we find someone."

"All right, man," sighed a defeated Cy.

Suddenly, the infrared setting on Clay's mask picked up something. He screamed: "Hey, dude! I think I got something or someone!"

"Really? Where to and how far?" responded Cy.

An automated female voice spoke: "Two hundred meters away."

"Two hundred meters away under that sheet of foil ahead," said Cy.

"Let's get there quick," answered Goob.

The two made their way across the abandoned land, where they picked up the location of a possible survivor. They crouched down to meet the gaze of a scared girl who was badly disfigured by the cleansing.

"P-Please don't hurt me!" she whimpered, curled up into a ball.

"It's okay," assured Goob, as he slowly lifted his mask off his head to show the girl that he wasn't one of them.

"We're here to help," he added, stretching out his hand toward her.

She slowly turned her head to look at Goob, hesitating to take his hand and murmuring, "H-how do I know I can trust you?"

"I know it may not look like it, but I'm clay, just like you—me and my partner over here," Goob explained, nudging his head toward Cy and reassuring her not to worry. She unclenched her expression a little.

"Come on." Goob stretched his hand to her.

Slowly, she took his hand to get up and dusted herself off. Goob handed her an aluminum cloak and mask. "Here, put this on, for protection from the drones."

She quickly put it on as Goob slid his mask back on. The three headed back the way Goob and Cy came, with Cy leading the way.

"Where are we going?" she asked.

"We're going somewhere safer than here, with others like us," Goob explained, scanning the sky to make sure all was clear.

They reached a big aluminum-covered vehicle. Cy opened the door and gestured for both to go in. They packed into the vehicle, started the engine, and sped away.

* * *

A moment of silence passed. Goob decided to break the silence. "What's your name?"

"I'm Riis. You?" she asked, glancing at the two sitting across from her.

"I'm Goob," he shared, then, signaling over to Cy, "That's Cy. It's nice to meet you."

"It's nice to meet you, too," she meekly replied, looking down at the two aluminum stubs where her hands once were and at her arms, where the last remains of her clay skin were chipping off. Riis clung to the aluminum cloak, concealing her arms in shame.

Goob moved closer to her, laying his hand on her shoulder to console her. "Hey, it's okay. It gets easier over time."

Her eyes then shifted to his other hand, clay intact, but from his wrist to shoulder, a dull gray aluminum. She asked: "How did you manage?"

He glanced at his hand and confessed: "I had to. I hated getting rid of my skin, but I had to, for protection."

"We really are scum, huh?" admitted Riis, as she lowered her head to hide her face and the tears that came.

Goob wrapped both his arms around her. "We're far from it, which is why our people need to rise up against the Aluminum Regime." He let go of her for a moment to meet her gaze.

"Which is why me, Cy, and others like us are trying to lead a resistance against them to bring Sculpticipica back to its old glory."

BRITNEY PHAN

YEARS AS MENTEE: 1

GRADE: Sophomore

BORN: Bronx, NY

LIVES: Bronx, NY

MENTEE'S ANECDOTE: *My relationship with my mentor reminds me of two plants growing beside each other. While one has some of its petals in full bloom, the other has just begun sprouting. Underneath, they are interlocked by the roots of their relationships, families, and experiences. The bigger plant reaches out once in a while to help the smaller plant, but at the end of the day it trusts her enough to know that she'll soon begin growing on her own.*

LINDSAY ZOLADZ

YEARS AS MENTOR: 4

OCCUPATION: Freelance Writer

BORN: Washington Township, NJ

LIVES: Brooklyn, NY

PUBLICATIONS AND RECOGNITIONS: *The New York Times*, *New York* magazine, and *Bookforum*

MENTOR'S ANECDOTE: *On a recent weekday, Britney and I took a field trip and visited one of my favorite places in the city, the main branch of the New York Public Library. It was the first time she'd been there, and it was an honor to introduce her to this magical place—half museum and half library. We were both in awe as we went through an exhibit of the many novels and nonfiction books that had been written inside the library. I could see how inspired Britney was, feeling all the creativity in that space—maybe it's a story she'll later tell if she one day writes a book there, too. She shared a piece with me later that day that proved she's well on her way as a writer.*

THIS IS

BRITNEY PHAN

"this is" is an answer to the question: "Where do you see yourself in ten years?" Just recently in history, women have the power to seize their opportunities and follow their dreams. This piece reflects on those dreams, and the future.

When I wake up in the morning, I want it to be to the sound of the birds chirping, perched high above the window of my bedroom on the branch of a tree overlooking my entire house. And I want my house to be big, so big it practically chokes all the scenery around it, so that when I lift that window open to let a portion of the summer breeze fly in, there'll be nothing else but blue skies to look forward to.

From below, I want to be able to smell the roses outside, twisted against the wiring of the fence of my patio, their thorns sharp but not enough to pierce my skin if I lean forward too much. Walking downstairs I'll hear, along with the birds, my mother making our favorite meal while my sister plays music in the living room. In this dream, I don't nearly want to be as alone as I say I do. I put a hand over my chest and notice that the hurt isn't there anymore, and every time I see a glimpse of myself in the reflection I'll stare straight ahead. Maybe somewhere hidden in my eyes there's a piece of my younger self that's looking back, and when I see her for the first time, I'll say *hello.* I'll say that I've been waiting for her, because I have, that her time is precious now, that it's a privilege not to realize how much of her life she'll spend thinking about it. In this dream, she won't have to worry.

It will always be summer here. The heat sticks to our skins in a layer of sweat built out of the days we spend just gazing at the sunset. The colors paint our arms the shade of purple descending into yellow. I reach over to pull out a dandelion and blow the petals to the wind, watching as each one disappears along with the sun over the horizon. My sister laughs at me, swatting away a fly that gets too close. Her face has gotten a little older, a little longer, stretched out at the edges, but then I'll look at her smile and be reminded of the time we were both children, equally striving for nothing, just as we are now. In this dream, my sleep is an endless black tunnel and when I come out, there's only sunlight ahead. Everything I wanted sits in front of me on platters I've already tried, and when it's all over, I'm sitting against my favorite couch in the corner of my living room. Television plays softly in the background while my mother nonchalantly hums a tune she heard in her younger days, and she'll tell me about it, running her hands through my hair as I fall asleep to her voice.

But no matter how invincible my dream seemed to be, life was keen on bleeding through.

"You know," she tells me quietly, her face reflecting the light on the ceiling overhead, like a planet from far away, "Grandma would be proud of you."

"Yeah," I'd say, suddenly opening my eyes to watch the stars up ahead. In this dream, in *this* living room, I'd put a window there just so I could see the way they moved every night, and I'd place my finger beside them, as if I'd grown large enough to catch constellations in my hands. "She would be proud."

My grandmother would die a beautiful death. Long after she'd gone, just like in life, she would continue giving parts of herself to others. When we were children, it was an extra hand that washed our bodies, our hair; a pair of eyes that oversaw our growth, making sure we were still alive by the time my parents returned home. In this dream, our roses would bloom from the pockets of her ashes. Every day would be a slow recline into an endless summer, and every morning I'd wake up to the sound of birds chirping, and I'd know, this is my dream.

TORI PHELPS

YEARS AS MENTEE: 1

GRADE: Freshman

BORN: Queens, NY

LIVES: Queens, NY

MENTEE'S ANECDOTE: *I love working with Laura. I feel like we have the same tastes in both reading and writing. One of my favorite memories is the first time that I met Laura, because she made me feel very comfortable and it was really easy to talk to her. When I handed her an essay that I wanted her to look over, I liked how she gave me things that she liked about it and things that she thought I could work on.*

LAURA GERINGER BASS

YEARS AS MENTOR: 4

OCCUPATION: Author

BORN: New York, NY

LIVES: New York, NY

PUBLICATIONS AND RECOGNITIONS: author of twenty books for children, preteens, and young adults

MENTOR'S ANECDOTE: *Tori and I meet each week at the Museum of Natural History (her choice), which was also one of my favorite places to hang out as a teen. The first time we met there at the Big Canoe, I was hit by waves of nostalgia. Our conversation ranged over Tori's love of music, lyrics of the songs she likes to sing, her experiences in one of the lead roles of her school's production of the musical* Oliver!, *short stories and novels we've both enjoyed, movies, shows, and writing prompts. With a backdrop of the Wall of Biodiversity, a reminder to observe, wonder, and improvise to the best of our creative abilities, I look forward to a second semester of writing and conversation with Tori at the museum.*

RECLAIMING MY TIME

TORI PHELPS

This essay is inspired by an essay prompt by an organization that I am in. With the help of my mom and Laura I was greatly inspired by all of the African American women that have made history.

I think about reclaiming our time, our history before slavery, the *culture* that was stolen from us. Before the slave trade, economic, political, and scientific developments were *superior* in Africa compared to other countries. African kingdoms had well-organized governments, as well as currency and international trade. Africans crafted *luxurious* items out of bronze, gold, ivory, and terra-cotta and excelled in science, technology, engineering, and math (STEM). Africa is acknowledged as the *birthplace* of many scientific developments. Engineering, mathematics, architecture, and medicine are associated with extensive political developments, such as the formation of states and monarchy.

To quote Bryan Stevenson: "Slavery gave America *fear* of black people and the taste for *violent punishment.*" The transatlantic slave trade *falsified* the views of the importance and history of the African continent.

In the words of Maxine Waters: *"We can reclaim our time"* by teaching students in schools about the true history and culture of the African continent. We must teach the *importance* of the culture and history of African Americans and introduce students to the *rich* and *vibrant* society that was Africa before slavery. We must acknowledge the *wealth* of *achievement* African Americans have made to a better society. We must acknowledge the strength of heroes like Harriet Tubman, who *escaped* slavery and came back to help others escape. We must teach children about Mary Jackson, Katherine

Johnson, and Dorothy Vaughan, *brilliant women* who worked with NASA to help beat Russia in the space race.

Simone Biles and Gabby Douglas are two *hardworking* gymnasts. As African Americans, they were *discriminated* against because of their skin color. This discouraged them, but they never gave up on what they loved to do. Recently, a fifteen-year-old African American girl named Cori Gauff, also known as Coco Gauff, won one singles title and two doubles titles on the Women's Tennis Association Tour. She is a former world No. 1 Junior Tennis player. Simone Biles, Gabby Douglas, and Cori Gauff are modern-day African Americans who are doing what they love and not giving up.

Michelle Obama, Simone Biles, Gabby Douglas, Cori Gauff, Harriet Tubman, Maxine Waters, Mary Jackson, Katherine Johnson, and Dorothy Vaughan have all *reclaimed* their time. They have *brought light* to the African American culture and they have made it known that African Americans are not just high school dropouts. They have shown people that African Americans are *not afraid to speak out* for what's right. With these women as inspiring examples, *I,* Tori Phelps, will reclaim my time.

MICAELA PINTO

YEARS AS MENTEE: 1

GRADE: Junior

BORN: Queens, NY

LIVES: Queens, NY

MENTEE'S ANECDOTE: *The first time I met Maddy, I felt somewhat intimidated. Not by her, but for my English, which I worried wasn't good enough. But with only a few words, I felt that good vibe Maddy carries with her. I learned we had more in common than I thought: we both speak Spanish, we've lived abroad, and we love cats. Maddy inspires me to grow as a writer, making me feel comfortable with my ideas and abilities. Together, we've created pieces that I proudly present to the world.*

MADELINE McSHERRY

YEARS AS MENTOR: 1

OCCUPATION: Marketing Manager, Amazon Web Services

BORN: Bronx, NY

LIVES: Queens, NY

PUBLICATIONS AND RECOGNITIONS: *Cambridge Review of International Affairs; Foreign Policy Rising*

MENTOR'S ANECDOTE: *The day I met Micaela at orientation, she shared her beautiful, perceptive reflection out loud, and when she finished, smiled and whispered, "That was scary." Micaela is thoughtful, intelligent, and inherently brave, pushing herself to the edge of what's comfortable in order to grow. Having decided to leave Peru and finish high school in the United States, she embodies what it means to choose challenge over comfort, and inspires me to do the same.*

505

MICAELA PINTO

After a visit to the doctor, "505" began in my imagination and ended as an exploration of a new genre and writing style for me.

The strong, stale smell of cleaning products and urine filled her nostrils as she took a deep breath in the hospital bed. She looked down toward her abdomen covered by bandages, an intense brown-reddish color from her dried blood. The harsh white lights reflected on her pale skin. The door opened and the tall doctor entered, holding a thick file of papers and wearing a yellow suit that covered every part of his body, including a mask for his face. All she could see were his blue eyes. "Was that suit necessary?" she thought.

Five other people wearing the same yellow suits entered the room and surrounded the bed. No one made eye contact with the patient. One began pressing hard on her belly. Another grabbed her wrist and took her pulse. Each minute felt like an eternity as they took notes and nodded their heads until finally the blue-eyed doctor spoke.

"How was your night, miss?"

"It was all right. I mean, the stomach pain was . . . tolerable," she said.

"That's good to hear," said the doctor as he opened the file. "As you know, we are still waiting for the blood work results."

She sighed, crossed her arms, and looked away from the doctor. "It's been five days. A week. I don't know. It's taking longer than it should."

The doctor, used to her forceful protests, ignored her and continued. "My team will check your vitals and your temperature, and look for any new symptoms. Every half hour."

"That's ridiculous. Let me at least sleep in peace."

"We wouldn't like to miss anything, or let it escalate," the doctor replied, making eye contact with her for the first time, his piercing blue eyes almost motionless.

The doctor left the room and accelerated his step toward the end of the hall, passing through four doors to the restricted area. There, he sat down and opened the patient's file. He began to speak as if someone else was there with him. "Phase one is complete. The patient did not reject the specimen. Phase two, incubation, has begun successfully."

"Proceed with caution and present your report tomorrow," said a distant voice from the dark screen before him.

How many days had she been there? She couldn't remember. Each day seemed longer than the previous one, the days long and the tomorrows longer. She began to forget why she ever came to the hospital. Each day, the assessments got longer and more uncomfortable, five pairs of eyes and hands touching her, grabbing her, as she came in and out of consciousness. What were they testing for? What was the diagnosis?

The only thing she knew was that she wanted answers and she wanted to get out of there.

So with all the courage she could put together, she ventured out into the corridor in search of that blue-eyed doctor to demand a diagnosis.

There were no signs. There were no other patients. In the darkness, she couldn't remember ever coming down this hallway. This wasn't the hospital she arrived in all those weeks ago.

A voice caught her attention. Quietly, she followed it down the hall, through several doorways, and peered through a small window to the last room.

Inside, the blue-eyed doctor was sitting in front of a gigantic monitor. She felt the hair on her body stand on end as she looked at pictures of her body covering the entire screen. Her face, arms, legs, lower regions, everything was photographed. Her eyes roamed the screen frantically until they stopped at one particular photo: Her abdomen was being cut by a long, large scalpel. She did not consent to having these pictures taken of her. Had she been asleep? Beside each photo, there were handwritten notes, in handwriting too small to read. However, it was the title, in large, red letters that made vomit begin to rise in her throat: Experiment 505.

Millions of questions raced through her mind as she tried to put the pieces together. She lacked air in her lungs, her body trembled, and her eyes grew larger and larger.

Then she looked away from the screen, and standing in front of the window was that pair of cold blue eyes and a knowing smile playing on the doctor's mouth.

DANIELA RAMOS

YEARS AS MENTEE: 1

GRADE: Senior

BORN: Bronx, NY

LIVES: Bronx, NY

PUBLICATIONS AND RECOGNITIONS: Scholastic Art & Writing Awards: Silver Key

MENTEE'S ANECDOTE: *Julia has taught me so much about how to find inspiration when it comes to trying to write a piece, and about the best coffee shops in New York City! I am eternally grateful to her in that she understands my weird passions and helps me think of ways to turn them into actual pieces I can be proud of.*

JULIA CARPENTER

YEARS AS MENTOR: 3

OCCUPATION: Journalist, *The Wall Street Journal*

BORN: Atlanta, GA

LIVES: Brooklyn, NY

PUBLICATIONS AND RECOGNITIONS: *The Wall Street Journal, Glamour Magazine,* 2019 Association of LGBTQ Journalists Excellence in Journalism Winner

MENTOR'S ANECDOTE: *When Daniela and I first met, she and I immediately bonded over family stories and our love of books and documentaries. We get together to drink coffees and hot chocolates and brainstorm new ideas for stories and poems. I am always so impressed with Daniela's energy and her ability to write in multiple formats and styles. I can't wait to read her work years into the future to see how it evolves and grows!*

BEAUTIFUL SKIN

DANIELA RAMOS

*This piece is meant to call attention to racial problems that don't exist
only in the United States. Just because people's experiences might be different doesn't mean that they aren't cut from the same cloth. People
should take pride in who they are because everyone is beautiful, not
different.*

Your mind shields the beauty of your dark skin from your eyes
Instead of seeing your skin as sweet as milk chocolate you see it as
   dirt
Just wishing you could dust it off
The fear of being black.
You read books like *The Invisible Man* with astonishment
Shocked that black people could be pushed to fight with other
   brothers back in the day and for what?
For brass coins, placed for you to get in an electrified rug.

But the thought that enters your mind first
That could never be me . . . not now and not in the past
You could never be stopped by the police for the color of your
   skin.
You think you're different because you've never had the
   conversation of "this is what you do if you have an encounter
   with the police . . . this is how you talk . . . this is how you
   breathe"
The fear of being black.
Those times will come soon, when you turn sixteen.
You're no different.
Actually no . . . maybe in one thing . . . in that you are not proud
   of the color of your skin.

Our color says a lot about us and the people before us.

We are descendants of patience, bravery and greatness.

Why would you deny that those three great qualities are in your blood?

The fear of being black is no longer inside your thoughts and it is not one of your problems to worry about.

Your biggest problem now is finding who you are.

What is the definition of "natural"?

Discontinuing payment to someone who is willing to let you lose your curls and damage your hair.

No longer hiding your curly and frizzy hair from the world

Losing the foundation that's three shades lighter than your actual skin color because you finally see the beauty in your skin.

Your beautiful dark skin.

JAYA RAO-HEREL

YEARS AS MENTEE: 1

GRADE: Sophomore

BORN: Brooklyn, NY

LIVES: Brooklyn, NY

PUBLICATIONS AND RECOGNITIONS: Scholastic Art & Writing Awards: Honorable Mention; music performances at Joe's Pub and Rockwood Music Hall

MENTEE'S ANECDOTE: *Before this year, I had never had a mentor in the formal sense. I always learned from those around me, and yet the label "mentor" seemed foreign. I was unsure of what to expect, but curious about how my time at Girls Write Now would help me define the term. Over the past year, Amanda has taught me that a mentor is someone you learn from, but also someone you laugh, reflect, explore, and smile with. I have learned a lot, and am so thankful that Amanda was the one to share it with me.*

AMANDA EKERY

YEARS AS MENTOR: 1

OCCUPATION: Musician, The New School, Jazz at Lincoln Center

BORN: El Paso, TX

LIVES: Brooklyn, NY

PUBLICATIONS AND RECOGNITIONS: 2020 Chamber Music America Inaugural Grantee for Performance

MENTOR'S ANECDOTE: *Jaya has a sense of self. She has great appreciation for her family and her ideas, and it's apparent in her writing and music. I deeply relate to her work, and often leave our sessions thinking about my own sense of self and identity, and wonder how I would put my thoughts into words as clearly and with conviction as Jaya has. She is a quiet force and I'm grateful to have her as a mentee who inspires and teaches.*

TWO WORLDS

JAYA RAO-HEREL

A memoir, a thought, a realization. Finding and defining my own identity.

I've grown up in two worlds. Falling asleep at kirtans, soft hums of Indian songs drifting in the air, and also listening to my dad's favorite Eagles song on repeat. I've grown up riding in rickshaws in India, and eating rice with my hands off banana leaves, but also learning where to place utensils to properly set a table on Christmas: forks on the left, knives and spoons on the right. I've grown up taking off my shoes at temples but also being told I can keep them on in my grandma's house, even on the carpet. I've grown up saying Grandma and Grandpa, Ajji and Aja. The latter always followed up by "That's Grandma and Grandpa in Kannada." I've grown up hearing people call me "jii-ya," but also learning about its Sanskrit origin from my mom. I've grown up with skin that made people say I looked more like my dad than my mom, but dark hair that resembles hers exactly. I've grown up watching cartoons about Hanuman, and reading Nancy Drew before bed. I've grown up with the familiar sound of my ajji's thick Indian accent, but also cringing at the roar of laughter when the class clown jokingly spoke in one, too. I've been angered by the way people let this slide, but also by the way *I* let it slide. I've grown up feeling like I wasn't a reflection of the diversity that I am.

I wonder if my light skin makes people think of me as *only white*; if they don't see the other 50 percent of me, does it even exist? The 50 percent that makes rangolis at Diwali and sings at pujas. The 50 percent that could eat paneer tikka masala and drink mango lassis every day. The 50 percent that is woven in my DNA and is dispersed through all aspects of my life. Yes, it does exist. I've grown up *in two* culturally rich worlds, *into* me.

LEADRA REEVES

YEARS AS MENTEE: 1

GRADE: Senior

BORN: Brooklyn, NY

LIVES: Brooklyn, NY

MENTEE'S ANECDOTE: *When I first met Baze, all of my past assumptions regarding mentorship and it being a formal arrangement disintegrated entirely. Our similar personalities, work ethic, sense of humor, and shared commitment to see each other succeed have drawn us closer. We regularly meet at the public library, where we have designated our own spot; it is a happy medium between the noise and the still silence. We gel so well together that doing work and spending time with her and her contagious smile is never a burden. I am so grateful to have met such an amazing person, mentor, and lifelong friend.*

BAZE MPINJA

YEARS AS MENTOR: 1

OCCUPATION: Senior Writer, SpotCo

BORN: Dover, NH

LIVES: Brooklyn, NY

PUBLICATIONS AND RECOGNITIONS: *Elle, Allure, Marie Claire*

MENTOR'S ANECDOTE: *Leadra is a smart, multitalented girl—she plays soccer, she performs in her school musicals, and she writes beautiful poems. On top of all that, Leadra received early admission into Brown University. I think the moment that our relationship deepened was the day that she first shared her poetry with me. Her poems were about heavy topics like police brutality and racial injustice. Talking about her work and those issues was a great bonding experience. I can't wait to see where Leadra's talent takes her.*

ROUGH EDGES

LEADRA REEVES

This poem speaks to all the forgotten women: the women with stories, with histories. I aim to give a voice to women who should have a place in history and should be recognized because of their struggles and how vital they are to society.

So kinky, so curly, so silky, so neat
The way she slicks back her dark brown strands;
concealing her roots underneath cakey coatings of clear gel;
Rougher than her edges,
that brown bristled brush lining her gifted palms is
Tougher than her mother who keeps her pledges
Not of allegiance to a flag that belittles her but
to her four kids she is raising all alone
in a neighborhood that instills a bloody cycle in young black lives,
no one knows otherwise
Than how to make children orphans
and have the streets teach them the do's and don'ts of a
    modernized society
She involuntarily inhales crack cocaine like it's oxygen
It's everywhere, she is choking,
Suffocating on this lifestyle
Still just a child she cannot part
like the part down the middle she traces with her comb
Her hot comb that is bigger than itself
Her hot comb that is a society uncooked, unseasoned, unflavored
Her hot comb places an expectation on who she should be
So she runs it through, burning any chance at self-love,
scorching any belief that she is a queen

Now eighteen, and still never even had a daddy around to hold
    up her crown
So she searches for him in all the wrong men
which either ends in her death
or leaves her lying at yet another ghettoed dead end.

JAYOLA REID

YEARS AS MENTEE: 1

GRADE: Junior

BORN: Portoviejo, Ecuador

LIVES: Bronx, NY

PUBLICATIONS AND RECOGNITIONS: Scholastic Art & Writing Awards: Silver Key, National Honor Society: Magna Cum Laude Academic Excellence Award

MENTEE'S ANECDOTE: *Getting to talk about things in our sessions every week that really excite me and introduce them to Ashley—things like my favorite music (yay, BTS!) and my closest friends and my plans for the summer—and to see that she was truly interested and enthusiastic and wanted to know more: That means a lot.*

ASHLEY OKWUOSA

YEARS AS MENTOR: 1

OCCUPATION: Journalist, Columbia University

BORN: Enugu, Nigeria

LIVES: New York, NY

MENTOR'S ANECDOTE: *Jayola is a gem, and being paired with her throughout this process has been incredible. She is smart, self-assured, and confident. She is not afraid to speak her mind and is constantly looking for ways to improve herself, whether it's with writing or the activities she does in her spare time, like debate. Jayola is bold and thoughtful. She came into the program sure of who she is, and I hope that she leaves the program even more sure that she belongs in every room she walks into and that the future is hers for the taking.*

MORNING ROUTINE

JAYOLA REID

A young girl of color is having a hard time educating her religious mother about the depression she silently struggles with.

Wake up and get ready for school anyway—I'm not working day in and day out to pay your tuition for nothing.

Straighten your hair and look presentable—I don't care if you cry when your ear is burnt.

If you can lie in bed and watch TV, you can get on the train to school. Failing should give you anxiety, not walking into the packed subway car.

You're faking it.

What do you have to be sad about? You have everything you need, I don't know what else you want. Stop crying before I give you something to cry about. Crying because you miss your father is not a valid reason.

Stop victimizing yourself—that's what our folk's problem is.

Don't blame your teachers for dress-coding you—blame yourself for believing you could wear that high skirt as if you were skinny enough not to be sexualized.

Why should I pay for a therapist when there is a Bible on your nightstand?

I don't care if you can't find friends that look like you. We don't deal with identity crises. We know who we are. Drugs are the only thing you can use as a coping mechanism?

I'm not paying for a therapist.

Now you depend on boys' love for your mental health?

I'm not paying for a therapist.

I'm not taking you to get diagnosed. I know what you have and it's just laziness.

Iron your white collared shirt, put on a longer skirt, make sure no curls are sticking out, and get on the crowded train to school.

ANNE RHEE

YEARS AS MENTEE: 1

GRADE: Junior

BORN: Brooklyn, NY

LIVES: Queens, NY

PUBLICATIONS AND RECOGNITIONS: Scholastic Art & Writing Awards: Honorable Mention

MENTEE'S ANECDOTE: *From talking about poetry and bonding over short fiction writers like Celeste Ng, to juggling junior year with our monthly meetings at the New Museum and Union Square Park alike, I'm so grateful for how transformative the Girls Write Now program has been in both expanding my perspective of writing and the world and also giving me the opportunity to meet my mentor, Sunny. She continually pushes me to be confident in my writing and offers amazing advice, but also challenges me to think outside of writing as I know it.*

SUNNY LEE

YEARS AS MENTOR: 1

OCCUPATION: Freelance Writer and Copy Editor

BORN: Ulsan, South Korea

LIVES: Brooklyn, NY

PUBLICATIONS AND RECOGNITIONS: *The Outline, Allure, Tenth Magazine*

MENTOR'S ANECDOTE: *Anne is staking her claim to history with her fierce ambition and nuanced ideas about what it means to be Korean American living in New York City today. Every time we meet, she has a million things going on (not an exaggeration), yet she carves out space to meditate on race, which, in turn, informs the way I think about my own identity. I'm in awe of Anne's poetry and constantly learn from her writing and ideas. And much like the great Asian American poets before her, I have no doubt her poetry and prose will make her a formidable force as she continues to write.*

CROSSING OVER

ANNE RHEE

This poem explores the generational gap that is felt by first-generation Asian immigrant parents and their children. While communication may seem difficult at first, it is still possible to find hope and reconciliation.

heavy, brittle, disembodied,
he struggles to form the breaks and snaps in this new language,
  longing,
for the comfort of the waterfall of his Korean,

but his daughter insists,
eyes sparkling of western conceptions and modernization,
her voice automated,
  metallicized,

  a silver cacophony of noise that never seems to fade,

the air lingering with its brilliance.

He stares at his daughter through a glass wall,
expanding in thickness and size,
his words are the barrier,
  his mouth,
    the barrier.

sometimes he is so frustrated,
that he wishes he could tear his mouth,
tear this imaginary border that has

dislocated him into
       isolation.
but

he cannot do it.

his words, alive,
       but dying.

      strangled

in the thick
abyss of his throat, buried in their graves
before they are borne into the world.

he knows that once
he releases his first word of English
      he will be confined to a prison
      of a language,
           caged, limited.

no,
he will clutch his roots and his homeland,
no,
he refuses to be jailed.

but his heart bleeds raw
with the prospect of knowing
that the price for not entering
is the wall.

he sees the secret embarrassment in her eyes
when he speaks in Korean.
for her father to be so foreign,
so Old World
she is confused.

she doesn't know how to live
between these two worlds,
fluttering from English to Korean,
wanting to not have to choose one
over the other.

she becomes angry,
        small liquid bursts,
                small petty arguments.

until one day, it becomes a flood of anger,
        warm and alive with years of choked resentment,

until she snaps back to reality,
snaps back to   loving her father.

she has become a demon,
feeding off a thirst of revenge
for what immigrating has done to her image
of her father.

another flood,
        a flood of tears,
salty and preserved
                it's too strong for her,
                too strong for her to stop and control,
        too incoherent
to bring back coherence.

she doesn't care anymore, doesn't
care about fitting in,

and her tears break down the wall,
break it until only fragments remain.

        too small to separate them now.

they stand there.
two souls.

one offers the other a hand.

the other takes it.

KATHY RIVERA

YEARS AS MENTEE: 1

GRADE: Senior

BORN: New York, NY

LIVES: Bronx, NY

MENTEE'S ANECDOTE: *Being in Girls Write Now and working with Mary has been a blessing and a great experience. She has opened me up to new things, such as different writing styles and different places to work around the city. I used to be shy with my writing and wanted to keep it to myself, but I can see the difference this past year has made. I am now much more open to sharing my writing with others, especially Mary. Mary and I have traveled to faraway places in immense crowds just so we can get to know each other and strengthen our bond, all while eating some chocolate and sipping hot chocolate.*

MARY DARBY

YEARS AS MENTOR: 2

OCCUPATION: Vice President, Burness

BORN: Peekskill, NY

LIVES: New York, NY

MENTOR'S ANECDOTE: *Kathy and I clicked right away. I knew I would love working with her. We laugh a lot together, and it's a joy to get together and just talk. Kathy is a young woman finding her voice and on the verge of taking her place in the world. She will, too. She's smart, she's eager, and she's worked hard to get where she is. She's looking forward to becoming more independent, extending her learning, and stretching herself as a person. I'm proud of her. She will go on to do more than she knows she can.*

STRANGE COMBINATION

KATHY RIVERA

Although this piece is not tied to the theme Taking Our Place in His-
tory, it does take place in my own history of living in a world where
someone of my shade of color grows up Hispanic.

I am a strange combination:

From my Spanish-speaking mother's attitude,
and my abandoned father's anger.
I am a strange combination.
I am fifty percent Nicaraguense and fifty percent Puerto Rican.
Not many people hear about my kind of mix.
I am a strange combination.

I can still hear the wind of my mom's chancleta flying across the
    room attempting to hit me or my sister to "give us something
    to cry about!"
The waves of her curly Central American hair gave away her
    lioness.
When she tells two out of her three daughters stories about her
    country, she speaks Spanish. The Spanish that flowed ever so
    smoothly out of her mouth.
We knew she was back home reliving her happiest moments.

Looking at the welkin here and looking at the welkin over in the
    Caribbean, I see myself trying to outlive my grandmother's life.
From teaching me my colors on a blanket with different flowers,
    to her gossiping to me in Spanish about her old children.
It is not flawed to outlive.

It is flawed to not try.

These two women are important in my life,
seeing that everyone else doesn't count.
There are no grandfathers, godparents, or third cousins you can
think of that I already have thought of.
Out of being from a Hispanic family household, you realize you
grow up similarly to other non-Hispanic families.

I do not have much of a heritage to uphold, however, living with
anxiety and instability was the only thing I was sure about up
until now.
I had to constantly tell my brain as well as my heart that
happiness is only a mood and not a destination.
Now, being from taboo and controversy,
I've learned how to walk away with compassion instead of
compulsion.

JANET ROJAS VAZQUEZ

YEARS AS MENTEE: 1

GRADE: Senior

BORN: Puebla, Mexico

LIVES: Brooklyn, NY

MENTEE'S ANECDOTE: *I honestly never saw myself as a writer, but Girls Write Now has taught me so many new methods of expressing myself through writing. Working with my mentor, Lily, has been incredible and she has taught me so many things. Getting to know her has been amazing because she's a confident woman I look up to. I have learned so much from Lily, and working with her always feels comfortable and creative. I'm so glad I got to join Girls Write Now, because it has given me the opportunity to write about things that matter to me.*

LILY BUTLER

YEARS AS MENTOR: 1

OCCUPATION: Director of Creative Strategy, *Slate*

BORN: Washington, D.C.

LIVES: Brooklyn, NY

PUBLICATIONS AND RECOGNITIONS: *Gawker, Jezebel, Slate*

MENTOR'S ANECDOTE: *Whenever someone asks me about Girls Write Now, the first thing I talk about is how much my mentee, Janet, inspires me. Despite juggling an array of extracurricular commitments, schoolwork, and family responsibilities, she always brings contagious enthusiasm to everything we do. "She's an inspiration" sums it up pretty well. She has taught me more than I ever imagined, and I can't wait to see (and read) what she accomplishes in the future.*

A PLANTED SCAR

JANET ROJAS VAZQUEZ

I dedicate this poem to my mom, Ana Vazquez. She sacrificed so much to help me become the woman I am. Even when we aren't together, I know she's giving me strength.

I was four years old
When my mom went to the grocery store
And didn't come back.

I am from the red roses my mom left me
That my abuelita told me to cherish.
I save them inside my soul.

I was born to a little girl playing with her doll
Dressing her up
And braiding her hair.

I am from "Don't come looking all messy and dirty"
In a big house with ten rooms
Where my toys are everywhere.

I grew up climbing mango trees
Looking for the green fruits
With the sour taste.

I was raised by my abuelita
Who believed in la llorona
And stories of men stealing young girls.

I was left with my mother's memories
That she planted in the backyard
before she moved to New York.

I was told not to open the box
Where my mother put a tea party
And the dolls she bought for me.

I am from neighbors blasting corridos,
Drinking cold cervezas,
Making carne asada that you can smell blocks away.

I can hear my abuelita saying
"Don't do this, don't touch that"
And that she would die if I left her.

I was nurtured by Virgen de Guadalupe
Who told me that my mom was coming
To get me in a dream.

JO ROSADO

YEARS AS MENTEE: 1

GRADE: Sophomore

BORN: New York, NY

LIVES: Bronx, NY

MENTEE'S ANECDOTE: *My relationship with my mentor is pretty good. Whenever we would meet up at Starbucks or the library it would always be chill and fun. We would crack some jokes and talk about stuff that's happening in our lives. She always makes me feel comfortable, and like I can trust her with just about anything. I am so glad I got to participate in this program with her.*

REGAN WINTER

YEARS AS MENTOR: 1

OCCUPATION: Assistant Editor, Little, Brown Books for Young Readers

BORN: West Lawn, PA

LIVES: New York, NY

MENTOR'S ANECDOTE: *In one of our first meetings, Jo told me about a recent experience she had with catcalling, and about how that experience made her feel. She wanted to write a poem about it to express her own emotions, and the emotions that all women who have experienced catcalling might have felt. Through brainstorming, we were able to relate this occurrence with the trials women have endured throughout history. Jo was able to write a truly poignant and powerful piece that I was proud to see her share with her family, friends, and teachers.*

FOR YOU

JO ROSADO

The following are lyrics to a song I wrote for someone I will forever love dearly and hold close.

When I wake up in the morning
And I get out of bed,
You're the first thing that I think about.
I can't get you out of my head.
Counting the minutes 'til I see you,
'Til I could hold your face.
You know my deepest wish is to stay in your embrace.

For you,
For you
I'd sail the seven seas,
Travel all the galaxies.
For you,
For you
I'd walk a million miles
Just to see you smile.

Tell me your hopes and dreams,
Tell me your darkest fears.
And when you're feeling down, I'll be right here to wipe your
    tears.
Sing me to sleep as the fire burns out
And stars begin to shine.
Tell me about the beauty of life,
Tell me I'm yours and you are mine.

For you,
For you
I'd sail the seven seas,
Travel all the galaxies.
For you,
For you
I'd walk a million miles
Just to see you smile.

The moment that I met you,
My world was filled with light.
I couldn't see before, but, girl,
You gave me my sight.
Ever since then I have a fire
That only you ignite.
Time spent without you,
It just isn't right.

For you,
For you
I'd sail the seven seas,
Travel all the galaxies.
For you,
For you
I'd walk a million miles
Just to see you smile.

TIFFANIE ROYE

YEARS AS MENTEE: 4

GRADE: Senior

BORN: Bronx, NY

LIVES: Bronx, NY

MENTEE'S ANECDOTE: *Working with Christine for four years now has definitely been a wonderful experience. It's weird to think about how much time has passed (when I first started the program I was fresh out of middle school, and when she started she was fresh out of college). She's the best mentor a girl could ask for and I wouldn't trade her guidance for the world. She has taken up a huge part of my high school history, and I will be forever grateful.*

CHRISTINE FLAMMIA

YEARS AS MENTOR: 4

OCCUPATION: PhD Candidate at Columbia University

BORN: Flemington, NJ

LIVES: New York, NY

PUBLICATIONS AND RECOGNITIONS: *Esquire, Cosmopolitan, Men's Health,* and more

MENTOR'S ANECDOTE: *Tiffanie and I have been working together for four (!) years and have had so much fun exploring writing styles, creative projects, and New York City. She is such a bright, creative person to be around. She is not afraid to jump into a new project, meet new people, or stand up for what she believes in. I'm excited to see all the awesome work she does!*

BRICK DISTRIBUTOR: THE INTERVIEW

TIFFANIE ROYE

This is a recording of my chat with Brick Distributor, an up-and-coming high school band with a vision of making music they love! They are in the midst of finding themselves in music history and have expressed that to me in this interview.

Q1: Give me a synopsis of how Brick Distributor was formed.

SOFIA: Okay, so basically we were like—Danny and I were dating and we knew that each other had musical abilities, so we decided first that we were going to cover a song and then we recorded it and put it on Reddit and the guy who wrote the song saw it and said he liked it. So Danny wrote a song and we decided we'd become a band. So we got Danny's friend who can play bass to join us and that's how we became Brick Distributor.

Q2: What song that you've written has been your favorite?

DANNY: I think "Just the Other Day." I like the way it makes me feel and how it tells a bittersweet story.

SOFIA: I'm biased toward the song "Girlfriend"'cause I wrote the lyrics and it's the most fun to sing. There's a part of the song where I get to scream and it's really intense. It's really fun while I'm performing to scream.

ZACH: My favorite song that I've written the bass part for is unreleased at the moment but is a mellow instrumental song that should hopefully come out soon.

Q3: Tell me a memorable and/or funny experience you've had at a show.

DANNY: Our first show was pretty memorable. It was in a Brooklyn backyard. There were five people present that weren't in a band. The memorable part of this was that the guitarist of the headlining band smashed his guitar. The experience was pretty crazy all around.

SOFIA: Hmm, let me think . . . I got very anxious before a show so I had to calm my anxiety right before going on and it was stressful, but my bandmates were there for me and we had a lot of fun. Another one is that at our most recent show we couldn't get our drum machine to work, so we started a few songs and the drums weren't coming in, which was annoying, but also really funny, and the sound guy at the venue was really pissed off.

ZACH: At our last show, the sound guy, who didn't like us very much, got his hair stuck in Danny's guitar . . .

Q4: Tell me the story surrounding your album *What's the Matter with You and Me??*

DANNY: Basically you write songs and put them all on the album. I feel like all the songs have themes and shit. I would say when we were writing this album there's existentialism and storytelling.

SOFIA: I mean, it's my favorite album out of the ones we've done so far. I think it has the most feeling and the most interesting story. I find that in our music that we're always playing characters and trying to embody the different feelings that those characters might feel. I guess the album itself is just a compilation of all the songs we've written since *Esteban B. Esteban B* was our first album under the old name we had. Actually the [album] that we wrote most recently is just called *Brick Distributor.*

ZACH: We had been working on the songs on the album for a long time and many of them had been finalized for a few months. The songs that were the newest, and in my opinion the best, were

"Girlfriend," "Another Personality," and "Just the Other Day" that closed out what would become our first album.

Q5: What's the hardest part about being in a band?

DANNY: I think being on stage is pretty stressful and I get pretty nervous on stages, so . . . performing is the hardest part. It's easy to record in a studio.

SOFIA: Um, the hardest part about being in a band . . . I would say collaborating because we're all really passionate and we all have a lot of opinions so sometimes compromising can be really difficult.

ZACH: The hardest part about being in a band is really just logistics. The act of playing with great people is so much fun that there really isn't a downside to it.

Q6: What are you most proud of in this band?

DANNY: Personally, I think we sound good, so I'm proud of that.

SOFIA: I'm most proud of the fact that we've not only come together as a band, but we came together as friends. We created a very important feeling of being in one collaborative and cohesive unit.

ZACH: I'm most proud of the songs we've written. It is one of the best feelings to create something that not only you enjoy playing, but also something that other people enjoy.

Q7: What are your future plans as a band?

DANNY: Well we have three shows this month [March]. I also want to perform at my job and make another album.

SOFIA: Um, well, since we're all going off to college, it's going to be pretty hard, but we're hoping to stay together as a band and send each other recordings through the internet.

ZACH: We plan to keep playing and releasing music that makes us happy to create.

LILLY SABELLA

YEARS AS MENTEE: 1

GRADE: Junior

BORN: New York, NY

LIVES: Queens, NY

PUBLICATIONS AND RECOGNITIONS: Scholastic Art & Writing Awards: Silver Key; Hypernova Lit; Sarah Lawrence Poetry Contest Winner

MENTEE'S ANECDOTE: *Before joining Girls Write Now, the thought of showing the most personal part of myself—my writing—to another person filled me with anxiety. But over coffee cups and bubble tea, I formed a relationship with my mentor that taught me I had nothing to be afraid of. Toni has not only helped me open up as a person, but she has helped open my world to a place where I feel confident to create, share myself, and grow as a writer. I truly look up to her and consider myself lucky to be her mentee.*

TONI BRANNAGAN

YEARS AS MENTOR: 1

OCCUPATION: Content Editor, Thinx Inc.

BORN: New York, NY

LIVES: Queens, NY

PUBLICATIONS AND RECOGNITIONS: *The Vagina Book: An Owner's Manual for Taking Care of Your Down There* (Chronicle, 2020)

MENTOR'S ANECDOTE: *This is my first year mentoring with Girls Write Now, and I could not have been luckier to be paired with Lilly. Besides the fact that she's one of the most talented poets I've ever read, I'm also lucky that we share the same taste in music, movies, internet drama, and bubble tea. (We might have a bubble tea problem; it's fine.) Working with her is always a highlight of my week, and I'm forever inspired by her maturity, work ethic, and ability to juggle the many things life throws her way.*

PUT YOUR ELBOWS INTO IT

LILLY SABELLA

*I've lived in the same home in Queens my whole life, and everything—
from cabinet doors to cereal boxes—reminds me of my childhood. This
is a poem about my parents and how I fit into our family.*

My mother washed dishes my whole life
her fingernails long and wet under suds of dish soap
and with each smear of Dawn over our plastic plates and cups,
she'd show me how to really put your elbow into it
When you're cleaning up after a man.
My father ate dry cereal every night before he went to bed
he'd take those plastic cups
leave every cabinet door open
every cereal box out
and fall into bed with a groan
his hip his back his knee always aching
and on the nights he'd cramp and twitch
I'd cry
because his screams were so loud it had to mean Trouble,
and with Cheerios crumbs pressed into his skin, he showed me
How to really be afraid of a man.
Some nights, lying in the middle of Mom and Dad
like a cigarette between teeth
they showed me broken glass in little girl feet
Kind of love
Knobby knees and questions from the police
Kind of love
All the neighbors hear nothing see nothing speak nothing
Of this Kind of love

But still, I remember Mom doing the dishes, Dad eating his
      cereal
and me
putting away cereal boxes and closing cabinet doors.

CLAUDIA SANCHEZ-JEAN

YEARS AS MENTEE: 1

GRADE: Sophomore

BORN: Queens, NY

LIVES: Bronx, NY

MENTEE'S ANECDOTE: *Sarah is a lot of things: giving, understanding, uplifting, and good at making banana bread. Every time we meet she becomes more and more relatable and pertinent to my everyday life. She was a break in my schedule that I very much needed. It's not that she only edited my work and told me what to fix but she showed me my strengths that I did not see and improved my expression more than my words.*

SARAH GRUEN

YEARS AS MENTOR: 1

OCCUPATION: Speechwriter, West Wing Writers

BORN: New York, NY

LIVES: Brooklyn, NY

PUBLICATIONS AND RECOGNITIONS: *McSweeney's Internet Tendency*

MENTOR'S ANECDOTE: *Not many sixteen-year-olds would spend their Saturday evening accompanying their far less cool twenty-five-year-old friend to see* Little Women. *Then again, Claudia isn't your average sixteen-year-old. An immensely talented artist (and little sister), Claudia proudly declared herself an Amy. But the truth is, I see something of each of the Little Women in Claudia: Along with Amy's ambition and skill, she has Meg's kindness and Beth's compassion, plus a whole lot of Jo March–esque humor, drive, creativity, and, of course, writing prowess. Look out world: With her art, her stories, and everything else she does, this (not so little) woman is going to make history.*

AN ODE TO WHO WE WILL BE

CLAUDIA SANCHEZ-JEAN

This is written for my mother, who built independence in me.

Thursday afternoon, the rain falls and won't stop until the next morning. School ended two hours ago and everyone is leaving their nine-to-five job. A girl sits on the steps at school, looking at the door, waiting for somebody to pick her up.

The door opens and it's her mother, soaked in rain the blue umbrella failed to shield. No worry, no fear, no relief the little girl showed. "It happens often"—the tardiness, the rain. Then why does it seem like you were really waiting?

Hand in hand (and on-sleeve to cross the street) to the train, pink rain boots and blue umbrella, the mother starts to ask, "How was your day?" The girl's day is always the same so that's all she says. They both know that.

Well, then how was the mother's day? Does she ever share? Full of coffee, emails, and phone calls? Maybe she should say that. So, go on, tell her something.

But the girl and I already know, because when "we" take the train and she'll wake you up at our stop, when "we" get home, "we" eat what's left over and "we" brush our teeth, and then the girl finally asks you to read her a book, you'll try not to fall asleep on her bed mumbling "One fish, two fish, red fish, blue fish." She'll always just find it amusing and read the book to you instead (One fish, two fish, red fish, blue fish).

She's not big enough to carry you to bed, so you do. But know that I know the girl can't wait to see you after school again. To see you try your best. Because the most she can do is give her love. Do you?

Well, the bigger she gets, the more she'll have, right? Now she can go home on her own. And now you get home after she's already had dinner. "We never have dinner together." Does she know this is for her and for the better? Yes she does, and she appreciates it, but I feel as if she rather it not be. What she does know is it's always going to be like this until she's grown enough, because you tell her a lot more often now.

She doesn't know if you love her. But soon she will know that you did and you still do.

ISABELLE SANDERSON

YEARS AS MENTEE: 2

GRADE: Junior

BORN: New York, NY

LIVES: New York, NY

MENTEE'S ANECDOTE: *When I first met Anna, I immediately noticed all of the colorful barrettes in her hair. Some were neon, some shaped like butterflies; there were even some sparkly ones. I just remember thinking to myself that this must be such a cool lady if she could pull off all these barrettes— and she was! She has been so wonderful in helping me with my writing, exposing me to new books, and even helping my life as a whole. Together, we've had discussions about cultural heritage, romantic objectification, and have plans to go to a roller derby match!*

ANNA WITIUK

YEARS AS MENTOR: 3

OCCUPATION: Grant Writer, Freelance

BORN: New York, NY

LIVES: Brooklyn, NY

MENTOR'S ANECDOTE: *I am so incredibly honored to be a mentor to Isabelle. The moment I met her I was struck by her mature poise, effervescent energy, and eagerness to learn all about the world and its people. I have very much enjoyed how willing she is to try new and different writing techniques and to explore the definition of what it means to write. Her poem "Encounters," which started out as a prompt in flash fiction, is a perfect example of this. She turned this single paragraph into a surging and evocative poem of descriptive senses and personal experience.*

ENCOUNTERS

ISABELLE SANDERSON

This poem is meant to capture the unfortunately timeless experience of girls who find themselves powerless and shamed by an attempt at romance. We can take our place in history by acknowledging these sometimes uncomfortable realities even when others refuse to do so.

Putrid and sour
at first the taste of morning
breath generously spread
over and inside her
mouth.
The smell of vanilla
shampoo melting scalding water.
Slow and thick
hot air.
Nutmeg soap
apple-rose body scrub
cinnamon body polisher
almond shaving cream.
More vanilla
something chocolatey
a tinge of ginger hair
oil deliriously sweet
hair spray saccharine hair
gel hands running
through strands of hair
so soft and so thin
running through fingers like water running through
over and over
cascading down pink freckles

and pink acne.
The dedicated movements of a dark mascara brush
and then
the smell of rain.

A cloud of vodka and urine.
something sour, something savory sticky
subway floor harsh
denim and canvas
blood
sweat
laundry detergent
Gatorade, black tea, aftershave, burnt cheese and acidic tomatoes,
    gasoline.
Then again,
the smell of rain. A whiff
of coffee
of almond milk, oat milk, 2% milk, cinnamon dust, chocolate
    powder, lemon tea, green matcha, clotted cream, thick jam,
    baked fruit, caster sugar.

The smell of cologne.

The jittering of legs.
The fidgeting in
scratchy pockets blush
spreads hot
across freckled cheeks.
One hand
inching closer
across a cool granite table top
desperate for
first
soft
touch.

Instead suddenly
something squishy
slimy vanilla chapstick
acidic mint gum
bitter coffee
slimy mint and bitter acidic and slimy acidic and acidic acidic and
    bitter slime and
slimy slimy
and cold damp hands
on burning skin
and burning cheeks
and still the oat milk and almond milk and cinnamon dust
still the coffee
pungent
still the cold
damp bitter acidic slime
spreading
like tentacles. Limp hands

till the slime recedes
and the smell of cologne grows fainter.
Replaced by rain
and salt water cooling burning cheeks.
Something else too, something
you can't quite
Place.

PRINCESA SANTOS

YEARS AS MENTEE: 2

GRADE: Sophomore

BORN: Cartagena, Colombia

LIVES: New York, NY

MENTEE'S ANECDOTE: *From the start, Camille and I had an immediate connection. I've learned so much from her talented, supportive, and equanimous persona. I enjoyed being able to bond over sports, adolescence, or social injustice we've similarly faced. I've felt the most confident while working with Camille on my poetry. I've enjoyed the weekly meets we spent working on new ideas and other writing genres. I'm so excited to further explore new themes and writing techniques as the year progresses!*

CAMILLE BOND

YEARS AS MENTOR: 1

OCCUPATION: Content Analyst/Contributing Writer, Thomasnet

BORN: Washington, D.C.

LIVES: Brooklyn, NY

MENTOR'S ANECDOTE: *As we discussed this year's program theme, Princesa and I found ourselves fascinated by the creative process of myth-making, and the ways in which contemporary writers have given voice to historically silent female characters. It was so much fun to geek out together over different interpretations of the Persephone myth—and so energizing to see Princesa stake her own claim on the character. I hope that she will continue to explore the act of giving voice and I'm excited to see where her writing takes her!*

WRAPPED IN RED

PRINCESA SANTOS

In my poem, I explore themes of self-identity and purpose through the eyes of the mythological character of Persephone. "Wrapped in Red" goes through Persephone's memories of a simple decision that altered her future.

Lost
I was.
Alone
I felt.
Taken
without conception,
I had no recollection.
What was my life?
My purpose?
Maybe
it was to be a porter,
rended beyond its borders.
Or a caretaker
forgotten,
to also be taken care of.
But was this all I was made for?
It couldn't be,
can't.
I must've been made for more,
than just this.
I give,
share
have no possession.
But when it comes to me

there's only pain,
deception.
Beauty is fallacy,
its presence wrapped in red.
The truth
revealed after a bite.
And my
long
last
freedom
is lost
every winter's night.

LULU SHA

YEARS AS MENTEE: 1

GRADE: Junior

BORN: Beijing, China

LIVES: Queens, NY

PUBLICATIONS AND RECOGNITIONS: Scholastic Art & Writing Awards: Gold Key

MENTEE'S ANECDOTE: *I feel like as women, we're pressured to prove ourselves and our writing skills to the rest of the world. We have to work twice as hard to sound half as smart as men, and it shouldn't be that way. I've always been shy and self-critical, so very little of my writing ever sees the light of day. Having Sophie as a mentor taught me to write as myself—to be as raw and candid in my writing as possible. Working with her allowed me to come out of my shell as a writer, because history deserves to see the genius bottled up inside each and every one of us.*

SOPHIE FLACK

YEARS AS MENTOR: 1

OCCUPATION: Author, Freelance Journalist, and Editor

BORN: Cambridge, MA

LIVES: New York, NY

PUBLICATIONS AND RECOGNITIONS: *Bunheads* (Little, Brown, 2011)

MENTOR'S ANECDOTE: *Lulu is a gifted short fiction writer, and because she takes on such weighty subject matter—exploring themes of entrapment, immigration, class struggles, gender and sexuality—I sometimes forget that she's only seventeen and treat her as a contemporary. We initially bonded over our shared love of flavored popcorn. But then I discovered her jaw-dropping storytelling abilities and now I mostly just sit in awe at how the words seem to effortlessly tumble out of her.*

EVACUATION

LULU SHA

*I have the craziest dreams, and this story was inspired by one I couldn't
understand. So I wrote it down.*

The war had been going on for months, but the schools stayed
open and Mom did her nine-to-five like always, and came home to
us and sunk into her armchair with a check in one hand and a cigarette in the other.

We were almost done with dinner by the time Mom turned on
the radio. The war would reach us by midnight.

"If only Dad were here," Lotte whined as Mom tried to shove a
spoonful of peas into her tight white lips.

Mom and I started to pack while Lotte played with her Barbie
dolls in the kitchen. The most we could take was one outfit each
and important documents sealed in a manila envelope. I wanted to
take more, but Mom said we could come back after the war.

It was almost ten when we started to move out. We didn't have
our own car, or even a bicycle, like the others, and there were no
taxis because all the cabbies were also trying to evacuate with their
own families.

Outside, people shuffled along, stopping occasionally because
someone had dropped something or something had to be left behind. The train station was about a mile and a half away. Mom and
I could have easily gotten there by ourselves, but Lotte dawdled,
humming and gaping at the other families, bundled up in big coats
and hunched over under their bulging backpacks.

The hardest part was making sure she didn't sit down in the
street, because it was covered in sewer muck from burst pipes, the
curb strewn with still-smoking cigarettes, and she was wearing her
princess dress. We were sticky with sweat from wading through the

thick air. The sky was the color of a bruise in the ten seconds before a stubbed toe started to bruise when you hoped that it wouldn't.

"Mommy, my tummy hurts," Lotte complained.

At the train station we were practically alone except for some female government bureaucrats in leather jumpsuits and red construction helmets waving signal flares at fighter jets that passed us in the sky. I thought they looked like femme fatales. If the invasion really did come at midnight, those ladies wouldn't be afraid.

"Lotte, we need to go! Goddamn it!" Mom screamed, her nostrils widening and closing rapidly.

Lotte started to cry. Snot dripped onto her lip, and she blew her nose in her lace sleeve.

"She's just a kid," I said.

We switched loads: Mom carried the laptop and documents, and I carried Lotte on my back.

The city was dark; the government had cut off the electricity. A stray dog howled at the moon. The brave biker ladies paid us no attention; I told myself that was because they were on official business and they had orders to follow. Meanwhile, Lotte was slipping down my back.

Then, I spotted an abandoned baby stroller, one wheel still spinning. We put Lotte in the stroller for Mom to push, while I carried the rest. The only sound was Mom's rubber flip-flops smacking the cement. I felt the trains humming beneath my feet—we were close to the station.

Suddenly, the front wheel of the stroller caught on a pebble and Lotte lurched out of the seat, while Mom tripped and crushed the handlebars. Surprisingly, Lotte hadn't woken up; she lay in a ball in the middle of the street, her dress muddy and torn. I tried to help Mom up, but in doing so dropped the laptop and documents, and they skidded along the pavement toward the sewer.

"Holy motherfucking Jesus Christ," I screamed, crawling on all fours and snatching them inches from disaster. I glanced up at Mom, expecting her to flick my head for cursing, but she was sitting on her heels in the middle of a puddle, her hair damp and matted on one side. She clutched a photo that I hadn't noticed her carrying before, of a twentysomething woman at the beach with wild hair. The other half of the photo was cut off, but a man's hand with long pianist's fingers rested on the woman's tanned shoulder. Even in the photo, she wasn't smiling.

"Let's keep going," I said. "We're almost there."

She nodded.

I wanted to apologize again, but I didn't. Instead I sat down next to them and pulled Lotte onto my lap, running my fingers through her thick, clumpy hair. Beneath us, the trains stopped humming. Even the biker ladies were long gone.

"Everything's going to be okay. Everything's going to be okay."

OLESYA SHANABROOK

YEARS AS MENTEE: 1
GRADE: Junior
BORN: New York, NY
LIVES: New York, NY

MENTEE'S ANECDOTE: *I remember the first time I met Karina. It was in the New-York Historical Society. Not only was it a beautiful place to meet someone with all of these colorful lamps lit around us, but I felt very nervous to meet someone new. But little did I know that Karina turned out to be this amazing, interesting mentor who sometimes is my confident about my social life outside of Girls Write Now. I'm quite happy that I got to spend a year with Karina, who can share my laughs and my opinions. Thank you, Girls Write Now and Karina.*

KARINA JOUGLA

YEARS AS MENTOR: 1
OCCUPATION: Donor Relations Manager, Girls Inc.
BORN: Cambridge, MA
LIVES: New York, NY

MENTOR'S ANECDOTE: *Olesya and I are both new to Girls Write Now this year, so it has been such a pleasure having her as a mentee as we've helped each other navigate the ins and outs of the program. I have been so impressed with Olesya's endlessly creative ideas for prompts and topics to try next. She has a gift for describing common emotions in completely novel, beautiful, and unexpected ways. Our pair sessions always go by too quickly—once we closed down a café but wanted to keep writing and talking, so we took our conversation to a donut shop.*

FALLING INTO THE DISEASE'S ARMS

OLESYA SHANABROOK

This piece is about a fictional outbreak in 2005 without the usage of smartphones and social media, and speaks about how diseases separate families. I was inspired by the coronavirus outbreak happening now in 2020.

王丽

Wang Li 2005–13–8

Falling into the Disease's Arms

Dear diary,

Yesterday, I held my grandma's hand as if I was the last source of her life energy left. I held her hand as tenderly as the first moment she held me in her arms. I remember opening the door and seeing her laying down on her bed next to a small chair that my dad would use when he plays dominos with his friends. As I walked closer to her bed, she slowly turned her head toward me. I saw the disease sneaking to her face, her throat covered with infected spots and rashes slowly crawling to her jawline. I was already wearing a pair of gloves and a white face mask. I was sitting there as the sun poured over my face like a glass of water. I felt her hand and gently turned it over, only to see the disease had already invaded her hand. I wished everything could go back to the way it was before, but now all the schools, grocery shops, and banks are closed. Really anything you can think of—all of it shut down. She turned her head toward me and said, "與其詛咒黑暗，不如燃起蠟燭." (Better to light a candle than to curse the darkness.) Then all of a sudden, I let all of my emotions out. Tears were falling like the drops from our weeping willow's branches that Grandma used to shake onto me after a rainy day. How could I let this happen? What have I *done to deserve this*? I felt like my world was falling apart. I remember all the laughs I had with her, the times I cried in her arms, the times she cooked for me, dressed me up for school, times I ranted to her because I felt angry. She was there for me in the times I needed her. She was like my second mother. You see, I didn't remember anything from my mother's funeral when I was a baby, but my grandma told me I held her hand the entire time. So this time I held her hand, wishing she could absorb my strength and wake up the next morning. She turned her head as I saw the life drain out of her body. She gradually closed her eyes. I placed her hand at her side and got up. I felt the chilly breeze coming in as I walked out of that room. I walked to my room and started to pack. Father wanted the siblings and me to stay with his sister out in the countryside as the disease spreads. He didn't say how long or when he would come back to see us. The government forced Father to stay in the city because he's a doctor. So Father is staying back so he can help others.

Now I am in a train car with my siblings, watching Father through the window. I think Father noticed me looking at him with such sorrow, so he tried to make a funny face to cheer me up. I slightly chuckled to make him feel like he is doing the best he can. My young siblings are looking up to me with hope and grief. I didn't know what to do and stared at them for a split second, then looked back at my father. The train conductor yelled, "All aboard." Quickly the train started to pick up the pace. My siblings and I waved to our father as the train started to move faster. Soon, I noticed Father in the distance and saw him leave. I stared back at my reflection in the window until we got out of the tunnel and saw the most beautiful sun.

SANJIDA SHEUBA

YEARS AS MENTEE: 2

GRADE: Senior

BORN: Sylhet, Bangladesh

LIVES: Bronx, NY

MENTEE'S ANECDOTE: *This year, working with my mentor, Megan, helped me to become a better editor. I realized that the "mistakes" I make in my work are something to be proud of. They help me turn my piece from a brainstorm into creative art. I've also learned to admire and be proud of my art.*

MEGAN WOOD

YEARS AS MENTOR: 2

OCCUPATION: Senior Editor, Oyster.com (a TripAdvisor Company)

BORN: Waupaca, WI

LIVES: New York, NY

PUBLICATIONS AND RECOGNITIONS: Cosmopolitan.com; Self.com; *Refinery29*

MENTOR'S ANECDOTE: *This year, I've enjoyed watching Sanjida come into her own as an artist. She's become a strong, confident writer with a powerful worldview and voice. I'm honored to read her work and watch her grow into a talented writer.*

TAKEN OUT

SANJIDA SHEUBA

Often, culture enforces us to make decisions that we don't want to make for the sake of family reputation.

The tiklis, the churis, the six-piece set of gold that lingers from her untouched lengha.

A moment of silence of her last day of freedom, her happiness rooted in the sacrifice of everyone around her.

Broken and completely empty.

The decision to either destroy the reputation of her family or to get married.

The thought of running away embroidered in her mind for the last year and a half.

The henna stains so deeply rooted, covering the several scars and marks on her body.

Silk rose, crystal chandeliers, her sorrows dripping down from the reflection of every light beaming on her.

Soft mellow fabric almost like the smell of the pillows she once cried on.

The sweet sound of the setted sari design being laid in the closet waiting for it to be taken out.

Her soul restless and pain left on her curly, but almost untouched hair, as every piece in her went missing.

The drip of the once soft-spoken glitter that sprinkles down her spine.

Beauty that resembles everywhere apart from her eyes.

Sorrows and sadness stays with her for the next few years as she is in a soul that does not belong to her, and a home that no longer screams her name.

Nothing left to recover from, and everything seems to be hidden,
  not a single thing left behind.
Everything shattered all at once.

ZAKIYYAH SINGLETARY

YEARS AS MENTEE: 1

GRADE: Senior

BORN: Brooklyn, NY

LIVES: Brooklyn, NY

MENTEE'S ANECDOTE: *When I first meet people, I am never quite able to give myself away to them. This was never much of a problem with Elizabeth. From the moment we met, I felt we were a good pair to work together. Elizabeth is incredibly supportive and a genuine person overall. She is a great person naturally and an even better mentor, I am blessed to have met her and worked alongside her. I know her guidance will help me get very far in life.*

ELIZABETH KOSTER

YEARS AS MENTOR: 4

OCCUPATION: Creative Writing Teacher, West Brooklyn Community High School

BORN: New York, NY

LIVES: New York, NY

PUBLICATIONS AND RECOGNITIONS: *The New York Times* "Modern Love" essay

MENTOR'S ANECDOTE: *Zakiyyah is passionate about writing, open and easy to talk to, and wonderful to work with. "I have a surprise," she wrote me one morning, and sent a poem that she'd started in the middle of the night and that she wanted to read for the first Girls Write Now Live reading. The poem—moving and powerful and filled with insight about racial injustice—made me weep for days. Her other work that I've read is similarly insightful and focused on charged, high-stakes issues. I'm looking forward to seeing what Zakiyyah has in store for Girls Write Now and beyond!*

FALLEN ANGELS

ZAKIYYAH SINGLETARY

Thank you to the fire inside of me that finally lit and allowed me to speak my truth.

For 400 years you kept us enslaved
raped us
beat us
tainted us
and killed us
yet somehow you are the ones that fear us
you see my skin color as a weapon
and shoot at every chance you get
because even though we are unarmed
we will always be viewed as armed with the melanin embedded in
    our skin
you stop every little brown boy with a hoodie on his head
racially profile every little brown girl with afros as big as your ego
you refuse to look within and see that you are the monsters
you so desperately are trying to run away from
you created this social construct called race
to identify my blackness as darkness
and your whiteness as pure
to you we are equal
as long as we don't commit a crime no matter how small
then we become slaves of the state again
with the 13th amendment
you have jail cells ready for little black boys as soon as they are
    suspended
they are 5x more likely to go to jail than white men
you're sitting in albany collecting the money

waiting for them to become another statistic
and I fear
for all seven of my brothers' lives
and pray for all of my sisters
that a picture of us will not end up under the next
#black lives matter
a mother is living without her child
wondering if she hadn't let them out
would they be here
a child is without a life
that barely ever began
now left to be six feet beneath
this is for the victims who didn't get the justice they deserved
thank you
Eric Garner
Trayvon Martin
Tamir Rice
Michael Brown
Freddie Gray
Aiyana Stanley-Jones
Terence Crutcher
Kimani Gray
Philando Castile
Sandra Bland
we are beautiful
deserving of life
and we matter
so does your story
may you all rest in heaven
sincerely the girl
who will never stay quiet again

SUHAYLAH SIRAJUL-ISLAM

YEARS AS MENTEE: 1

GRADE: Freshman

BORN: Brooklyn, NY

LIVES: Brooklyn, NY

PUBLICATIONS AND RECOGNITIONS: Scholastic Art & Writing Awards: Silver Key

MENTEE'S ANECDOTE: *Ruey-yah is great. I love meeting with her in BRIC multimedia house after school because sometimes, even if we don't get any work done, we talk a lot. And it feels productive! Whether we're talking about community or I'm ranting about gentrification, Ruey-yah's input is always appreciated. It's just so refreshing to see her because her perspective on things is really interesting. I also love hearing the little snippets about her life from her roommates to her work because it doesn't seem like there's ever a dull moment for her. Honestly, I love writing and meeting with her and I could not have asked for a better mentor.*

RUEY-YAH TANG

YEARS AS MENTOR: 1

OCCUPATION: Freelance Artist and Writer, Yaymaker, Fobo, Sage

BORN: Taipei, Taiwan

LIVES: Brooklyn, NY

MENTOR'S ANECDOTE: *Every time I see Suhaylah she is on her phone, furiously tapping away. I am usually walking in. But then we spend way too much time talking. I think Suhaylah and I are both embedded within such a strong network of community, which I believe has instilled and reminded us to stay engaged, active, communicative, and grateful for all that we have. When it feels as if we are too exhausted to care about everyone and everything, words are powerful.*

A MOMENT IN HISTORY; A FAVORITE

SUHAYLAH SIRAJUL-ISLAM

It's the little moments that count. This poem is about one of my favorite moments in my history.

knee deep wading in the water.
September 22nd, 2018.
do you remember?

laughter and cloudy bright blue skies
our wind strewn hijabs matching the mess
of our salt water soaked maxi dresses—
it's bliss.

our faces are flushed with happiness
bodies shivering, both cold and warm
as the sunlight hits the water,
wet sand curling beneath our toes
you are a stranger to me.

my friends decide to go farther.
they scream as the waves push them back
and i topple

do you remember?
how my hands dropped the bunched-up skirt
as i fell

my wrist burns.

"Woah,
I got you."
you say,

and i'm left staggering onto you.

ASHLEY SOTO

YEARS AS MENTEE: 1

GRADE: Senior

BORN: New York, NY

LIVES: Bronx, NY

MENTEE'S ANECDOTE: *My year in Girls Write Now has been very amazing. It was not only great because of the many new things I learned and did but also because of my meetings with my mentor. It has been a huge pleasure to have a mentor like Karen. She has guided me through my college process and even helped me with my schoolwork with her amazing suggestions and comments. I'm still surprised at how much we have in common.*

KAREN PENNAR

YEARS AS MENTOR: 1

OCCUPATION: Freelance Writer and Editor

BORN: New York, NY

LIVES: New York, NY

MENTOR'S ANECDOTE: *A year ago I might not have imagined that one day I'd be chatting with a Latinx high school senior from the Bronx about the number of cats on an island in Japan—for a paper she was writing on the topic. But here we were, Ashley and me, talking about Japan, which she wants to visit and I'd recently been to. And about medicine—she wants to be a doctor, I studied public health. Oh, and we've talked about poetry, too. Our meetings have been great, and I can't wait to see what you do next, Ashley!*

LOVE YOURSELF;
THE TOUCH OF DARKNESS

ASHLEY SOTO

LOVE YOURSELF

Oh beautiful rose
stemmed into the ground.

No sunshine.
No rain.

Will save you
Will cure you

from your
Deep

Melancholy.

So beautiful but
so sad.

Dreading your own looks.
Crying intensely,
big rain drips
slipping, sliding down your petals.

Such an intense beautiful red
but

at the very middle
where your heart is
resides
the color

Black

Slowly spreading onto the radiant red
Like a plague

You,
blinded by anger.
Immense sadness.

You don't realize your beauty,
your worth.

When will you come to love yourself?

THE TOUCH OF DARKNESS

How to escape this darkness?

Crying intensely
My heart
aching.
My head
Spinning.

Salt roads carved onto my cheeks.

Sitting in the darkness,
engulfed by it.

Far too deep.

It feels like two soft hands
sliding slowly around my neck

A soft
deceiving touch.

With true horrific intentions.

I turn my eyes away

Paralyzed.

Not the slightest light.
Not the slightest sound.

Only my silent sobbing.
My body quivering both in fear and sadness.

My shaky breaths.
My heart pounding,
Tirelessly.

How to get out?

How to escape this darkness that moves me when it flows?

Manipulating my thoughts.
My emotions.

How to escape I ask?

No one . . .

No one answers.

With this realization I gain control.
The hands slip away from my neck

in a caressing,
almost loving way.

Too confused . . .
What to do?

I lay down
fully believing that

I am truly here

To stay.

SHYANNE SPENCER

YEARS AS MENTEE: 1

GRADE: Junior

BORN: New York, NY

LIVES: Brooklyn, NY

MENTEE'S ANECDOTE: *Mrs. Sherrill has helped me a lot. When I struggle with believing in myself, she pushes me to be my best. Mrs. Sherrill has spent hours working with me because she says that I am here in the world for a reason and that my voice will touch many one day. If I had to choose who my mentor would be all over again, I would pick her every single time. My writing has elevated because of her. I've been reading so people can ride the waves of my journey and experience something powerful.*

SHERRILL COLLINS

YEARS AS MENTOR: 1

OCCUPATION: Program Administrator, New York University

BORN: New York, NY

LIVES: New York, NY

MENTOR'S ANECDOTE: *When I met Shyanne, I wasn't sure how things would work out. She was not fully trusting the Girls Write Now concept—or me, for that matter—and I, eager to be a mentor, had committed to this young lady in front of me, and was challenged to figure things out. "What do you like to write?" I asked. Sitting, Shyanne said, "I can read a poem that I've written, but I have to turn around so you can't look at me." Quickly taking control, I said, "Well, that's not happening, so just stand up, face me, and read." And as I listened to her read her life, a tear dropped, and my heart adopted her on the spot!*

WESTSIDE OF HARLEM/FLOWER

SHYANNE SPENCER

This poem that I share comes from a familiar place that me and other teenagers experience growing up. I remind myself daily of my self-worth, and, like others, I can live my best life and pursue my gift. My voice speaks for many as we take our Place in HerStory!

Where a flower grew
Where you see people shooting dice
I said the west side of Harlem
Where babies cry cause
Mom didn't have enough for milk
Where you walk out your house and that
Gun decides if you live
Or get killed
As you sit on that bench . . . think, think
For a minute
Think about how much time you spent in
That house
Waiting for your mom to get home
You look on the side of you and you see two blunts that's
Been rolled and burnt
You see the beer cans
And hoping she
Doesn't hit you again
I said the west side of Harlem where
You see the fresh boys
And fly girls
Where having the best shoes makes you
or learning how to shoot a gun

Man I feel like that shit takes you
And know that your mom has a
Issue with substance abuse
Remember your still that flower that
Grew on the west side of Harlem

CONFUSED

Sucking in my tears to breathe
The fire that burns in me
Angry at the world
Because of something I could've
Did Better or something I could've done
The ways of the world is unknown
My darker days are becoming cold
Death is my option
Staying alive is not
I try to hold back my words and hoping
Someone sees this teenage girl who is
Crying . . . crying for help
When you see these big scars these embarrassing scars you may
    understand Why or maybe not
You sit there as she speaks jotting down
Her thoughts and pills she need to take
Or maybe wondering why she cuts with a blade . . . and as she
    watches you she wonders if you really understand why she
Chooses death or living
But who is she kidding
The numbness creeps in our veins
See me and this girl are the same
And we understand that humankind may never understand our
    pain
And you know what . . . it's okay

HOLDING ON

Cry myself to sleep sometimes
Cut myself to sleep sometimes
Just feelin like i wanna die
Feeling empty inside
Tryin to be numb and ignore
The rejection and depression
Holding on to memories that
Aren't what they seem to be,
In reality they're nightmares
And I stare
I stare into darkness
Hoping for a better life
I feel coldness creeping in my veins
And it's makin me go insane
Because my heart is beating . . .

Just tryin to hold on

KILHAH ST FORT

YEARS AS MENTEE: 1

GRADE: Junior

BORN: Brooklyn, NY

LIVES: Queens, NY

PUBLICATIONS AND RECOGNITIONS: Climate Speaks at The Apollo

MENTEE'S ANECDOTE: *I knew Amber and I were a perfect mentee-mentor pair at the Friday Night Salon. The one we attended focused on slam poetry, one of my favorite forms of writing. Yet I found myself self-conscious and questioning whether I even deserve to be in the same room as all these other writers. Amber, without having to say a single word, saw all my insecurities and worries. She listed reasons why I should share my work and be proud of it. I've never had someone blatantly tell me my writing was valid. It's been a great year of overcoming my demons with Amber's help.*

AMBER LOVELESS

YEARS AS MENTOR: 1

OCCUPATION: Assistant Manager, Queens Public Library

BORN: Litchfield, IL

LIVES: Queens, NY

PUBLICATIONS AND RECOGNITIONS: American Library Association Emerging Leaders 2019

MENTOR'S ANECDOTE: *I knew Kilhah and I were perfectly matched when she dropped a musical theater reference into conversation at our first meeting. She has graciously, imperturbably, worked her schedule around mine to meet at the library. Our meetings aren't always peaceful, but that doesn't stop her from being productive. Kilhah has an intense understanding of herself and the human condition, which she is able to portray in ways that instantly connect to the reader. It has been a privilege helping her hone her words into a captivating message this year.*

DEEPLY ROOTED MEMORIES

KILHAH ST FORT

My piece shows the strength and perseverance of women by using a rose as the subject.

zoom in.
strawberry petals
branching off of a
willowy stem,
stripped of her natural defenses;
disconnected from her roots.
holding her breath underwater, but
half free to gulp in air.
tiptoeing the lines of asphyxiation and liberation.
beauty drowns out her screams.

zoom out.
porcelain vases flank her,
celebratory of daily wins
(silent in times of woe)
together basking in the celestial bodies' affections,
preening under human wonder,
stowing the finite praise
away to
dissect in their minds until gasping sobs
become the symphony of their nights.

zoom in.
strawberry darkens crimson, crimson darkens black.
shriveled brittle tips.
hunched over into herself;

shielded from cold indifference.
a petal falls off.
then two.
then three.
what is she worth now?

zoom out.
crowded in by dark plastic walls
and foul odor,
she was moved.
rejected, forgotten, expendable.
a younger, newer plaything
holds her spot between the vases.
day by day, night by night
a fresh rose is plucked, put on display and thrown away.
each one's story is told
to their admirers,
mixed together in a facade of being the same.
but before the replacement
a whisper is exchanged:

"fret not little one,
for the thorns, the patience and the love
of our ancestors flow through your stem.
you will not be forgotten."

zoom in.
The rose is tall, sturdy and glossy
against the gazes.
tales of her predecessors' fear and courage keeps her standing
and when it's her time to go
she does not wilt, she is not broken.
she is tired but standing.
she passes the stories of their past to the next
and whispers make them proud.

SYLVI STEIN

YEARS AS MENTEE: 3

GRADE: Junior

BORN: New York, NY

LIVES: New York, NY

PUBLICATIONS AND RECOGNITIONS: Scholastic Art & Writing Awards: Silver Key, National Honor Society, Magna Cum Laude Academic Excellence Award

MENTEE'S ANECDOTE: *My mentor, Nan, and I meet weekly in Le Pain Quotidien for some good chatting and good poetry. We always have something new to share, to laugh about, or to discuss in righteous indignation. We both enjoy reading and erasing poetry to make something entirely new.*

NAN BAUER-MAGLIN

YEARS AS MENTOR: 6

OCCUPATION: Writer/ Editor

BORN: New York, NY

LIVES: New York, NY

PUBLICATIONS AND RECOGNITIONS: *Widows' Words* (Rutgers University Press, 2019)

MENTOR'S ANECDOTE: *I have been a mentor to Sylvi for two years. In terms of history, I expect in maybe four or five years to see Sylvi's name on a book cover entitled:* The Next Wave of Young Women Poets.

SUMMER CAMP LOVE LETTER

SYLVI STEIN

Summer camp carries a particular kind of magic in your life. I wanted to capture the whimsical romance of teenage relationships in this prose poem.

I will never love you as much as the ocean—or, I will love you in a different way. I hope you can understand that. Being with you will be like the summer after third grade—waking up every morning and not knowing why I'm so happy, and then remembering all over again. I will cut the crusts off your sandwich at lunch in the dining hall, something small and tender amid all this chaos. I will paint my toenails for you. I will use my nice conditioner for you. I will shave my legs for you (but you won't care if they're shaved, we'll sit on my bed and laugh about hairy ape legs). It's okay if you don't like the beach. It's okay if you like smooth jazz. I will make you get your hair wet, and you will make me listen to Miles Davis on the car ride home. I want you to ask me to the dance. I want to spend a ridiculous amount of time getting my outfit ready and then just sit outside the rec hall and play cards with you. I want to learn to braid hair and then practice on you. I want to sign up for yoga by the lake and then skip it to go swimming with you. I want to eat mint chocolate chip ice cream outside with you as the sun melts us into dripping puddles. I want to hand you the water pitcher at dinner and feel your fingers brush mine, a secret language only the two of us understand. I want to draw charcoal designs on the back of your hands with the ashy remains of Friday night campfire. I want to make crappy friendship bracelets with you on the art porch while it rains. I want to sit on the splintery picnic benches with you after dinner and talk until the mosquitoes chase us inside. I want to be late to evening activities because we were watching the sun go down. I want to hold your hand and pretend it's not a big deal, even though I think it is. I want you to leave me notes under my pillow. I want to wake you up to look at the full moon. I want all the clichés you can give me.

MARGARETA STERN

YEARS AS MENTEE: 1

GRADE: Senior

BORN: Miskolc, Hungary

LIVES: New York, NY

MENTEE'S ANECDOTE: *My mentor and I have a relationship where I can tell them anything and have deep intellectual conversations with them. My mentor encourages me to express my ideas, thoughts, and feelings. My mentor and I both feel very strongly about women's rights and we both love going to cafés. I'm glad I got the opportunity to work with them and they have inspired me to never stop writing.*

JEN STRAUS

YEARS AS MENTOR: 2

OCCUPATION:
Development Coordinator, U.S. Holocaust Memorial Museum

BORN: Washington, D.C.

LIVES: Brooklyn, NY

MENTOR'S ANECDOTE: *Getting to know Margareta over the last year has been an absolute joy. I wondered what to expect with a new mentee, but we quickly developed a rich and meaningful rapport. It is a privilege to have watched Margareta grow as a writer, and to share in the many exciting milestones as she gets ready to graduate. I can't wait to see what the rest of the year holds for her and our time at Girls Write Now!*

I WISH LOVE WAS SIMPLE

MARGARETA STERN

These poems are inspired by my experiences with love. Through writing these pieces I was able to express myself and get closure from the past, which has made me the person that I am today.

"EXPOSED TO A UNIVERSE OF UNIMAGINABLE EMPTINESS"

Why can't you just trust what we have?
because i couldn't give that love to you.
Bring me back to a time where my brain wasn't hungry no more
because i need energy
energy
i need energy
before i turn zombie.
My identity was crushed because i was in pain
and i knew my heart had shattered
because when i try so hard
i turn zombie.
And because you loved her
i could not hold on to my sanity no longer
so i fall to my emptiness
my unimaginable emptiness.
which formed through experiences turned my life to an obstacle
    course.
Exposure to when i couldn't find love in anything or anyone
and
closure to when i sought out the reasons why.
Exposed to the universe.
Vulnerable to criticism.

to criticize and compare ourselves to others.
The drug of desire.
The addiction for human desire.
Exposed to the universe that is constantly expanding
and when the dark side is lost in our nature
the closure is unimaginable.

"LONG GONE FROM A MEMORY"

Why do you have to be the way that you are?
I must resist my temptations of pure anger and lust
so that you don't become long gone from my memory
because when you were gone my heart yearned for that
    affectionate love
which was our love
a crossroad type of love formed through our internal struggles
and even though we witness the stop signs
we choose to ignore them.
We accelerate on the highway of passion
and oh baby our love is in flames
save me before i'm long gone.
I love you.
Tell me I'll be ok.
I'm sorry that I crashed
but do you still love me?
I'll be ok.
Because my insecurities they are on me
and the voices in my head they are inside me.
I'm scared of feeling not good enough
memories in the past have shown me what it's like to feel
long gone
long gone
long gone.
So i'm sorry that I crashed
I just needed a way out.

"I WISH SOMEONE HAD"

And I'm reaching the limit
you've got me floating on love
and I wish someone had warned me about how much it hurts
to fall in love with someone who isn't in love with you.
I wish someone had warned me
that the freshman boy would only break my heart
and that the mysterious stranger from the corner of the room
    would kiss me in the basement closet
and only break my heart.
Oh and the girl that showed interest in me
well somebody could've warned me
that I'd only break her heart too.
My curiosity when I look at you and know you're not the one
and I wish someone had told me that life goes on even when you
    don't want it to.
Do you remember how you made me feel?
I had grown numb to the way you treated me
because i wanted so much
even when you continued to ignore me and put me down
because you were taken by a memory of love that took your life
    away.
You're not the one.
because drifting to the arms of the deceased
cuts my soul so deep
so please when you open your eyes can you see that I'm not the
    one?
as you're not the one for me.

"WHY CAN'T YOU LOVE ME?"

Why can't you love me like you loved her?
because I'm not her
and I'm sorry.

I tried to convince myself that I wasn't just a rebound to you
but everybody is someone's rebound at some point
and our paths just happened to cross one another.
Why can't you love me like you loved her?
because you lie to yourself
while I'm left to piece together the truth
but you don't notice me doing so
because you only notice her and she's a dead girl
so it must be my fault.
I'm not good enough.
Why can't you love me like you loved her?
because I'm not her
and I'm sorry.
but before I leave I need to tell you my truth
which is that it just really hurts to know that i'll never be the one
    for you
because when I look at you i want to hold you in my arms
so that you don't leave me
but I didn't want to accept that you were never mine
because you were already gone.

ALIN SUAREZ

YEARS AS MENTEE: 2

GRADE: Senior

BORN: New York, NY

LIVES: Bronx, NY

MENTEE'S ANECDOTE: *Throughout my wonderful year at Girls Write Now, the highlight has been going on diner dates together on Saturday mornings!*

KIELE RAYMOND

YEARS AS MENTOR: 1

OCCUPATION: Faculty, Parsons School of Design

BORN: Miami, FL

LIVES: Brooklyn, NY

MENTOR'S ANECDOTE: *One winter morning, Alin and I stumbled into a Midtown diner after our first plan fell through. We ordered coffee and mozzarella sticks and started talking. Ever since, it has been our tradition to seek out the unassuming diners of Manhattan. I love hanging out with Alin because of her breadth of curiosity. She is an expert on* The Twilight Zone *and Jamaica Kincaid and K-pop. It's clear that she feels a deep love and loyalty to her mom and siblings. Most of all, I love seeing how her voice transforms when she turns to the page. She has the wisdom and insight to turn an everyday dialogue with friends into rhythmic prose poetry. This piece especially speaks to Alin's widened sense of self and how she discovered that her reserved nature comes not from an absence of empathy but from a fear of how powerful that empathy could be. I for one cannot wait to see what she does next.*

LETTING GO

ALIN SUAREZ

This piece is dedicated to the past me who struggled so hard to find her place.

When I was four, my father died. I don't remember much, but I remember feeling lost because I was too young to sympathize with everyone. The only thing I did cry over was the cookie my brother ate that was meant for me to feel better about not having a dad anymore. And even after some time had passed and everyone had finally gotten over my dad dying, I knew there was no shaking the feeling of being lost.

When I was eight, my friends decided to join a dance program. Out of spite and to make myself feel better, I joined their dance program *and* a gymnastics program. I just wanted to be able to say, "I am better than you." I thought it would make me feel a little less bad, but it left me feeling the same. A few years later, I joined the soccer team with them while also swimming and playing tennis. I did everything I could to be the best, and I was still left feeling empty. Because it was all just something I did to thrive off the sadness of others, and to forget about the fact that I was sorry for myself for feeling so devoid of joy.

When I was thirteen, my friend told me she was depressed. All I could think to say was, "Oh, wow." I don't think I could have been less interested in her struggles, because I was obsessed with the idea that I was the one with *real problems*. That was the last time we really had a conversation before she threw a Chick-fil-A sandwich at me. She told me straight to my face how crappy I was and how miserable I'd become since I made it my life goal to be better than everyone else. She also thought it was worth noting how great she had been to me despite everything. Even in an argument, she bought me a Chick-fil-A sandwich. The same one she later threw at me.

When I was fifteen, I had to sit down and ask myself, "What is wrong with you? Why must you just push people's buttons?" It's true that I loved getting a rise out of people and pretending that I was dripping with confidence. But mostly I just felt so so so bad about myself all the time. Not long after that, I was asked about the first event that changed my idea of normal. I ignored the question, until everything came flooding back to me. All the times I was a jerk to someone I loved, all the terrible jokes about my dad, all the anxiety of having most of my teenhood spent dwelling in my own sadness and boredom and discontent. My normal didn't change when my dad died but my normal changed when I decided that happiness had to die with him. Happiness doesn't die when someone dies. Happiness dies when you decide you can't let the trauma go.

When I was four, my dad died. And from four to fifteen, I decided that I was dead, too. I figured nobody would care, nobody would cry, and most important, nobody would miss me. That is a shitty contrast to how well my father is remembered. How nice everyone talks about him, the respect they gave him even years after his death, the love everyone carries for the guy. I remember the good times I had with him. The vague memories of lying on a small Dora bed with him while watching *Dora*. The time he yelled at a nurse for telling him that chickenpox only happen once when there were clearly chickenpox on my body again. And I know he would have loved me regardless of my achievements. I know I am the last thing my mom has of him. I am the living embodiment of the love they once shared and how, to her, everything about me is love.

When I was sixteen, I cut my hair, I dropped out of all those extracurriculars, and I let myself breathe. For the first time I had to sit there and endure the agony of figuring out how to enjoy being with myself. The awkwardness and the rage slowly became happiness. I realized that when you decide to leave that cage of trauma and self-pity and arrogance, you can finally see the beauty in everything. *You can finally let it go.*

SANDY TAN

YEARS AS MENTEE: 1

GRADE: Junior

BORN: New York, NY

LIVES: New York, NY

MENTEE'S ANECDOTE: *Barnes & Noble is one of those magical places that is filled to the brim with all different types of stories. It's also the first place where Claudia taught me how to tell mine. From using writing prompts in our much-referenced "What If" book to editing pieces at Parsons School of Design, Claudia has changed my whole perspective on writing. Every week, Claudia and I are always working on something new in the small café within Barnes & Noble. Sometimes we're editing, other times we're writing, but we're always laughing over the weirdest things.*

CLAUDIA MARINA

YEARS AS MENTOR: 1

OCCUPATION: Faculty, Parsons School of Design

BORN: Miami, FL

LIVES: Brooklyn, NY

MENTOR'S ANECDOTE: *Sandy is incredibly talented at telling stories. When we first met, she expressed an interest in writing creatively but felt restricted by the formats and rules taught in school. Our conversations centered on the role of voice in storytelling. She played with conventions, finding her balance between respect for great works of fiction and a confidence to challenge the way these stories are told. Her work explores the role of dialogue, and her characters take their place in history.*

ASIAN AMERICAN

SANDY TAN

This poem is an exercise in claiming my place in history—as a member of a community but also as an individual. It explores some thoughts I frequently have about my Asian American identity and living in New York.

Are you a Banana or a Twinkie?
If you're Asian, it doesn't make a difference
At least that's what the stock clerk told Mom
when we were shopping at the supermarket.
After 15 minutes spent in the orange pile,
She drifted to the bananas
"Bananas are bananas," he interjected
Mom laughs at his ignorance and picks up two of them
She waves her right hand
holding the yellow-skinned fruit
"This American"
She shows him the other one
it was short, stout
"This Asian."
Maybe it was the condescending glance
the clerk gave me or the murderous smell of durian
but at that moment
I felt ashamed
Ashamed that Mom had spoken out about a banana
in her broken English.
We didn't appear to him as American,
but in this moment I didn't feel
Asian either.

If you ask for a fork in the restaurant to eat a bowl of rice,
If you can't communicate with your grandparents in Taishanese,
If you don't understand the old lady asking for directions on
    Mott Street,
If you don't get straight A's,
If you don't play the piano,
If you can't read the newspaper your parents read,
If you don't cook rice in a rice cooker,
If you don't aspire to be a pharmacist,
If you don't wash dishes by hand,
then what kind of Asian are you?
The ones they call Bananas
or Twinkies.
Yellow,
but white.

I ask Mom what she thinks of this, but she doesn't care much.
She says
I am American and I should be proud
She says it's okay
to not use chopsticks
She says it's okay
to talk to my grandparents in broken Chinese
She says it's okay
to not understand the old ladies in Chinatown
to be less than perfect
to not know "Clair de Lune"
to read *The New York Times* instead of 星島日報
to make rice on the stovetop.

She says it's okay I don't want to be a doctor
dishwashers are a scam
The only type of Asian I
should be is me—
her daughter.
Asian,
but American.

HANNAH THOMAS

YEARS AS MENTEE: 2

GRADE: Senior

BORN: Arima, Port of Spain, Trinidad and Tobago

LIVES: Brooklyn, NY

MENTEE'S ANECDOTE: *Meeting Stephanie has been life-changing. Within these two years, she's been able to recognize my style of learning and process of creating. As a pair, we understand each other so well which allows us to work so quickly! We can spend hours working on a piece while sharing funny family stories with each other. Stephanie pushes me past limits I thought I could never get around by encouraging me to never use the words "I don't know." She has taught me and given me room to grow as a writer, editor, and creator.*

STEPHANIE GOLDEN

YEARS AS MENTOR: 6

OCCUPATION: Freelance Author, Journalist, Book Doctor

BORN: Brooklyn, NY

LIVES: Brooklyn, NY

PUBLICATIONS AND RECOGNITIONS: The Startup at Medium; aeon.co

MENTOR'S ANECDOTE: *This was our second year together, and I've watched Hannah grow as a writer and a person. ("I don't know" has vanished from her vocabulary.) This year, I never need to tell her anything twice. She gets my suggestions and tips instantly and starts applying them in new contexts. Plus, her work has gotten subtler and more sophisticated. We work intensely on Hannah's writing, but we also have fun. When we recorded a podcast interviewing each other, we laughed so hard I was afraid it would get picked up on the phones of other pairs recording nearby.*

A TRADITIONAL WIFE

HANNAH THOMAS

This story was inspired by a Girls Write Now workshop where we spoke about outdated taboos. The inspiration for my piece was the complicated yet consistent dynamic between my two Caribbean grandparents.

Cynthia sat on the rocking chair facing the television—turning over her wrist and reading her small silver watch. She noticed it was nearing 8 p.m.—her husband's usual time. Just then she heard Papa strutting through their small hallway. He entered their living room, his long body hunched over. He picked up his fedora and Cynthia jumped up to help him put on his coat. He turned to face her as she fixed his scarf over his collar. Both stayed silent. She took her seat again and he turned to leave, tipping his fedora toward her before closing the door behind him. Cynthia turned her gaze to the television screen while she heard the door close.

Hours passed and like always she hadn't heard from him. She was the furthest thing from worried because she knew where he was. Every night Papa received a phone call, got dressed, and left—all in silence. She'd never asked him where he was going, she was raised not to. But she wanted the satisfaction of him telling her. Every time she built up the courage to ask, she could hear her mother's voice in the back of her head: "You should never ask a man where he's going after eight p.m." Cynthia was torn between this taboo and what she felt entitled to as a wife.

She decided to call her granddaughter, Hailey. Papa and Cynthia had never had kids, so Hailey was the closest thing Cynthia had to a daughter. Hailey picked up the phone quickly. "Hey, Ma, what's going on?"

"Hailey, did Papa happen to mention where he was going tonight?"

Cynthia looked around the room, anticipating Hailey's answer. "Ma. You do know all you have to do is ask Papa, right?"

"I just wanted to know if he told you," Cynthia asked, sounding like a small child.

"You're kidding, right? I feel like I'm speaking to kids," Hailey responded, clearly annoyed.

"Well, then, what the hell do you think I should do? He just gets up, and picks up his old coat, and tilts his stupid hat and leaves! He doesn't even say a word! Not a bye, not a 'Hey, babe, I'm leaving.'"

Hailey chuckled on the other end of the line. "Well, Ma, do you just want me to call and tell him—"

"NO!" Cynthia responded before Hailey could finish. "He can't think I'm just some lady waiting until he comes through the door. Mother always said you shouldn't ask a man where he's going after eight p.m."

"Ma . . . it's 2020! You're his wife, for God's sake, you should be able to ask him whatever you please," Hailey protested.

"You may be right." Cynthia began thinking maybe it was possible to ask him.

"You think about that. I have some work to finish up, so you go ask Papa and let me know how it goes. Love you." Hailey hung up. Cynthia sat back into her rocking chair trying to think about what good would come of asking. Would he get mad and storm off? Would he think less of her? But most of all she wondered if she would be violating her culture, her mother, and everything she knew and thought to be true.

She glanced at her watch once again. It was 1 a.m. She heard the jingle of Papa's keys from outside. He opened the door, turning his back to his wife, took off his fedora, placed it on the staircase railing, and began to take off his coat. Cynthia's anxiety grew as she tried working up the nerve to ask, telling herself it couldn't be that hard. Papa threw his coat over the railing and started toward their hallway. Without thinking, she yelled after him, "Papa, where were you?" Papa looked at Cynthia from over his shoulder, without turning around. He raised his eyebrow at her, as if he hadn't understood her question. Cynthia came closer. "I said, where were you?" She spoke in a stern tone, but Papa could see right through her. He turned to face her and raised his head, looking down at her. Papa chuckled and shook his head, then turned away from her and walked back down the hallway. Cynthia stayed still, watching. She stuck her hands on her hips. "I'm going to ask again tomorrow," she said to herself.

KENIA TORRES

YEARS AS MENTEE: 2

GRADE: Senior

BORN: Queens, NY

LIVES: Queens, NY

MENTEE'S ANECDOTE: *Without Hannah, this piece would have just been one more document stored on my computer. Not only does Hannah support my writing by sacrificing so much of her time to work with me, she also gives me the confidence to share my work with others. She gives me thoughtful feedback and never judges me for my ideas. Whether we're working on meeting deadlines or just talking about life, I always look forward to our pair meetings.*

HANNAH SHELDON-DEAN

YEARS AS MENTOR: 2

OCCUPATION: Freelance Writer and Writing Consultant, Columbia University School of Social Work

BORN: Burlington, VT

LIVES: Brooklyn, NY

PUBLICATIONS AND RECOGNITIONS: five licensed children's books with Penguin Young Readers

MENTOR'S ANECDOTE: *Kenia was already a great writer when we met, but what's been amazing for me to witness in our second year together is how much her confidence in her own voice has grown. She revises her work fearlessly, digging through the pieces she's created and pushing them to do exactly what she wants, whether it's a bold experimental poem or a perfect college essay. And Kenia does it all while being one of the most original, hilarious people I know— every week I wonder when the Queens Central Library librarians are going to tell us to quiet down and quit laughing, but I hope we (and they) never do.*

THOUGHTS IN TRAIN TRAFFIC

KENIA TORRES

When I was told I would have to write an essay about myself as part of my college application, I was convinced I couldn't do it. I had always avoided writing that involved telling my own story; however, in the end I was surprised and proud of the outcome.

"Ladies and gentlemen, please excuse the train traffic ahead of us; we will be moving shortly."

The words no one wants to hear on a busy Monday morning echoing through the loudspeakers of the E train. The cause of a chain reaction of sighs and frustrated expressions that become more and more desperate as time moves on and we don't. The word "shortly" does nothing more than reassure those who don't speak the second most popular language of New York City: subway. Even then, after twenty minutes, it is evident that the word is nothing more than a false hope used to keep passengers calm in this time of utmost despair.

A man in a blue tuxedo leans back on the subway car doors, disregarding the signs that clearly advise him not to. His expression reveals nothing more than the tapping of his foot does, annoyance and disappointment toward the subway system that has once again let him down. In his head he thinks of the excuse he will use this time, daring not to blame his tardiness on the MTA for the third time this week, although it is indeed the only culprit.

A teenager across from him fumbles through his bookbag, pulls out a spiral notebook, and carefully analyzes the writing that has been neatly scripted onto the lined pages. He has forgotten that there's no school today and will now arrive at an empty high school with no other choice than to return home after a miserable two-hour journey. The conductor's attempt to communicate with us once more comes out in muffled sounds and high-pitched screeches. The tourist next to me doesn't speak subway, so I translate for her, "He apologizes for the inconvenience and says that we will be moving shortly." She sighs, as does everyone else except for me. Judging by her neon-pink suitcase and matching neck pillow, she's worried she'll miss her flight and will have to wait hours, days, or weeks to catch another one.

I look around, capturing everyone's expressions and taking mental notes. The pregnant lady sitting on the other side of me—she's on the way to her maternity photo shoot. The man standing in the corner with the guitar strapped across his back—he's performing at a pub later that night for the first time.

In reality, they each have their own story that defines them in one way or another, and if I were to be made aware of that story, I would honor it. However, uninformed about the lives of others and curious for answers, I create my own stories for them. Without knowing it, they become main characters in my novels, the inspiration behind my poems, and the heroes in my fairytales. They are given a new name, new hobbies, and a new life. All of this because of a delayed train and a teenage girl with an imagination that is too wild for her own good.

With a slight jerk forward the train begins moving again, slowly at first, as if threatening to stop again, but then quickly regaining its speed. Alas, the next stop is reached, and the train opens its doors to welcome in new inspiration.

D TOWNES

YEARS AS MENTEE: 2

GRADE: Senior

BORN: New York, NY

LIVES: Bronx, NY

MENTEE'S ANECDOTE: *Chaya is honestly amazing and so supportive of all my ventures. When she's not attempting to convince me not to dye my hair, she's trying to thrust me into the world of scriptwriting. Working with Chaya has forced me out of my comfort zone and taught me that sometimes "showing, not telling" isn't an effective writing strategy. Chaya is amazing and unapologetically herself. Her life hasn't been easy, and she's taken every challenge in stride and honestly is the best role model I could ever have.*

CHAYA WILKINS

YEARS AS MENTOR: 2

OCCUPATION: Content Strategist, Brooks Brothers

BORN: Bronx, NY

LIVES: New York, NY

MENTOR'S ANECDOTE: *When I first met D, I was immediately impressed by her ability to unapologetically express herself. She said, "My name is DeAnna, but I go by D." In those few words, she made a declaration; she defined herself in the way that she saw fit and she's been doing that in her writing. She's creating her place in history by staying true to herself through her storytelling, by developing new organizations at her school, and by simply being D—no matter what.*

AGATHA AND THE NAMING

D TOWNES

"Agatha and the Naming" is the story of me, in a way trying to claim my place in my family's history. While Agatha's struggle is name-based, mine is skill- and future-based. She gets to meet her namesake while I still question mine.

Agatha Persephone Murrow believed that she didn't deserve her name. It was a name that came along with a legacy that was passed down over centuries. The first Agatha, who was actually named Aga'ta, was a slave who emancipated herself in a manner similar to that of Frederick Douglass. Once free she did everything to remain free, and for that the family decided that she and her name would live on forever.

Agatha Persephone was her generation's Agatha; a remnant of her ancestors, and for that Agatha would never forgive her family. With the name came the crushing pressure, the pressure to be a martyr or a power of her own; as the fifth Agatha of her bloodline she had very little to work with. Agatha knew that she would never be good enough in her family's eyes. All she had managed to attain in her seventeen years of life were a few minor spelling bee wins. As well as a determination of what she would major in at Clark Atlanta, which she considered no small feat.

But the Murrow family didn't think that they needed another science major, and that made Agatha, to their standards, undeserving of her name. Her passion for toxicology was deemed meaningless and with that her accomplishment was stripped away.

The previous Agatha was an accomplished writer, a MacArthur Genius Award winner, Pulitzer Prize winner, and let's not forget botanist. The other Agatha helped save an endangered species; to the Murrows, Agatha Persephone's awards were worthless.

It was a typical afternoon at home, Agatha had been avoiding questions from her parents about which organizations she would enroll in during her freshman year. When suddenly, Agatha asked her mother, "Ma, can I visit Grandpa?"

Her mother responded hastily, "Sure, leave."

Agatha left, needing space, as she often did in these moments. She needed to speak to the only person who ever appreciated her accomplishments.

Her grandfather lived in South Carolina, in a small town that often served as her escape from reality.

She made her way to South Carolina, and eventually found herself standing in front of the white house with the dark green door. Worn down, but as strong as her grandfather, the house had seen hurricanes and tornadoes. The paint was chipped and worn, but still the house stood. The door opened into the only place she considered to be her true home. She would always admit that her grandfather was a little racist. He hated everyone who wasn't black, but he had his "reasons." Agatha respected him enough not to ask any questions.

Agatha knocked on the door and picked at her nail polish while she waited. It was about two minutes later that her grandfather opened the door with the type of smile that she never received from her parents.

"Come on in, babygirl," he said, gesturing for her to enter.

They talked for hours, as they always did, and she vented her frustrations with family. She questioned how he, her mother's biological father, could be part of the Murrow family.

Eventually, the witching hour drew near and she decided to rest. Her grandfather sent her to a room on the top floor, shrouded in darkness, but she still felt safe. From the single window in the room she could see a tree that sat atop a hill.

She heard a noise—*Was it a scream?*—and saw a flash of light, and suddenly she was no longer in the house, but in a field.

She looked at the hilltop where the tree was, and saw her Aga'ta, the original, the almighty.

"They lie, on me and my name," she said.

"They shame me, you shame me," she continued with rage in her eyes.

"You allow them to shame YOU, bearer of mine name," she bellowed.

Agatha turned to her, despair in her voice. "I don't understand. How do we shame you? Aga'ta, please tell me how to do right by you."

Aga'ta looked at her sharply—it felt as though she had been sliced through with a sword. She felt the wind around her pick up as the tree swayed dangerously. The wind practically screamed her name.

"I died for nothing if you do not liberate yourself!" Aga'ta's voice boomed, as her eyes glowed red; while the world dimmed the wind's scream carried into a crescendo.

And then there was nothing.

KAYLA WALFORD

YEARS AS MENTEE: 1

GRADE: Sophomore

BORN: New York, NY

LIVES: Brooklyn, NY

MENTEE'S ANECDOTE: *Allison has always been encouraging in all subjects and hobbies I've talked about—whether it be writing, drawing, sewing, or managing my Dungeons & Dragons campaign. We continually find similarities between us, from pastimes to just having the same computer. Allison has never hesitated to compliment my work, and it only motivates me to make more pieces that we can both be proud of. I'm so grateful to have her as my mentor!*

ALLISON CONSIDINE

YEARS AS MENTOR: 2

OCCUPATION: Senior Editor, *American Theatre*

BORN: Dallas, PA

LIVES: Brooklyn, NY

PUBLICATIONS AND RECOGNITIONS: *Backstage, HelloGiggles, Epicurious*; 2017 Critic Fellow at the Eugene O'Neill Theater Center National Critics Institute

MENTOR'S ANECDOTE: *Kayla continually impresses me with her confidence and boundless imagination. Whether she's crafting a Dungeons & Dragons campaign, teaching herself a new language, or writing a novella, she gives it her all. I'm inspired by the worlds she builds through her writing. Our time together has taught me to set goals and to feed my creative spirit, and I'm so grateful.*

WITH ROUNDED EDGES

KAYLA WALFORD

"With Rounded Edges" is a piece made to capture the childlike, nostalgic feeling of the most simplistic version of love. This excerpt is the end of the story, leaving an open-ended finish that encourages the reader to continue the story of Paige and Amara on their own.

I have taken an affinity for shooting at the whales in the sky.

It's not like the bullets hit anywhere near them. The bullets probably landed somewhere farther off, down into the forest, behind Amara's vacation house. I didn't shoot for my accuracy. It was for the thrill of the *bang!* and the backfire, like someone roughly shoving my shoulders, and the smell of the muzzle after the bullet had shot off. I squinted again and focused.

Bang!

Bang!

Footsteps thudded down the steps inside the house, and the screen door flapped open. Light footsteps joined me on the porch. "You know, the target range is always an option."

I shrugged. "I like the scenery here more." I raised the pistol again and she shuffled closer. I lowered my arms and sighed. "Amara, if you stand too close I can't concentrate."

"I regret giving you my dad's gun." Amara shook her head. "But I came out to see if you wanted any of this!" She thrust a large cardboard box at me so forcefully the pistol in my hand clattered out of my grasp.

I laughed. "Shut up, I don't need that! My apartment's too full of your stuff now, you know." I took the box anyway.

While I ruffled through the hand-me-downs, Amara plopped down next to me. "Those whales sure are something, huh?" I hummed. "God, they're so beautiful. They look lovely against the sunset, too. Imagine if we were up high with them; we could, like, run on their backs, or look at how small people are below, or watch the sunsets without any trees blocking the view." She paused, then laughed. "I'm sorry, that sounded so silly."

I laughed with her. "Yeah, a little."

We watched the whales in silence as the sunset started to deepen in color. I picked out a pretty dress from Amara's box and a weird little cat sculpture I found funny. When the sky reached a deep red, the whales started their cries. "Frickin' amazing," Amara commented. "What're they doing, a, uh, whaddayacallit, a mating call? Paige, you're the one with the marine biology major."

I scoffed, "Yeah, but I'm only a freshman." I paused. "But yeah, they're mating calls."

Amara laughed and hefted herself up. "You're silly. I want to see them closer up, wanna come?"

I followed her into the kitchen. Amara pulled out a bottle of wine her parents forgot to take out of the cabinet last year. She wiggled it and grinned, like we weren't nineteen.

We trudged up the hill we used to sneak out to as kids. It felt strange, being allowed to come up here now. We laid down on the grass and watched the whales pump their fins and glide on the breeze. I thought of Amara's dad's pistol, *bang, bang, bang*, and the bullets flying into the forest. We left the wine forgotten at our side and just talked instead. Sometime around when the sky was painted navy blue on the edges, our hands got tangled together. The whales started up a cry that was unlike anything I've ever heard before. Amara fell silent.

"Man, that's weird. Do whales really make that sound?"

"Huh?"

"Do whales sound like that? Like the actual ones, under the sea."

"I have no idea."

SHARNICE WALKER

YEARS AS MENTEE: 1

GRADE: Senior

BORN: Bronx, NY

LIVES: Bronx, NY

MENTEE'S ANECDOTE: *Deenie and I meet every Friday at the Girls Write Now headquarters in one of the recording booths and talk about anything and everything on my mind. I've come to her with many personal things and she's helped me deal with a lot of resentment I hold toward my parents. She's helped me realize my dreams and who I want to be in life. I couldn't have asked for a better mentor.*

DEENIE MATTHEWS

YEARS AS MENTOR: 1

OCCUPATION: Freelance Writer

BORN: Kingston, Jamaica

LIVES: New York, NY

PUBLICATIONS AND RECOGNITIONS: *Amsterdam News, Los Angeles Sentinel, The Baltimore Times*

MENTOR ANECDOTE: *I'm continually blown away by Sharnice's incredible amount of talent and her focus as well as discipline. I was nervous before starting the program, but must say I have been pleasantly surprised. I tend to worry about her because of the challenges that women face in general and the particular challenges Black girls face, but her unflappability and determination to be positive make me confident that she will end up doing just fine. She is a wonderful and unstoppable force!*

DEVOTION

SHARNICE WALKER

There has been a time in all of our lives where we've placed our significant other above ourselves and our responsibilities. I wanted to show how we as women often lose who we are while trying to help someone figure out who they want to be.

"What are you devoted to?"

"My love."

"Why would you devote yourself to another human?"

"Because he loves me."

It was midnight. The moon was full and shining bright above me as I walked through town. I first stopped at our old house. It had a lawn with weeds that roamed wild. He said that he'd mow it at some point but he never got to it I guess. The house itself used to be all white, but now the paint was peeling and turning a gray color, why hadn't he been repainting the house? I tried opening the door and wasn't surprised to find it unlocked. Jordan always did forget to lock the door when he was home; he would probably get mugged if I wasn't around to remind him. As I stepped into the house I was taken aback by how empty it was. The big TV that my dad had given us was gone, the couch we got at that garage sale down by Mrs. Johnson, his PlayStation, our fridge, table, and chairs were all gone. The only things that stayed were the juice stains on our carpet and the rat holes.

"Jordan," I yelled, as I walked up the stairs to our bedroom.

Our door was wide open and everything was gone.

"Jordan!" I yelled, as I ran through the house. My breathing was getting heavier and heavier. I walked around, looking in the bathroom: not there. Basement: not there. Our living room: not there. And our bedroom again: not there.

"Okay . . . Okay. Everything is fine, he's around here some-where, everything is fine," I said, cradling my head and trying to calm down. After a minute of heaving and trying to stop the tears from pouring out, I looked up and through the window to see me and Jordan riding down the street in a blue 1987 Toyota Corolla he borrowed from his friend. He was driving wearing his gold chains, white button-up, blue jeans, and snakeskin shoes. I was wearing a blue dress and white slippers, and holding a picnic bas-ket. We were smiling and holding hands. We looked down the road, ringing with excitement to reach our destination. I ran down the stairs and tried following the car before it disappeared. It was some ways up the road, but I followed it about a mile across town, when it disappeared in front of Jordan's parents' house.

His house looked so disgraceful. The beautiful garden his mom had was filled with weeds and dead flowers, the lawn was un-kempt and wild, the car tires were missing, and the windows were boarded up. It looked so neglected, I walked up the front steps and knocked on the door. No one answered. I banged on the door. No one answered.

"Jordan!" I yelled, banging on the door. I tried opening the door only to see it swing open, slamming against the wall. The in-side was even sadder, all the furniture they didn't care to take was covered in a dusty tarp and the walls looked like they were halfway through being knocked down. I felt the tears running down my face as I ran out of the house. Holding my knees and heaving, I could feel my chest tighten and my vision become blurry. Looking up I see the Toyota Corolla riding past the house, me and Jordan smiling like we had no care in the world. I stand up straight, wipe my eyes, and follow the car. I follow it to Jordan's friends' house, the park where he used to play basketball and the pizzeria he always went to. He wasn't there, no one was there. My feet felt sore from walking up and down the town all night, my eyes were bloodshot from all the tears, and I was so tired. In the middle of the sidewalk, I cradled myself in the fetal position and started whimpering in the street.

"Jordan, where are you? I need you, please," I said through my pathetic sobs, and after a few minutes I heard the sound of laughter. Looking up, I saw myself laughing in the car and holding the basket, and instead of disappearing in front of a different building it stopped in front of a forest. Since when was there a forest that close to town? I saw myself and Jordan walking hand in hand, we looked so happy so beautiful. I started following them. As I stepped into the forest, rays of light peaked through the trees. It was like it became early morning, but as I looked back at the town it was still the middle of the night.

I tried to follow them, but the forest was so dense. I got lost along the way, and I could feel the tears threatening my eyes again.

"Jordan! I'm here! Please come here!" I yelled, stumbling through the forest. My legs finally caved under me and I fell to the ground, scraping my knees as I yelled out for my love. He was so close, why didn't he hear me? I'm so tired and sick, I want him here to hug me and take me back to our home, to cuddle me in our bed. I lay down in the wet grass, too weak to leave and too tired to cry again. I laid there crying out to him but my voice was too sore until I felt energy above me. I looked up to see me. I was wearing the same blue dress I saw myself wearing in the car. She reached her hand out to me, but I sat up and swatted it away. I got up from the ground dusting off my dress and asked: "Do you know where Jordan is?"

Her face didn't move, but her eyes looked so disappointed. She pointed to the left of us and as she did, it was almost like the trees parted themselves to show a clear path.

"Thank you," I said, as I ran down to see Jordan.

KATHY WANG

YEARS AS MENTEE: 1

GRADE: Sophomore

BORN: New York, NY

LIVES: Brooklyn, NY

MENTEE'S ANECDOTE: *Nicole has honestly been an absolute role model. I look forward to every single one of our meetings. She's soft-spoken and very kind, and never runs out of good writing ideas I could adapt. I love talking about her dog the most! We both bond over the fact that we're the oldest siblings of the family, and what it's like to be a girl while being the eldest. Overall, I think Nicole is super fun. My writing has improved greatly because of her.*

NICOLE JONES

YEARS AS MENTOR: 1

OCCUPATION: Writer and Editor

BORN: Charlotte, NC

LIVES: Brooklyn, NY

PUBLICATIONS AND RECOGNITIONS: *The Paris Review; Low Country* (Catapult Press, 2021)

MENTOR'S ANECDOTE: *I was so impressed with Kathy from the moment we met. Her intelligence and enthusiasm are an inspiration. The afternoon of orientation at the New-York Historical Society, after oohing and aahing over paintings and Tiffany lamps, I remember talking about books she loved and bonding over how reading had opened up the world for both of us. Kathy and I meet at the Center for Fiction now, and getting to know her has been the most fun. It's a joy to watch her writing grow and a privilege to be entrusted with reading her work!*

SPRINGFIELD CEMETERY

KATHY WANG

Before I moved, I lived in front of a cemetery for most of my childhood. In one of Girls Write Now's Friday Night Salons, I remembered the cemetery and thought it would be fun to spin a ghost story about it. Cemeteries are always so spooky!

When I biked to school and back every day, I would always have to pass by Springfield Cemetery. For a cemetery, it was surprisingly cheery, with the red and white flowers that adorned rows and rows of graves. Mr. Porter, the groundskeeper, made sure no grave looked empty. As I stopped and visited at least once a week, sometimes every afternoon, we would talk every now and then. He told me bringing flowers always made the spirits happy.

One day, I was riding home from school as usual and looked to the cemetery out of habit as I passed. Almost instantly, I noticed a grave that was just a little hidden by the overgrown vegetation of the place; it was a new one, and odd for sure, as Mr. Porter himself said that Springfield was overcrowded.

There was a man standing over the grave. He was extremely tall and thin, wispy-looking, almost as if the wind could just pick him right up and drop him off someplace miles and miles from here. It was winter around this time, but the man wore no overcoat, just a simple black turtleneck and jeans. He wore no shoes. If he was bothered at all by the cold, he didn't show it.

Despite fear nipping at my sides, I decided to approach the man, curiosity getting the better of me. My mother would be yelling at me right now, telling me to stay away, but paranormal things weren't exempt from my inquisitive nature. He looked strange from far away and even stranger up close. He had half a mustache and looked awfully familiar, but I couldn't quite put my finger on it. I opened my mouth to speak, but the words got caught in my throat the moment I made eye contact with him. He looked right through me, gazing sadly at something in the far distance, muttering under his breath. I turned by instinct to follow his gaze, only noting the distant nothingness in the horizon.

Perplexed, I looked back to the man, only to see that he had vanished along with the grave!

Red and white, from the flowers on top of the graves, were the usual colors in my peripheral that stood out when I whizzed by Springfield Cemetery. Occasionally, some families would leave yellow or pink flowers behind for their loved ones. That day as I was biking, a bright burst of purple stopped me in my tracks. It was a dahlia in front of the same grave where I had seen the tall, wispy-looking man three weeks ago.

Dahlias were known to represent one who believed strongly in their sacred values. They were my mother's favorite; she would insist on getting a summer bouquet every time we passed the florist shop after church on a Sunday. But no one really leaves dahlias at a grave.

Almost as if a force was pulling me, I stepped into Springfield Cemetery. The crumbly soil felt like quicksand under my feet; my legs became jelly, but I could not stop—I kept going. The dahlia was even more gorgeous up close, but the fact that it looked so new and recent left an unsettling feeling in my stomach.

Right then, the same man I had noticed a few weeks before appeared, this time dirtier than I remembered. This close, I saw that his hair was long and matted, his feet bare as before—only caked in dirt this time, and his hands were dark from digging through earth. He walked past me, and I caught a glimpse of his face, his expression as sad as a kicked puppy. He had a scar under his chin that resembled a knife wound.

I shuddered at the thought of being so close to a spirit, my mother's clear-as-day scolding resounding in my head. Though I haven't been back to the church in ages, I recited a chant in my head for protection against whatever evil may be lurking around. I glanced back at the grave.

It read "Jeremie, 1957."

ABENA WIREKOH

YEARS AS MENTEE: 1

GRADE: Senior

BORN: Kumasi, Ghana

LIVES: New York, NY

MENTEE'S ANECDOTE: *During these past few months, meeting up with Mareesa has been one of the best highlights of my week. I feel extremely lucky to have Mareesa be a constant part of my life who I see every week. Our free write sessions are my personal favorite and some of my best works have been from flash-fiction pieces we have done together. I look forward to the weeks we have left of this year and cry in advance for the end of our time together.*

MAREESA NICOSIA

YEARS AS MENTOR: 1

OCCUPATION: Independent Journalist

BORN: Oneonta, NY

LIVES: New York, NY

PUBLICATIONS AND RECOGNITIONS: *Wired, The Atlantic, The Huffington Post*

MENTOR'S ANECDOTE: *Witnessing Abena explore her voice and share her unique life experiences in her poetry, college essay, and other creative projects this year has been a wonderful privilege. She radiates quiet strength and tackles difficult subjects with courage and grace—producing beautifully compelling pieces in the process. Our weekly writing sessions followed by our meandering walking-to-the-subway chats reliably make me laugh and cry, and our time together has inspired me to renew my own creative writing practice.*

BECAUSE THIS IS MY FIRST LIFE

ABENA WIREKOH

This is a piece about being a seventeen-year-old. An ode to myself reflecting on the experiences of my teenage years while acknowledging some of my personal heroes.

Because I am 17
Because I am a female who is 17
Because the nights are restless and the days too short—

Too short to live the fairytale life
Of basketball games and walks along the beach
Of dancing on rooftops and long nights spent partying

Because the long nights are shared with lonely cries
Cries of pain and anger for everything—Myself, school,
    parents, friends—
Everyone
And hatred for the world
Filled with the tears of innocence
Bathed in racism, sexism, classism, and every other ism
Hatred for the world that suffocates me
That binds me useless and helpless

So I lay awake in bed
As slow, sad songs play in the background
As I reminisce on the times of childlike innocence
When all was bliss with sprinkles of joy

Until the sun ascends and my sleep descends
Until my fears are romanticized away

And the echoes of darkness are colored in pink and purple hues

Because I am a 17-year-old Who is sometimes an adult
And other times a child
Coerced into the role that best fits the narrative

When will I become an adult?
When do I stop being a child?
Is there a moment when one leaves childhood for adulthood?
For all the troubles it brings?
And for the termination of ignorance?

Because I am 17
And I do not live a life of passion fighting for a grand cause
Like Martin Luther King dreaming of liberation
Fighting for the freedom of my brothers and sisters

A life of standing my ground like Claudette Colvin
Of taking my place in history
Or a life of silence with my work stolen like Rosalind Franklin
Plundered as my body lies beneath granite stone

But because I am 17 and although I don't march for a cause?
Or sacrifice my youth for my country
I have fought my own battles
And persevered to be here

Therefore my stories deserve to be heard,
The stories of uncertainty and indecisiveness,
The stories of my teenage years—

As days whirl by, I sink into sloth
And dreams bleach before my eyes,
Drifting away, existing . . . not living

CHELSEA YAN

YEARS AS MENTEE: 1

GRADE: Junior

BORN: Xiamen, China

LIVES: Staten Island, NY

PUBLICATIONS AND RECOGNITIONS: *YCteen* magazine; cofounder of Redefy Stuyvesant

MENTEE'S ANECDOTE: *The first time KK and I met, we unraveled our thoughts about culture, music, and food, and were excited to find so much in common. Our conversations provided me with confidence and an outlet to express my opinions freely. Without KK, a lot of my ideas wouldn't grow to what they are today. Through working with her, I came to understand the significance of mentorship. KK's patience, humor, and open-mindedness taught me how to be confident with my voice and I feel so lucky to have had the chance to work with her.*

KK APPLE

YEARS AS MENTOR: 6

OCCUPATION: Comedian & Freelance Copywriter

BORN: Indianapolis, IN

LIVES: Brooklyn, NY

PUBLICATIONS AND RECOGNITIONS: *Vulture, Funny or Die*; writer and house performer at the Upright Citizens Brigade Theatre

MENTOR'S ANECDOTE: *Getting to know Chelsea has been such a joy this year. She makes me laugh every week as she shares the latest from school or her thoughts on the world around her. When she sits down to write, she's incredibly honest and brings a thoughtful curiosity to her work. Being her mentor has been a lesson in constantly being impressed. Chelsea is so ambitious and her academic drive inspires me. And, of course, I feel lucky to be schooled in all the best parts of BTS.*

EPIPHANY OF HOTPOT

CHELSEA YAN

*Moving from city to city at a young age, away from my family and rel-
atives, shaped my passions and how I view the world. These two chants
connect blurry fragments of my childhood to my hopes for the future.*

Beware!
A Chinese dinner banquet is a total war zone.
Flying chopsticks,
Clashing dishes,
Passing soy sauce bottles,
Mixing aromas of exquisite spices,
Some tables even rotate.

They said,
Don't make so much noise when you drink soup,
Don't talk with food in your mouth,
Don't move your feet around,
Don't sit there like a dumb girl while the adults make a toast,
Don't you dare stick your chopstick in your food,
Do you want your ancestor's ghost coming for you tonight?

They said,
the neighbor
Of the uncle
Of the pet
Of the cousin
Of the aunt
Of the sister
Of the nephew

Of my mother
Might be getting married,

They said,
This is your auntie,
She changed your diaper once when you were two.
This is your fourth cousin,
She got into Yale last spring.
This is your great-great-great-uncle,
He brought you a cup of bubble tea when you went to elementary
    school.
Go say hi! Go have a conversation! Now!
Be a good girl.

They said,
Shush!

Mama threw me a look
here and there.
Not to warn me or shut me up,
But to signal a delicious dish was coming up
and it is time to stay focused
on the food.

For she was just like me,
Sincerely confused by the
Subtle flexes,
Mind games,
And calculations
under the smiling faces of our relatives.

When I was young,
I dreaded the ride back home after a large dinner party.
I had no idea if I
did anything wrong, or
said anything impolitely, or

ate anything too ferociously, or
sat in a chair that significantly violated the feng shui of the table.
Did I act like the girl I've been raised to be tonight?

The older I grew,
The more I wanted to escape.
No more dirty looks,
or evil smirks.
No more superstitious rules,
and exaggerated cultural taboos.
Please.

Baba couldn't believe that
His only daughter can't even get along
With her own family.
It's all because she's not a boy.
He explained to them.

Only Mama understood me
In this big wide world,
And that was enough.

[2]

I pretend to scroll my phone
But I can barely focus,
so I stare at my toes instead.

I hear the summer breeze playing with my siblings,
I hear my mama's broken English conversation with the movers,
But I can't hear your voice.
It's almost time,
Aren't you going to say goodbye?

How I adored your scent of fresh paint and new wooden
    furniture;

How I ran my fingers through the textured pink wallpaper;
How I dropped my palette and painted you a colorful tattoo;
How I winced and whined all night when I first returned from
    the orthodontist;
How I rolled off my bed accidentally
and cuddled with your hardwood floors until my neck hurt the
    next day;
How I cooked my first bowl of spicy instant noodles when Mama
    went to look for a new job;
How I planted the little cherry branch sneakily behind the pool,
With high hopes that it would grow taller than me;
How I anticipated you to love and nurture me,
And now I thank you.

The mere existence of you
reminds me of the dedication in our hearts
when Mama took me by the hand and left that dinner party.
The women of China deserve a different path,
A chance to shine.
Even if it means stepping out of the comfort of being provided
    for.
Even if it means applying for a job for the first time.

Clutching on to our suitcases,
Mama rushed me onto the airplane to New York City,
And we said goodbye to everything we've ever known.

Zai Jian, Shanghai City Tian-An Dong seventh building.
Gao ci, Yong-Sheng The Hill twenty-third floor.
See you, Sunset Park Fifty-Second Street.
Bye-bye, Forest Hills 103rd Street.
So long, Flushing 6002 Lawrence Street.
Farewell, Richmond 141 Cranford Avenue.

To me, you are not hardened cement,
wood, and bricks.
When Mama had to work late nights,

You were my quiet companion,
Teaching me how to be comfortable *alone*.

I turned up with hopes for the future,
Now I depart with more hope
and your warm blessings.
No, you are not a gleaming, luxurious mansion,
But your humble rooms provided way more than shelter.

Click!
The door locks behind me.
I leave with more than I came with.
One last glance, moving on.
I'm going to soar higher.
I bid you adieu.

Alright, here I go.

CHRISTINE YAN

YEARS AS MENTEE: 1

GRADE: Junior

BORN: Queens, NY

LIVES: Queens, NY

PUBLICATIONS AND RECOGNITIONS: Redefy Stuyvesant

MENTEE'S ANECDOTE: *From the start, it was obvious that Avery and I were a perfect match. Like how a book is incomplete without its cover, what would Christine do without Avery? Week after week, Avery continues to encourage and support me. She is empathetic, adventurous, and not afraid of the "what ifs." Avery constantly inspires me to take bold actions—to bring my story to places I could have never imagined before. With someone as skilled as Avery, there is never a dull moment. I am extremely grateful to Girls Write Now for introducing me to such a wonderful person and talented writer.*

AVERY CARPENTER FORREY

YEARS AS MENTOR: 1

OCCUPATION: Contributing Editor, *theSkimm*; NYU MFA candidate

BORN: Greenwich, CT

LIVES: New York, NY

PUBLICATIONS AND RECOGNITIONS: *How to Skimm Your Life* (Ballantine Books, 2019)

MENTOR'S ANECDOTE: *Christine's quiet brilliance and poise amaze me every week. She's a triple threat: a budding photographer, writer, and businesswoman. Recently, she let slip that she won an entrepreneurship competition and even owns stock in Slack (and here I am still reminding myself to check Slack for updates)! Her love of music and photography shines through her writing, and it's inspired me to weave similar themes into my own pieces. I'm so grateful to her and to the program for introducing us.*

STOLEN SOUND

CHRISTINE YAN

In the midst of our busy lives, we find time to pursue our interests outside of work and school. I wanted to explore one young woman's creative passion and what happens when an unexpected force interferes with that sacred time.

It was just before 2:00 a.m. when Lili wrapped up her nightly jam session. This was how she usually spent her late nights: experimenting with melodies and stringing different beats together. Lili preferred the comforts and stillness of her own apartment in Manhattan to the house parties full of other girls her age. She just wanted to prove to her parents that moving away from Hawaii wasn't a mistake.

A few years ago she started uploading instrumental covers of pop songs and her own pieces to YouTube as an escape from university. While she majored in biology, music was Lili's true passion.

It wasn't until she uploaded her rendition of "Gypsy" by Fleetwood Mac that she started accumulating tens of thousands of subscribers. As her following grew, Lili received more sponsorships and royalties. It was only then that her parents caved and granted Lili's request to drop out of college.

Suddenly, a faint but noticeable knock sounded through her studio door—a snap back to reality. Lili froze in her living room, sheets of music clutched close to her heart. After what felt like eternity, a slightly wrinkled piece of paper with a messy note scrawled on it slipped under the door.

Her heart pounded as she walked over. Could it be a noise complaint? Now that she thought about it, her next-door neighbor never seemed to like her. She bent down and picked up the note with slightly shaky hands.

Struggling to make out the words, Lili read: *Hey, this is your next-door neighbor. I'm actually a record producer. Would love to talk more tomorrow or in the next few days. Business card attached. Feel free to contact me.*

She flipped over the paper and looked at the card: Brad Stilton. If school had taught her one thing, it was to always do research. She'd heard of the major labels, but never of his.

He must be trustworthy though, Lili thought to herself. A scammer couldn't possibly afford to live in Manhattan and it wasn't unheard of for underground artists to join unknown labels. As she walked back to her room, Lili wrote a reminder to continue looking online tomorrow.

A hammering sound from the floor above woke Lili up before her alarm. This routinely happened in the mornings, yet there was never a set pattern. Lili could never bring herself to ask them to quiet down. Instead, she interpreted it as a forecast for her day: loud with a chance of annoyance.

Lili immediately started her day to avoid having her mood killed in the morning. She checked her inbox, but only to delete forty-five new spam emails. These didn't bother her like they usually did. Brad Stilton's offer had already consumed her thoughts. She decided to go out on a limb and shoot him an email.

Not even ten minutes later, her phone buzzed. A reply from Brad. Lili anxiously opened the message. *4:00 p.m. today at the Starbucks across the street. How does that sound?*

Lili was caught off guard by both his casual language and the sudden appointment. She glanced at her clock, just a little after three. Brad was cutting it a little too close, but who was Lili to complain? Though she had reminded herself to conduct an unofficial background check on Brad, those reservations faded with the idea of him getting her voice on Spotify. Lili replied, *Not a problem. I'll bring my recent piece on a CD. Looking forward to meeting you.* Sent.

The next half-hour flew by, and before Lili knew it, she was rushing out of the apartment with her CD in hand. No matter how early she thought she was, she always managed to end up being a little late.

As Lili rounded the corner of her building, she slammed right into a stranger. Her CD clattered onto the floor along with the rest of her belongings from her tote bag.

"I'm so sorry," Lili said. "I'll pick up my stuff."

"You good?" the stranger asked. "Let me help."

Lili quickly shoved her phone, compact mirror, and water bottle back into the bag. She picked up her phone, checking to make sure there were no scratches.

Without missing a beat, the stranger slipped the CD into his jacket pocket and reached out to offer Lili a hand. She thanked him, and both parted their separate ways: one back to the building and another to Starbucks.

A year later, Lili sat ready for another night session. Her life hadn't changed much since that day in Starbucks when Brad stood her up. He remained unresponsive to her emails and became a professional ghost who Lili had mostly forgotten about.

To begin her night session, Lili turned on Spotify for inspiration. The "All-New Indies" playlist blared through her room as she closed her eyes and leaned back into her chair.

Her eyes shot open to a familiar melody being sung by a different artist, her words placed in a different mouth.

KAITLYN YANG

YEARS AS MENTEE: 3

GRADE: Junior

BORN: New York, NY

LIVES: New York, NY

PUBLICATIONS AND RECOGNITIONS: Scholastic Art & Writing Awards: Gold Key, Silver Key, and Honorable Mention

MENTEE'S ANECDOTE: *Meg and I always have fun brainstorming future stories together. After our weekly free-writes, we build on each other's ideas and create new worlds and obstacles to challenge our characters and push them to overcome. I can always count on Meg to help me work through any roadblocks I face in my writing and introduce me to new exercises to jump-start my creativity.*

MEGHANN FOYE

YEARS AS MENTOR: 3

OCCUPATION: Digital Content Director, Parade.com

BORN: Lynn, MA

LIVES: Jersey City, NJ

PUBLICATIONS AND RECOGNITIONS: Published on Parade.com, Brit + Co, Working Mother; author of *Meternity*, which has been optioned for TV by Paramount

MENTOR'S ANECDOTE: *I have no doubt in my mind that my mentee, Kaitlyn, will be taking her place in history soon with her many writing accomplishments, including a fantasy YA novel she's been working on throughout our time at Girls Write Now, as well as a series of essays that speak to the themes of family, loss, and memories. In our work together, Kaitlyn always comes prepared with a new piece she's been working on. Our favorite thing to do is build on each other's ideas to get it to an even more impactful place. Her work is far beyond her years already and her particular skill is connecting the history of the character to the present conflict in incredibly imaginative ways.*

RASPBERRY HEART

KAITLYN YANG

"Raspberry Heart" reflects the importance of being in touch with our emotions and remaining humans in a time when technology is becoming more and more prevalent in our lives. My piece connects to this year's theme by questioning this impact on human interaction in the near and distant future.

My heart hurts like it's being squeezed, I tell Lily.
Like heartbreak? Symptoms of heartbreak are exhaustion and body pains.
No, like something's grabbed it and pushed all the air out.
Like loneliness? Symptoms of loneliness are sadness and feelings of isolation.
No, like my heart's being strangled. Lily doesn't understand. Like most others, she doesn't have a heart. She has a central control system, wired to handle her inputs and outputs. A central control system is cube-shaped and silver—I saw a few when I went to the hospital earlier today. They were laid out on a tray, all shiny and gleaming.
One of those is going to be implanted into your brother today, the doctor said when he caught me staring. *It's going to save him from relying on his heart.*
What do hearts look like?
Nothing like these. They're bumpy and red—
Like a raspberry?
I suppose. Horrid, aren't they? All sour and staining my fingers—
Have you ever implanted a heart before?
Oh no, child. Hearts are for removing. It's much too risky to rely on a heart.

I turn to Lily.

Have you ever seen a heart?

There was a picture of one on record in the laboratory. And I have seen models.

Can you show me some time?

Certainly. Observation is crucial for understanding. But you are going to get your heart removed soon, aren't you?

I guess.

Would you like it if I booked you an appointment?

That's okay. I'll do it later.

But why keep something that causes you so much pain?

Skip a beat.

Have you ever had a raspberry?

No.

They're sweet and tart—

They are not a very efficient source of energy.

And juice runs out when you squeeze them between your fingers—

They are not a very reliable source of fuel.

And you eat so many at a time that your fingers are still red even after you wash your hands. Skip a beat.

Have you ever had a heart?

I must have. Some time ago.

I guess I'm the only one left, then.

I am right here.

The only one left with a heart.

Most choose not to rely on a raspberry.

I know. But I'm scared to live without one.

It's much too risky to rely on a heart.

But what if it's worth it?

Skip a beat.

CLAIRE YU

YEARS AS MENTEE: 2

GRADE: Sophomore

BORN: New York, NY

LIVES: Queens, NY

PUBLICATIONS AND RECOGNITIONS: Scholastic Art & Writing Awards: Gold Key, Silver Key, and Honorable Mention; *The DESK* Magazine

MENTEE'S ANECDOTE: *Jesse and I bonded on the first day we met when we found out how similar we were. Talking to Jesse, I found out that we both write poetry, dance, and play(ed) the flute! It's honestly been so reassuring to know that I have someone to talk to who understands and can get advice from someone who has been through everything I'm going through now. Our weekly meetings at a café in downtown Manhattan always seem to go by so quickly when we chat about my writing and our lives.*

JESSE CHEN

YEARS AS MENTOR: 1

OCCUPATION: Account Director, Water & Wall Group

BORN: Edison, NJ

LIVES: New York, NY

PUBLICATIONS AND RECOGNITIONS: Crain's; Gramercy Institute 20 Rising Stars; Academy of American Poets University & College Poetry Prize

MENTOR'S ANECDOTE: *Claire is what would happen if you took high school me, made her Gen Z, notched up the work ethic to 200 percent, and took a few inches off the top. We're both poets, flutists, former ballet dancers turned hip-hop dancers, Asians, women, the daughters of immigrants, sisters, wearers of round glasses, resistant to the idea of ever leaving New York City; the list goes on. I'm thankful to get to work with someone so intelligent, articulate, and ambitious, and to cultivate her voice as one of a growing number of Asian women of color in the writing community.*

INTERLUDES

CLAIRE YU

This piece is inspired by my love for dance and my team. It is a reflection on the moments from dance I find myself thinking about and the reasons for my passion for it.

1. Moments of
Dimensions
Chemistry
Tension in the air,
tension in your arms and legs and between your fingers and
behind your eyes
The space between our bodies is sacred when we move we press
against that bubble
I can feel your heartbeat echoing in waves
We stretch out the rhythms between us
elastic
Your push and my pull
balance
catch me if I fall
Music so loud you can feel the vibrations in the floor
or is that your heart
beating, the blood
pulsing through your veins in rhythms you feel so deeply
has it been a part of you all along?
Staccato breaths we crescendo
Let your soul, elated, rise
The weight of your shadow draped heavy around my shoulders
Your gravity holds me
to this world

2. Moments like this
When you close your eyes and feel the presence of the people
     around you
Happy in that moment
Happy to exist
To be there, and alive, and breathing
The look in your eyes that one time
Your heartstrings reaching out
Wrapping around mine, the intensity
Of my passion meeting yours
And since that wordless moment there is something
more between us, something
not tangible, but less empty, something
more inside my chest when I meet your eyes

3. Moments when we celebrate
the beauty
the harmony of intertwining limbs
the passion for movement
our passion for each other
energy we pass to one another without ever touching
The amalgam of you and me
Who says you can't
find beautiful things in tragedy? The hope
still blossoming in your breast after the sky
falls down
The brightness of the sun when the world
comes to an end
This is when we dance, spinning so fast
to match the dizzying pace of our lives
claiming significance to every cadence, every note, every bass,
every beat—
every heartbeat
every life
every breath

GRACE YU

YEARS AS MENTEE: 2

GRADE: Sophomore

BORN: New York, NY

LIVES: Queens, NY

PUBLICATIONS AND RECOGNITIONS: Scholastic Art & Writing Awards: Honorable Mention

MENTEE'S ANECDOTE: *When I first met Sarah, we bonded quickly over our favorite literary heroes and found out that we shared an intense love of bookstores. Since then, Sarah and I have met every week at Barnes & Noble, where we write, laugh, and obsess over her cat, Cricket. Through her guidance, I've been able to experiment with cross-genre writing, and even completed a sixty-page portfolio! Our meetings are the highlight of my week and Sarah is a friend as well as an amazing writing mentor. We have so much fun together and she inspires me to be my best self.*

SARAH McNAUGHTON

YEARS AS MENTOR: 1

OCCUPATION: Executive Editor, LIVESTRONG.com

BORN: Denver, CO

LIVES: New York, NY

MENTOR'S ANECDOTE: *I look forward to Friday all week long: the brisk walk to Barnes & Noble, the comforting smell of books and coffee, the shy smile of a brilliant, talented young writer and musician. How lucky am I? Knowing Grace's carefully crafted scenes are created within the rare, tiny windows of free time she has makes me appreciate her work even more—how does she do so much (and so well)? I relish our discussions about her characters' backstories and wish our hour of thoughtful creativity lasted longer. On my brisk walk home I start looking forward to next Friday.*

SAYONARA, HELLO

GRACE YU

"sayonara, hello" is a cross-genre piece that explores the discrimination and isolation immigrants face. It is told from the perspective of a young Japanese girl who searches for acceptance from the people around her.

in my dreams i am in japan. there is a small village in the corner of somewhere, maybe nowhere. we are in fields and fields and the flowers are blooming. we are here. we are all here. chiyoko and ena and hibiki are here, with their wispy cloud hair, and shiori, with her little dog. he has a little blue collar and he chases us as we run. aoi and kinata are twins with matching ebony eyes and dark charcoal lashes. they stand here too. kaito has a limp and pretty legs. pretty but crooked. in my dreams he tries to run and falls down. he looks down at his pretty white legs and looks sad, for his legs are thin like reeds and he cannot properly stand. i am sorry for him, but when i wake up it is all gone. i wake up and it is cold and windy. the fields are replaced by softly falling snow. my dreams are of japan and they fade away into my pillow.

canada is a barren land. the people here are tall with sharp faces and light hair. when they speak their lips are sharp, the words harsh. spindly spider fingers, pale arms with peachy prickly hairs, sharp. they are the beautiful ones in this strange foreign land. they let out harsh cries when they see me and touch my dark dark hair. in this land, i am all alone. my almond eyes and my golden skin. i am a yellow rose in the middle of a blizzard.

she said, promise me you won't leave me. yakusoku, i promise. this girl has promised me. she will never go. i tell her in return. i will always stay here, yakusoku, and i never see her. i am gone in the night and i don't say bye to her.

there were houses, i know. dirt houses and small pots over a stove. the rice was so warm. the grains settling in my stomach and everything small and cozy. i don't remember anymore. fields and fields drift into my mind. i don't remember. someone is stumbling and falling down.

drifts of snow settle outside. everyone making snowballs and they are icy bullets in my hands. so round, make me shiver. when the people are throwing them i don't know why. snowflakes are pretty. i hate it when they break all the little crystals and push them into a ball. it feels like a storm. everyone throws them and they hit me with icy bullets in my heart. i don't think anything. i am trembling and on the ground. i am crushed rose in the middle of a blizzard.

hide. under my warm coat. i can see my breath here, the air sharp like icicles. i am huddling underneath the blankets. i thought i was warm once. i don't remember anymore. i thought someone had a dog. everything small and cozy. were there fields anywhere? it is so cold. i stop dreaming and using my pillow.

ebony eyes and charcoal lashes. my hair is dark, skin yellow like summer. the only girl who talks to me has yellow hair like a spring flower. she nods her head like a daffodil in a warm breeze. bright gold dust curls fall to her shoulders. i finger my straight hair.

where was everyone? i think back then i wasn't so alone. children in small villages. sit here in the middle of nowhere. i am trying to run somewhere i can't remember.

tissues white like roses at a funeral. her hair is bright. i look up and she is watching me. where did she come from? i don't know. she asks me why i'm not indoors. i am so far from home. i follow her. there is a little house and something over a small stove. slowly everything is warm. something cozy settling in my stomach and i thought it was like this in some other world. i don't know if i can remember. flowers and flowers all blooming, a corner in a far-away field. pretty legs white like snow. promise me you will never leave me, promise me i'll never go. she smiles like a different girl that i used to know. what did i say to her?

snowflakes are like fields of crystal flowers. we are running into the distance. golden hair ahead of me and mine wispy like a cloud. we are laughing. almond eyes bright and everything soft. i am starting to remember. i left in the night. couldn't see in the dark. there is something shining in the distance. i am so warm. i am running to her, smiling at her. what did i say to her? i remember now.

arigato, thank you.

JENNY ZHENG

YEARS AS MENTEE: 1

GRADE: Junior

BORN: New York, NY

LIVES: New York, NY

PUBLICATIONS AND RECOGNITIONS: Scholastic Art & Writing Awards: Gold Key

MENTEE'S ANECDOTE: *I'm addicted to tea now. And those thin Whole Foods meat strips. I love your giant neon jacket. My brother stalked your LinkedIn for me. I loved our visit to the International Center of Photography. I don't think I would've visited a museum for photos. And I can't believe it's a five-minute walk from my house! I do appreciate New York City a little more now. That might also be because I plan to leave for college. Thanks for putting up with all my college questions. I hope over the summer we do get to go see Shakespeare in the Park together.*

SAIRA KHAN

YEARS AS MENTOR: 1

OCCUPATION: Senior Platform Editor

BORN: Karachi, Pakistan

LIVES: Brooklyn, NY

PUBLICATIONS AND RECOGNITIONS: *The New York Times, The New Yorker*

MENTOR'S ANECDOTE: *Jenny and I went to see the Tyler Mitchell exhibit at the International Center of Photography, where one of the artworks is a multimedia piece that you experience by lying on the ground on a bean bag to watch a short film being projected on the ceiling. I watched one loop and then got up to leave. Jenny wanted to stay, so we both lay on the floor for five minutes watching the film. The experience of watching that film on loop was beautiful and I'm so glad I stayed. Sometimes you need someone to remind you to slow down, and I'm glad Jenny was that person for me that day.*

A MULTIGENERATIONAL WOMAN

JENNY ZHENG

This piece came from something in my life. I didn't have an ending, though. What I observed were random glimpses of probably normal behavior. The plot (the hardest) eventually came, inspired from the anthology title.

An elderly lady stands idle outside my apartment building. I keep a hand firm on the cast iron door, painted blue-gray, and she does come in—I am not mistaken. I flash back a kind smile, I try. Moments later we stand facing the closed doors of an elevator. I stare stiffly at the screen above, the boxy red number it displayed, her small hairy head in my peripheral vision. I hold my breath at the stench from the garbage cans lining our esteemed lobby, which isn't usually this unbearable in the late afternoon (on the starkest day of December, no less!)—mornings are when most take out the previous day's trash on their way to work or school.

In the elevator, I press 5. The old lady reaches over, presses 7. Twice; her large index finger missing on the first try. I get an adequate view of the rolls of heavily creased fat on her fingers and their thick, no-frills nails, all yellowed and the same inch-long length.

This time she catches my not-so-subtle stare, and smiles back like a struggling child, lips pulled back, corners turned down. There's a mark on her gums. The top left. It's large and gray. Unsettling. I'm staring. I tilt up my lips at her forehead and reorient my eyeballs back to the buttons.

The elevator feels rickety. Only then am I reminded it was broken for the past three months, fixed just last week. As normal, convenient, and regal it became, the daily elevator rides when I first moved here, normal it became when the metal junk broke, the daily climbs of five flights, reassuring myself of burnt calories, but mostly resenting the too tall steps of the stairs until my backpack was off and on my bedroom couch, after which the sense of triumph arrives, only after, and within the span of an afternoon, normal was again taking the elevator home.

* * *

Days later, I'm tasked to buy family breakfast. A young lady holds the elevator for me as I scurry down the hallway to catch the ride. I guess I owe her. Her hand firmly locks back the automated metal door, which, sensing humanity in its path, jolts and lazily slinks back.

I'm squished in the corner of the elevator, a large green laundry bag pushing me farther in as the lady enters.

I flash a hopefully grateful smile. She lives in apartment 14. I know. The one with its door always open, located next to the elevator. It has a single bedroom, if I overheard correctly. It houses large numbers despite this.

Apartment fourteen came to my attention one late night, after flossing and brushing; with anti-aging night cream thickly slapped on, I was ready to crash, only to notice a dreadful bag of trash still hooked on my bedpost. I responsibly trudge to the dumpster on the first floor, unashamed of my hospital gown pajamas and matching pink kitty slippers. In front of apartment 14, a lady, fragile-looking, possibly in her thirties, stood casually smoking.

It was a terrible first impression; our building's supposedly smoke-free and I certainly didn't appreciate the secondhand lung damage. She looked away at the ceiling, sheepish. I approached, a blank look aggressively willed onto my face. I opted for the stairs.

The woman was gone by the time I stepped out of the elevator I rode up, the door of fourteen also closed, though the smell lingered. Tobacco smells good occasionally, a thought I immediately beat up upon realization; I could grow used to anything.

That following morning I beseeched Mother to tattle on the smoking lady to our landlord, but my family likes to stay out of trouble, as we are used to, and the hazard soon slips my mind.

* * *

The young lady, quite perky I find, not at all resembles that willowy smoker I previously encountered—her roommate, I presume.

"How long have you lived here?" she asked me with a huge smile. Very toothy. I must look extremely approachable. "Awhile."

"Who are you living with?"

"My family."

"Are you close?"

"Mhm. Yeah."

My sister-in-law, who told me one time when she shared the elevator with this girl from 14, she smelled something strange from the duffel bag that they had.

"It was like, you know the thing in hospitals, they use on dead bodies."

And she says she knows how corpse preservative smells.

The girl has a mark in her mouth. I know from my sister-in-law's reportings. It's ugly.

Maybe they're a cult. Or they all have gum disease.

After the elevator lands, I recount the conversation, triple-checking that I didn't expose my suspicions. Then I stare at the back of the young lady, who is penguin-walking down toward the blue-gray door, lugging her giant green bag behind her. I feel guilty for my discrimination. It is unlikely she was collecting information to massacre my family with.

Before she exits the building, the lady turns back, flashing a familiar awkward grin. A black mark looks back at me.

GIRLS WRITE NOW CURRICULUM

Take **Your** *Place in History*

Taking Our Place in History is exactly what the Girls Write Now Class of 2020 mentees are doing each time they put pen to paper, fingertips to keyboards, and voices to microphones. They are visualizing their identity through graphic design, profiling their mentors using techniques of journalism, dashing off flash fiction, crafting lunes, slamming their words into poetry, and erasing exclusion from noninclusive texts. They are making their mark on the world.

They are writing speeches to themselves about self-love and penning tributes to those they admire. They are voicing their outrage and celebrating their passions, flipping the switch on what ails us, and turning this world from hate to love with humor and candor. They are saying, We are here and we have things to say.

The lesson plans in this section inspired Girls Write Now mentees to create the original content in this anthology. The plans are adapted from Girls Write Now Workshops and Salons, taught in collaboration with staff by professional writers who have both expertise in a particular genre or medium and experience applying it in the real world, representing both the craft and industry side of writing, and embodying how crucial writing is no matter what art form or career you aspire to.

Girls Write Now's curriculum reflects what writing means today—multigenre, multimedia, multiplatform communication—everything from storytelling to coding. Mentees create at the intersection of language, technology, and art. Taken with the book's multimedia companion, the boundaries are no longer decipherable as they bend and blend genres and media, sharing their stories to optimize interaction with the audience. The exercises here can be applied in analog or digital terms.

Step into history by creating your own stories and experience the power of your voice.

—ERICA SILBERMAN,
Director of Curriculum and Engagement

PROFILES

with Zaina Arafat

Zaina is a Palestinian American writer whose debut novel, You Exist Too Much, *is forthcoming in June from Catapult Books. Her stories and essays have appeared in publications including the* New York Times.

Profiles 101

A profile is a type of feature story that usually focuses on a person and what's important or interesting about that person at that moment. Although profiles usually focus on people, like celebrities, you can also profile entities like sports teams or companies. It's also not necessary for subjects of profiles to be public figures. They can be anyone who might make an interesting story that readers can relate to.

Opening Lines

If you could meet any important woman in history, who would it be, and why? History means a long time ago, but it also means today! You are part of history just as much as your ancestors. And you don't have to be famous to be part of history! Who is important to you?

The Craft of Profiles

Observation:

How do we render a person on the page? Profile writing is based around the fundamental writing tenet of *show, don't tell.* You want your reader to be able to see the person you are writing about on the page, and this means using specific details to render them real.

Ways to reveal character based on observation:

Appearance: What are some notable visible characteristics of the person you're writing about? What color hair do they have? Is it short, long, shoulder-length? Do they dress in a distinctive way?

Speech: This is where dialogue and quotes come in, and where you get to hear from the person you are profiling in their own voice, and to hear some of their thoughts and motivations directly.

Actions: Does the person you're profiling have any notable mannerisms or gestures? This is especially important when describing the particular incident you are focusing on. For example, if you're profiling a person who just won the WNBA championship, you will want to describe any notable actions they took on the court, or even before the game (did they eat a giant bowl of pasta, did they wear mismatched socks for good luck?).

Interviewing:

Research: Usually, it's beneficial to read and obtain background information about the subject, source, or topic at hand before interviewing so that you can ask informed questions.

Ask simple questions: Keep your questions short, to the point, and focused. Otherwise you risk distracting or confusing your subject. Break down complicated questions into shorter, simpler questions.

Try to use mostly open-ended questions: Open-ended questions often begin with "Why?" and "How?" or phrases such as "Tell me about . . ." or "How does that make you feel?" They invite longer, more insightful responses.

Ask follow-up questions based on their responses: Listen to the answers before moving on to your prepared questions. Often it is during a follow-up question that the right quote falls into your lap. Based on their responses, sometimes you'll be led down a different path than intended, and that's okay! Often we don't know exactly what we're looking for when we begin a profile.

Take notes: While having an audio recorder is helpful, always keep a notebook handy and use it to jot down quotes, statistics, or facts that strike you. You might also want to write down physical details about your environment and your subject's appearance, facial expressions, and voice. But be sure to look up from your notebook and maintain eye contact.

Think of the interview as a conversation: Keep the interview informal and casual, not overly scripted, and go with the flow, allowing your subject to switch directions—as long as you remain in control of the interview and are prepared to steer it back to your topic as needed.

Telling a larger story: Often, the person you profile can speak to a larger subject. For example, YazTheSpaz and her experience also speaks to the larger subject of the Muslim Americans and inclusivity in the United States. To find what this larger story is, it can be helpful to think about why this person's story is significant outside of just their immediate circle, why this person's story would matter to anyone who doesn't personally know them.

Profile Free-write

Write a profile of someone you know or admire. Focus on something notable they have accomplished, and that they feel proud to have achieved. It can be as major as winning a prestigious writing award, or as simple as flossing every night for a week. In addition to describing them and their experience, be sure to capture why this accomplishment is significant to them, and any challenges they faced along the way.

Begin by listing at least three or four questions to help you tell your subject's story. *Jot down observations that will help your reader see this person. Be sure to include direct quotes. You can begin by creating a scene. For example, "When she opened the medicine cabinet and saw the dental floss staring back at her, she knew it was time."*

FLASH FICTION

with Susanna Horng

Susanna is a mother, writer, teacher, and Girls Write Now mentor alumna who lives in New York City. She teaches writing and critical creative production at NYU, was a 2018 NYSCA/NYFA Artist Fellow in Fiction, and her work has appeared in the Bennington Review.

Flash Fiction 101

Flash fiction, also known as microfiction and sudden fiction, are stories told in just a few paragraphs, or sentences, or in some cases just a few words. Sometimes experimental in form, and often reading like poems, these compressed stories usually pack an emotional punch.

Opening Lines

List up to three taboos that you have heard, been told, or know from your experience. The sources can be your friends, family members, culture, religion, popular culture, gender, et cetera.

The Craft of Flash Fiction

Character and Setting: How do you render a character on the page?

Details: What are notable details about the character you're creating? Scars, piercings, tattoos, makeup, deformities? What are notable details about the setting in your story? Flora or fauna?

Speech: This is where dialogue and quotes come in, and where you get to hear the character speak in their own voice, and to hear some of their thoughts and motivations directly.

Actions: What mannerisms or tics does the character have? How does the character behave? Especially when they get or don't get what they want?

Stakes: What does the character want, and why is it important to them?

Storytelling: How do you write a memorable short short?

Structure: Stories need to have a clear beginning, middle, and end. For your beginning, start in the middle of the action/scene. Middle needs tension/stakes. At the end, leave your reader wanting more.

Stakes: What does the character want?

Tension: How does the character get, or not get, what they want? What are the obstacles? How does the character react?

Flash Fiction Free-write

Write a short short using one of the taboos you wrote about.
Use two characters only in your short short. Your characters should be specific, and should want something specific from the other in the story that they either get or don't get by the middle of the story. The two characters can want the same thing or different things. The two characters can tell each other what they want or not. If they don't tell the other, what they want must be clear to readers. The end of the story is how the character(s) deal with getting, or not getting, what they want.

SHORT FORM POETRY

with Melanie Goodreaux

Melanie is a poet, playwright, fiction writer, actor, and director-dramatist from New Orleans, Louisiana. She has been living and creating art in New York City since the late 1990s. Her plays include Enough VO5 for the Universe *and* The White Blacks. *She published* Black Jelly, *her first book of poetry, in collaboration with photographer Nikki Johnson.*

Poetry 101

Many people think writing poetry is about being deep, mysterious, and abstract. Many poets would disagree—it might be more about creating an image for the reader to attach to, or choosing just the right words to communicate with your reader.

Opening Lines

Pick any random word. Explode your word into a poem! Expand your idea. Write five to seven lines, with just *one or two words* per line to see if you can create good word choices that are descriptive and concrete. You *cannot* use any part of your chosen word in your poem.

Skinny Poems: The Craft and Free-write

Skinny poems are poems that have one or two words in a line. Using Melanie's skinny poem below as inspiration, write your five to seven lines:

Elder
Mamma
Wrinkled memories
Rocking-chair
Queen
Of
Family
Whispering
Prayers
Yester-year

—Melanie Goodreaux

Lunes: The Craft and Free-write

A lune is a short poem with three lines. It is a cousin to the haiku. These forms can be poems on their own, or they can be used to enhance other writing. There are a few kinds of lunes.

LUNE FORM:

3
5
3
—

Total: 11 Words

Using Melanie's lune below as inspiration, create lunes that have a word count, not a syllabic count. Your lunes will have three words in the top line, five words in the second line, and three words in the last line—a total of eleven words. Try to write between three and five lunes on various topics. The goal of the lune is to create an image for the reader—not to be "abstract."

Wrinkled hands reaching
Toward my face, last day
Hospital bed, goodbyes

Burgundy lips screaming
Bloodshot eyes, piercing stares, jealousy
Stolen dreams, revenge

Pink clouds floating
Metal wings travel above earth
Taking me home

—*Melanie Goodreaux*

Possible topics for your lune: a person in your family, food, an emotion, a historical event or person, something beautiful in nature, something/someone you've seen on the train.

ERASURE POETRY

with Arriel Vinson

Arriel is a Tin House Winter Workshop alum and Midwesterner who writes about being young, black, and in search of freedom. She earned her MFA in Fiction from Sarah Lawrence College and a BA in Journalism from Indiana University. Arriel is a Girls Write Now mentor.

Erasure Poetry 101

An erasure poem, sometimes called a "blackout poem," is a form of found poetry where a poet takes an existing text and erases, blacks out, or otherwise creates an entirely new work from what remains. A pure found poem consists exclusively of outside texts: the words of the poem remain as they were found, with few additions or omissions. Decisions of form, such as where to break a line, are left to the poet. Usually the result is something dramatically different from the original.

Opening Lines

What is one thing you want to erase or get rid of completely? It can be a song, a movie, a textbook, an idea, or something else meaningful to you.

The Craft of Erasure Poetry

Approaches: How do you use someone else's words to make your own point? Erasure/blackout poetry can be used as a means of collaboration, creating a new text from an old one and thereby starting a dialogue between the two—or as a means of confrontation, a challenge to a preexisting text. We can erase/blackout to resist, or to create a conversation. We are writing to say something new with something old. We are erasing to debate, to fight with our words.

Why would you want to erase/blackout a text?

> **Resisting:** What is the writer saying that you don't agree with? What do you want to change about this text?
>
> **Agreeing, but furthering the point:** If you agree with the writer, what more do you want to say about what they wrote? How can you say that only using the text? How can you add your voice to the piece?
>
> **Creating something entirely new:** Are you finding something to say that doesn't have anything to do with the text? Are there words on the page that you find intriguing, confusing, or strange? Are there words that you use often that you want to get rid of? How can you create a new work from the piece?

Erasure Poetry Free-write

Make an erasure poem *yours*!

Read the piece a few times: First, figure out what the writer/narrator is trying to say in the original text. That way, you have an idea of what is being said, how it's being said, and what might be missing. This can give you an idea of where to go in your erasure.

Figure out what you want to say: Have an idea in mind after reading the piece? Circle the words in pencil that you really want to use. Figure out what phrases/sentences/words stand out to you.

Choose an erasure/blackout method: Decide whether or not you want the reader to see the rest of the text. Are those words important to the reader's understanding of your erasure poem? Are those words you disagree with? Is the context important?

Try a few different erasure methods: Start working on the piece in pencil. Don't Sharpie away the words just yet. If Wite-Out doesn't work, try making the other words gray (let's do a light shading for now). If blackout makes the work too confusing, try crossing a line through the words. Maybe you want to rewrite it on a new piece of paper. Maybe you want to highlight the words instead. Sometimes poets highlight because they don't want to "damage" a text. Maybe it's a sacred text, or a text that is special or historical. Figure out what method works best for your poem!

Think about what your poem sounds like: Read it to yourself as you choose the words you're erasing. Is there a rhythm? Does it read smoothly? If not, consider using some of the words you erased (or alternatively, getting rid of some of the ones you didn't).

Think about what your poem looks like: Consider what your poem looks like as you're erasing. Does it look too bare? Too full? Think about what you're trying to say, and how the form can complement that.

Write a poem that fits you and your voice: How can you make the original text YOU? How can you insert your thoughts, emotions, and feelings? If you're a person of few words, erase a lot. If you're a person of a lot of words, erase only a little.

TRIBUTES

with Natalie Douglas

Natalie is an eleven-time MAC (Manhattan Association of Cabarets) Award, Nightlife Award, two-time Backstage Bistro Award, and BroadwayWorld Cabaret Best Vocalist Award winner. Her recent appearances include Birdland Jazz Club, Carnegie Hall, Café Carlyle, the Town Hall, the Crazy Coqs & the Pheasantry in London, and numerous cabaret conventions.

Tributes 101

A tribute is an exploration and a celebration of an artist, their work, and their life. It also usually features one's personal connection to the artist. Ideally the person who has watched and listened to your tribute knows a bit more about the artist you've chosen, a bit more about you, and hopefully a bit more about themselves, too.

However, there are other occasions ripe for tributes: award ceremonies, birthdays, anniversaries, weddings, memorials, readings, graduations, and cabarets (which blend music and stories).

Opening Lines

Song: Think of a song that meant or means something to you. What was going on in your life when you heard it?

Artist: Name a female artist from the twentieth century who means something to you.

Issue: What is your top issue of concern: climate change, racial justice, economic justice, immigration, gender and LGBTQ+ justice, or others . . .

The Craft of Tributes to Singers

Why singers? You pay tribute to singers if you really admire them and if they've influenced your development as an artist and, more important, as a human being.

Connecting with the audience: Bring songs and stories to life for a varied audience—some devoted fans of the artist who know more, and some newbies who are utterly unfamiliar with the artist, and everyone in between. The show has to entertain and hopefully move them all.

Songs and stories: Using a combination of humor, truth, and honest emotion, try to include original stories never heard before, or never heard in this context.

Anecdotes about the person: A human story. For example, How did Sammy Davis Jr. get started in show business? What was Nina Simone's first singing gig? How did the song "Why?," about Martin Luther King's assassination, come to be written? How did Cole Porter write "Miss Otis Regrets"? What influenced Dolly Parton's writing of "I Will Always

Love You" or "Coat of Many Colors"? Who wrote "Strange Fruit"? Who or what is "Mr. Bojangles" about?

Connecting your own story to the person: How does this story relate to your life, or how did you feel when you first heard this story? Does it tell you more about the world or the era in which it took place, or more about yourself or the human condition?

Playing their music (song selection): Which songs speak to you and why?

Tributes Free-write

Tribute show: Imagine you are a cabaret singer doing a tribute show. Introduce the singer you will tribute and one of the singer's songs that you will sing. It doesn't matter if you sing in front of an audience or if you only sing alone in the shower. *Pretend you are a singer!*

Awards ceremony: Imagine you are paying tribute to a singer at an awards ceremony. How would you introduce them?

Useful things to include in your tribute: Why this singer speaks to you; What this singer has to say and how that resonates in your life or in our modern world; quote the singer or their lyrics; humor.

SKETCH COMEDY

with KK Apple and Nikki Palumbo

KK is a writer and comedian in Brooklyn, and a Girls Write Now mentor. She performs sketch comedy around New York City, and very often dances on stages, or large/small/living rooms. You can find her writing and producing at Vimeo by day, or performing at Upright Citizens Brigade Theatre by night. She loves being a part of the community of passionate writers who share their words through Girls Write Now.

Nikki is a writer and comedian in New York, and a Girls Write Now mentor and member of the Girls Write Now Anthology Committee. She writes, directs, and teaches sketch comedy at the Upright Citizens Brigade Theatre, and contributes to The New Yorker, McSweeney's, *and* Reductress. *She wrote this in third person, with the help of a fourth person.*

Sketch Comedy 101

When it comes to writing a comedy piece it's important to remember that you do not need to try to be funny, or even worry about whether you know how to tell a joke. The funniest moments are the real ones, so think about something that happened to you that you found funny. Sketch comedy is a type of writing that allows you to have commentary about the events that you see occurring around you. It's when you point out the unusual to an audience by creating a piece of theater.

Opening Lines

Think of an anecdote from the past week—something that really happened in your life that made you laugh in the moment, or after the fact. Break it down: What was funny about it?

The Craft of Sketch Comedy

Skits are written in a set of small moments or "beats." Each beat is meant to heighten the sketch. Usually a sketch is three beats with a button on the end. The goal is to end the beat on the funniest line or funniest moment. However, you can't go too big on a beat too soon because then you won't be able to top it in the end!

Vocabulary of comedy: The tools you need to write a comedic sketch.

Game: What is funny or unusual about your scene.

Premise: The beginning of a road for your game. A premise should be specific and you should be able to write it down in a single sentence.

Beats: The separate moments throughout your scene that accentuate the game for laughs.

Heightening: The process of making sure that each beat has higher impact and is naturally funnier than the one before.

Explore: To explain the logic behind the unusual and answer "Why?"

Pattern: Pattern is the best way to use your game by creating a logical world, isolating one unusual thing (your game), and then using patterns to see how that game affects other aspects of that world.

"If, then": "*If* that is true, *then* what else would be true?" This technique is used to play out patterns. Once you isolate something funny or unusual about your scene, you should ask yourself: If that thing is true, what else would be true in this world?

Voice of reason: The character grounded in reality (of the world as we know it to be) and therefore able to call out what is unusual in the scene. The "Wait, what?" of the sketch. By questioning unusual actions or beliefs, the voice of reason often sets up another character to defend the unusual logic and explore the game of the scene.

Callback: Referencing something specific from earlier in your scene or show.

Character point of view: Perception of different people and characters.

Relationships: Character connections, backstory, feelings for each other.

Repeated action: Catchphrase, physical action, voice, tone.

Editing: The process of choosing the best moment to end your scene, and the process of revising and removing portions of your scene to improve it.

Buttons/blackout lines: A strong ending, hopefully a big laugh, so the scene doesn't just fizzle out. Often a callback to something earlier in the scene, an ultimate heightening of the game of the scene, or something unexpected.

Sketch Comedy Free-write

Traditions: Think about the traditions of your family/friends around the holidays. Is there a special food you eat? A way that your uncle always starts dinner? A song that *must* be played? Take that tradition and make it the unusual thing in your sketch.

Commercial: Write a commercial parody for your favorite product or brand. Start with what you know about the brand, what you love, and who buys it. How can you use tropes of typical commercials to flip all of these things on their heads?

SLAM POETRY

with Brittany Barker and Savannah Lucas

Brittany is a poet, an educator, and a Girls Write Now mentee alumna. She is a New York Knicks Poetry Slam Finalist and the Program Director for Third Space Initiative HS Arts Program. She is the Founder and Executive Producer of BlackGirl ThirdSpace Productions.

Savannah is a slam poet, a Girls Write Now mentee, and a senior at City-As-School High School in New York City.

Slam Poetry 101

In the 1920s, performance poetry emerged from the jazz poetry movement in the Harlem Renaissance. In the 1960s it became a powerful way for voices to be heard during the Civil Rights Movement. In the '70s political black poetry created the foundations of hip-hop. In 1984, the first-ever poetry slam took place in Chicago, and from there it took off to become something so much bigger than itself.

Opening Lines

Complete these sentences:

Poetry is . . .
If poetry were a metaphor, it would be . . .
Poetry and I went on a lunch date . . .

I use poetry to . . .

Poetry feels like . . .

I found poetry when . . .

The Craft of Slam Poetry

The thought of unmasking yourself and going deep into problematic situations may sound uneasy at first, but it usually brings this feeling of peace and release to your being. It allows you to turn your darkest days into something beautiful.

Delivery is a key part of a good spoken-word poem. Think about your poem like a script, and you are the actor. Say each word like you mean it. Don't only write your truth, say your truth.

Slam Poetry Free-write

Confront your inner world . . .

Explore what is being closed off or protected. Imagine how you are feeling. What is it like in this world?

Tell the truth about something you once lied about.

GHOST STORYTELLING

with Kathleen Scheiner

Kathleen is a freelance writer and editor, specializing in horror, sci-fi, and fantasy. She also edits a lot of manga. She's written for Publishers Weekly, L'ecran Fantastique, Toxic, *and* Penny Blood. *Her novel* The Collectors *was published in 2013. Kathleen has been a Girls Write Now mentor for nearly a decade.*

Ghost Stories 101

Ghost stories are tales told about the soul of a deceased person or a disembodied spirit visiting a place or living persons. The ghosts can be emotionally tethered to a person, place, or object.

Opening Lines

Have you ever seen a ghost? What was it like? Where were you? What did it feel like? *What do you think they wanted?*

The Craft of Ghost Stories

Atmosphere and Setting: Ghost stories rely on atmosphere and setting to create chills. For example, you're in a place you go to frequently, such as the library, maybe waiting for your turn at one of the computers. This is a setting you're familiar with: rows of bookcases filled with books; in the background a librarian reads a book to children; and in front of you are tables populated with people reading. In this most normal of settings, you hear pages flipping and the sound of a book being dropped behind you. But when you turn around, there's no one there. The library has a ghost.

Ghost Stories Free-write

The setting is New York City. New York is one of the oldest cities in the United States, and many places and buildings here are known for their ghosts. Near Times Square, there's the Belasco Theatre, which is supposedly haunted by its namesake David Belasco, who will appear in the balcony during rehearsals watching the show, or in the hallways. The McCarren Park Pool in Brooklyn is said to be haunted by children who drowned there in the 1930s when the pool first opened. And the first stop in the United States for many immigrants, Ellis Island, was sometimes their last one. It's supposedly haunted by people who died there after being quarantined with illnesses such as measles and scarlet fever.

Place: Take a building or place in the city you know well. Think about what may have happened in its history and why a spirit might be hanging out there. Tell a story where you describe its setting and then have a ghost make a surprising appearance.

Point of view: Write a story from the ghost's point of view, in which you are haunting a particular building or place in New York. How do you appear to people? What are you trying to tell them?

Experiential: Maybe you've had a brush with the other side. Write about a visit you had from a ghost, paying particular attention to the setting.

SPEECHWRITING

with Anna Humphrey and Sarah Gruen

As a field organizer for Barack Obama's first presidential campaign, Anna learned how to ask tough questions—and how to answer even tougher ones. She brings these same skills to West Wing Writers, where she helps visionary leaders match messages to moments. Anna has written for the Chief Information Officer at the White House, facilitating decision-making on technology issues by senior leaders and other non-technical staff, as well as the Pentagon's Chief Technology Officer. Anna is a Girls Write Now mentor.

As a speechwriter at West Wing Writers, Sarah has penned remarks for Fortune 500 CEOs, toasts for award-winning actors, and keynote addresses for philanthropic leaders. Her words—on topics ranging from diversity and inclusion to higher education to artificial intelligence—have been delivered at conferences, commencements, and conventions around the world. Sarah is a Girls Write Now mentor.

Speechwriting 101

Speechwriting is the art of conveying an informational, entertaining, and/or persuasive message in front of a live audience. It is about expressing your vision, exciting people, and maybe even getting them to act.

Opening Lines

Speech: What's a speech that's especially meaningful to you? It can be a movie monologue or a State of the Union, an address at a protest or pump-up speech—anything! What makes it so memorable?

Speaker: Who is your favorite speaker? Think about coaches and teachers, friends and family, politicians and celebrities. What makes them so good?

The Craft of Speechwriting

Audience: Ask yourself . . . Who's in the audience? Are there multiple audiences? Are people in the audience a prop, or are they the true target of the remarks? What's the key idea the audience needs to hear?

Tone and voice: Ask yourself . . . What's the relationship between the speaker and the audience? How does the audience currently view the speaker? How do you want them to view the speaker? Does the speaker need to be credentialed? Or do they already have credibility with the audience? What kind of voice should I be using?

Monroe's Motivated Sequence for persuasive speeches: Techniques for organizing persuasive speeches that inspire people to take action. Ask yourself . . .

Attention: What emotion do I want the audience to feel? Happy? Alarmed? Respected? Moved?

Problem: What's the macro problem? What's the micro problem? Examples of macro/micro problems: climate change/California wildfires, workplace gender inequality (not enough mentorship opportunities for women), erosion of democracy (voter disenfranchisement). What emotion do I want the audience to feel?

Solution: Does the solution mirror the problem? If not, redefine the problem. What emotion do I want the audience to feel?

Vision: Does the solution solve the macro problem? If so, what does the new world look like once achieved? If not, what does the world look like once it's solved the micro problem? And how does solving the micro problem further the effort to solve the macro one? What emotion do I want the audience to feel?

Call to action: Is there something specific the audience must do? If so, what is it? If not, what role does the audience play? Is there a final piece of advice they should heed? What emotion do I want the audience to feel?

Monroe's Motivated Sequence for rom-com speeches: Ask yourself . . .

Setting: What else is happening around me? Who else is watching or listening, if anyone? Is the location meaningful? If so, why?

Tone and voice: What's the relationship between the speaker and the audience? How does the audience currently view the speaker? How do I want them to view the speaker? What kind of voice should I be using?

Attention: Does the audience want to listen to me? If not, how will I grab their attention? If so, how will I hold it?

Anna and Sarah's Motivated Sequence: Ask yourself . . .

Hold up a mirror: What does this observation say about the audience? How will it make them feel? What form should that observation take? A hard truth? A compliment? Something they may not know about themselves?

Callback: How did the audience feel when they first experienced whatever I'm calling back to? How will it make them feel now?

Promise a happy ending: What does the audience want? What does this promise say about me, the speaker?

Speechy Speech Free-write

Write a speech about a cause that's important to you. Think about the audience, tone, and voice, and the motivated sequences above.

ABOUT GIRLS WRITE NOW

For more than twenty years, Girls Write Now has been a nationally respected leader in arts education as New York's first and only writing and mentoring organization for girls. Girls Write Now matches underserved teens—over 90 percent of color, 90 percent high need, 75 percent immigrant or first generation, and 25 percent LGBTQ/gender-nonconforming—with professional writers and digital media makers as their personal mentors. Mentees' multigenre, multimedia work is published in outlets including *Teen Vogue*, *BuzzFeed*, and the *New York Times*; performed at Lincoln Center and the United Nations; and wins hundreds of Scholastic Art & Writing Awards. One hundred percent of Girls Write Now seniors are accepted to college—armed with confidence, portfolios, and lifelong bonds. Through Girls Write Now's Writing Works workforce development program, we prepare young adults to be skilled communicators and competitive candidates, creating a diverse pipeline into the schools and industries most in need of their talents.

Girls Write Now has been distinguished three times by the White House as one of the nation's top youth programs, twice by the Nonprofit Excellence Awards as one of New York's top ten nonprofits, by NBCUniversal's 21st Century Solutions for Social Innovation, by Youth INC for Youth Innovation, and as a DVF People's Voice Nominee. Reaching over 6,000 youth annually, Girls Write Now is a founding partner of the STARS Citywide Girls Initiative, now in its seventh year. Girls Write Now earned the 2019 HI Impact Award, ranking in the top 4 percent of programs nationwide for outstanding performance driving social-emotional growth for youth. With features in *Bustle*, *People*, *Newsweek*, and more, Girls Write Now's annual anthology has received numerous awards and recognitions.

GIRLS WRITE NOW 2020

SENIOR TEAM

Maya Nussbaum, *Founder and Executive Director*
Molly MacDermot, *Director of Special Initiatives*
Erica Silberman, *Director of Curriculum and Engagement*
Natalie McGuire, *Controller*

COMMUNITY TEAM

Ariah Dow, *Community Coordinator*
Lisbett Rodriguez, *Community Coordinator*
Anjali Misra, *Community Fellow*
Teresa Mettela, *Community Intern*
Louisa Campbell, *Multimedia Adviser*
Richelle Szypulski, *Events Producer*
Spencer George, *Special Initiatives Assistant*

DEVELOPMENT TEAM

Kelsey LePage, *Development and Operations Associate*
Elizabeth Baribeau, *Senior Grant Writer*

BOARD OF DIRECTORS

Tayari Jones, *Honorary Board Member*
Bestselling author of *An American Marriage*

Rupi Kaur, *Honorary Board Member*
Internationally bestselling poet, author, illustrator, and
  performer

TEACHING ARTISTS

KK Apple, *Sketch Comedy*

Zaina Arafat, *Profile Writing*

Brittany Barker, *Slam Poetry*

Anne Beal, *Stop Motion Animation*

Amber and Tiffany Davis, *Empowerment Coaching*

Natalie Douglas, *Tributes*

Melanie Goodreaux, *Short Form Poetry*

Sarah Gruen, *Speechwriting*

Susanna Horng, *Flash Fiction*

Anna Humphrey, *Speechwriting*

Sammi LaBue Hatch, *Therapeutic Writing*

Yunxuan Lin, *Multimedia*

Savannah Lucas, *Slam Poetry*

Kelly Moffitt, *Podcasting*

Andrea Plasko, *Wellness*

Nikki Palumbo, *Sketch Comedy*

Kathleen Scheiner, *Ghost Stories*

Arriel Vinson, *Erasure Poetry*

Sofia Von Hauske Valtierra, *Multimedia*

AGENTS OF CHANGE HONOREES*

Julie Schwietert Collazo, *coauthor of* The Book of Rosy: A Mother's Story of Separation at the Border

Robyn Crawford, New York Times *bestselling author of* A Song for You: My Life with Whitney Houston

Rupi Kaur, *internationally bestselling poet, author, illustrator, and performer*

Laurie Liss, *Executive Vice President and Managing Partner, Sterling Lord Literistic, Inc.*

Rosayra Pablo Cruz, *coauthor of* The Book of Rosy: A Mother's Story of Separation at the Border

Danielle Paige, New York Times *bestselling author of the* Dorothy Must Die *and the* Stealing Snow *series, and the graphic novel* Mera: Tidebreaker

Kiley Reid, New York Times *bestselling author of* Such a Fun Age

Umi Syam, *Graphics/Multimedia editor at* the New York Times

Cleo Wade, *American artist, poet, activist, and bestselling author of* Heart Talk: Poetic Wisdom for a Better Life

Lauren Wilkinson, *author of* American Spy

List in formation as of spring 2020.

LITERARY PARTNERS

Alliance for Young Artists & Writers

Alloy Entertainment

Amazon Literary Partnership

Berkley

Blanchette Hooker Rockefeller Fund

The Blue List

The Book Group

Creative Artists Agency

Catapult

Comcast NBCUniversal

Context & Co.

Diane von Furstenberg

Dutton

Feminist Press

Find Your Light Foundation

Fletcher & Company

Forbes

Ford Foundation

Fresh

G. P. Putnam's Sons

GFP Real Estate

Harman Family Foundation

HarperCollins Publishers

HBO/WarnerMedia

HG Literary

Houghton Mifflin Harcourt

Infosys Foundation

Inkluded

Jane Rotrosen Agency

Macmillan

News Corp

New-York Historical Society

Open Road Integrated Media

Paragraph

Parsons The New School for Design

Penguin Random House

The Pinkerton Foundation

RBC Capital Markets

The Rona Jaffe Foundation

Scholastic

Soapbox Inc.

SparkPoint Studio

StoryBundle

Table 4 Writers Foundation

Tin House

VIDA: Women in Literary Arts

West Wing Writers

The Wing

Women of Letters

Workman Publishing

Writers House

Young to Publishing Group

Youth INC

ANTHOLOGY SUPPORTERS

We are grateful to the countless institutions and individuals who have supported our work through their generous contributions. Visit our website at girlswritenow.org to view the extended list.

Girls Write Now would like to thank Dutton, including Christine Ball, Maya Ziv, Marya Pasciuto, Hannah Feeney, Susan Schwartz, Claire Sullivan, Dora Mak, and Sabrina Bowers for their help producing this year's anthology, and Amazon Literary Partnership, which provided the charitable contribution that made this anthology possible.

The anthology is supported, in part, by public funds from the National Endowment for the Arts; the New York State Council on the Arts, a state agency; and the New York City Department of Cultural Affairs, in partnership with the City Council and the New York City Department of Youth and Community Development.